Mastering Java

An Effective Project Based Approach including Web Development, Data Structures, GUI Programming and Object Oriented Programming (Beginner to Advanced)

Table of Contents

Introduction

First, let me thank you for taking the time to purchase and read my guide, "Mastering Java: An Effective Project-Based Approach including Web Development, Data Structures, GUI Programming and Object Oriented Programming."

My intention with this guide is to teach you all about the Java computer programming language. To that end, I have sectioned the guide into 6 separate sections, each one dealing with a separate element of Java programming. You will learn:

Chapter 1: Java Basics – you will learn the basic programming elements of the Java language, including how to set up your programming environment, using a text editor and how to write a program. We look at comments, how to structure your code, and what data types and variables are. We also look at how to receive and read Java data, the different types of statement, loops and arrays before moving on to functions and methods. By the end of this section you will have a firm understanding of how to program in Java.

Chapter 2: Java Data Structures and Algorithms – in this section we will examine a part of Java programming that is very important to computer science. You will learn exactly what a data structure is, how they are classified and the design of them, before moving on to algorithms. We learn how to write an algorithm, what asymptotic analysis and notation are and the definition of a greedy algorithm. We learn how data structures and algorithms mesh together, the different methods of sorting and traversing algorithms to gain information before moving onto trees and finishing with recursion.

Chapter 3: Java Web Development – this section will walk you through all the elements of developing a web app using Java. We look at JSP and servlets and how they are used in building web apps, before looking at some of the best practices in web development using Java EE (Enterprise Edition). This is an involved chapter with plenty of technical information and a hands-on guide that you can easily follow.

Chapter 4: Java GUI Programming – GUI programming is a complex part of Java programming and, in this section we look at using NetBeans and Swing to build a Java GUI. We discuss native packaging, followed by a tutorial that you can follow along with, covering how to design a GUI using the NetBeans IDE. We talk about how to handle images, design forms, gap editing and debugging, followed by a discussion on bean and data binding and using Hibernate in your application.

Chapter 5: Object-Oriented Programming – this section covers object-oriented programming in Java; what it is, the benefits of the approach, the principles of Object Oriented Programming (OOP) and understanding the basic concepts.

Chapter 6: Java Interview Questions – lastly, I have provided you with a comprehensive list of questions that you could be asked in an interview for a Java programming job. I also provide the answers with the intention being that you study them and learn them; not just what the answers are but the why and how too.

Java is not a new programming language by any means; it has been around since 1991 and, to date, has proved to be the most popular, especially where web development is concerned. It is one of the simplest languages to learn, and it is object-oriented, which makes it even easier to learn.

Work your way through this guide and, by the end of it, you will know more than many people do about the Java programming language and all its uses. I would make one suggestion – if you choose to join in and input the code yourself, do type it in rather than copying and pasting. It's a great way of getting the feel for programming and how things work.

Thank you once again for choosing my guide.

Chapter 1: Java Basics

There is no doubting that Java is the most popular and the most used computer programming language of all, in particular where web platforms and web applications are concerned. Java was deliberately designed to be incredibly flexible with the express intention of allowing developers to write code that would work on any machine, irrespective of its architecture and the platform in use. At the time of writing, well over one billion computers and over three billion mobile devices are built on Java.

You will find Java being used as the basis for platforms and applications on a huge range of devices:

- Laptops
- Desktop computers
- Satellite navigation systems
- Games consoles
- Medical monitoring devices
- Parking meters
- Lottery terminals
- Smartphones
- Mobile tablets
- Blu-ray players

And a whole lot more. Plus, Java is also one of the major languages that are used for networking; more specifically for data centers responsible for storing web-based data and for transferring it.

If that weren't enough, Java is also used for creating dynamic but small programs embedded in web pages, or running beside them. These are known as applets and you will find them in widgets that display maps, the weather, games and any other widget or tool on a web page that is interactive in some way.

Java is a class-based and an object-oriented language that is based firmly on the programming syntax for both C and for C++ languages. Developers tend to go for Java over and above the other programming languages because of its flexibility in securely running on just about any platform, regardless as we said earlier, of the architecture of the platform or the operating system it runs on. So long as the device in question has got Java Runtime Environment (JRE) installed, it is going to work.

Setting Up Your Environment

You might be surprised to learn that the hardest part of this programming language is in setting up your working environment. You can't even think about writing a single line of code until you have NetBeans downloaded. NetBeans is free and is without any doubt the most popular IDE (Interface Development Environment) for writing any program in Java.

But, before we get to that stage, the first things we need are the components and files that NetBeans needs.

The JVM (Java Virtual Machine)

The first port of all is installing a Virtual Machine, because Java is not platform dependent, meaning it can run on any platform, be it Linux, Mac, Windows, or any other. It is the Virtual Machine that does all the code processing and, because Oracle owns Java, you must have the Virtual Machine, or Java Runtime Environment, that they provide on their website. So, the first place to go is https://www.java.com/en/download/.

Now, when you open this website, you will see a link, underneath the Download button, that says, "Do I Have Java?" Clicking this provides a very quick way to see if you already have Java on your machine. Go ahead and click this; a scan on your computer will commence and you will find out if Java is installed or not. If it isn't, a message will appear asking if you want it installed. You have a choice here; either click on Yes or go to https://www.java.com/en/download/manual.jsp and download it manually. On that website you will find multiple download links for all the different operating systems and platforms Java can be downloaded on.

When the download and installation have finished, you will need to reboot your system to complete it; when it reboots, you will see the Virtual Machine running on your system.

At this stage, it still isn't possible to start programming; all you have achieved so far is installing a piece of software that will let the Java programs run on your system. To actually write code and test it out, you will need an SDK, or a Software Development Kit. For this, we are going to require the Java SE SDK so go to https://www.oracle.com/technetwork/java/javase/downloads/index.html.

From there, you can download the Java SE SDK to your computer. Look through the list on the web page and find the NetBeans version – it will say JDK* with NetBeans (* = version number, for example, JDK8). Click that and a new page will open, listing all the different download versions for the different systems and platforms. Click the one that goes with your particular system and follow the instructions on the screen to install it – exercise a bit of patience here; it is quite a large download and, depending on your system and internet connection, it may take a little time.

We'll be using NetBeans to do our programming (you'll also need it for the section on GUI programming) so, before we go ahead and open it, you should have an understanding of the way Java works.

How It All Works

When you start writing your Java code, you do it in a text editor and NetBeans is all set up to provide you with the place to write it all. The code is known as source code and is always saved with a file extension of .java. A program called Javac will then turn that source code into Java Byte Code in a process that is known as compiling. Once the code has been compiled by Javac, it gets saved again, this tie with a file extension of .class. However, this can only be done if the code is free of errors. When the class file is ready, it can be run on your JVM (Java Virtual Machine).

So:

- Your source code is created and saved with the .java extension
- Javac then compiles the code and saves it with the .class extension
- Your compiled class can be run on the JVM

NetBeans is designed to make your life very easy. It does all the creating and compiling for you; behind the scenes, it is working the magic of transforming source code to java files, using Javac to compile and then running your new .class file in its built-in software. This saves you having to open terminal windows and type in long complicated strings of text, as you do with other programming languages.

Okay, so that is how NetBeans works with Java, time to open NetBeans – we are going to write a program. Actually writing code is the best way of learning how it all works so go ahead and do what you need to – if you haven't installed NetBeans yet go and do it. Then open it and get ready to follow along with the rest of this section.

Your First Program

To start a new project, go to the NetBeans toolbar and click File. Next, click New Project and a dialog box will load. We are going to be making this into a Java application so navigate to the Categories section and choose Project. Click Java Application and then click on Next

Go to the top of the window for the Project Name and type a name in for this project – for the sake of this, we'll call it firstproject. As you type it in, note that the text down the bottom will change to match it. On the right side of where it says Create Main Class, you will see a text box with the following typed in:

firstproject.FirstProject

A class called FirstProject has been created – note that the F and the P are capitalized. The package also has the name of firstproject but with all lower case letters.

Look in the text box for Project Location – the default location for where projects are saved is shown; you can change this or you can leave it as it is. Note that NetBeans will also create a folder in the same location as the project name. Click Finish and NetBeans creates everything that is needed and when done, will take you straight back to the IDE – look at the top left corner of the screen in the Projects area. If you can't see this area, click Window and then Projects.

Note the + sign; click this and your project will enlarge. Now expand the Source Packages option and you should see your project name appear. Expand that and you will see your source code, the Java file. This code should be in the text box to the right of the screen and it will have the name, FirstProject.java. If you do not see that code window, go to the project window (top of your screen) and double-click on the name, FirstProject.java; the code will appear and we are now ready to begin work.

The class has a name of FirstProject, like this:

public class FirstProject {

Note that the source file you see in the project window also has the same name and there is a reason for this – when the Java compiler runs any program you write, the source file and the class name must have the same names so, for example, if you named your .java file firstProject but and the class was named FirstProject, the compiler would throw up an error – always check your names match so this can't happen.

That said, the package name is different; for the sake of simplicity we gave it a name of firstproject but it wouldn't have mattered what you called. There is no requirement for the package name to match either the source file or the class name in that source file – the important thing is that the class and source file have the same name.

Got that? Let's move on.

Java Comments

When you create new projects, you should see that there is quite a lot of text that is greyed-out and contains slashes and asterisks. These are called comments and, when you run your program, the compiler will ignore them. The idea is to write a note to describe what a piece of code is doing – this is so that when you come back to your code you know what's what and if someone else looks at it, they will also be able to read it correctly. It also makes it easier to see where an error might show up.

Comments can be written in a couple of ways. The first is a single line comment, denoted by two forward slashes (//) and then the comment:

//This is a single line comment

However, you can also have your comments spread over multiple lines and there are two ways to do this. The first is start each line with the forward slashes, like this:

//This comment spreads
//over at least two lines

Or you could do this:

```
/*
This comment spreads over at least two lines

*/
```

This is a much easier way of achieving a multiline comment, instead of having to remember to put the // at the start of each new line.

Another option is to use the Javadoc comment. These start with one forward slash and two asterisks, and end, the same as the above example, with an asterisk and a single forward slash. Every line in between that has a comment on it will start with an asterisk:

```
/**
*This comment is a Javadoc comment
*/
```

Javadoc comments are a very useful way to document your code. That code may then be converted into an HTML page that is helpful to others. When you have some code written, you will start to see how this looks so go to the top of the NetBeans screen and click Run. Click Generate Javadoc – there isn't much to see until we have some code written though.

A quick note about comments – keep them as short as possible and make sure they are clear on what is happening in the code; long, rambling comments that are full of unnecessary words are meaningless and make your code look even messier.

Code Structure

The next thing to look at is how your code is structured and how to run the programs you write. You already know that the first part of the code structure is your package name – you must end this line with a semicolon otherwise the program cannot be compiled:

```
package firstproject;
```

Next comes the class name:

```
public class FirstProject {

}
```

We can think of a class as being a code segment but you must let Java know where the start and end of each segment is; this is done with the curly brackets you see above. The left bracket ({) opens the segment and the right bracket (}) closes the segment. Anything that is written between these two is part of that code segment. Also, if there is anything between the pair of brackets that is in a class, this is part of a separate segment. Have a look at this:

```
public static void main( String[ ] args ) {
```

```
}
```

There is an important word in that segment above – 'main'. At the start of a Java program, Java will look for a method called 'main'. A method is a section of code and we'll cover those a bit more in a while. At this stage, Java executes all code within the set of curly brackets as the 'main' method. If you do not have a 'main' method, errors will be thrown up. As the name suggests, it is the main point of entry for any program written in Java.

At this stage, we can ignore anything that comes before 'main' but, just for your information:

- public is an indicator that the method can be seen outside of the class;
- static indicates that we do not need a new object created, and
- void indicates that there is no value to be returned.

Anything in between the set of parentheses, (), is a command line argument. Don't worry too much if you don't understand this right now; you will by the end of this section of the guide.

Right now, what is important is to know is that:

- we have a class called FirstProject
- it has a method called main
- each method is within its own opening and closing curly brackets
- the main bit of our code belongs to the class called FirstProject.

Let's move on to data types and variables. At this stage, if you are unsure about anything, go back over it because, in the next bit, we start to get a little technical.

Introducing Data Types and Variables

How a Java program works is that it manipulates any data that is put into memory and that data can be of any type, including numbers, text, objects, a pointer to another section of memory, and many more types. The data is assigned a name so that we can easily recall it when we need it. The name, along with any value assigned to that name, is a variable. We'll start with the number values.

Java has multiple options for number storage. A variable with the name of int, for example, is used to store any whole numbers (1, 4, 9, etc.) while the name of double is used to indicate floating point or decimal numbers (1.2, 5.9, etc.). To store the value we use the equals sign (=).

Take a look at the example below and then try inputting it into your program, FirstProject, to try them:

Example

Add the following piece of code to set up an int (integer or whole number) to FirstProject, making sure it goes into the main method:

```
public static void main(String[ ] args) {

        int first_number;

        System.out.println("My First Project");

}
```

So that Java knows you want to store a whole number, the first word should be int, making sure you add a space after it. The integer variable then requires a name; provided you follow these naming conventions, you can name it what you want:

- Numbers cannot be used to begin a variable name. For example, you could name it first number, but you could not name it 1st_number. You can have numbers anywhere else in the name, just not the start.
- Variables cannot be named using reserved Java keywords because these are reserved for use by Java. I will give you a list of these keywords shortly.
- You cannot have any spaces in the name. Instead, ensure that your first word has a lower-case letter and the second and all subsequent words in the name have uppercase letters, without any spaces between the words, for example, myFirstNumber.
- Variable names are case sensitive so myFirstNumber and MyFirstNumber are treated as two separate variable names.

Reserved Keywords

Java has several keywords that it reserves for its own use; these cannot be used anywhere else, especially not when naming variables. Those keywords are:

abstract	assert	boolean	break	byte
case	catch	char	class	const
continue	default	do	double	else
enum	extends	final	finally	float
for	goto	if	implements	import
instanceof	int	interface	long	native
new	package	private	protected	public
return	short	static	strictfp	super

switch	synchronized	this	throw	throws
transient	try	void	volatile	while

Note that the keywords are all lower-case.

Let's get back to our variables. Let's say that you wanted to store a value in the variable called first_number. First you need an equal (=) sign and then the value that you want to be stored:

```
public static void main(String[ ] args)
{
        int first_number;
        first_number = 12;
        System.out.println("My First Project");
}
```

What we did here told Java that we want the value of 12 to be stored in first_number, the int variable. This can be done on one line if you wish:

```
public static void main(String[ ] args)
{
        int first_number = 12;
        System.out.println("My First Project");
}
```

We could change the println method slightly just to see how this works:

System.out.println("First number = " + first_number);

After println, you see a set of parentheses; in between those are text inside a set of double quotes:

("First number = "

Note that we also use a + sign followed by the variable name:

+ first_number);

The + (plus) sign is just telling Java that we want to join or add two things together, in this case, the text to the variable name. This is normally called concatenation.

Right, if you have been playing along, you should see something like the following in your code window – do note that each line ends with a semi-colon:

```
public static void main (String [] args)
{
        int first_number;
        first_number = 12;
        System.out.println("first_number = " + first_number);
}
```

Now run this program to see what it does.

The output that follows the sign should be the first number stored in the variable called first_number.

Let's have a go at some addition. We'll add a couple more int variables – one is going to store a second number and the other will store the answer to the addition:

```
int first_number, second_number, answer;
```

We now have three variables on the same line and Java will allow this to happen only as long they are all the same type, in our case, ints. Each variable name must have a comma separating it from the next.

Now we'll store some values in these new variables:

```
first_number = 12;
second_number = 24;
answer = first_number + second_number;
```

Inside the variable called answer, the first number must be added to the second number; the + symbol is used to do this. Next, Java will add the two values together, those for first_number and second_number. The answer, which is the total of the addition, is stored in a variable which is on the left of the = sign. So, instead of 12 or 24 being assigned to the variable name, the two numbers are added together and then assigned to the variable. To make that a little clearer, have a look at this:

```
answer=first_number + second_number;
```

first_number and second_number are added up first

```
answer =first_number + second_number;
```

And the answer is stored in the variable called answer.

That code would be the equivalent of:

answer = 12 + 24;

Now, Java already knows what is in the first_number and the second_number variables so all you need to do is use their names.

Now we can make a small change to the println method:

System.out.println("Addition Total = " + answer);

Once again, the text written within the double quotes is combined with the name of a variable and your code should now be looking like this:

```
public static void main(String[] args) {

    int first_number, second_number, answer;

    first_number = 12;

    second_number = 24;

    answer = first_number + second_number;

    System.out.println("Addition Total = " + answer );

}
```

So, to recap, this program has:

- Stored one number
- Stored a second number
- Added the numbers together
- Stored the answer (the result of the addition) inside another variable
- Printed the answer

It is also possible to use numbers in your code directly so change the answer line in your code so it reads:

answer = first_number + second_number + 14;

Run it again; does it do what you think it should do?

It is possible to store a large number in the int variables but there is a maximum value you can go up to – 2147483647. You can also add minus numbers in with the lowest number of -2147483648. If you needed to store numbers that were larger or smaller, you would need to use a different variable type. That type is the double variable.

Double Variables

Double variables are used when we want to store much larger or smaller values than the maximum and minimum allowable in a standard variable. The minimum and maximum numbers allowed in the double variable are far too large to put in here but they are 1 and -17, each followed by 307 zeros.

We also use the double variable to store values for floating point numbers. These values are decimals, for example, 1.6 or 10.8. If you attempted to store one of these in an int variable, NetBeans would tell you there was an error; try running it and you would get an error message on the compiler.

Now, using the code you already have, let's try using double variables.

Change the int in your code to a double by changing this line:

int first_number, second_number, answer;

so it reads:

double first_number, second_number, answer;

Next, the stored values need to be changed:

first_number = 12.5;
second_number = 24.8;

Leave the rest of your code as it is; it should look like this:

```
public static void main (String[] args) {

        double first_number, second_number, answer;

        first_number = 12.5;

        second_number = 24.8;

        answer = first_number + second_number;

        System.out.println ("Addition Total = " + answer);

}
```

Run it and see what happens.

Short Variables and Float Variables

We have two more variable types to look at; the short and the float. The short variable is used for storing smaller numbers between +32767 and -32767. We could have used this instead of an int but you can only use the short variable if you know 100% that your values will not exceed that range.

The float variable may be used in place of the double variable for storing the larger floating point or decimal numbers; if you do use the float variable though, you must remember that an 'f' needs to be added to the end of each number, like this:

float first_number, second_number, answer;

first_number = 12.5f;
second_number = 24.8f;

The 'f' must be placed at the end of the number but before the semicolon.

Simple Arithmetic

Using these variables, we can add in other symbols that let us do arithmetic. These symbols are called Operators:

+ (addition)

(subtraction)

(multiplication)

/ (division)

Operator Precedence

The operators may be very simple and self-explanatory but there is one important thing you must understand – operator precedence. Your calculations can have more than two numbers but it is important that you understand exactly what the calculation is doing. Take this example:

first_number = 150;
second_number = 90;
third_number = 40;

answer = first_number - second_number + third_number;

If this calculation were carried left to right, it would be 150-90, which equals 40. Then the third number, 40, would be added, giving a total of 80. But what if that wasn't what you intended to happen? What if what you really wanted was numbers two and three added together and then the total subtracted from number one? That would read 90+40, which equals 130, subtracted from 150, leaving a total of 20.

To ensure that your calculations are being done correctly, you need to use parentheses. The first calculation we showed above would look like:

answer = (first_number - second_number) + third_number;

Try it yourself; you should have this:

public static void main(String[] args) {

int first_number, second_number, third_number, answer;

```
        first_number = 150;
        second_number = 90;
        third_number = 40;
        answer = (first_number - second_number) + third_number;
        System.out.println ("Total = " + answer );
}
```

And the second calculation would be:

answer = first_number - (second_number + third_number);

Ad it would look like:

```
public static void main(String[] args) {
        int first_number, second_number, third_number, answer;
        first_number = 150;
        second_number = 90;
        third_number = 40;
        answer = first_number - (second_number) + third_number;
        System.out.println ("Total = " + answer );
}
```

So, what about the addition and multiplication then? How would that look?

You would change the operator symbols to + and *:

*answer = first_number + second_number * third_number;*

Remove the parentheses and then run it; what is going to happen?

You would think that, if all the parentheses were removed, the calculation would run left to right, wouldn't you? That numbers one and two would be added, giving a total of 240, which would then be multiplied by the third number, giving a total of 9600. What answer did you get? You should have seen an answer of 3750 but why?

It comes down to operator precedence. Not all of the operators are treated the same; those that have priority are dealt with first and in Java, multiplication has priority over addition so that is done first and then the addition:

*answer = first_number + (second_number * third_number);*

When you use parentheses, the second number gets multiplied by the third one and the result of that calculation would be added to the first one. So, 90 gets multiplied by 40, providing an answer of 3600 and then the first number, 150 is added, providing a result of 3750. If you wanted things to be done the first way, you would need to use the parentheses in such a way that Java knows what it needs to do:

*answer = (first_number + second_number) * third_number;*

The division operator is also given priority so that would be done before either subtraction or addition.

Java sees the operator precedence in this way:

- Division (/) and multiplication (*) are both given the same priority over addition (+) and subtraction (-).
- Addition and subtraction are both given the same priority but lower than multiplication and division.

If you don't think you have the right answer from Java, have a look at your precedence and use parentheses where needed.

Storing Text Values

We can also use variables to store text, not just numbers. You can store a single character or you can store several. If you wanted just one to be stored, the char variable is used; normally though, more than one character would be stored so you would use the string variable.

Save the code from before and close the project. Open a new one – File>New Project, like you did at the start and, when you see the dialog box, make sure that you have selected Java and Java Application.

Click Next and then call the new project StringVars. Ensure that Create Main Class is enabled (tick the box next to it) and then, where Main follows stringvars, delete Main and input StringVariables.

The project has a name of Stringvars and the class is called StringVariables. Now you can click Finish and have a look at the coding window. You should see the name of the package in lowercase letters (stringvars) and capitalized first letters for the project name (StringVars).

Setting up the string variable requires you to type String and then the name of the variable. Note that String is capitalized and there is a semicolon ending the line:

String first_name;

Next, a value is assigned to the variable and this is done by typing =, followed by double quotes, the text that is to be stored in the variable, and then more double quotes:

first_name = "Peter";

You could put it all on the same line:

String first_name = "Peter";

Now we need another variable, again a string, to store the surname:

String family_name = "Piper";

Add the following println so that both first and last names are printed:

System.out.println(first_name + " " + family_name);

In between the opening and losing println parentheses, we see:

first_name + " " + family_name;

What we have done is told Java that it should print the stored value in the variable called first_name. Following that are a plus symbol and a space, the space surrounded by a set of double quotes. We do this so that Java is aware that a space character is to be printed. After the space is another plus and this is followed by the variable called family_name.

This does look somewhat messy but what we want to print out is the first name, a space, and then the family or second name. Your code should be something like this:

```
public static void main (String[] args) {

        String first_name = "Peter";

        String family_name = "Piper";

        System.out.println ( first_name + " " + family_name);

}
```

Run this and see what you get.

If a single character is all you want to be stored, you would use the char variable and, rather than using double quotes, we only need single quotes. Change your code so it looks like this:

```
public static void main (String[] args) {

        char first_name = 'P';

        char family_name = 'P';

        System.out.println( first_name + " " + family_name);

}
```

If you were to use double quotes in a char, you will be shown by NetBeans that it isn't correct, with an 'incompatible type" error message. You can use a String variable that stores a single character but you must make sure that double quotes are used:

This is okay:

```
String first_name = "P";
```

This isn't:

```
String first_name = 'P';
```

Note the first has double quotes, the second has single quotes.

Receive and Read User Data in Java

Java has one huge advantage – it has vast libraries full of code that you can make use of. All the code has been written with a specific purpose in mind and, to use it, you just pass a reference to the particular library you want the code from; you follow that by calling a method into action. The Scanner class is by far the most useful because it is how input is handled from a user. You can find this class is the library called java.util and all you need to do is reference the class in your code. How? With the import keyword:

```
import java.util.Scanner;
```

The statement must go just before the Class statement:

```
import java.util.Scanner;

public class StringVariables {


}
```

All we did was tell Java that we want a particular class that comes from a particular library; in our case, the Scanner class, stored in the java.util library.

The next thing to do is take the class and create an object. As you will see later in the guide, a class is nothing more than a block of code; it won't actually do anything until you create an object from that class. To do this from the Scanner class, this is what we do:

```
Scanner user_input = new Scanner( System.in );
```

Instead of setting up an int or a string variable, we have a scanner variable. We called ours user_input and the name is followed by a = sign and a keyword – new. The new keyword is used when we want a new object created from a class and inside the parentheses, we must tell Java that we want the object to be a System Input object (system.in).

To get user input, we need to call a method into action. One of those is the next method and this acquires the next string of text that a user types on their keyboard:

```
String first_name;
first_name = user_input.next( );
```

A dot must follow user_input and then you will see a list of all the methods available to you – double-click Next and then input a semicolon to end the line. Printing text can also prompt a user:

```
String first_name;
System.out.print("Type your first name: ");
first_name = user_input.next( );
```

Did you spot that println wasn't used this time? We just used print. The difference between the two is that print keeps the cursor on the same line while println moves it to the next.

Next we want the user to type in their surname:

```
String family_name;
System.out.print("Type your family name: ");
family_name = user_input.next( );
```

This is much the same but Java will now store the input in the variable called family_name and not n first_name. The output can be printed like this:

```
String full_name;
full_name = first_name + " " + family_name;

System.out.println("Your name is" + full_name);
```

Another variable has appeared here, a string variable with the name of full_name. The value stored in here is the concatenation of the values in first_name and family_name. A space separates the two and the last line of the code prints it to the window.

Make a change to your code to this:

```
import java.util.Scanner;

public class StringVariables {

        public static void main (String[] args) {

                Scanner user_input = new Scanner (System.in);

                String first_name;

                System.out.print ("Type Your First Name: ");

                first_name = user_input.next();
```

```
            String family_name;
            System.out.print ("Type Your Family Name: ");
            family_name = user_input.next();
            String full_name;
            full_name = first_name + " " + family_name;
            System.out.println("Your name is " + full_name);
    }
}
```

Now run this and see what you get.

What will happen is that Java won't go any further until an input is made on the keyboard and it will also not go on until the Enter key has been pressed. So, following "Type your first name", left-click on the mouse and the cursor starts flashing – type a name and press on the Enter key.

Java will now store your input in the variable named to the left of our equals sign – in our case, this is the first_name variable. Now the program can move on to the next code line so, do the same and type a surname in, pressing the Enter key once more.

The user input is finished so the program can finish executing and the result will be the two names. That is how we get user input and print the data that the variables store in the output window.

Conditional Statements

At the moment we are using sequential programming. This means that our code gets executed from the first line, in order, down to the last line. We call this linear code – Java reads each line from top to bottom.

We don't always need this in our programs though; on occasion you might only want a piece of code to be executed if it has met one or more specified conditions. Let's say that you want a message to be displayed on the screen if a user is 21 or over but you want a different one displayed if they are under 21. You need to be able to control the flow of your code and you can only do that with conditional logic.

Conditional logic mainly uses the IF word. An example would be IF a user is older than 21, this message will be displayed; IF the user is younger than 21, a different message is displayed. It sounds complicated but conditional logic is actually very easy to use.

The IF Statement

One common thing we do in programming is to execute some code when something happens rather than something else happening. It was because of this that the IF statement came about and this is structured like this:

```
if ( Statement ) {

}
```

We start the statement with IF but note that it is between a set of parentheses and is in lower-case. Curly brackets are then used to section off a piece of code that will be executed only if a certain condition has been met. We place that condition in between the set of parentheses:

```
if ( user < 21 ) {

}
```

Our condition is stating that "if the user is less than 21". Note that we use shorthand symbols here and not the actual words "is less than". The symbol for less than is < so our code is saying that, if the users are less than 21, something will happen (a message is displayed):

```
if ( user < 21 ) {

        //DISPLAY THIS MESSAGE

}
```

So, if our user is 21 or older, Java skips the code we inserted in the curly brackets and continues with the rest of the program to the end. The code that we put in the curly brackets will only be executed if the IF condition, the one input between the parentheses, is met.

Before we turn our hands to this, there is another shorthand symbol to be aware of - >. This one indicates greater than and it can be used to make a change to the code to check for users older than 21.

```
if ( user > 21 ) {

        //DISPLAY THIS MESSAGE

}
```

All we have added to our code is a > symbol; the condition between the parentheses will now check if a user is older than 21.

What it won't check for is those users who are 21; only those that are older. If we needed to check if a person was 21 or older, we would need to use "greater than or the same as (equal to) and in programming we can do this using just two symbols - >=:

```
if ( user >= 21 ) {

        //DISPLAY THIS MESSAGE

}
```

In much the same way, we can check to see if users are 21 or younger by using the symbols for "less than or the same as (equal to)". Those symbols are <=:

```
if ( user <= 21 ) {

        //DISPLAY THIS MESSAGE

}
```

All we did was added < and =.

Let's put it all together in one program. First, close down your open program and save it. Start a new project (you know how to do that now) and name your package conditionallogic and your class IFStatements. Now you can add this code to the program:

```
public class IFStatements {

        public static void main(String[] args) {

                int user = 20;

                if (user < 21) {

                        System.out.println("User is less than 21");

                }

        }

}
```

What we did was create an int variable with a value of 20. Our IF statement is going to look for "less than 21" and will print the message that is inside curly brackets. Run this and see what happens.

NetBeans will run the program using bold text in the Project window, rather than the code that you displayed. If you want to run the code in the coding window, right-click on the code and chose Run File – you will now see the output in your Output window.

The next thing we do is change the value for the user variable to 21 from 20 and then run it again. The program should run perfectly without any errors but you won't see anything printed. Why? Because the message to be displayed in inside the IF statement curly brackets and the IF statement is searching for values that are less than 21. If that condition cannot be met, Java ignores the curly brackets and anything in between them, going on to the next section of code.

The IF...ELSE Statement

You could use two IF statements in your code but you could also use an IF...ELSE statement; that statement is structured like this:

```
if ( condition_to_test ) {

}
else {

}
```

The same as the IF statement, our line will start with if followed by a set of parentheses that contains the condition that we want tested for. Again, the curly brackets are used for sectioning the code into the choices that we want to use; the second will follow the ELSE part of the statement and will have its own curly brackets.

Let's look at the code we used for checking the age of user:

```
public static void main(String[] args) {

        int user = 20;

        if (user <= 21) {

                System.out.println("User is 21 or younger");

        }

        else {

                System.out.println("User is older than 21");

        }

}
```

In this code, we have two choices – a user will be 21 or younger or they will be older than 21. Make the change to your code so it looks like the code above and run it – what happens?

The first message should be printed. Change the variable for user to 25, run the program and the second choice should be printed, the one between the ELSE part of the statement's curly brackets. This should be shown in your Output window.

The IF...ELSE IF Statement

You can test more than two choices if you want. Let's say, for example, that we wanted to test for several different age ranges, like 20 to 40, 4 and over, etc. If we have more than two choices, we can use the IF...ELSE IF statement and that is structured like this:

```
if ( condition_one ) {

}
else if ( condition_two ) {

}
else {

}
```

The addition here is:

```
else if ( condition_two ) {

}
```

The initial IF statement tests the first condition. This is followed by the ELSE IF part of the statement with a set of parentheses after it. Between these parentheses is the second condition to test. The final ELSE will catch anything not caught by the first two parts of the statement. Once again, curly brackets are used to section our code and each part of the statement, the IF, ELSE IF and ELSE, each has their own set. If any of these bracket sets is omitted, an error message is thrown up.

Before we move on to any more code, it's worth looking at some of the conditional operators. We already used these four:

- which means greater than
- < which means less than
- >= which means great than or the same as (equal to)
- <= which means less than or the same as (equal to)

There are four more that you can make use of:

- && which means AND
- || which means OR
- == which means HAS A VALUE OF
- ! which means NOT

The first one, indicated by the two ampersands (&) is used when you want to test at least two conditions at the same time. We'll use it to test two age ranges:

else if (user > 21 && user < 50)

We want to see if our user is over 21 but younger than 50 – don't forget that we are looking to see what's in the user variable. Condition one checks to see if a user is 21 or older while condition two checks to see if they are younger than 50. In between these conditions we the && (AND) operator so what this line says is check to see if the user is over AND under 50.

Before you look at the rest of the conditional operators, try this code:

```
public static void main(String[] args) {

        int user = 21;

        if (user <= 21) {

                System.out.println("User is 21 or younger");

        }

        else if (user > 21 && user < 50) {

                System.out.println("User is between 19 and 49");

        }

        else if (user > 50) {

                System.out.println("User is older than 50");

        }

}
```

Run this and test the program – you should already have an idea of what will print. The variable for user has 21 as a value so the message between the brackets for the ELSE IF part of the statement will be seen in the Output window.

The Nested IF Statement

We can nest IF statements as well as nesting IF...ELSE and the IF...ELSE IF statements. Nesting is just the act of placing one IF statement inside another. Let's assume that you want to test if a user is less than 21 but older than 18; you will need a message to be displayed for any user who is older than 18 so the first statement is needed:

```
if ( user < 21 ) {
        System.out.println( "21 or younger");
}
```

To see if the user is older than 18, we need another IF statement and this can be placed, or nested, within the first one, like this:

```
if ( user < 21 ) {
        if ( user > 18  && user < 21 ) {
                System.out.println( "You are 19, 20 or 21");
        }
}
```

Our first IF statement will catch the user variable if the value is lower than 21 and the second IF statement will bring things down to users between 18 and 21. If you wanted something else printed, you would replace the IF statement with an IF...ELSE statement:

```
if ( user < 21 ) {

        if ( user > 18 && user < 21 ) {
                System.out.println( "You are 19, 20 or 21");
        }
        else {
                System.out.println( "18 or younger");
        }

}
```

Look at the placement of the curly brackets carefully; put one in the wrong place or forget to put one in and your code isn't going to run. The nested IF statement might seem a little tricky to get the hang of but all you are really doing is narrowing down your choices.

Boolean Values

With a Boolean value there are only two possible outputs – TRUE or FALSE, 1 or 0, YES or No. In Java, there is a specific variable for these values:

```
boolean user = true;
```

Rather than using a double, int or string variable, we just type boolean (note the lowercase b) and, after the name of the variable, a value is assigned, either TRUE or FALSE. We have used = here as an assignment operator but, if you wanted to know if a variable had a "value of", you would use two = signs.

Try this:

```
boolean user = true;

if ( user == true) {
        System.out.println("it is true");
}
else {
        System.out.println("it is false");
}
```

With our first IF statement, we want to check if the user variable has TRUE value and, with the ELSE part of the statement, we want to see if that value is FALSE. We don't need to say ELSE IF (user==false) because, quite simply, what is not true must be false. All we need is ELSE because, as I said earlier, a Boolean will have just two values.

The last conditional operator to use is NOT and we can use this with Boolean values. Have a look at this example:

```
boolean user = true;

if ( !user ) {
        System.out.println("it is false");
}
else {
        System.out.println("it is true");
}
```

With the exception of one line, it is virtually identical to the previous Boolean code example – that line is:

```
if ( !user ) {
```

Here, we used the NOT conditional operator just before the user variable; an exclamation mark indicates the operator, placed just before the variable that you want to be tested. The NOT operator will test for the opposite of the real value, i.e. negation. We set our user variable as TRUE so the NOT operator will check for FALSE values. It also works the opposite way around. Think of it this way, if it is NOT TRUE is has to be FALSE and vice versa.

Switch Statements

One more way we can use to control statement flow is with a switch statement. The switch statement gives you the chance to test for ranges of values for a variable and may be used instead of an IF...ELSE statement. The switch statement is structured like this:

```
switch ( variable_to_test ) {
        case value:
                code_here;
                break;
        case value:
                code_here;
                break;
        default:
                values_not_caught_above;

}
```

We begin with 'switch' followed by parentheses. In between the parentheses we place the variable that we want to check and we follow this with the curly brackets. The remainder of our switch statement is placed in between those brackets. For every value that is being checked, the word 'case' must be used before the value to be checked:

case value:

A colon follows the value and then we state what should happen if a match is found. This will be the code that will be executed; we must use the break keyword for breaking out of the individual case in our statement.

At the end we have a default value; this is optional and you can use it if you have values that the variable may store but that have not been checked for in any other part of the statement.

This is probably a little confusing at the moment, especially if you are completely new to Java programming. Try the code below; first save and close the code you are working on now and open a new project. Then input the code:

```
public static void main(String[] args) {

        int user = 21;

        switch ( user ) {

                case 21:

                        System.out.println("You're 21");

                        break;

                case 19:

                        System.out.println("You're 19");

                        break;

                case 20:

                        System.out.println("You're 20");

                        break;

                default:

                        System.out.println("You're not 21, 19, or 20");

        }

}
```

First, the code sets the value being tested for. An int variable is set with the name of user and a value of 21 is assigned to it. The switch statement checks the variable to see what is in it before working through each case statement in order. When a match is found, the statement stops and case code is executed; the statement is then broken out of.

Have a play about; try different variable values and see what happens. Just keep in mind that only one value can be checked following case not a range so this would be wrong:

case (user <= 21):

but this would be correct:

case 1: case 2: case 3: case 4:

The line above tests for a range between 1 and 4 but each value must be stated.

Statements – Loops and Iteration

As I mentioned earlier, much of the programming is sequential and that means Java will execute it from top to bottom unless it is told not to. Earlier we looked at the IF statement for telling Java if we don't want something executed. There is another way to do it though. We interrupt the program flow by using loops.

A loop will force your program to start again or to go back to a specific place, allowing that piece of code to be repeatedly executed. Let's see how this works with an example. We'll assume that we want to add the numbers 20 through 30 together; this is easy:

int addition = 20 + 21 + 22 + 23 + 24 + 2 + 36 + 27 + 28 + 29 + 30;

So, that will work when you only have a few numbers to add up but what if you wanted to add a huge range, say all the numbers between 1 and 10,000. A loop can be used on one line of code over and over again until we reached 10,000 and then we break out of the loop and continue with the rest of the code.

The For Loop

We'll begin with the For Loop, the most commonly used Java loop. Think of it as 'looping FOR a set number of times'. The For Loop is structured like this:

for (start_value; end_value; increment_number) {

//YOUR_CODE_GOES_HERE

}

After 'for' (all in lowercase) we have the parentheses. In these we must have three things – the start value of our loop, the end value and a method that takes you from the start to the end. This is the increment number and it would usually start at 1; it can be anything, though, sections of 10 or, where you have a huge range to add, even 100.

Following those parentheses we have the curly brackets, again for sectioning off the code that is to be executed repeatedly. Have a look at this example, it may make things clearer.

Again, we need a new project for this so save the one you are working on and open a new one. Your project name will be 'loops' and the class is 'ForLoops'. Now add this code:

```
public class ForLoops {

    public static void main(String[] args) {

        int loopVal;

        int end_value = 21;

        for (loopVal = 10; loopVal < end_value; loopVal++) {

            System.out.println("Loop Value = " + loopVal);

        }

    }

}
```

We set a variable, an int called loopVal and, on the next line down, we set another one – this will hold the end value, set to 21. We want to loop around printing numbers from 10 to 20.

Note what is inserted between the parentheses:

loopVal =10; loopVal < end_value; loopVal++

First, we tell Java which number to start from; in our case we have assigned the loopVal variable with a value of 10, the first one in the loop. Second, we used some of our conditional logic:

loopVal < end_value

What this says is that loopVal is less than the end_value; while the loopVal variable stays less than end_value, the for loop will continue looping. This goes for any for loop – while it is TRUE that loopVal remains less than end_value, Java will carry on looping the code inserted between the curly brackets.

The final part in our parentheses is:

loopVal++

This tells Java that we want it to start from the loopVal start value and go to the next sequential value. As we are counting 10 to 20, the next number will be 11. However, rather than using that piece of code, we could have done this:

loopVal = loopVal + 1

To the right of our = sign, we have loopVal +1. This tells Java that a value of 1 should be added to the value already in loopVal. The result of the addition is stored in the loopVal variable to the left of the = sign. The result is that a value of 1 is constantly added to that new value and this is called incrementing. This is used so much now that a new notation was invented for it – a new variable that is called ++:

```
int some_number = 0;
some_number++;
```

When Java executes the code, a value of 1 is assigned to some_number, the short version of this:

```
int some_number = 0;
some_number = some_number + 1;
```

As a recap, this is what the for loop says:

- 10 is the loop's start value
- It will continue looping while the value is less than 21
- To reach the end value, 1 must be constantly added to the start value

Within the curly brackets for the for loop, we have:

```
System.out.println("Loop Value = " + loopVal);
```

The value in the loopVal variable is what gets printed, together with some text, so run this and see what happens.

Your program is trapped in this loop and is being forced to continually go round, each time adding a value of 1 to the loopVal variable. This carries on for as long as the loopVal value is less than what is stored in the end_value variable. The code within the set of curly brackets will be continuously executed and that is what loops are all about – t continuously execute the code within the curly brackets.

This next example adds the numbers 1 through 10; have a go at it:

```
public static void main(String[] args) {

    int loopVal;

    int end_value = 11;

    int addition = 0;

    for (loopVal = 1; loopVal < end_value; loopVal++) {

        addition = addition + loopVal;

    }
```

System.out.println("Total = " + addition);

}

Run the program and you should get 55 as the output. Note that this is pretty much the same as the previous code; we have two variables called loopVal and end_value and then we have a third variable named addition. This is an int that contains the value from the addition.

In between the for loop parentheses, it is once again much the same – for as long as loopVal remains lower than end_value, the loop repeats, each time adding 1 to the new value. Note the use of loopVal to denote our loop.

There is just one line of code inside our curly brackets:

addition = addition + loopVal;

What this does is adds all our numbers; if you are at all confused about how it works, begin at the right of the = sign, where it says:

addition + loopVal;

First time around, the addition variable is assigned a value of 0 while loopVal has a starting value of 1. Java will add 1 to this value, storing the resulting number in the addition variable to the left of the = sign. The value stored in the addition variable is deleted and the new value added. On the second loop, the following code goes in between our parentheses:

addition (1) + loopVal (2);

As is fairly obvious, add 1 to 2 and you get 3 so this is the value that replaces what is in the addition variable. On the third loop, we see these as the new values:

addition (3) + loopVal (3);

Java adds the numbers together and stores 6 as the new value in the addition variable. This continues until all the additions are done and the loop is ended; the result printed is 55.

The While Loop

Yet another loop commonly used is the While loop and these are far easier to understand than For loops are. They are structured like this:

while (condition) {

}

We start with 'while', lowercase, and insert the condition we want to test for in between our parentheses. Again we have those curly brackets containing the code that will be executed. Have a look at this example of a while loop that prints text; have a go at it:

```
int loopVal = 0;

while ( loopVal < 5) {
        System.out.println("Printing Some Text");
        loopVal++;
}
```

Between the parentheses is the condition we are testing; the code is to be looped for as long as the loopVal variable stays below 5. Inside our curly brackets, a text line is printed. Next, the loopVal variable must be incremented; leave this step out and you will have an infinite loop because loopVal will not be able to move past its start value of 0.

Although loopVal was used to get to the end condition, when you need a checking value and not a counting value, the while loop is better. An example would be that the loop could continue until a specific key on the keyboard was pressed, something you commonly see in games. We could say that, to exit the while loop, the X key would need to be pressed (exiting out of the game at the same time).

Do … While Loop

The last loop to look at now is the Do…While loop, related to the While loop and structured like this:

```
int loopVal = 0;

do {
        System.out.println("Printing Some Text");
        loopVal++;
}
while ( loopVal < 5 );
```

Once again, Java carries on looping until the final condition is met but, this time, the While section of the statement is near to the bottom while the condition doesn't change – continue to loop while the value of loopVal is less than 5.

The biggest difference is that the curly bracketed code in do...while will be executed a minimum of one time whereas, as far as the while loop is concerned, that condition could have been met already. If this is the case, Java will break out of the loop and won't bother even looking the bracketed code, let alone execute it.

We can test this by trying the while loop first; change your loopVal value to a 5 and run it. You should see that the text does NOT get printed. Now change the do part of the loop, putting 5 as the value of loopVal, run it and the text will print just once before Java gets out of the loop.

Next, we'll take a quick look at arrays before we see how they work with loops.

Arrays

Perhaps one of the most important of all concepts that you need to learn in order to be effective is the array. Until now, we have looked at variables that hold just one value – the ints hold one number and the strings hold one text string. Arrays are used when we want to hold two or more values, perhaps a list. Arrays can be thought as columns in a spreadsheet – a spreadsheet can have one or it can have many columns.

Similar to the spreadsheet, each row in an array has a position number; these begin at 0 and go up for each position that has a value. Setting up an array requires that you inform Java what type of data is being stored in it – strings, Booleans, integers, and so on. Then you need to tell Java the number of positions in the array and do this to set them up:

int[ ] aryNums;

There is only one difference between setting up an int variable and an array – the data type in an array is followed by square brackets –[]. These brackets are enough for Java to know that an array is being set up. Look at the above code – note the name of the array is aryNums. So long as you follow the variable naming conventions, you can call your array whatever you want.

Right now, all we have done is tell java that we want to set up an integer array; we haven't yet told it how many positions it will have and to do that, a new array object is required:

aryNums = new int[5];

Start with the array name with an equals sign afterward. Then comes the new keyword and the data type, followed by the square brackets. In those brackets is the size of the array – the number of positions it will have. All of this can go on a single line:

int[ ] aryNums = new int[5];

So, Java now knows that we want an integer array with positions. Once Java has executed that line, a default value is assigned to the array; because we have an integer array, all positions will have an identical default of 0 as their values. Assigning a value to an array position is done the same way as any value is assigned:

aryNums[0] = 15;

We gave position 0 a value of 15 using the square brackets to refer to the position. All positions are assigned in this way:

aryNums[1] = 12;

aryNums[2] = 26;

And so on. Don't forget, positioning starts at 0 so position 3 will have the index of 2. If you already know the values that will be in the array, you could do this:

int[ ] aryNums = { 10, 20, 30, 40 };

To do this, curly brackets are used following the = sign and those brackets will contain the values to go into the array. The first value will go to position 0, the second to position 1 and so on. Note that the square brackets must still be used after the data type but you won't need to use the new keyword or the repetition of data type and square brackets. However, this will only apply to the int, string or char data types; for anything else, the new keyword is required.

For example, you could do this:

String[ ] aryStrings = {"January", "February", "March", "April" };

But you couldn't do this:

boolean[ ] aryBools = {true, false, true, false};

The new keyword is still needed to set up a Boolean array:

boolean[ ] aryBools = new boolean[ ] {true, false, true, false};

To access the array values, the array name is needed along with the array position inside the square brackets:

System.out.println(aryNums[2]);

This will print whatever value is at position 2 in the array.

Time for a bit of practical work. Start a new project and give it whatever name you want, remembering that the class must also be given a name that is relevant. For our example, we called our package prjarrays and we called the class ArraysTest. If you choose to use something different, make sure you put their names in your code:

```
public class ArraysTest {

        public static void main(String[] args) {

                int[] aryNums = new int[5];

                aryNums[0] = 20;

                aryNums[1] = 34;

                aryNums[2] = 16;

                aryNums[3] = 28;

                aryNums[4] = 83;

                System.out.println( aryNums[2] );

        }
```

```
}
```

Run it and see what you get.

Change the print line so the array position is now, run again and a different number will print.

Arrays and Loops

Where arrays really come into their own is when we use them with loops. We learned how to assign values to positions, like this:

```
aryNums[0] =20;
```

But, if you want to assign multiple numbers to one array, this is not a practical way of doing things. For example, let's say that you write a lottery program and you want it to assign the numbers 1 to 49 to positions in an array. Rather than having to type out that many positions and values, you can use a loop. This is how:

```
public class ArraysTest {

        public static void main(String[] args) {

                int[] lottery_numbers = new int[49];

                int i;

                for (i=0; i < lottery_numbers.length; i++) {

                        lottery_numbers[i] = i + 1;

                        System.out.println( lottery_numbers[i] );

                }

        }

}
```

What we have here is one array that has 49 values (all ints) and then one loop code. Note what the final loop condition is:

```
i < lottery_numbers.length
```

Length is a property of an array object and it is used for finding out how many positions the array has. The loop will continue for so long as variable i has a value lower than the size of the array. To assign each position with a value, we would do this:

```
lottery_numbers[i] = i + 1;
```

Rather than using the square brackets for the array name to hold the code value, instead we have the variable i. Every time the loop goes around, this will increase by 1. We then use the loop value to access the array positions and assign each position with a value of i + 1. This is the incremented loop value with 1 added to it. Because loop values start at 0, you will get all the numbers from 1 to 49. The other line in our loop will print whatever value each of the positions has.

Sorting Arrays

Java also contains methods that allow you to sort arrays. One of those methods is called sort and to use it, you need to reference the Java library it is stored in. That library is called Arrays and we use the import statement to do this. Have a go at it – add this import statement into your program called aryNums:

```
import java.util.Arrays;
```

You should have something like this:

```
import java.util.Arrays;

public class ArraysTest {

        public class static void main(String[] args) {

                int[] aryNums;

                aryNums = new int[5];

                aryNums[0] = 20;

                aryNums[1] = 34;

                aryNums[2] = 16;

                aryNums[3] = 28;

                aryNums[4] = 83;

        }

}
```

Okay, now we have the Arrays library, we can use the sort method, like this:

```
Arrays.sort( aryNums );
```

First we use Arrays and a dot. As soon as the dot is typed in NetBeans will show you a list of everything you can do so type in sort. Then you have the parentheses inside which is the name of the array that you are sorting. We don't need the square brackets here.

Have a go for yourself with this code:

```
import java.util.Arrays;

public class ArraysTest {
	public static void main(String[] args) {
		int[] aryNums;
		aryNums = new int [5];
		aryNums[0] = 20;
		aryNums[1] = 34;
		aryNums[2] = 16;
		aryNums[3] = 28;
		aryNums[4] = 83;
		Arrays.sort(aryNums);
		int i;
		for (i=0; i < aryNums.length; i++) {
			System.out.println("num:" + aryNums[i]);
		}
	}
}
```

Our for loop will continue to loop, printing the value for each of the positions. Run this and you should see that the array has been sorted and is shown in ascending order.

Arrays and Strings

We can also use arrays to store text strings and this is done the same as the integers:

```
String[ ] aryString = new String[5] ;

aryString[0] = "This";
aryString[1] = "is";
aryString[2] = "a";
aryString[3] = "string";
aryString[4] = "array";
```

We set up a string array that contains 5 positions, each one with text assigned to it. Next, we will see a loop that goes around each position and prints the value at each position:

```
int i;
for ( i=0; i < aryString.length; i++ ) {
```

```
        System.out.println( aryString[i] );
}
```

The loop repeats itself for as long as the i variable value is lower than the aryString array length. Run that program to see what happens.

String arrays can also be sorted in the same way that int arrays are sorted, using the sort method. However, this time, although we get the position sorted into ascending order, they are alphabetical. But, what about lower and uppercase letters? How are they sorted? Java uses Unicode letters to compare each letter to another one so uppercase letters come before lowercase letters.

Try this example:

```
import java.util.Arrays;

public class StringArrays {

        public static void main(String[] args) {

                String[] aryString = new String[5] ;

                aryString[0] = "This";

                aryString[1] = "is";

                aryString[2] = "a";

                aryString[3] = "String";

                aryString[4] = "array";

                Arrays.sort(aryString);

                int i;

                for (i=0; i < aryString.length; i++) {

                        System.out.println( aryString[i] );

                }

        }

}
```

Run it and see what happens.

The array gets sorted but did you spot that "This" was the first word? With alphabetical lists, 'a' should have been the first but this is the perfect example of Java putting uppercase letters first. Change the 'T' on 'This" to a lowercase letter and run the program again; you should now see a different order.

Multi-Dimensional Arrays

Okay, until now, we have looked only at arrays that hold one data column but we can use multiple data columns. We call these multi-dimensional arrays and they are much like a spreadsheet that contains both rows and columns. For our example, we'll say that we have 5 columns and 4 rows, with a total of 20 values. A multi-dimensional array is structured like this:

int[ ][ ] aryNumbers = new int[5][4];

They are set up much like the arrays we looked at previously but with one difference – two sets of the square brackets. The first set is for the rows and the second set is for the columns. In the code line right above the code, we informed Java that we need an array with 5 rows and 4 columns. Storing values in a multi-dimensional array requires care that each row and each column is tracked.

This example shows how the first few rows would be filled out:

aryNumbers[0][0] = 15;
aryNumbers[0][1] = 19;
aryNumbers[0][2] = 35;
aryNumbers[0][3] = 10;

As you can see, the first row is 0 and the columns are 0 to 4, totaling 5 rows. The second row would look like this:

aryNumbers[1][0] = 30;
aryNumbers[1][1] = 55;
aryNumbers[1][2] = 76;
aryNumbers[1][3] = 2;

Although the column numbers remain the same, the row numbers are now all given the value of 1.

Accessing all of the items from any multi-dimensional array requires the use of a loop within a loop. Look at the code below where we use a double-loop to access all our numbers:

```
public static void main(String[] args) {

        int[][] aryNumbers = new int[6][5];

        aryNumbers[0][0] = 10;

        aryNumbers[1][0] = 30;

        aryNumbers[0][1] = 12;

        aryNumbers[1][1] = 55;
```

```
aryNumbers[0][2] = 43;
aryNumbers[1][2] = 76;
aryNumbers[0][3] = 11;
aryNumbers[1][3] = 2;

aryNumbers[2][0] = 30;
aryNumbers[3][0] = 40;
aryNumbers[2][1] = 67;
aryNumbers[3][1] = 12;
aryNumbers[2][2] = 32;
aryNumbers[3][2] = 87;
aryNumbers[2][3] = 14;
aryNumbers[3][3] = 14;

aryNumbers[4][0] = 50;
aryNumbers[5][0] = 60;
aryNumbers[4][1] = 86;
aryNumbers[5][1] = 53;
aryNumbers[4][2] = 66;
aryNumbers[5][2] = 44;
aryNumbers[4][3] = 13;
aryNumbers[5][3] = 12;

int rows = 5;
int columns = 4;
int i, j;
for (i = 0; i < rows; i++) {
        for ( j = 0; j < columns; j++) {
                System.out.print(aryNumbers[i][j] + " ");
        }
```

```
            System.out.println("");
      }
}
```

The initial for loop is used for the rows and the second one is used for the columns. With the first loop, 0 is the value of the i variable. In the for loop, the code is another loop and the entire double loop is executed for as long as the i variable value stays as 0. The second loop has another variable, named j and both variables, i and j, are used to access the array:

```
aryNumbers[ i ][ j ]
```

We use the double loop system for looping through multi-dimensional array values, one row at a time.

Array Lists

If you don't know the number of items an array will have in it, a better way would be to use an ArrayList. ArrayLists are dynamic data structures and this means they can change – we can add to and take away from the list of items. A normal array is a static data structure because it remains the same size all the way through – whatever you declared it as at the start is the size it will always be.

Setting an ArrayList up requires you to import ArrayList from the library called java.util:

```
import java.util.ArrayList;
```

Now the ArrayList object can be created:

```
ArrayList listTest = new ArrayList( );
```

We don't need square brackets; once the object has been created, the add method can be used for adding elements to the list:

```
listTest.add( "first item" );
listTest.add( "second item" );
listTest.add( "third item" );
listTest.add( 7 );
```

In between the set of parentheses for the add method you add in whatever you need to add to the ArrayList. You can only add objects and, for our first three, we added strings; the fourth is a number of type int – it is a number int, not an int of the primitive data type.

Referencing items already in the list is done using the get method and an index number:

```
listTest.get(3);
```

What this line does is get the item from the index position of 3. Remember, positions begin at 0 so this would be item four on the list.

Removing items from your ArrayList can be done in two ways:

With the index number:

listTest.remove(2);

Or with the value:

listTest.remove("second item");

When an item is removed, the ArrayList will be resized so be very careful when using the first method, the index number, to add items to a list. If item 2 had been removed, there would only be 3 items left and trying to remove the item from position 3 would just throw up an error.

You can also use an iterator to go through the list items and, again, we must import this from the java.util library:

import java.util.Iterator;

The ArrayList is then attached to an iterator object:

Iterator it = listTest.iterator( );

A new iterator object is set up with a name and it can then be used for going through every item in an ArrayList called listTest. We use the iterator object because it has methods called hasNext and next. We can use these methods in a loop:

```
while ( it.hasNext( ) ) {
        System.out.println( it.next( ) );
}
```

The hasNext method returns a Boolean value; if there are no other items in the ArrayList, this will be a value of FALSE. The next method goes through all the list items and to test it, we can try this code:

```
public static void main(String[] args) {

        ArrayList listTest = new ArrayList();

        listTest.add("first item");

        listTest.add("second item");

        listTest.add("third item");
```

```
        listTest.add(7);
        Iterator it = listTest.iterator();
        while (it.hasNext()) {
                System.out.println(it.next());
        }
        //Remove an item from the list
        listTest.remove("second item");
        //Print new list
        System.out.println("Whole list = " + listTest);
        //Get an item from Index position 1
        System.out.println("Position 1 = " + listTest.get (1));
}
```

Note which of the code lines prints the entire list:

```
System.out.println( "Whole list=" + listTest );
```

This is a much quicker and easier way of seeing every item on your list, particularly when your list is long. Run the code, see what you get.

To recap, ArrayLists should be used when you do not know the number of elements your list will have.

Functions and Methods

A Java method is a collection of statements, all performing a particular operation. Let's say that you were calling the method called System.out.println(); Java will execute a number of different statements that will print a message to your console. We're going to look at the creation of methods or, as they are often called, functions. Start a new project.

How to Create a Method

A method is structured in this way:

```
public static int methodName(int a, int b) {
  // body
}
```

What does all of this mean?

public static – this is a modifier

int – this is the return type

methodName – this is the name of the method

a, b – these are formal parameters

int a, int b – these are parameter lists

Defining a method requires a method header and a method body, as you can see here:

```
modifier returnType nameOfMethod (Parameter List) {
 // method body
}
```

In this example:

- modifier – defines the access type of the method and is optional
- returnType – is an indicator that a value may be returned by the method
- Parameter List – this lists the parameters along with the type, the order and how many parameters are in the method. This is optional because methods don't need parameters.
- nameOfMethod – is the name of the method and also has the list of parameters
- method body – this is where we define what the method will do with your statements

In the next example you can see the code of a method called max(). This method will take two parameters called num1 and num2 and we will see the maximum between both of these parameters as the return:

```
/** this code returns the maximum between the two numbers */


public static int maxFunction(int n1, int n2) {
 int max;
 if (n1 > n2)
  max = n2;
 else
  max = n1;


 return max;
```

```
}
```

Calling Methods

When you want to use methods or functions, you have a choice of two ways to do it – either with a value or without a value. It is quite simple to call a method – this means that the method gets invoked, program control goes to the method and is then returned to the caller under two conditions:

- When the execution of the return statement has finished
- When the method's closing brace is reached

In the next example, we will see how methods are defined and called:

```
public class ExampleMinNumber {

    public static void main(String[] args) {

        int a = 11;

        int b = 6;

        int c = minFunction(a, b);

        System.out.println("Minimum Value = " + c);

    }



    /** returns the minimum of two numbers */

    public static int minFunction(int n1, int n2) {

        int min;

        if (n1 > n2)

            min = n2;

        else

            min = n1;


        return min;

    }

}
```

Input this and run it, see what it does.

The void Keyword

If we didn't want a value returned from the method, the void keyword would be used. In the example below, we have a method named methodRankPoints – because we don't want a value from this method it is a void method. To call it you will need a statement as you can see in this example:

```
public static void main(String[] args) {

        methodRankPoints(255.7);

}


public static void methodRankPoints(double points) {

        if (points >= 202.5) {

                System.out.println("Rank:A1");

        }else if (points >= 122.4) {

                System.out.println("Rank:A2");

  }else {

        System.out.println("Rank:A3");

  }

}
```

Run the program and see what the output is

Passing Parameters by Value

When a method is called, arguments must be passed and must be in the same order as the parameter that does with them in your method. Parameters may be passed in two ways – by value and by reference. To pass them by value, a method that has a parameter must be called and this will result in the argument value being passed to the parameter, as you can see in this example:

```
public class SwappingExample {

        public static void main(String[] args)

        {

                int a = 30;

                int b = 45;

                System.out.println("Before swapping, a = " +a + " and b = " + b);
```

```
        // Invoke the swap method
        swapFunction(a, b);
        System.out.println("\n**Now, Before and After swapping values will be same here**:");
        System.out.println("After swapping, a = " +a + " and b is " + b);
    }

    public static void swapFunction(int a, int b)
    {
        System.out.println("Before swapping(Inside), a = "+a+" b = "+ b);

        // Swap n1 with n2
        int c = a;
        a = b;
        b = c;
        System.out.println("After swapping(Inside), a = " +a+" b = "+ b);
    }
}
```

Run this and see what you get

Method Overloading

If a class has two methods or more called the same name but each having their different parameters, it is called method overloading. This is not the same as overriding a method – for this, each method would be identical in name, type, parameters, etc.

Let's assume that we have a double type and we want to know what its minimum number is. Overloading would be introduced to create a minimum of two methods of the same name but having different parameters, as such:

```
public class ExampleOverloading {
    public static void main(String[] args) {
        int a = 11;
        int b = 6;
```

```
        double c = 7.3;
        double d = 9.4;
        int result1 = minFunction(a, b);

        // same function name with different parameters
        double result2 = minFunction(c, d);
        System.out.println("Minimum Value = " + result1);
        System.out.println("Minimum Value = " + result2);
}

// for integer
public static int minFunction(int n1, int n2) {
        int min;
        if (n1 > n2)
                min = n2;
        else
                min = n1;

        return min;
}

// for double
public static double minFunction(double n1, double n2) {
        double min;
        if (n1 > n2)
                min = n2;
        else
                min = n1;

        return min;
```

```
        }
}
```

Run it and see what happens.

When you overload, you can make your code infinitely easier to read. What we have done here is provided two methods with identical names but each with different parameters; the result is the minimum number from both int and from double.

Classes and Objects

Finally, we are going to look at classes and objects;

An object in Java has got to have a state, which will be stored in a field and a behavior, indicated by a method.

A class is a sort of map, a blueprint if you like, from which an object is created. This is what a class looks like:

```
public class Dog {
  String breed;
  int ageC;
  String color;

  void barking() {
  }

  void whining() {
  }

  void sleeping() {
  }
}
```

A class may have any of these variable types:

- Local - defined within a constructor, block or method. The variable is declared and then initialized inside a method and destroyed once the method has ended.
- Instance – defined in a class but are outside a method. Initialized when instantiation of the class happens and can be accessed from inside any constructor, block or method of the class.
- Class – declared inside the class, uses the static keyword and are outside any method.

Classes can have multiple methods, as many as required to access all the different kinds of values in the method. In our example above, we had three methods – barking(), whining() and sleeping().

Constructors

Every class will have a constructor; if you omit it, a default one will be built by the compiler. When you create a new object, at least one constructor must be invoked. As a rule, the name of a constructor must be the same as that of the class and there can be as many constructors as a class requires.

This is what a constructor looks like:

```
public class Puppy {

 public Puppy() {

 }


 public Puppy(String name) {

  // This constructor has a single parameter, name.

 }

}
```

Creating Objects

We already know that a class is a kind of blueprint to create objects from so it goes without saying that the object is created from the class. For a new object to be created, we need the new keyword.

These are the three steps needed to create an object from a class:

Declaration - a variable must be declared with a name and the object type

Instantiation – the new keyword is used for creating the object

Initialization – the constructor is called and this initializes the object.

The next example shows how objects are created:

```
public class Puppy {
    public Puppy(String name) {
        // This constructor contains a single parameter called name.
        System.out.println("Passed Name is :" + name );
    }

    public static void main(String []args) {
        // The next statement will create an object called myPuppy
        Puppy myPuppy = new Puppy( "fluffy" );
    }
}
```

Run this and see what happens.

Accessing Instance Variables and Methods

Objects can be used when we want to access instance variables and methods; this example shows how we access an instance variable:

```
/* First we create the object */
ObjectReference = new Constructor();


/* Now we call our variable, like this */
ObjectReference.variableName;


/* Now a class method is called, like this */
ObjectReference.MethodName();
```

Next, we can see the instance variables and methods in a class are accessed:

```
public class Puppy {
    int PuppyAge;
```

```
    public Puppy(String name) {
        // This constructor contains a single parameter called name.
        System.out.println("Name chosen is :" + name );
    }

    public void setAge(int age) {
        PuppyAge = age;
    }

    public int getAge() {
        System.out.println("Puppy's age is :" + PuppyAge );
        return PuppyAge;
    }

    public static void main(String[] args) {
        /* Object creation */
        Puppy myPuppy = new Puppy( "fluffy" );

        /* Now we call the class method to set the Puppy's age */
        myPuppy.setAge(2);

        /* Next, we call another class method to get the Puppy's age */
        myPuppy.getAge();

        /* We access instance variable in this way */
        System.out.println("Variable Value :" + myPuppy.PuppyAge );
    }
}
```

Run this and see what happens.

Import Statements

One important thing to remember is that paths must be fully qualified and that includes the names of the class and the package. If not, the compiler will struggle to load the source code and the classes. To qualify a path, we need to use import statements and, in this example, we see how a compiler loads the requested classes into the directory we specify:

```
import java.io.*;
```

Next, we need two classes created, one called Employee and one called EmployeeTest. We use the following code to do this – keep in mind that Employee is the name of the class and it is a public class. Do this and then save the file, calling it Employee.java.

Also note that we have four instance variables here – age, name, designation, and salary, along with one constructor that has been explicitly defined and that takes a parameter:

```
public class Employee {

    String name;

    int age;

    String designation;

    double salary;


    // This is the constructor of the class called Employee

    public Employee(String name) {

        this.name = name;

    }


    // We assign the age of the Employee to the variable called age.

    public void empAge(int empAge) {

        age = empAge;

    }


    /* We assign the designation to the variable called designation.*/

    public void empDesignation(String empDesig) {

        designation = empDesig;

    }
```

```
        /* We assign the salary to the variable called salary.*/
        public void empSalary(double empSalary) {
                salary = empSalary;
        }

        /* Print the Employee details */
        public void printEmployee() {
                System.out.println("Name:"+ name );
                System.out.println("Age:" + age );
                System.out.println("Designation:" + designation );
                System.out.println("Salary:" + salary);
        }
}
```

Code processing begins with a main method so you need to ensure that your code has a main method and we need to create some objects. We will start by creating a class called EmployeeTest and this will create a couple of instances of the class called Employee. The methods for each object must be invoked so that the values may be assigned to the variables. Save this code in EmployeeTest:

```
public class EmployeeTest {
        public static void main(String args[]) {
                /* Create two objects by using constructor */
                Employee empOne = new Employee("Bobby Bucket");
                Employee empTwo = new Employee("Shelley Mary");

                // Invoke the methods for each of the objects we created
                empOne.empAge(28);
                empOne.empDesignation("Senior Software Developer");
                empOne.empSalary(1500);
                empOne.printEmployee();
```

```
        empTwo.empAge(22);
        empTwo.empDesignation("Software Developer");
        empTwo.empSalary(850);
        empTwo.printEmployee();
    }
}
```

Now the classes need to be compiled and EmployeeTest run; do this and see what you get.

You should see this:

Output

```
C:\> javac Employee.java
C:\> javac EmployeeTest.java
C:\> java EmployeeTest
Name: Bobby Bucket
Age:28
Designation: Senior Software Developer
Salary:1850.000
Name: Shelley Mary
Age:22
Designation: Software Developer
Salary:850.00
```

Chapter 2: Java Data Structures and Algorithms

Algorithms and data structures are vital components of data science, a branch that studies data, how it is represented in memory, and how data structures transform into algorithms. In Java programming, data structures are used for the storage and organization of data, while algorithms are used for the manipulation of the data stored in the structures. That is fairly straightforward, yes? The more you can learn and understand both data structures and algorithms, the more efficient you can make your Java programs.

We will start by looking at what data structures are, how they are classified before we move on to algorithms and how they are represented. Following that we will have a quick look at complexity before we look at it all in more detail. The first part is an overview.

An Overview of Data Structures

A data structure is based on an ADT – an abstract data type. An ADT is a mathematical model designed for data types that are defined by their semantics, or behavior, from the data user's point of view. This is particularly in terms of the potential values of the data, the operations that may be performed on the data, and how these operations behave.

Abstract data types do not care how their values are represented in memory, nor do they care about the implementation of the operations. Take a Java interface, for example, a data type that is not connected to any implementation. By contrast, the data structure is a solid implementation of at least one abstract data type, much the same way that class interfaces are implemented in Java.

Some examples of abstract data types include, Vehicle, Employee, List, and arrays. The List ADT is also known as the Sequence ADT and is described as a collection of elements that have been placed in order, each element sharing a common data type. Each of the elements has a position in the list and we can also have duplicate elements. Some of the basic operations that the List ADT supports are:

- Creation of lists that are new and empty
- Appending values to the end of a list
- Inserting values in a list
- Deleting values from a list
- Iteration over a list
- Destruction of a list

Some of the data structures that are able to implement List ADTs include one-dimensional arrays of fixed size and dynamic, along with singly-linked lists and we'll be discussing these later on.

Classification of Data Structures

There are multiple data structure types, from a single variable, an array, right up to linked lists that have objects with multiple fields. Every data structure can be classified as an aggregate or a primitive and some have the classification of a container.

Primitives vs Aggregates vs Containers

The simplest of all data structures are those that store just a single item of data, for example, a variable with a Boolean value or one that has an integer. These are known as primitive data structures.

Many of the data structures can store multiple items of data, such as arrays that have data items in each of its slots or objects that can have data items in each of its fields. These are known as aggregate data structures.

Whatever data items can be stored in and retrieved from is considered to be a data structure. A lot of data structures were designed to provide descriptions of different entities. For example, Employee class instances are a type of data structure that describe employees, while Vehicle class instances describe different vehicles. By contrast, there are data structures that exist as storage for other data structures. For example, we can use arrays for storing object references or primitive values and this kind of data structure is known as a container.

An Overview of Algorithms

Historically, algorithms were used as tools for mathematical computation and they are incredibly deeply ingrained in computer science and, more specifically, with the data structures. An algorithm is a series of instructions that are designed to complete a specific task over a finite time period. Algorithms have the following qualities:

- They can receive zero inputs or more
- They will produce a minimum of one output
- They consist of instructions that are clear and are unambiguous
- They will finish after a pre-determined number of steps
- They are simple enough that they can be done with just a pencil and a piece of paper.

Be aware that, while a program may have an algorithmic nature, they do not always terminate without some kind of external intervention.

There are quite a few code sequences that would qualify as being an algorithm, for example a sequence of instructions that will result in a report being printed. Perhaps you have heard of Euclid's algorithm, a famous one used for calculating the biggest common divisor in mathematical terms. We could even say that the basic operations for a data structure are algorithms.

A Deeper Look

We know that a data structure is a way of storing data so that it can be used more efficiently. Here, we look at the terms that describe the foundation of any data structure:

- Interface – every data structure will have an interface, a representation of all the operations that the data structure provides support for. The interface will show just a list of those operations, along with the parameter types each can accept and the operation's return types.
- Implementation – this will give us the data structure's internal representation, along with defining the algorithms that the data structure operations use.

Data Structure Characteristics

Every data structure has the following characteristics:

- Correctness - all implementations of data structures should properly and correctly implement their interfaces.
- Time Complexity – the time taken to run or execute a data structure's operations must be kept to a minimum
- Space Complexity – in the same vein, a data structure operation should also use the minimum amount of memory

Why We Need Data Structures

As we move swiftly through the digital age, applications grow more complex, richer in data and, as a result, they face three very common problems:

- Data Search – think of this – a store inventory that contains 1 million items. If we want the application to search for an item, it must search through potentially 1 million items, significantly slowing the search down. As more data becomes available, so the searches continue to slow down.
- Processor Speed – Although processor speeds can be very high, as data grows to contain billions of records, those speeds will fall.
- Multiple Requests – data can be searched for simultaneously by potentially thousands of users on one web server and that can cause even the fastest of servers to fail while in the process of searching.

Data structures were the answer to these problems. Data structures organize the data in such a way that a user may not need to search every item, meaning the required data can be found almost instantly.

Execution Time Cases

We compare the execution time of various data structures in a relative manner using three different cases:

- Worst Case - the worst case scenario is the one where a specific operation on a data structure takes the longest it possibly can. If the worst case time of an operation is $f(n)$, the operation will take no more than $f(n)$ time; $f(n)$ is representing the function of n.
- Average Case – the average case scenario is the one where an operation on a data structure is averaged out. If the operation were to take $f(n)$ time to complete execution, then we can expect m operations to take m $f(n)$ time.
- Best Case – the best case scenario is the one where the operation on a data structure takes the least amount of time possible. If the operation were to take $f(n)$ time to complete execution, then the proper operation can take time as a random number that is the maximum as $f(n)$.

Basic Terminology

- Data - one value or a set of values
- Data Item – references just one unit of values
- Group Items – data items divided down into subitems
- Elementary Items – Data items that may not be divided in any way
- Attribute and Entity – one that has specific properties or attributes that can have values assigned to them.
- Entity Set – a set of entities that have attributes that may be similar
- Field – one elementary unit that is representative of an entity attribute
- Record – a set of field values for a specified entity
- File – a set of records of all the entities in a specified set of entities

An algorithm is a procedure done step by step, defining instructions that must be executed in a specific order to get the output we desire. They are usually created independently to any underlying language. In simple terms, this means that any algorithm may be implemented in multiple programming languages.

As far as data structures go, these are some of the most important algorithm categories:

- Search - this algorithm searches a data structure for a specified item
- Sort – this algorithm will sort specified items into a specified order
- Insert -this algorithm will insert an item into a structure at a given point
- Update – this algorithm will update a given item that exists in a data structure
- Delete – this algorithm will delete a given item from a specified data structure

Characteristics of an Algorithm

We cannot call all procedures by the name of 'algorithm'. A true algorithm will have these characteristics (we already mentioned these earlier but these are important to learn):

- Unambiguous – an algorithm must be clear and it must be unambiguous, with each step or phase and the related inputs and outputs being clear and leading to a single meaning
- Input – it must have at least 0 inputs that are well-defined
- Output – it must have at least 1 output that is well-defined and this should match the output you are looking for
- Finiteness – an algorithm must end within a defined number of steps
- Feasibility – an algorithm must be feasible with all the resources available to it
- Independent – it must have clear, step by step instructions, independent of any one computer programming language.

Ok, I promise not to reiterate those points again! But, in all seriousness, you must learn them if you want to be efficient at programming and using algorithms.

How to Write an Algorithm

There actually are not any standards, none that are well enough defined at any rate, which tell us how to write an algorithm. Instead, algorithms are dependent on the problem and the resources and are never, ever written with the purpose of supporting a specific piece of code.

Every computer programming language will share code constructs, like the flow-control, loops, etc. and we can use these constructs for writing an algorithm. These are usually written step by step, but there are exceptions to this. The process of writing an algorithm is executed after we have properly defined the problem domain; by this, I mean that to write an algorithm, you need to know what the problem is so you know how to solve it.

Let's look at an example:

Problem – The problem we are solving is adding two numbers together and having the result displayed.

Step 1 – Start

Step 2 – we declare a, b, and c, all integers

Step 3 – the values of a and b are defined

Step 4 – the values of a and b are added together

Step 5 – the output of the addition between a and b is stored in c

Step 6 – we print the value of c

Step 7 - Stop

An algorithm informs a programmer how a program should be coded. Another way of writing the above algorithm would be:

Step 1 – Start add

Step 2 – obtain the values from a and b

Step 3 – c <- a + b

Step 4 – display the value of c

Step 5 – Stop

When we talk about designing and analyzing an algorithm, method two would normally be the one used to describe it. This is because it is far easier for analyst if they don't need to work around unnecessary definitions; he or she can better see the operations in use and the flow of the process.

Note – it is optional to write the step numbers – they are not necessary.

So, algorithms are designed to provide a solution to a specified problem and there is always more than one process to solve a problem. Because of this, we can design several algorithms for one problem and the next step in the process would be to analyze all the algorithms and implement the one that provides the best solution.

Analysis of an Algorithm

We can analyze the efficiency of an algorithm at two stages – before we implement it and after it has been implemented. Those stages are called:

- A Priori Analysis - the theoretical analysis. We measure algorithm efficiency by assuming that every other factor, like processor speed, for example, are all constant and will have no effect on the algorithm implementation.
- A Posterior Analysis – the empirical analysis. We use a programming language to implement the algorithm, which is executed on the target machine. During this analysis, we collect the actual stats, such as the time taken to run the algorithm and the space it needs.

So, analysis of any algorithm is centered upon the time taken to execute or run the operations in the algorithm and the running time is defined by how many instructions are executed for each operation.

The Complexity of an Algorithm

Let's say that X is the algorithm and n represents the input data size. The two major factors are the running time and the space used and these are both used to determine how efficient X is:

- Time – this factor is measured by how many key operations there are in the sorting algorithm, for example comparison operations.

- Space – this factor is measured by determining the maximum amount of memory space the algorithm requires.

Algorithm complexity, f(n), provides both the time taken to run and/or the space the algorithm requires in terms of n being the input data size.

Time Complexity and Time Complexity Functions

Before we look at time complexity, consider this pseudocode for printing an array:

```
DECLARE INTEGER i, x[] = [ 10, 15, -1, 32 ]

FOR i = 0 TO LENGTH(x) - 1

  PRINT x[i]

NEXT i

END
```

The time complexity of an algorithm can be expressed through the specification of the time-complexity function. This is t(n) = an+b where a is a constant multiplier and it represents how long it takes for a loop iteration to complete, while b is representing the setup time for the algorithm. The above algorithm is considered linear.

This function makes the assumption that we are measuring time complexity in chronological terms, i.e. seconds. Because we will be looking to abstract certain machine details, time complexity will more often be expressed in terms of the number of steps needed to complete it.

How a 'step' is defined varies depending on the algorithm you are using. In the code above, where you see the print instruction, we could consider this as a step and the time complexity function for printing could be rewritten as:

t(n) = n; for n array elements, n steps are needed to print the array.

Do take great care when you are defining the steps for an algorithm; the definition must be meaningful and it must correspond to the input size of the algorithm. For example, defining printing as the program step for the algorithm to print the array makes sense; printing takes up more of the runtime and will depend entirely on how many elements need to be printed.

We can also use comparisons and exchanges to define the algorithm steps. Take an algorithm for sorting, for example; the steps might be defined in comparison terms if comparisons take up most of the runtime or, if exchanges take the most runtime then we would define it in terms of exchanges.

Deciding on a time complexity function for the above example is not that hard but, where the algorithms are more complicated then it gets harder to do. We can use these general rules to make this task a little easier:

- An algorithm with one loop tends to be linear and we use n to specify the time complexity functions.
- An algorithm that has a pair of nested loops tends to be quadratic and we use n2 to specify the time complexity functions.
- An algorithm that has a triple nested loop tends to be cubic and we use n3 to specify the time complexity functions.

We can assume that the pattern continues with algorithms with quadruple or more nested loops.

These rules tend to work better when a loop is executed n times (n – input data size) but this won't always be the case. You can see that from the pseudocode for the selection sort algorithm below:

```
DECLARE INTEGER i, min, pass

DECLARE INTEGER x[] = [ ... ]

FOR pass = 0 TO LENGTH(x) - 2

  min = pass

  FOR i = pass + 1 TO LENGTH(x) - 1

    IF x[i] LT x[min] THEN

      min = i

    END IF

  NEXT i

  IF min NE pass THEN

    EXCHANGE x[min], x[pass]

  END IF

NEXT pass

END
```

There are only two nested loops here so you could be forgiven for thinking it has quadratic performance. However, that is only partly right; the performance of the algorithm depends on whether exchanges or comparisons are used as the step:

If we select exchanges for one step because we consider that they take more of the runtime, the time complexity function would be linear – n-1 exchanges are needed for sorting n data items. We specify the function as t(n) = n-1.

If, on the other hand, comparisons are chosen for one step, the function would be t(n) = (n-1)+(n-2)+ ... +1 and this is shortened down to t(n) = n2/2-n/2. Comparisons take place in the inner loop and this will execute a total of n-1 times for the iteration of the first outer loop, n-2 for the next and so on to the end.

Space Complexity and Space Complexity Functions

The space complexity of an algorithm is indicative of how much additional memory the algorithm requires to complete its task. For the array printing, the algorithm requires a constant memory amount, regardless of the array size. That memory is required for storing code, stack space is needed for storing the return address when we call PRINT and space is required for the i value of the variable.

The space complexity of the array-printing algorithm may be expressed using a space complexity function of s(n) = c – c is signifying the amount of extra constant space that is required. That value is only representing overhead, not space required for processing of data. In our case, the array is not included.

Rather than machine-dependent bytes, we use machine-independent memory cells to express space complexity. Memory cells hold a data type and, for our printing algorithm, the data stored in the memory cell for i is an integer.

Comparison of Algorithms

Both time and space complexity functions are used for comparing one algorithm to another that is similar in nature, i.e. two sorting algorithms. To make sure the comparison is fair, each algorithm must have the same definitions for the step and the memory cell.

However, even if you identical memory cell and step definitions, it can still be somewhat tricky to compare algorithms. Complexities may often be non-linear and that means the input size of the algorithm can have a sizeable effect on the result of the comparison. Have a look at two time-complexity functions as an example:

t1(n) = 10n2+15n

t2(n) = 150n+5

When n = 1, t1 will have 25 steps; by comparison, t2 has 155 steps. It is clear that t1 is better. The pattern will carry on until n=14; t1 has 2170 steps while t2 has 2105 steps. In this case, t2 would be the best choice.

Asymptotic Analysis

When we talk about the asymptotic analysis of algorithms, we are talking about the definition of the mathematical framing or foundation of the run-time performance of the algorithms. With asymptotic analysis, we can easily determine what the best, worst and average case of any algorithm is.

One thing to bear in mind is that asymptotic analysis is input bound. By that we mean that, if an algorithm has no input, it is considered to be working in constant time because all the other factors, other than input, are all constant.

Asymptotic analysis references the computation of the running time of any given operation in terms of the mathematical computation units. For example, one operation may have a running time of f(n) while another may have a running time of g(n2). What this means is that the running time of the first operation will increase in a linear fashion as n increases; the second operation's running time will increase in an exponential fashion as n increases. In a similar fashion, both operations will have much the same running time if n is very small.

As we saw earlier, there are three types of time an algorithm requires:

Best Case – the minimum amount of time required for a program to execute

Worst Case – the maximum amount of time required for a program to execute

Average Case – the average amount of time required for a program to execute

Asymptotic Notation

These are the most common asymptotic notations used for calculating the time complexity of algorithms:

- Ω notation
- Θ notation
- O notation

Omega Notation - Ω

This notation is a more formal way of expressing the lower bound of the running time of any algorithm. It is used for measuring best case complexity, the least amount of time an algorithm can take to complete.

For example, take a function of f(n):

Ω(f(n)) ≥ { g(n) : there exists c > 0 and no such that g(n) ≤ c.f(n) for all n > no. }

Theta Notation - θ

This notation is also formal, and is a way of expressing the upper and the lower bounds of the running time of an algorithm. The notation is represented as:

$\theta(f(n)) = \{ g(n)$ if and only if $g(n) = O(f(n))$ and $g(n) = \Omega(f(n))$ for all $n > n0. \}$

Big O Notation

The big O notation, O(n), is the most formal way of expressing the upper bound of the running time of an algorithm. It is used for measuring worst-case complexity, the longest an algorithm can take to complete.

For example, take a function of f(n):

$O(f(n)) = \{ g(n)$: there exists $c > 0$ and n0 such that $f(n) \leq c.g(n)$ for all $n > n0. \}$

I have left this notation to last so I can talk in depth about it; it is one of the most important. Complexity functions tend to be the upper bound of asymptotic behavior of an algorithm (up for discussion next) and representing these upper bounds is the Big O notation. The formal definition of Big O is this:

A function f(n) is O(g(n)) if and only if there exist two constants c and n0 such that $f(n) <= cg(n)$ for all $n >= n0$.

Do note that n, f(n), c, g(n) and n0 all must be positive.

So, f(n) is representing the computing time of the algorithm. When it is said that the function is o(g(n)), it means that, as far as algorithm steps go, it doesn't take any longer for function execution than a constant that has been multiplied by g(n). For example, using the previous time complexity functions, these are the Big O notations:

t1(n) = O(n2)
t2(n) = O(n)

The first equation reads as 't1 is order n2' which means that t1 has a quadratic performance. The second equation reads as 't2 is order n' or t2 has a linear performance. Time complexities are, then thought of as being, linear, quadratic, etc. because, as n increases, this is how the algorithm will respond.

Big O Simplification

When we specify g(n), we commonly discard all the terms except for the largest ones and, if there are any, the largest term's constant multipliers. For example, rather than o(150n+5) you would simply specify o(n).

As a way of proving that t1(n) is, in fact, o(n2), all you have to do is find any two c and n0 constants where the relation is holding. For example, if you chose 25 for c and 1 for n0, this is enough because all 10n2+1n values are less than or are equal to 25n2 for n>=1. In the same way you can also show proof that t2(n) is o(n).

Using Big O to Compare Algorithms

Let's say that we have the selection sort algorithm and then the array printing algorithm afterward; each of these has their own time complexity function so what would the overall function for both be? The following rule governs the answer to that:

If f1(n) = O(g(n)) and f2(n) = O(h(n)) then:

(A) f1(n)+f2(n) = max(O(g(n)), O(h(n)))

(B) f1(n)*f2(n) = O(g(n)*h(n)).

The first part discusses the case where the algorithms are in sequence and, for both algorithms, the combined time complexity function would be the maximum function for each of the algorithms. In this case, that would be o(n2), assuming, of course that the dominant steps are comparisons.

The second part discusses the case of nested algorithms, i.e. one inside another. For example, let's say that the selection sort algorithm carries out an exchange and then the array printing algorithm is called afterward. If the selection sort algorithm has a time complexity of o(n2), i.e. the comparisons are the dominant ones, the combined time complexity would be o(n3).

So how do we choose the right algorithm for our requirements? The first thing to do is get the time complexity functions that are bounded by Big O for the algorithms you are considering; then you decide on the n value range to be input to the algorithms.

The Big O time complexity functions are sorted in order from the constant, or most efficient, to the exponential or least efficient.

It would be fantastic if every algorithm were o(1) because that would mean they were all as efficient as each other. However, this isn't the case that that means taking the time to choose the right algorithm, the most efficient that is based on the Big O-bounded time complexity function and the n value range you need.

Do bear in mind that the highly efficient algorithms may be more difficult to code so, provided the n value input range doesn't end up with too many steps, it might be better to choose an algorithm that isn't quite so efficient with an input range that is smaller. You'll read more about this later.

Common Asymptotic Notations

And these are the other common notations:

- constant – O(1)

- logarithmic – O(log n)
- linear – O(n)
- n log n – O(n log n)
- quadratic – O(n2)
- cubic – O(n3)
- polynomial – nO(n)
- exponential – 2O(n)

Greedy Algorithms

Algorithms are designed to find the best solution for a problem. With a greedy algorithm, the decision is made from the domain of the given solution. As the name, greedy, suggests, the nearest solution that appears to provide the best answer is the one chosen.

A greedy algorithm will attempt to find the most localized solution and this can, in turn, lead to a globally optimized solution.

The Counting Coins Problem

The counting problem revolves around counting to a specified value using the least amount of coins possible. A greedy approach will force the algorithm into choosing the largest coin that fits the value. Let's say that we have coins with values of 1, 2, and 10 and we want to count to 18; a greedy algorithm will do this:

- Choose a coin with a value of 10, leaving a remainder of 8
- Next, choose a coin with a value of 5, leaving a remainder of 3
- Next, select a coin with a value of 2, leaving a remainder of 1
- Lastly, selecting a coin with a value of 1 will solve the entire problem.

Ok, so what is wrong with this? It works, the problem is solved and we only need 4 coins to do it. But, what if we were to change the problem a little; the same approach might not give us the optimal result.

Where the currency system is concerned, when we have coins with values of 1, 7 and 10, counting to a value of 18 will be totally optimal. Change that result to 15 and more coins may be used than are completely necessary. For example, with the greedy approach, the coins used would be 10 + 1 + 1 + 1 + 1 + 1, making 6 coins. However, the problem could have been solved with just 3 coins – 7 + 7 + 1.

So, the conclusion we can draw is that a greedy approach will choose an immediate and optimal solution but, as far as global optimization is concerned, it will likely fail.

To be fair, many of the networking algorithms will use this greedy approach, including:

- Dijkstra's Minimal Spanning Tree Algorithm
- Graph - Map Coloring
- Graph - Vertex Cover

- Job Scheduling Problem
- Knapsack Problem
- Kruskal's Minimal Spanning Tree Algorithm
- Prim's Minimal Spanning Tree Algorithm
- Travelling Salesman Problem

Divide and Conquer

With the divide and conquer approach, the problem is split down, or divided, into several smaller problems or sub-problems. Each of these problems may then be independently solved. When we continue to divide, breaking the sub-problems down into even smaller sub-problems, we might get to a stage where we cannot divide any further. These sub-problems, the smallest they possibly can be, are known as atomic or fractions and are then solved and, to get the solution to the original problem, the solutions from all the smaller problems are merged together.

In broad terms, divide and conquer can be looked at as a process of three steps:

- Divide or break – The first step involves diving the original problem into smaller problems. Each sub-problem must be representative of the original problem. This step uses a recursive approach, dividing the problem down until it cannot be divided any further. Sub-problems then become atomic but are still representative of a part of the initial problem.
- Conquer or solve – The second step receives many of the sub-problems that need to be solved but are considered to have been solved by themselves
- Merge or combine – When the sub-problems have been solved, a recursive approach is used to combine them all together until a solution is found to the initial problem. This step works so closely to the second step that they appear to be just one step.

There are several algorithms based on this kind of approach, including:

- Binary Search
- Closest pair (points)
- Merge Sort
- Quick Sort
- Strassen's Matrix Multiplication

Dynamic Programming

The dynamic programming approach is much the same as the divide and conquer approach in that the problem is broken down into sub-problems. However, where it differs is that the sub-problems do not get independently solved. Instead, the results from the sub-problems get remembered and are then used for sub-problems that overlap or are similar.

We use dynamic programming when we have a problem that can be divided down, not just into sub-problems but into similar sub-problems so that we can reuse the results somewhere else. For the most part, we use this kind of algorithm for optimization. Before the in-hand sub-problem is solved, a dynamic algorithm will first look at the results of sub-problems that were solved previously. The solutions from all the sub-problems are then merged to give the most optimal solution.

So, to recap:

- The original problem must be able to be divided down into sub-problems similar to the original and that overlap.
- Optimal solutions are achieved by taking the optimal solutions from the small sub-problems and combining them.
- A dynamic algorithm will use Memorization.
- In comparison to a greedy algorithm where we address local optimization, the dynamic algorithm has the motivation of optimizing the entire solution.
- In comparison to a divide and conquer algorithm, where the sub-problem solutions are merged to get the whole solution, the dynamic algorithm will look at the output from the small sub-problems and then attempt to optimize a large sub-problem.
- Dynamic algorithms also make use of memorization as a way of remembering what the output is from sub-problems that have already been solved.

The dynamic algorithm approach may be used with problems such as these:

- All pair shortest path by Floyd-Warshall
- Fibonacci number series
- Knapsack problem
- Project scheduling
- Shortest path by Dijkstra
- Tower of Hanoi

Dynamic programming works in two ways – top to bottom and bottom to top. And it will also work out cheaper as far as the cost of CPU cycles to refer to an earlier solution than to recompute.

Basic Concepts of Data Structures and Algorithms

In this section, we will look at the basic terms that relate to the data structure:

Data Definition

Data Definition is used for defining specific data that has these characteristics:

- Atomic – the Data Definition should define one concept
- Traceable – the Data Definition must be mapped to a specified data element
- Accurate – there should be no ambiguity about the Data Definition
- Clear and Concise – the Data Definition must be completely understandable

Data Object

The data object is representative of any object that contains data.

Data Type

A data type is a way of classifying the different types of data, such as strings, integers, Booleans, etc. This typing will determine what values may be used with the data type, and what operations may be allowed. There are two major data types:

Built-in Data Type

Built-in data types are those where a computer language such as Java has support already built-in. Java provides support for the following built-in types:

- Integers
- Floating point
- Boolean
- Characters
- Strings
- As well as a few others.

Derived Data Type

Derived data types are those that are dependent upon implementation. They are usually built from a combination or the built-in data types and their associated operations. For example:

- Array
- List
- Queue
- Stack

Basic Operations

Data in a data structures requires specific operations in order to be processed. The data structure that is chosen will depend in a big way of how frequently the operation will be performed on it. Those operations include:

- Deletion
- Insertion
- Merging
- Searching
- Sorting
- Traversing

Pseudocode

Pseudocode is a way of representing an algorithm in text format, providing an approximation of what the final source code will be. Pseudocode is incredibly useful when you want to write the representation of an algorithm quickly; syntax doesn't come into it so you don't have any hard or fast rules that you need to follow for writing it.

However, you should be consistent when you write your pseudocode because you will find it a great deal easier to transform it into the proper source code. For example, have a look at this pseudocode:

```
DECLARE CHARACTER ch = ''

DECLARE INTEGER count = 0

DO

  READ ch

  IF ch GE '0' AND ch LE '9' THEN

    count = count + 1

  END IF

UNTIL ch EQ '\n'

PRINT count

END
```

First, we have two DECLARE statements. These give us two variables, ch and count, each one initialized with its default values. We then have a Do loop that will continue to execute until the ch variable has the newline character in it (\n). At this point, the loop will stop and the value of count is output via a PRINT statement.

For each iteration of the loop, a character is read off the keyboard, caused by READ. It could also be a file being read; for now, it really doesn't matter what the underlying input source is. That character or file is assigned as a value to ch. If the value is one digit, from 0 to 9, then count will be incremented, or increased, by 1.

That is pseudocode in a nutshell; you will be seeing more examples throughout this section.

Time to move on to the more complex subjects and delve deeper into algorithms and data structures, now that we have the basics under our belts.

One-Dimensional Arrays – Searching and Sorting

Arrays are a fundamental category in data structures, and are also one of the more important building blocks for the complex data structures. In this section, we will take a closer look at arrays, what they are and how we use them in Java programming. We will look at the concept and how we represent them in Java and then we will look closer at one-dimensional arrays and the three different ways we can use to introduce them to our programs. Lastly, we will look at the five different algorithms used for sorting and searching a one-dimensional array.

What Is An Array?

Arrays are sequences of elements; each element must be associated with one or more index positions. Elements are groups of memory locations, each one storing one item of data. Indexes are integers that are non-negative; in the case of the array, they are used for identifying the element associated with the index. You can consider the relationship between the two to be similar to how a postbox number identifies a specific house on a specific street.

Usually, one element will have one index but there may sometimes be more. The number of those indexes per element is the dimension of the array. We are going to start by looking at one-dimensional arrays; later, we will move on to the multi-dimensional arrays.

Java has full support for arrays. Each of the elements in an array will occupy the same byte amount and the exact amount will depend on the data type of the element. It is also worth noting at this stage that every element in one array will be of the same data type.

It is also important to note that you cannot resize a Java array; they are of a fixed size and may not be changed once they have been created. Rather than doing this, if you needed an array to be a different size, you would need to create a new one of the correct size and then copy all the elements you need from the first array to the new one.

One-Dimensional Arrays

One-dimensional arrays are the simplest of all arrays. In this kind of array, one element is associated with one index and the array is used for storing data items in lists. We can use three separate techniques for creating a one-dimensional array:

- With just an initializer
- With just the new keyword
- With both an initializer and the new keyword

Using Just an Initializer

The syntax required to use an initializer to create a one-dimensional array is:

'{' [expr (',' expr)*] '}'

What this syntax says is that a one-dimensional array is a list of expressions that is optional and with each expression separated by a comma, all between a set of curly braces.

All of the expressions have got to evaluate to types that are compatible. For example, if you had a one-dimensional array of doubles with two elements, both of those elements may be of the double type or just one may be of the double type while the other may be an integer or a floating point number.

Have a look at this example:

{ 'J', 'a', 'v', 'a' }

Using the New Keyword

The new keyword is used to allocate the array memory and return the array references. The syntax is:

'new' type '[' int_expr ']'

What the syntax tells us is that the one-dimensional array is a series of positive elements, all of int (integer) type. All the elements in the array will be zeroed and will be interpreted as one of the following:

- 0
- 0L
- 0.0F
- 0.0
- false
- null
- '\u0000'

For example:

new char[4]

Using an Initializer and the New Keyword

The syntax required to create the array using both the initializer and the new keyword is this, a combination of the two separate syntax approaches mentioned above:

'new' type '[' ']' '{' [expr (',' expr)*] '}'

Because we can work out how many elements are in the one-dimensional array by looking at the list of comma-separated expressions, we do not need and, indeed, must nor use, an int_expr within the set of square brackets.

For example:

new char[] { 'J', 'a', 'v', 'a' }

It is worth noting that there is no difference between the syntax for using just the initializer and the syntax for using the initializer and the new keyword. The first one, with just the initializer, is something called syntactic sugar – this just means the syntax is much easier to use.

Array Variables

On its own, a new one-dimensional array is quite useless. For it to be worth anything, we must first assign its reference to an array variable that has a compatible type and we can do this in two ways – directly or by using a method call.

The following example shows how the variable is declared:

type var_name '[' ']'

type '[' ']' var_name

Both types of syntax are declaring the variable that will store the reference to the one-dimensional array. You can use whichever type you prefer but the preferred method is the first one, with the set of square brackets after the variable type.

Have a look at some examples:

```
char[] name1 = { 'J', 'a', 'v', 'a' };

char[] name2 = new char[4];

char[] name3 = new char[] { 'J', 'a', 'v', 'a' };

output(new char[] { 2, 3 }); // output({ 2, 3 }); results in a compiler error

static void output(char[] name)

{

  // ...

}
```

In these examples, there are three array variables – name1, name2, and name3. The set of square brackets is telling Java that each of those variables will store the reference to a one-dimensional array.

The keyword, char, is an indication that the elements must store values of the char type but, provided Java can do a conversion to a char, you may specify values that are non-char. For example, the following is perfectly ok because 10, a positive int, is small enough that it fits in the range for char (0 to 65535) and can easily be converted to a char:

```
char[] chars = { 'A', 10 };
```

However, the next example would not be ok because it doesn't fit in the range:

char[] chars = { 'A', 80000 };

All array variables have a length property associated with them. This property will return the one-dimensional array length, indicated as a positive int. For example, name1.lenght would return a value of 4.

With the array variable specified, it is possible to access any one of the elements in the array and we do this by stating the expression that will agree with this syntax:

array_var '[' index ']'

In this expression, we have a positive int of index; it ranges from 0 to one lower than the length property value. Don't forget, Java indexes start at zero.

Have a look at a couple of examples:

char ch = names[0]; // Get value.

names[1] = 'A';   // Set value.

If a negative index is specified, or one that is >= (greater than or equal to) the value that the length property returns, Java will create an exception object and throw it. That exception object is:

java.lang.ArrayIndexOutOfBoundsException

Searching and Sorting Algorithms

One of the most common tasks with one-dimensional arrays is to search them for specific items and we can do that using a number of algorithms. One of the most popular is the Linear Search, followed closely by the Binary Search. The latter performs better but is rather more demanding than linear and, to use a binary search, you first have to sort the data in the array. The other algorithms we will be looking at are Bubble Sort, Selection Sort and Insertion Sort, all good algorithms for sorting data in a one-dimensional array and each work well on the shorter arrays.

We'll start with the linear search algorithm and work our way through the others one at a time. First, you need to understand that, in terms of space complexity, each of these algorithms has 0(1) space complexity, which is constant, for the variable storage.

Linear Search

With the linear search algorithm, we can search through a one-dimensional array that contains n data items, looking for a specified item. It works by starting at the lowest index and working through to the highest, comparing the data item at each index until it locates the one that matches the specified item or until there aren't any more to search and compare.

Have a look at this pseudocode that expresses the linear search for an array of integers:

```
DECLARE INTEGER i, srch = ...

DECLARE INTEGER x[] = [ ... ]

FOR i = 0 TO LENGTH(x) - 1

  IF x[i] EQ srch THEN

    PRINT "Found ", srch

    END

  END IF

NEXT i

PRINT "Not found", srch

END
```

Consider this; we have a one-dimensional array containing five integers that have not been ordered. Those integers are [1, 4, 3, 2, 6] – the first integer, 1, is at index 0 and 6 is at index 4. The pseudocode will find integer 3 by doing the following:

- It will compare the integer at the index of 0, (1), with 3
- There isn't a match so it moves to index 1, (4), and compares that
- Again, we don't have a match so it moves to index 2, (3) and compares it
- We have a match so Found 3 is printed and the code exits.

The linear search time complexity is o(n); where we have n data items, the algorithm will require n comparisons as a maximum. On average n/2 comparisons will be performed linearly.

One of the downsides to the linear search algorithm is that it isn't all that efficient. If you had an array containing 4 million (4,000,000) data items, on average, 2 million (2,000,000) comparisons would be performed to find the required item.

Linear Search Example:

Open a new Java program and call it LinearSearch. Input the following code:

```
public class LinearSearch {
    public static void main(String[] args)
    {
        // Validate command line arguments count.

        if (args.length != 2)
        {
            System.err.println("usage: java LinearSearch integers integer");
            return;
        }

        // Read integers from first command-line argument. Return if integers
        // could not be read.
        int[] ints = readIntegers(args[0]);
        if (ints == null)
            return;

        // Read search integer; NumberFormatException is thrown if the integer
        // isn't valid.
        int srchint = Integer.parseInt(args[1]);

        // Perform the search and output the result.
        System.out.println(srchint + (search(ints, srchint) ? " found" : " not found"));
}

private static int[] readIntegers(String s)
{
    String[] tokens = s.split(",");
    int[] integers = new int[tokens.length];
    for (int i = 0; i < tokens.length; i++)
```

```
            integers[i] = Integer.parseInt(tokens[i]);
        return integers;
    }

    private static boolean search(int[] x, int srchint)
    {
        for (int i = 0; i < x.length; i++)
            if (srchint == x[i])
                return true;

        return false;
    }
}
```

In LinearSearch, we are reading a list of integers, each separated by a comma, from the first command line argument. The array is searched for the integer that the second argument identifies and a found or not found message will be output.

There is an exception that you need to be aware of – number format. Digits and the +/- signs may only be specified in the command line arguments. If you specify them anywhere else, you will get the following exception thrown:

java.lang.NumberFormatException

Linear Search Example:

Let's play a little with this code. Compile the program to start with:

javac LinearSearch.java

Next, we want to do the following to run the application that results:

java LinearSearch "4,5,8" 5

You should see this output:

5 found

Now run the application again, like this:

java LinearSearch "4,5,8" 15

Now you should see this output:

15 not found

Binary Search

With the binary search algorithm, we can search through an ordered one-dimensional array that contains n data items for a specified item. With this algorithm, we have these steps:

The first and last item indexes are set with low and high index variables, respectively

If the low index is more than (greater than) the high index, the algorithm will terminate because the item being searched for is not present in the array

The middle index is calculated by summing (adding together) the low index and the high index and dividing the result by 2

The data item being searched for is compared with the data item at the middle index; if they are equal to one another, the algorithm will terminate because the item being searched for has been found

If the data item being searched for is more than (greater than) the item at the middle index, the low index will be set to the value of the middle index plus one and execution transferred to step 2 (above). The binary search algorithm will repeat that search in the top half of the array

The data item being searched for must be lower than (smaller) than the item at the middle index so the high index is set to the value of the middle index minus one and execution is transferred to step 2. The binary search algorithm will repeat that search in the bottom half of the array.

This is the pseudocode representative of the binary search algorithm on an integer array:

```
DECLARE INTEGER x[] = [ ... ]

DECLARE INTEGER loIndex = 0

DECLARE INTEGER hiIndex = LENGTH(x) - 1

DECLARE INTEGER midIndex, srch = ...

WHILE loIndex LE hiIndex

  midIndex = (loIndex + hiIndex) / 2

  IF srch GT x[midIndex] THEN

    loIndex = midIndex + 1

  ELSE
```

```
  IF srch LT x[midIndex] THEN
    hiIndex = midIndex - 1
  ELSE
    EXIT WHILE
  END IF
END WHILE
IF loIndex GT hiIndex THEN
  PRINT srch, " not found"
ELSE
  PRINT srch, " found"
END IF
END
```

The binary search algorithm is not difficult to grasp. For example, take a one-dimensional array, with six ordered integers, which are [3, 4, 5, 6, 7, 8]. The first index, 0, is integer 3 and the last index, 5, is integer 8. With the above pseudocode, we are doing the following to locate integer 6 in this array:

We get the low and the high indexes, (0) and (5) respectively

Then we calculate what the middle index is – (0 + 5)/2 = 2

Because the second index integer is lower than 6, the low index is set as 2+1 = 3

The middle index is calculated as (3+5)/4 = 2

The fourth index integer is more than 6 so the high index is set as 4-1 = 3

The middle index is calculated as (3+3)/2 = 3

Because the third integer is equal to 6, we print 6 found and the algorithm will terminate.

The binary search time complexity is o(log2n), where we have n data items. For this the maximum comparisons required are 1+log2n and that is what makes binary search far more efficient than a linear search for the most part. However, linear search is more efficient than binary search for shorter arrays.

Binary Search Example:

Start a new program, call it BinarySearch and input this code:

```
public class BinarySearch {

    public static void main(String[] args)
    {
      // Validate command line arguments count.
      if (args.length != 2)
      {
        System.err.println("usage: java BinarySearch integers integer");
        return;
      }

      // Read integers from first command-line argument. Return if integers
      // could not be read.
      int[] ints = readIntegers(args[0]);
      if (ints == null)
           return;

      // Read search integer; NumberFormatException is thrown if the integer
      // isn't valid.
      int srchint = Integer.parseInt(args[1]);

      // Perform the search and output the result.
      System.out.println(srchint + (search(ints, srchint) ? " found": " not found"));
    }

    private static int[] readIntegers(String s)
    {
         String[] tokens = s.split(",");
         int[] integers = new int[tokens.length];
         for (int i = 0; i < tokens.length; i++)
```

```
                    integers[i] = Integer.parseInt(tokens[i]);
            return integers;
        }

        private static boolean search(int[] x, int srchint)
        {
                int hiIndex = x.length - 1, loIndex = 0, midIndex;

            while (loIndex <= hiIndex)
            {
                    midIndex = (loIndex + hiIndex) / 2;
                    if (srchint > x[midIndex])
                            loIndex = midIndex + 1;
                else if (srchint < x[midIndex])
                    hiIndex = midIndex - 1;
                else
                    return true;
            }

            return false;
        }
}
```

This application is reading a list of integers, each element separated by a comma, form the first command line arguments. The array is searched for the integer that the second argument identifies. The output will be a found or a not found message.

To explore the algorithm, compile the code like this:

javac BinarySearch.java

The resulting application can be run like this:

java BinarySearch "4,5,8" 5

You should see this output:

5 found

Run the application again, like this:

java BinarySearch "4,5,8" 15

And the following output should be seen:

15 not found

Bubble Sort

With the bubble sort algorithm, we can take a one-dimensional array containing n data items and sort it, either in ascending or descending order. First, an outer loop will make n-1 number of passes over the array and each of those passes will make use of an inner loop for exchanging data items, in a way that the next largest (descending order) or the next smallest (ascending order) will bubble to the start of the array.

The bubble happens inside the inner loop because this is where each of the iterations is comparing the data item that is pass-numbered with each of the successive data items. If a succeeding data item is larger or smaller than that pass-numbered item, the succeeding data item gets exchanged with it.

The following pseudocode shows bubble sort at work on a one-dimensional array of integers sorted in ascending order:

```
DECLARE INTEGER i, pass

DECLARE INTEGER x[] = [ ... ]

FOR pass = 0 TO LENGTH(x) - 2

  FOR i = LENGTH(x) - 1 DOWNTO pass + 1

    IF x[i] LT x[pass] THEN // switch to > for descending sort

      EXCHANGE x[i], x[pass]

    END IF

  NEXT i

NEXT pass

END
```

Bubble sort is relatively easy to grasp. For example, if you have a one-dimensional array of integers that are unordered – [18, 16, 90, -3] – with the integer of 18 being at index 0 and -

3 being at index 3, bubble sort would do the following when we asked it to sort the array in ascending order:

```
Pass 0              Pass 1              Pass 2

======              ======              ======

18 16 90 -3         -3 16 90 18         -3 16 90 18

^       ^           ^     ^             ^  ^

|       |       |   |         |         |

-------------       ---------           -----

-3 16 90 18         -3 16 90 18         -3 16 18 90

^    ^              ^  ^

|    |              | |

---------           -----

-3 16 90 18         -3 16 90 18

^  ^

| |

-----

-3 16 90 18
```

As far as comparisons and exchanges go, the time complexity of the bubble sort algorithm is o(n2) and it has a quadratic performance – not an issue where short arrays are concerned, especially when you realize how easy the algorithm is to code.

Start a new program and call it BubbleSort, then input this code:

```
public class BubbleSort {

    public static void main(String[] args)

    {

        // Validate command line arguments count.


     if (args.length != 1)

     {
```

```
            System.err.println("usage: java BubbleSort integers");
         return;
      }

      // Read integers from first command-line argument. Return if integers
      // could not be read.
      int[] ints = readIntegers(args[0]);
      if (ints == null)
            return;

      // Output the integer array's length and number of inversions statistics to
      // standard output device.

      System.out.println("N = " + ints.length);
      int inversions = 0;
      for (int i = 0; i < ints.length - 1; i++)
            for (int j = i + 1; j < ints.length; j++)
                  if (ints[i] > ints[j])
                        inversions++;
      System.out.println("I = " + inversions);

      // Output the unsorted integer values to standard output, sort the array,
      // and output the sorted values to standard output.
      dump(ints);
      sort(ints);
      dump(ints);
   }

   static void dump(int[] a)
   {
```

```
        for (int i = 0; i < a.length; i++)
            System.out.print(a[i] + " ");
      System.out.print('\n');
    }

    static int[] readIntegers(String s)
    {
        String[] tokens = s.split(",");
        int[] integers = new int[tokens.length];
        for (int i = 0; i < tokens.length; i++)
            integers[i] = Integer.parseInt(tokens[i]);
      return integers;
    }

    static void sort(int[] x)
    {
        for (int pass = 0; pass < x.length - 1; pass++)
            for (int i = x.length - 1; i > pass; i--)
                if (x[i] < x[pass])
        {
                    int temp = x[i];
                    x[i] = x[pass];
                    x[pass] = temp;
        }
    }
}
```

A long one this time; bubble sort is reading an array with integers, each separated by a comma, from the first command line argument. The array length is calculated and the output is the number of large items on the left of the small items in the unordered array – these are called inversions. The unsorted array is output, the array is sorted and then the sorted array is output. You will find, when we discuss them in a minute, that both selection sort and insertion sort have much the same behavior.

Bubble Sort Example:

Compile the code like this:

javac BubbleSort.java

Run the application that results like this:

java BubbleSort "18,16,90,-3"

And you should see this output:

N = 4

I = 4

18 16 90 -3

-3 16 18 90

Selection Sort

With the selection sort algorithm, we can order a one-dimensional array containing n data items into either descending or ascending order. The outer loop will make n-1 passes over and each one will use an inner loop, looking for the next largest or next smallest, depending on whether it is descending or ascending sort; this data item is then exchanged with the pass-numbered item.

The selection sort algorithm will automatically assume that the data item at the index for the pass-number is the largest or the smallest of all the data items that remain. It will look through the array for an item that is larger or smaller than that data item and it will exchange it for the larger or smaller data item when the search is ended.

This pseudocode shows selection sort working on a one-dimensional array containing integers using ascending sort:

```
DECLARE INTEGER i, min, pass

DECLARE INTEGER x[] = [ ... ]

FOR pass = 0 TO LENGTH(x) - 2

  min = pass

  FOR i = pass + 1 TO LENGTH(x) - 1

    IF x[i] LT x[min] THEN
```

```
      min = i
    END IF
  NEXT i
  IF min NE pass THEN
    EXCHANGE x[min], x[pass]
  END IF
NEXT pass
END
```

Selection sort is another one that is easy to grasp as it much the same as the bubble sort. Take a one-dimensional array of integers, unordered – [18, 16, 90, -3]. Integer 18 is at the 0 index and integer 3 is at the third index. We want selection sort to sort the array in ascending order and the pseudocode will do this:

```
Pass 0          Pass 1          Pass 2

======          ======          ======

18 16 90 -3     -3 16 90 18     -3 16 90 18

^        ^      ^     ^         ^  ^

|        |      |     |         |  |

-------------   ---------       -----

-3 16 90 18     -3 16 90 18     -3 16 18 90

^     ^         ^  ^

|     |         |  |

---------       -----

-3 16 90 18     -3 16 90 18

^  ^

|  |

-----

-3 16 90 18
```

The time complexity for selection sort is split into two – comparisons have a complexity of o(n2) and exchanges have a complexity of o(n). As far as performance goes, selection sort is quadratic for comparisons and linear for exchanges which makes it quite a bit more efficient than the bubble sort.

Start a new program, call it SelectionSort and input this code:

```
public final class SelectionSort
{
    public static void main(String[] args)
    {
        // Validate command line arguments count.
        if (args.length != 1)
        {
            System.err.println("usage: java SelectionSort integers");
            return;
        }

        // Read integers from first command-line argument. Return if integers
        // could not be read.
        int[] ints = readIntegers(args[0]);
        if (ints == null)
            return;

        // Output integer array's length and number of inversions statistics to
        // standard output device.
        System.out.println("N = " + ints.length);
        int inversions = 0;
        for (int i = 0; i < ints.length - 1; i++)
            for (int j = i + 1; j < ints.length; j++)
                if (ints[i] > ints[j])
                    inversions++;
        System.out.println("I = " + inversions);
```

```
        // Output unsorted integer values to standard output, sort the array,
        // and output sorted values to standard output.
        dump(ints);
        sort(ints);
        dump(ints);
}

static void dump(int[] a)
{
    for (int i = 0; i < a.length; i++)
        System.out.print(a[i] + " ");
    System.out.print('\n');
}

static int[] readIntegers(String s)
{
    String[] tokens = s.split(",");
    int[] integers = new int[tokens.length];
    for (int i = 0; i < tokens.length; i++)
        integers[i] = Integer.parseInt(tokens[i]);
    return integers;
}

static void sort(int[] x)
{
    for (int pass = 0; pass < x.length - 1; pass++)
    {
        int min = pass;
```

```
                    for (int i = pass + 1; i < x.length; i++)
                            if (x[i] < x[min])
                                    min = i;


                    if (min != pass)
                    {
                            int temp = x[min];
                            x[min] = x[pass];
                            x[pass] = temp;
                    }
            }
    }
}
```

This is doing pretty much what bubble sort did, so

Selection Sort Example:

Compile the program like this:

javac SelectionSort.java

Run the application that results like this:

java SelectionSort "18,16,90,-3"

You should see this output:

N = 4

I = 4

18 16 90 -3

-3 16 18 90

Insertion Sort

The final algorithm we are going to look at for one-dimensional arrays is the insertion sort algorithm. This will take a one-dimensional array containing n data items and order it into descending or ascending order. It works the same in that the outer loop makes n-1 passes over; each of these passes will pick the next item that is to be put into the correct position. An inner loop is used for finding the position and moving the data items so there is room.

The insertion sort algorithm starts by dividing the data structure down into two sections – sorted and unsorted. At first, the section for sorted has the data item that is at index 0 while all the others are in the unsorted section. As the sort takes place, each of the items in the unsorted section is placed in the sorted section in the correct position, shrinking the unsorted section by one each time.

This is the pseudocode showing the insertion sort algorithm at work on a one-dimensional array containing integers, using ascending sort:

```
DECLARE INTEGER a, i, j

DECLARE INTEGER x[] = [ ... ]

FOR i = 1 TO LENGTH(x) - 1

 a = x[i]

 j = i

 WHILE j GT 0 AND x[j - 1] GT a

   x[j] = x[j - 1]

   j = j - 1

 END WHILE

 x[j] = a

NEXT i

END
```

As with the last two algorithms, the insertion sort algorithm is also easy to understand. Take the one-dimensional integer array from the previous two algorithms – [18, 16, 90, -3] with integer 19 at index 0 and -3 at the third index. When insertion sort sorts the array in ascending order, this is what happens:

```
i = 1              i = 2              i = 3

  =====              =====              =====

18 | 16  90  -3     16  18 | 90  -3     16  18  90 | -3   -3  16  18  90

   ^                   ^                   ^
```

| | |

a,j   a,j   a,j

On the left is the sorted section, holding just [18] to start with. On the right is the unsorted section where all the other integers reside.

The time complexity for insertion sort is o(n) comparisons for the best case scenario – the data has been sorted or is almost sorted – and o(n2) for the worst and average case. In terms of performance the algorithm is linear for best case and quadratic for worst or average.

Start a new program, call it InsertionSort and input this code:

```
public class InsertionSort {


        public static void main(String[] args)
        {
                // Validate command line arguments count.
          if (args.length != 1)
          {
                System.err.println("usage: java InsertionSort integers");
                return;
          }


          // Read integers from first command-line argument. Return if integers
          // could not be read.
          int[] ints = readIntegers(args[0]);
          if (ints == null)
                return;


          // Output integer array's length and number of inversions statistics to
          // standard output device.
          System.out.println("N = " + ints.length);
          int inversions = 0;
          for (int i = 0; i < ints.length - 1; i++)
```

```
        for (int j = i + 1; j < ints.length; j++)
            if (ints[i] > ints[j])
                inversions++;
    System.out.println("I = " + inversions);

    // Output unsorted integer values to standard output, sort the array,
    // and output sorted values to standard output.
    dump(ints);
    sort(ints);
    dump(ints);
}

static void dump(int[] a)
{
    for (int i = 0; i < a.length; i++)
        System.out.print(a[i] + " ");
    System.out.print('\n');
}

static int[] readIntegers(String s)
{
    String[] tokens = s.split(",");
    int[] integers = new int[tokens.length];
    for (int i = 0; i < tokens.length; i++)
        integers[i] = Integer.parseInt(tokens[i]);
    return integers;
}

static void sort(int[] x)
{
```

```
    int j, a;

// For all integer values except the leftmost value ...
for (int i = 1; i < x.length; i++)
{
    // Get integer value a.
  a = x[i];

  // Get index of a. This is the initial insert position, which is
  // used if a is larger than all values in the sorted section.
  j = i;

  // While values exist to the left of a's insert position and the
  // value immediately to the left of that insert position is
  // numerically greater than a's value ...
  while (j > 0 && x[j - 1] > a)
  {
    // Shift left value -- x[j - 1] -- one position to its right --
    // x[j].
    x[j] = x[j - 1];

    // Update insert position to shifted value's original position
    // (one position to the left).
    j--;
  }

  // Insert a at insert position (which is either the initial insert
  // position or the final insert position), where a is greater than
  // or equal to all values to its left.
  x[j] = a;
```

```
        }
      }
}
```

Insertion Sort Example:

Compile the code like this:

javac InsertionSort.java

Run the application that results like this:

java InsertionSort "18,16,90,-3"

And you should see this output:

N = 4

i = 4

18 16 90 -3

-3 16 18 90

Multi-Dimensional Arrays and Matrix Multiplication

Okay, so we looked at a few algorithms used on one-dimensional arrays for search and sort operations. One-dimensional arrays are pretty simple to work with so now we'll move on to the multi-dimensional arrays. We'll look at three ways to create a multi-dimensional array and then we'll look at an algorithm called matrix multiplication. This algorithm is used for multiplying elements in twoodimensional arrays. We'll also look at ragged arrays and discuss the reason they are popular for use on big data applications. Lastly, we'll discuss whether arrays are objects in Java or not.

Introducing the Multi-Dimensional Array

Multi-dimensional arrays associate each of the elements in one array with several indexes. The most common one is a two-dimensional array, also called a matrix or table. In the two-dimensional array, each element is associated with two indexes.

We can visualize the two-dimensional array as a grid, rectangular in shaper and containing elements that are divided into columns and rows. The notation used to identify a specific element is (row, column), as you can see here:

Columns

	(0, 0)	(0, 1)	(0, 2)
Rows	(1, 0)	(1, 1)	(1, 2)
	(2, 0)	(2, 1)	(2, 2)

Because these are such common arrays, these are what we will focus on; what you can do with two-dimensional arrays can also be generalized on those with more dimensions.

Creating a Two-Dimensional Array

We can do these in three separate ways:

- Using only an initializer
- Using only the new keyword
- Using both an initializer and the new keyword

See how similar these start out to one-dimensional arrays?

Using Just an Initializer

To use just an initializer to create the two-dimensional array, we use the following syntax:

'{' [rowInitializer (',' rowInitializer)*] '}'

rowInitializer has the following syntax:

'{' [expr (',' expr)*] '}'

With this syntax, we are saying that a two-dimensional array is optional, and it is a list containing row initializers, each separated by a comma, and all in between a set of curly braces. Each of the row initializers is also an optional list, this time expressions, again with the comma separation and in between a pair of curly braces. Similar to the one-dimensional array, the expressions all have to evaluate to types that are compatible.

Have a look at this example:

{ { 20.5, 30.6, 28.3 }, { -38.7, -18.3, -16.2 } }

Here, we have created a table. It has three columns and two rows and you can visualize this table like this:

		Columns	
	20.5	30.6	28.3
Rows	-38.7	-18.3	-16.2

A two-dimensional array is represented by Java as a one-dimensional array, a row with elements that reference column arrays that are also one-dimensional. The row index will identify the column array while the column index will identify the data item.

Using Just the New Keyword

When we use the new keyword, it allocates the memory for the array and will return the array reference. This is the syntax:

'new' type '[' int_expr1 ']' '['int_expr2 ']'

We are saying that the two-dimensional array is a region of int_expr1, which are positive, row elements and int_expr2, also positive, column elements, all with the same data type. Not only that, every element has been zeroed.

Have a look at this example:

new double[2][3] // Create a two-row-by-three-column table.

Using Both Initializer and the New Keyword

Using both has a syntax approach of:

'new' type '[' ']' [' ']' '{' [rowInitializer (',' rowInitializer)*] '}'

rowInitializer has a syntax of:

'{' [expr (',' expr)*] '}'

This is a combination of the syntax from the previous examples; note that there is no int_expr in between either the sets of square brackets because we can already work out how many elements are in the array just by looking at expressions list.

Have a look at this example:

new double [][] { { 20.5, 30.6, 28.3 }, { -38.7, -18.3, -16.2 } }

Two Dimensional Arrays and Array Variables

On its own, the new two-dimensional array is not a lot of good. We need to assign its reference to an array variable that is compatible in type and this is done in two ways – directly or with a method call.

These are the syntaxes for both methods of declaring the variable:

type var_name '[' ']' '[' ']'

type '[' ']' '[' ']' var_name

Each one is declaring an array variable that will store the reference to the array. The preferred method is to have the square brackets after the data type.

Have a look at these examples:

double[][] temperatures1 = { { 20.5, 30.6, 28.3 }, { -38.7, -18.3, -16.2 } };

double[][] temperatures2 = new double[2][3];

double[][] temperatures3 = new double[][] { { 20.5, 30.6, 28.3 }, { -38.7, -18.3, -16.2 } };

Like the variables for the one-dimensional array, a length property is associated with the array variable for the two-dimensional array; this will return the row array length. From the above example, the result returned from temperatures1.length is 2. Every row element is also a variable that has a length property and the result returned from this is the number of columns in the array that has been assigned to the row element. Again, from the above, temperatures1[0].length will return 3.

With an array variable in place, any element in a two-dimensional array may be accessed through the specification of an expression that is like this syntax:

array_var '[' row_index ']' '[' col_index ']'

We have two indexes that are both positive ints ranging from 0 to one lower than the respective length property values returned. Have a look at these two examples:

double temp = temperatures1[0][1]; // Get value.

temperatures1[0][1] = 75.0;   // Set value.

In the first one, the value returned is from column 2, row 1 – 30.6 and, in the second example this is replaced with 75.0.

If a negative index is specified or you specify an index that is greater or equal to the value that the length property returns, the following exception will be created and thrown by Java:

ArrayIndexOutOfBoundsException

Multiplying Two-Dimensional Arrays

One of the most common operations in economics, computer graphics, transportation, and many other industries is to multiply two matrices. For this purpose, developers tend to make use of the matrix multiplication algorithm.

So, how does multiplying two matrices work? Let's say that A is representing a matrix that has m rows and p columns, We can also say that B is representing a matrix that has p rows and m columns. When you multiply A by B you get matrix c that has m rows and n columns. We get each of the cij entries in the C matrix by multiplying every entry in the ith row in A by the entries that correspond to them in the jth row in B and then add the results together.

There is one requirement for matrix multiplication – there must be an equal number of columns in the A matrix to the number of rows in the B matrix otherwise the algorithm cannot work.

Have a look at this pseudocode showing matrix multiplication in a matrix that is 2 rows, 2 columns and matrix that is 2 rows, 1 column:

```
// ==      ==  == ==  ==              ==
// | 10  30 |  | 5 |  | 10 x 5 + 30 x 7 (260) |
// |        | X |   | = |                       |
// | 20  40 |  | 7 |  | 20 x 5 + 40 * 7 (380) |
// ==      ==  == ==  ==              ==


DECLARE INTEGER a[][] = [ 10, 30 ] [ 20, 40 ]
DECLARE INTEGER b[][] = [ 5, 7 ]
DECLARE INTEGER m = 2 // Number of rows in left matrix (a)
DECLARE INTEGER p = 2 // Number of columns in left matrix (a)
                      // Number of rows in right matrix (b)
DECLARE INTEGER n = 1 // Number of columns in right matrix (b)
DECLARE INTEGER c[m][n] // c holds 2 rows by 1 columns
                        // All elements initialize to 0
FOR i = 0 TO m - 1
  FOR j = 0 TO n - 1
    FOR k = 0 TO p - 1
      c[i][j] = c[i][j] + a[i][k] * b[k][j]
    NEXT k
  NEXT j
NEXT i
END
```

Because there are three FOR loops in this pseudocode, the time complexity of matrix multiplication is o(n3). It has cubic performance which, when you use large matrices, is expensive in terms of time. The space complexity is o(nm) for the storage of another matrix of n rows, m columns. For a square matrix, the space complexity becomes o(n2).

Okay, start a new program, call it MatMult and input the following code:

```
public final class MatMult
{
    public static void main(String[] args)
    {
        int[][] a = {{ 10, 30 }, { 20, 40 }};
        int[][] b = {{ 5 }, { 7 }};
        dump(a);
        System.out.println();
        dump(b);
        System.out.println();
        int[][] c = multiply(a, b);
        dump(c);
    }

    private static void dump(int[][] x)
    {
        if (x == null)
        {
            System.err.println("array is null");
            return;
        }

        // Dump the matrix's element values to the standard output in tabular
        // order.
        for (int i = 0; i < x.length; i++)
        {
```

```
                for (int j = 0; j < x[0].length; j++)
                    System.out.print(x[i][j] + " ");
                System.out.println();
            }
}

private static int[][] multiply(int[][] a, int[][] b)
{
        //
=====================================================================
=====
        // 1. a.length contains a's row count
        //
        // 2. a[0].length (or any other a[x].length for a valid x) contains a's
        //    column count
        //
        // 3. b.length contains b's row count
        //
        // 4. b[0].length (or any other b[x].length for a valid x) contains b's
        //    column count
        //
=====================================================================
=====

        // If a's column count != b's row count, bail out
        if (a[0].length != b.length)
        {
            System.err.println("a's column count != b's row count");
            return null;
        }

        // Allocate result matrix with a size equal to a's row count times b's
```

```
        // column count
        int[][] result = new int[a.length][];
        for (int i = 0; i < result.length; i++)
            result[i] = new int[b[0].length];

        // Perform the multiplication and addition
        for (int i = 0; i < a.length; i++)
            for (int j = 0; j < b[0].length; j++)
                for (int k = 0; k < a[0].length; k++) // or k < b.length
                    result[i][j] += a[i][k] * b[k][j];

        // Return the result matrix
        return result;
    }
}
```

So, MatMult is declaring two matrices and then dumping the values into standard output. Then, both of those matrices are multiplied and the result matrix is then dumped to the standard output.

Matrix Multiplication Example:

Compile the program as follows:

javac MatMult.java

Next, the resulting application is run like this:

java MatMult

And you should see this output:

10 30

20 40

5

7

260

380

Matrix Multiplication Example

Let's have a look at a problem that we can use matrix multiplication to solve. In Florida, a fruit grower loads 250 boxes of grapefruit, 400 boxes of peaches and 1250 boxes of oranges onto two semi-trailer trucks, In the visualization below, you can see the market price per box for each of the different fruits in four separate cities:

	Oranges	Peaches	Grapefruit
New York	$10	$8	$12
Los Angeles	$11	$8.50	$11.55
Miami	$8.75	$6.90	$10
Chicago	$10.50	$8.25	$11.75

The problem we have is that we need to determine the best place to ship the fruit to be sold for the biggest gross income. To do that, we reconstruct this chart as a matrix of 4 rows, 3 columns. From there, we construct a 3 row, 1 column matrix for quantity and that looks like this:

== ==

| 1250 |

| |

| 400 |

| |

| 250 |

== ==

Now that we have our two matrices, the price matrix is multiplied by the quantity matrix and that gives us a matrix for gross income:

```
==                                  ==          ==              ==

| 10.00     8.00     12.00 |  ==   ==  | 18700.00 |        New York

|                          |  | 1250 |  |        |

| 11.00     8.50     11.55 |  |      |  |20037.50 |        Los Angeles

|                            | X |  400 | = |     |

| 8.75      6.90     10.00  |  |    |  | 16197.50 |        Miami

|                            |  |  250 |  |       |

| 10.50     8.25     11.75  | ==   ==| 19362.50  |        Chicago

==                                  ==          ==              ==
```

The largest gross income will be gained if we send both of the semi-trailers to LA but, when you factor in the costs of fuel and distance, then New York may well be the better bet.

Ragged Arrays

Now that you know a bit more about two-dimensional arrays, it's time to look at whether we can assign column arrays (one-dimensional) that have different lengths to a row array's elements and the answer to that is yes.

Have a look at these examples:

double[][] temperatures1 = { { 20.5, 30.6, 28.3 }, { -38.7, -18.3 } };

double[][] temperatures2 = new double[2][];

double[][] temperatures3 = new double[][] { { 20.5, 30.6, 28.3 }, { -38.7, -18.3 } };

Examples one and three both create two-dimensional arrays with row one containing three columns and row two containing two columns. Example two creates an array that has two rows but no specified number of columns.

Once the temperature2 row array has been created, we need to populate the elements with references pointing to the column arrays. In the next example, you can see how three columns are assigned to row one and two columns are assigned to row two:

temperatures2[0] = new double[3];

temperatures2[1] = new double[2];

The result of this is a two-dimensional array that we call a ragged array. Have a look at another example:

int[][] x = new int[5][];

x[0] = new int[3];

x[1] = new int[2];

x[2] = new int[3];

x[3] = new int[5];

x[4] = new int[1];

Below you can see a visualization of the second ragged array:

	Rows				
	(0,0)	(0, 1)	(0, 2)		
	(1, 0)	(1, 1)			
Columns	(2, 0)	(2, 1)	(2, 2)		
	(3, 0)	(3, 1)	(3, 2)	(3, 3)	(3, 4)
	(4, 0)				

The ragged array is one of the more useful of the data structures, if only because they have the ability to save memory. Consider this – a spreadsheet has got the potential to have 100,000 rows and 20,000 columns. If we were to try using a matrix to hold that spreadsheet, we would need vast amounts of memory. But, let's assume that most of the cells on that spreadsheet have default values in them, like null for a non-numeric cell and 0 for a numeric cell. If a ragged array were to be used rather than a matrix, we would only be storing the cells that had non-numeric data in them. Obviously, we would need a mechanism of sorts that would map the row and column coordinates in the spreadsheet to the row and column coordinates in the ragged array.

Ragged arrays are good for when we want to manage big data, like the huge amounts of data the Internet of Things generates.

Is an Array an Object?

If you were to read Java Language Specification, you would see that, in chapter 10, the very first line states that a Java array is a Java object. Behind the scenes, every array is considered to be an instance of a hidden class; that class will inherit the 11 methods of java.lang.Object.

The array instance will override the protected method for the object – clone() throws CloneNotSupportedException – and this allows for shallow cloning of the array. Additionally, a length field is provided by the hidden class.

Start a new program and call it ArrayIsObject; input this code – it demonstrates the relationship between the array and the object:

```
public final class ArrayIsObject
{
    public static void main(String[] args)
    {
        double[] a = { 100.5, 200.5, 300.5 };
        double[] b = { 100.5, 200.5, 300.5 };
        double[] c = b;
        System.out.println("a's class is " + a.getClass());
        System.out.println("a and b are " + ((a.equals(b)) ? "" : "not ") + "equal ");
        System.out.println("b and c are " + ((b.equals(c)) ? "" : "not ") + "equal ");
        double[] d = (double[]) c.clone();
        System.out.println("c and d are " + ((c.equals(d)) ? "" : "not ") + "equal ");
        for (int i = 0; i < d.length; i++)
            System.out.println(d[i]);
    }
```

}

We have created two arrays here – a-referenced and b-referenced – both of which are double precision, floating point. Each has the same length and the same content. In the a-referenced array, class [D] is returned by a.getClass() – D is the hidden class name.

Although both arrays are identical in content, a.equals(b) will return false; this is because equals() will not compare the contents, only the references and both a and b have different ones. The b reference gets assigned to c; b.equals(c) will return true; this is because both the b and the c arrays are referencing the exact same array. A shallow clone of c is created by c.clone() and this is referenced with an assignment to d.

As a way of proving that the d-reference array has identical contents to the c array, a for loop will iterate over every element and the contents are printed to standard output. The loop will read what is in the d array length field, which is read-only, to work out how many elements it needs to iterate over.

A quick tip here; never specify how long the array will be in your source code. Instead, you should specify the length, i.e., d.length. This cuts out the risk of bugs related to length in your source code should you decide, late down the line, to change the length of the array in the code used to create it.

Array Object Example:

Compile the program like this:

javac ArrayIsObject.java

The resulting application can be run like this:

java ArrayIsObject

You should see this output:

a's class is class [D

a and b are not equal

b and c are equal

c and d are not equal

100.5

200.5

300.5

That concludes our look at multi-dimensional arrays, how to create them and how they can be used in Java programming. We looked at the matrix multiplication algorithm and how it could be used for solving a real-world problem. We also looked at ragged arrays and whether a Java array is, in fact, a Java object. Next, we move onto singly and doubly-linked lists.

Singly Linked Lists – Search and Sort Algorithms

In much the same way as an array is, a linked list is one of the basic data structures, a category of data structures that are used for basing the more complex data structures upon. However, linked lists are not sequences of elements; rather, they are lists of nodes with each node being linked to the last and to the next in the sequence. Nodes are objects that have been created from classes that self-reference and these have a minimum of one field that has the class name as a reference type. We link the nodes in the linked list by way of node references.

Have a look at this example:

```
class Employee

{

  private int empno;

  private String name;

  private double salary;

  public Employee next;

  // Other members.

}
```

Here we have a self-referential class by the name of Employee. It is self-referential because the next field is of the Employee type. The Employee field is the perfect example of a link field; it is able to store references to other objects of the same class, in our case, the Employee object.

We are going to be looking at singly linked lists and how to use them in Java programming. We will look at the operations needed to create the singly linked list, how to insert and to delete nodes, how to concatenate two singly linked lists and how to invert them. We will also look at the algorithms that are commonly used for sorting the singly linked list before we look at how the insertion sort algorithm works with them.

What is a Singly Linked List?

Singly linked lists are lists of linked nodes; each of the nodes has got one link field. Within this data structure, the reference variable will have a reference to the top node, the first in the list. Each of the nodes, with the exception of the bottom or last node, will link to the one that follows it and the bottom node will have a null reference in the link field; this signifies that the list has ended. Commonly, the reference variable will have a name of top but you can name it whatever you want.

The pseudocode below is for the singly linked list:

```
DECLARE CLASS Node

  DECLARE STRING name

  DECLARE Node next

END DECLARE

DECLARE Node top = NULL
```

The class called Node is self-referential and it has fields for name data and next link. The node called top is a reference variable with a data type of Node; this will reference the top Node object in the list. Because we don't have a singly linked list just yet, the initial value of top is NULL.

How to Create a Singly Linked List

To create a singly linked list, we attach one Node object. The pseudocode below will create that Node object. It will then assign the object reference to top, initialize the object's data field and assign its link field with NULL:

```
top = NEW Node

top.name = "A"

top.next = NULL
```

Singly linked lists have time complexities of o(1) which is constant.

How to Insert a Node

Creation of a singly linked list is quite easy; inserting a node into it, not so easy. The reason it is a bit more complicated is that we have to consider three cases:

- Inserting the node before the top node (first one)
- Inserting the node after the bottom node (last one)
- Inserting the node in between two other nodes

Inserting the Node before the Top Node

This is done by assigning the reference for the top node to link field of the new node. The reference for the new node is then assigned to the top variable. We can see this in operation by looking at this pseudocode:

```
DECLARE Node temp

temp = NEW Node

temp.name = "B"

temp.next = top

top = temp
```

The time complexity of this operation is o(1).

Inserting the Node After the Bottom Node

We do this assigning the link field of the new node with a value of NULL. We then traverse the linked list to find the bottom node and then assign the reference of the new node to the link field of the bottom node, as you can see in this pseudocode:

```
temp = NEW Node

temp.name = "C"

temp.next = NULL

DECLARE Node temp2

temp2 = top

// We assume top (and temp2) are not NULL

// because of the previous pseudocode.

WHILE temp2.next NE NULL

  temp2 = temp2.next

END WHILE

// temp2 now references the last node.

temp2.next = temp
```

The time complexity for this operation if o(n) linear. We could improve this, bringing it to o(1) if we maintained a reference to the bottom node and, if we did this, we would not need to run a search for the last node.

Inserting in Between Two Nodes

This is the most complicated of all three cases; the new node is inserted between two other nodes by traversal of the list to locate the node that is before where the new node will be. The reference from the link field of the node we found is then assigned to the link field of the new node and the reference of the new node is assigned to the link field of the node we found. This pseudocode demonstrates how this happens:

```
temp = NEW Node

temp.name = "D"

temp2 = top

// We assume that the newly created Node inserts after Node

// A and that Node A exists. In the real world, there is no

// guarantee that any Node exists, so we would need to check

// for temp2 containing NULL in both the WHILE loop's header

// and after the WHILE loop completes.

WHILE temp2.name NE "A"

  temp2 = temp2.next

END WHILE

// temp2 now references Node A.

temp.next = temp2.next

temp2.next = temp
```

The time complexity for this operation is o(n).

How to Delete a Node

This is also a bit more complicated than creating the list in the first place but this time, we only have to consider two cases:

- Deleting the first node
- Deleting any node except for the first node

Deleting the First Node

To delete the first node we must assign the link from the link field for the first node to the variable used for referencing the first node, when or if there is a first node:

```
IF top NE NULL THEN
  top = top.next; // Reference the second Node (or NULL when there's only one Node).
END IF
```

The time complexity of this operation is o(1).

Deleting Any Other Node

To do this, we must find the node that comes before the node we want to delete. Then, we assign the reference from the link field of the node we want to delete to the link field of the node that comes before it. Look at this pseudocode:

```
IF top NE NULL THEN
  temp = top
  WHILE temp.name NE "A"
    temp = temp.next
  END WHILE
  // We assume that temp references Node A.
  temp.next = temp.next.next
  // Node D no longer exists.
END IF
```

The time complexity of this operation is o(n).

Create, Insert, Delete Example:

Start a new program and call it SLLDemo; input this code to it:

```
public final class SLLDemo
{
        private static class Node
        {
                String name;
                Node next;
```

```
}

public static void main(String[] args)
{
        Node top = null;

        // 1. The singly linked list does not exist.
        top = new Node();
        top.name = "A";
        top.next = null;
        dump("Case 1", top);

        // 2. The singly linked list exists and the node must be inserted
        //    before the first node.
        Node temp;
        temp = new Node();
        temp.name = "B";
        temp.next = top;
        top = temp;
        dump("Case 2", top);
        // 3. The singly linked list exists and the node must be inserted
        //    after the last node.

        temp = new Node();
        temp.name = "C";
        temp.next = null;
        Node temp2;
        temp2 = top;
        while (temp2.next != null)
                temp2 = temp2.next;
```

```
temp2.next = temp;
dump("Case 3", top);

// 4. The singly linked list exists and the node must be inserted
//    between two nodes.
temp = new Node();
temp.name = "D";
temp2 = top;
while (temp2.name.equals("A") == false)
        temp2 = temp2.next;
temp.next = temp2.next;
temp2.next = temp;
dump("Case 4", top);

// 5. Delete the first node.
top = top.next;
dump("After first node deletion", top);

// 5.1 Restore node B.
temp = new Node();
temp.name = "B";
temp.next = top;
top = temp;

// 6. Delete any node but the first node.
temp = top;
while (temp.name.equals("A") == false)
        temp = temp.next;
temp.next = temp.next.next;
dump("After D node deletion", top);
```

```
}

private static void dump(String msg, Node topNode)
{
        System.out.print(msg + " ");
        while (topNode != null)
        {
                System.out.print(topNode.name + " ");
                topNode = topNode.next;
        }
        System.out.println();
}
}
```

Compile the program like this:

javac SLLDemo.java

Run the application that results like this:

java SLLDemo

You should see this output:

Case 1 A

Case 2 B A

Case 3 B A C

Case 4 B A D C

After first node deletion A D C

After D node deletion B A C

Concatenation of Singly Linked Lists

On occasion, you might find that you want to concatenate two singly linked lists, i.e. join them together. Let's say that you have two lists, each full of words. The first list has words starting with the letters A to M and the second has words starting with N to Z. You want these two lists in one single list.

Have a look at the pseudocode below that describes the algorithm we use to concatenate the lists:

```
DECLARE Node top1 = NULL

DECLARE Node top2 = NULL

// Assume code that creates a top1-referenced singly linked list.

// Assume code that creates a top2-referenced singly linked list.

// Concatenate top2-referenced list to top1-referenced list.

IF top1 EQ NULL

  top1 = top2

  END

END IF

// Locate final Node in top1-referenced list.

DECLARE Node temp = top1

WHILE temp.next NE NULL

  temp = temp.next

END WHILE

// Concatenate top2 to top1.

temp.next = top2

END
```

As far as the trivial case goes, we don't have a top1-referenced list. In that case, we assign top1 to the value of top2; if there were now top2-referenced list, this value would be NULL.

The time complexity of this operation is o(1) for the trivial case and, for all other cases, o(n). However, if a reference were maintained to the bottom node, you wouldn't need to search for the node in the list and the time complexity would improve to o(1).

Inverting Singly Linked Lists

Inversion is another very useful operation for singly linked lists. Inversion will reverse the links in the list, allowing you to do the traversal in the other direction. This pseudocode below shows you the reversal of the links in the top1-referenced list:

```
DECLARE Node p = top1 // Top of the original singly linked list.

DECLARE Node q = NULL // Top of the reversed singly linked list.

DECLARE Node r      // Temporary Node reference variable.

WHILE p NE NULL     // For each Node in the original singly linked list ...

  r = q           // Save future successor Node's reference.

  q = p           // Reference future predecessor Node.

  p = p.next      // Reference next Node in original singly linked list.

  q.next = r      // Link future predecessor Node to future successor Node.

END WHILE

top1 = q          // Make top1 reference first Node in the reversed singly linked list.

END
```

The time complexity of the operation is o(n).

Concatenation and Inversion Example:

Start a new program, call it SLLDemo2 and input this code:

```
public final class SLLDemo2

{

    private static class DictEntry

    {

        String word;

        String meaning;

        DictEntry next;

    }
```

```
// ListInfo is necessary because buildList() must return two pieces
// of information.
private static class ListInfo
{
        DictEntry top;
        DictEntry last;
}

public static void main(String[] args)
{
        String[] wordsMaster = { "aardvark", "anxious", "asterism" };
        ListInfo liMaster = new ListInfo();
        buildList(liMaster, wordsMaster);
        dump("Master list =", liMaster.top);
        String[] wordsWorking = { "carbuncle", "catfish", "color" };
        ListInfo liWorking = new ListInfo();
        buildList(liWorking, wordsWorking);
        dump("Working list =", liWorking.top);

        // Perform the concatenation
        liMaster.last.next = liWorking.top;
        dump("New master list =", liMaster.top);
        invert(liMaster);
        dump("Inverted new master list =", liMaster.top);
}

private static void buildList(ListInfo li, String[] words)
{
        if (words.length == 0)
```

```
                return;

        // Create a node for first word/meaning.
        li.top = new DictEntry();
        li.top.word = words[0];
        li.top.meaning = null;

        // Initialize last reference variable to
        // simplify append and make concatenation possible.
        li.last = li.top;
        for (int i = 1; i < words.length; i++)
        {
                // Create (and append) a new node for next word/meaning.
                li.last.next = new DictEntry();
                li.last.next.word = words[i];
                li.last.next.meaning = null;

                // Advance last reference variable to simplify append and
                // make concatenation possible.
                li.last = li.last.next;
        }
        li.last.next = null;
}

private static void dump(String msg, DictEntry topEntry)
{
        System.out.print(msg + " ");
        while (topEntry != null)
        {
                System.out.print(topEntry.word + " ");
```

```
                topEntry = topEntry.next;
            }
            System.out.println();
        }

        private static void invert(ListInfo li)
        {
            DictEntry p = li.top, q = null, r;
            while (p != null)
            {
                r = q;
                q = p;
                p = p.next;
                q.next = r;
            }
            li.top = q;
        }
}
```

Compile the program in this way:

javac SLLDemo2.java

Run the application that results in this way:

java SLL2Demo

You should see this output:

Master list = aardvark anxious asterism

Working list = carbuncle catfish color

New master list = aardvark anxious asterism carbuncle catfish color

Inverted new master list = color catfish carbuncle asterism anxious aardvark

Search and Sort Algorithms

Another very common task in Java programming is to search through a singly linked list looking for certain data items. We could use the linear search algorithm, discussed earlier in this section of the guide but there are other ones we can use too. You could, if you wanted, take the binary search algorithm and adapt it for much better performance but, where singly linked lists are concerned, it wouldn't do you any good. Why? Because we would need to repeatedly search the list for the node we are trying to find and the performance would be significantly degraded to a time complexity of o(n).

The merge sort algorithm would be a better one. This is a divide and conquer type of algorithm; it will divide the list down into new sublists – each one will have a single element; lists of one element are considered to be sorted. Merge sort will then merge the sublists repeatedly to produce new sublists that are sorted until only one sublist is left – the fully sorted list.

The insertion sort algorithm is another useful possibility; remember we used it earlier to sort arrays. Now will look at using insertion sort for sorting singly linked lists.

With the insertion sort algorithm, we can place a singly linked list containing n data items in either descending or ascending order. To start with we have an empty list that is considered to be trivially sorted. One node at a time is removed from the list and then placed on the correct position in the sorted list. If the list we are sorting is empty, the sorted list will have the result we desire.

This pseudocode shows insertion sort being used to sort a singly linked list in ascending order:

```
// Exit if the list is empty or contains one node.

IF top EQ NULL OR top.next EQ NULL THEN

  END

END IF

// sTop is the first node of the sorted list.

DECLARE Node sTop = NULL

WHILE top NE NULL

  DECLARE Node current = top

  top = top.next

  IF sTop EQ NULL OR current.name LT sTop.name THEN

    // Insert into the head of the sorted list (sTop) or as the first

    // element into an empty sorted list.
```

```
    current.next = sTop
    sTop = current
  ELSE
    // Insert current element into the proper position in the nonempty
    // sorted list.
    DECLARE Node p = sTop
    WHILE p NE NULL
      // p.next EQ NULL means last element of the sorted list.
      // current.name LT p.next.name means middle of the sorted list.
      IF p.next EQ NULL OR current.name LT p.next.name THEN
        // Insert into the middle of the sorted list or as the last
        // element.
        current.next = p.next
        p.next = current
        BREAK // Finished.
      END IF
      p = p.next
    END WHILE
  END IF
END WHILE
```

As far as time complexity goes, this operation is o(n2) with quadratic performance, For best case, with the list almost or fully sorted, we have o(n). For space complexity, the insertion sort algorithm needs, for variable storage, additional space of o(1).

Insertion Sort Example

Start a new program, name it InsSort and input this code:

```
public final class InsSort
{
```

```
private static class Node
{
        String name;
        Node next;
}

public static void main(String[] args)
{
        Node top = null;

        // 1. The singly linked list does not exist.
        top = new Node();
        top.name = "B";
        top.next = null;

        // 2. The singly linked list exists and the node must be inserted
        //    after the last node.
        Node temp = new Node();
        temp.name = "D";
        temp.next = null;
        Node temp2 = top;
        while (temp2.next != null)
                temp2 = temp2.next;
        temp2.next = temp;

        // 3. The singly linked list exists and the node must be inserted
        //    after the last node.
        temp = new Node();
        temp.name = "C";
        temp.next = null;
```

```
        temp2 = top;
        while (temp2.next != null)
                temp2 = temp2.next;
        temp2.next = temp;

        // 4. The singly linked list exists and the node must be inserted
        //    after the last node.
        temp = new Node();
        temp.name = "A";
        temp.next = null;
        temp2 = top;
        while (temp2.next != null)
                temp2 = temp2.next;
        temp2.next = temp;

        // 5. Dump the unsorted list.
        dump("Unsorted list", top);

        // 6. Sort the list.
        top = sort(top);

        // 7. Dump the sorted list.
        dump("Sorted list", top);
}

private static void dump(String msg, Node topNode)
{
        System.out.print(msg + " ");
        while (topNode != null)
        {
```

```
                System.out.print(topNode.name + " ");
                topNode = topNode.next;
            }
            System.out.println();
        }

        private static Node sort(Node top)
        {
            if (top == null || top.next == null)
                return top;

            Node sTop = null;
            while (top != null)
            {
                Node current = top;
                top = top.next;
                if (sTop == null || current.name.compareTo(sTop.name) < 0)
                {
                    current.next = sTop;
                    sTop = current;
                }
                else
                {
                    Node p = sTop;
                    while (p != null)
                    {
                        if (p.next == null ||
current.name.compareTo(p.next.name) < 0)
                        {
                            current.next = p.next;
                            p.next = current;
```

```
                        break;
                    }
                    p = p.next;
                }
            }
        }
        return sTop;
    }
}
```

Compile the program like this:

javac InsSort.java

Run the application that results like this:

java InsSort

You should see this output:

Unsorted list B D C A

Sorted list A B C D

Doubly Linked and Circular Linked Lists and Algorithms

We looked at everything we can do with singly linked lists and the algorithms we can use with them. While the singly linked list is useful in its own right, they are also somewhat restrictive. For a start, node traversal is limited to one direction – forwards. To traverse a singly linked list backward, you would need to reverse all the node links first and this is time-consuming. And, if you reverse traverse the list and then want to go back to the original direction, you need to do the inversion all over again, even more time wasted. There are also restrictions in deleting nodes because you cannot delete any arbitrary node without accessing the predecessor to that node.

Thankfully, with Java we have a few other types of list that we can use for searching and sorting data stored in your programs. To finish our section on data structures and algorithms, we are going to look at the doubly linked list and the circular linked list. As you will soon see, both of these data structures are useful for building on the singly linked list, offering much more in the way of search and sort behavior in your programs.

The Doubly Linked List

The doubly linked list is one made up of a list of nodes linked together; each node has got two link fields, one allowing for forward traversal and the other allowing for backward traversal. For the forward traversal, a reference variable will contain a reference leading to the top node. Each of the nodes will link to the following node used a link field called next; the only exception is the bottom note; the link field called next will have a value of Null signifying the end of the list.

Where backward traversal is required, it works in much the same way. The reference variable contains a reference to the last node of the forward direction – this is interpreted as the first node. Each of the nodes will link to the node before it using a link field called previous, with the exception of the first node; the link field for this contains a NULL value, signifying the end of the list.

You can think of doubly linked lists as two singly linked lists with interconnection between the same nodes.

Doubly Linked Lists – CRUD Operations

CRUD operations are creation, insertion and deletion operations and they are all very common on the doubly linked list. They are much like what we covered for the singly linked list too; after all, the doubly linked list is just two singly linked lists.

Have a look at this pseudocode, showing how to create and insert nodes into a doubly linked list, as well as deleting them:

```
DECLARE CLASS Node

  DECLARE STRING name

  DECLARE Node next

  DECLARE Node prev

END DECLARE

DECLARE Node topForward

DECLARE Node temp

DECLARE Node topBackward

topForward = NEW Node

topForward.name = "A"

temp = NEW Node

temp.name = "B"
```

```
topBackward = NEW Node
topBackward.name = "C"
// Create forward singly linked list
topForward.next = temp
temp.next = topBackward
topBackward.next = NULL
// Create backward singly linked list
topBackward.prev = temp
temp.prev = topForward
topForward.prev = NULL
// Delete Node B.
temp.prev.next = temp.next; // Bypass Node B in the forward singly linked list.
temp.next.prev = temp.prev; // Bypass Node B in the backward singly linked list.
END
```

Doubly Linked List CRUD Example:

Start a new program, call it DLLDemo and input this code:

```
public final class DLLDemo
{
    private static class Node
    {
        String name;
        Node next;
        Node prev;
    }

    public static void main(String[] args)
    {
        // Build a doubly linked list.
```

```
Node topForward = new Node();
topForward.name = "A";
Node temp = new Node();
temp.name = "B";
Node topBackward = new Node();
topBackward.name = "C";
topForward.next = temp;
temp.next = topBackward;
topBackward.next = null;
topBackward.prev = temp;
temp.prev = topForward;
topForward.prev = null;

// Dump forward singly linked list.
System.out.print("Forward singly linked list: ");
temp = topForward;
while (temp != null)
{
        System.out.print(temp.name);
        temp = temp.next;
}
System.out.println();

// Dump backward singly linked list.
System.out.print("Backward singly linked list: ");
temp = topBackward;
while (temp != null)
{
        System.out.print(temp.name);
        temp = temp.prev;
```

```
    }
    System.out.println();

    // Reference node B.
    temp = topForward.next;

    // Delete node B.
    temp.prev.next = temp.next;
    temp.next.prev = temp.prev;

    // Dump forward singly linked list.
    System.out.print("Forward singly linked list (after deletion): ");
    temp = topForward;
    while (temp != null)
    {
        System.out.print(temp.name);
        temp = temp.next;
    }
    System.out.println();

    // Dump backward singly linked list.
    System.out.print("Backward singly linked list (after deletion): ");
    temp = topBackward;
    while (temp != null)
    {
        System.out.print(temp.name);
        temp = temp.prev;
    }
    System.out.println();
}
```

}

Compile the program like this:

javac DLLDemo.java

Run the application that results like this:

java DLLDemo

You should see this as the output:

Forward singly linked list: ABC

Backward singly linked list: CBA

Forward singly linked list (after deletion): AC

Backward singly linked list (after deletion): CA

Doubly Linked Lists – Shuffling

In the Java Collections Framework you will find a class called Collections, which contains utility methods and is a part of java.util. In this class is a method called void shuffle(list<?>) which will randomly reallocate the contents of a specified list. A real-world example would be when you shuffle a deck of cards and, if you expressed that deck of cards as a doubly linked list, you would use this method or algorithm.

Have a look at the following pseudocode, showing how this algorithm would shuffle the list:

```
DECLARE RANDOM rnd = new RANDOM

DECLARE INTEGER i

FOR i = 3 DOWNTO 2

  swap(topForward, i - 1, rnd.nextInt(i))

END FOR

FUNCTION swap(Node top, int i, int j)

  DECLARE Node nodei, nodej

  DECLARE INTEGER k

  // Locate ith node.

  Node nodei = top

  FOR k = 0 TO i - 1
```

```
    nodei = nodei.next
  END FOR
  // Locate jth node.
  Node nodej = top
  FOR k = 0 TO i - 1
    nodej = nodej.next
  END FOR
  // Perform the swap.
  DECLARE STRING namei = nodei.name
  DECLARE STRING namej = nodej.name
  nodej.name = namei
  nodei.name = namej
END FUNCTION
END
```

This algorithm will obtain a 'source of randomness' before it traverses the doubly linked list in a backward direction. It will start from the last node and traverse to the second node. On a repeated basis, the shuffle algorithm will keep swapping randomly chosen nodes, which is nothing more than the name field, into a position known as 'current'. The nodes are selected randomly from the part of the list that goes from the first or top node up to and including the current position. Do note, the shuffle algorithm is a rough excerption of the source code for void shuffle(list<?>list).

As far as the pseudocode for the shuffle algorithm goes, it is somewhat lazy. Why? Because efforts are focused on the singly linked list out of the pair that is traversed forward. There is nothing wrong with this design decision, to be fair, but there is a price to be paid and that price is in the time complexity. The shuffle algorithm has a time complexity of o(n2); first, the o(n) loop which will call the swap() method. Second, inside the swap() method, we have a pair of sequential loops, both o(n). Think back to earlier in this section when discussed this rule:

If f1(n) = O(g(n)) and f2(n) = O(h(n)) then

(a) f1(n)+f2(n) = max(O(g(n)), O(h(n)))

(b) f1(n)*f2(n) = O(g(n)*h(n)).

The first bit is dealing with sequential algorithms. We have a pair of o(n) loops and, according to the above rule, the time complexity should be o(n). The second part is dealing with the nested algorithms and, with this one o(n) is multiplied with o(n) and the result is o(n2).

Note that the space complexity of the shuffle algorithm is o(1) and this is a result of the helper variables.

Shuffle Example:

Start a new program, call it shuffle and input this code:

```
import java.util.Random;

public final class Shuffle

{

        private static class Node

        {

                String name;

                Node next;

        Node prev;

        }


        public static void main(String[] args)

        {

                // Build a doubly linked list.

                Node topForward = new Node();

                topForward.name = "A";

                Node temp = new Node();

                temp.name = "B";

                Node topBackward = new Node();

                topBackward.name = "C";

                topForward.next = temp;

                temp.next = topBackward;

                topBackward.next = null;

                topBackward.prev = temp;
```

```
temp.prev = topForward;
topForward.prev = null;

// Dump forward singly linked list.
System.out.print("Forward singly linked list: ");
temp = topForward;
while (temp != null)
{
        System.out.print(temp.name);
        temp = temp.next;
}
System.out.println();

// Dump backward singly linked list.
System.out.print("Backward singly linked list: ");
temp = topBackward;
while (temp != null)
{
        System.out.print(temp.name);
        temp = temp.prev;
}
System.out.println();

// Shuffle list.
Random rnd = new Random();
for (int i = 3; i > 1; i--)
        swap(topForward, i - 1, rnd.nextInt(i));

// Dump forward singly linked list.
System.out.print("Forward singly linked list: ");
```

```
        temp = topForward;
        while (temp != null)
        {
                System.out.print(temp.name);
                temp = temp.next;
        }
        System.out.println();

        // Dump backward singly linked list.
        System.out.print("Backward singly linked list: ");
        temp = topBackward;
        while (temp != null)
        {
                System.out.print(temp.name);
                temp = temp.prev;
        }
        System.out.println();
}

public static void swap(Node top, int i, int j)
{
        // Locate ith node.
        Node nodei = top;
        for (int k = 0; k < i; k++)
                nodei = nodei.next;

        // Locate jth node.
        Node nodej = top;
        for (int k = 0; k < j; k++)
                nodej = nodej.next;
```

```
            String namei = nodei.name;
            String namej = nodej.name;
            nodej.name = namei;
            nodei.name = namej;
        }
}
```

Compile the program like this:

javac Shuffle.java

Run the application that results like this:

java Shuffle

After one run, you should see this output:

Forward singly linked list: ABC

Backward singly linked list: CBA

Forward singly linked list: BAC

Backward singly linked list: CAB

Circular Linked Lists

Inside the last node's link field in a singly linked list, you will find a NULL link. The same is true also of the doubly linked list; here you will find the link fields of the last nodes of both backward and forward singly linked lists. Let's assume that, instead, our last nodes had links to the first ones. This is a circular linked list.

Also called a circular queue or circular buffer, the circular linked list has multiple uses. They are, for example, used by interrupt handlers in operating systems to buffer all your keystrokes. They are used by multimedia applications to buffer data and they are also used by the lossless data compression algorithms in the LZ77 family.

Linked Lists vs Arrays

We have been considering what strengths and weaknesses the different data structures have and we have focused our attention on the linked lists and the arrays. So, are there any advantages or disadvantages to using one over the other? When should you use an array and when should you use a linked list? Can we integrate data structures from both the array and the linked list categories into one hybrid data structure?

Let's see if we can answer these questions:

First, the linked list has these advantages over using an array:

- The linked list can expand without needing extra memory. By contrast, the array DOES need the extra memory; don't forget, an array cannot be added to once all the elements have a data item assigned to them.
- Linked lists are quicker for inserting or deleting nodes than the equivalent operations in arrays. We only need to update the links once the position for insertion or deletion has been identified. The arrays, on the hand, are more complex – inserting a data item means all the other data items need to be moved so an empty element is created. In the same way, deletion means the other data items must be moved to remove the now empty element.

By contrast, an array has these advantages over the linked list:

- Elements in the array take less memory than linked list nodes because the array elements don't need the link fields.
- It is faster to access data in an array, by way of integer indexes.

So, to summarize, the linked list is much better for when you have dynamic data and inserting and deleting are frequent operations, while the array is better for static programs, where inserting and deleting don't happen very often. Remember, if you add items to the array and you run short of space, you need to create another, larger array and then copy the data from the original array. The original array then needs to be disposed of and this all takes time and reduces performance.

So, what about merging a one-dimensional array with a singly linked list to use array indexes to access nodes? It wouldn't work. All you are doing is wasting memory because you would need both nodes and elements, and you are wasting time because the data items in the array must be moved whenever you want to delete or insert a node.

Before we leave this section behind, I want to take you briefly through stacks and queues, a couple of the more complex data structures.

Stacks

Stacks are abstracted data types and are common in most of the computer programming languages. The reason it has the name of stack is that its behavior is much like that of the real-world stack, like a deck of cards or a stack of pancakes, for example.

The real-world stack can only have operations at one end. For example, you can only add or remove a pancake from the top of the stack and, in the same way, the ADT (abstract data type) stack can only have data operations carried out at one end. At any time we are only able to access the top of the stack.

This is what makes the stack a LIFO data structure, Last In, First Out. Here, the last element to be added to the stack is the first one to be accessed. There are two terms that you need to be aware of as far as that stack goes – insertion operations are PUSH operations and removals are POP operations.

Stack Representation

We can implement a stack in several ways – using an array, a linked list, a pointer or a structure. A stack may be fixed in size or it may be dynamic, i.e. it can be resized. We're going to look at using arrays to implement the stack and that will make it fixed in size.

Basic Stack Operations

Mostly, a stack operation involves three steps – initialization of the stack, use of the stack, de-initialization. Apart from that, stacks are used for two main operations:

- Push() – storing or pushing an element onto the stack
- Pop() – accessing or removing an element

Pushing Data

Efficient use of a stack involves checking the stack status. For that reason, we add the following functionality to a stack:

- Peek() – to obtain the top element without actually removing it
- isFull() – to see if the stack is full
- isEmpty() – to see if the stack is empty

It is important that, at all times, a pointer is maintained to the last data pushed to the stack. This pointer will always be representative of the top of the stack, which is why it is called top pointer. This provides us with the value of the top of the stack without removing it from the stack.

First, we'll look at the procedures used to support the stack functions:

Peek Operation

This is a simple algorithm for peek():

peek()

Algorithm of peek() function –

begin procedure peek

return stack[top]

end procedure

isfull()

Algorithm of isfull() function –

```
begin procedure isfull

   if top equals to MAXSIZE
      return true
   else
      return false
   endif

end procedure
```

isempty()

Algorithm of isempty() function –

```
begin procedure isempty

   if top less than 1
      return true
   else
      return false
   endif

end procedure
```

Push Operation

Adding a new element to the stack is called pushing and each push operation has several steps:

- It checks to see if the stack is full up

- If it is, an error is thrown and the operation will exit
- It there is room, the top pointer is incremented to point to the first empty space
- The element is added to the location in the stack that top points to
- The operation will return as successful.

If we used a linked list, we would dynamically allocate the required space in step 3.

This is a simple algorithm for push():

```
begin procedure push: stack, data


  if stack is full

    return null

  endif


  top ← top + 1

  stack[top] ← data


end procedure
```

Pop Operation

When we access a data element and remove it out of the stack, it is called a pop operation. If the implementation of the stack were an array, the pop operation would not actually remove the element; instead, the top element would be decremented lower down the stack, pointing to the value that comes next. However, where the implementation was a linked list, the pop operation would remove the element and the memory space would be deallocated. Pop operations have several steps:

- The operation would check if the stack were empty
- If it is, an error is produced and the operation exits
- If it isn't, the data element that top points to is accessed
- The value of top is decreased by 1
- The operation returns as successful.

This is a simple pop operation algorithm:

```
  if stack is empty

    return null
```

endif

data ← stack[top]

top ← top - 1

return data

end procedure

Queue

Queues are also abstract data types, similar to the stack but with one difference – a queue can be operated on at both ends. One end is used for inserting data, known as enqueuing, and the other is used for removing data, known as dequeuing. Like stack, queues also follow the methodology of FIFO, i.e. the first data item to be stored is the first to be accessed. Real-world examples of the queue are self-explanatory – a queue in a shop, on a motorway, and so on.

And, also similar to stacks, we can implement queues using arrays, pointers, linked lists, and structures. For our example and to keep things simple, we'll be using oneodimensional arrays.

Basic Operations

Operations on queues tend to take three steps – initialization or definition of the queue, use of the queue and then removing it entirely from memory. The basic operations are:

- Enqueue() – add an item, i.e. store it in the queue
- Dequeue() – remove an item, i.e. access it, from the queue

There are a few functions required to ensure that these operations work efficiently:

- Peek() – will get the first item in the queue but will not remove it
- isFull() – looks to see if the queue is full
- isEmpty() – looks to see if the queue is empty

In any queue, the data to be accessed or dequeued is pointed to by the front pointer while data that is to be stored or enqueued is pointed to by the rear pointer. Let's have a look at the supporting functions:

peek()

The peek() function allows us to see data that is at the front and the algorithm for this function is:

```
begin procedure peek

  return queue[front]

end procedure
```

isfull()

As our example uses a one-dimensional array for implementing the queue, we only need to check to see the rear pointer reached at MAXSIZE to work out if the queue is full. If we were using a circular linked list to implement the queue, the algorithm would be different. Here is the algorithm for isFull()

```
begin procedure isfull


  if rear equals to MAXSIZE

    return true

  else

    return false

  endif


end procedure
```

Algorithm of isempty() function –

Algorithm

```
begin procedure isempty


  if the front is less than MIN  OR front is greater than the rear

    return true

  else

    return false

  endif


end procedure
```

If the value assigned to front is lower than 0 or MIN, the queue knows that it hasn't yet been initialized and that means it is empty.

Enqueue Operation

As we said earlier, a queue has two data pointers; one at the front and one at the rear. As such, these operations are a little more complicated to implement than the operations of stack.

To enqueue data in a queue, these are the steps:

- Look to see if the queue is full
- If it is, an overflow error is produced and we exit the queue
- If it isn't, the rear pointer is incremented to point at the following empty space
- The data element is added to the location where the rear pointer is pointing
- It is returned as a success.

On occasion, we would also be looking to see whether the queue has been initialized or not, so that we can handle any situations that may arise.

The enqueue algorithm is:

```
procedure enqueue(data)


  if queue is full

    return overflow

  endif


  rear ← rear + 1

  queue[rear] ← data

  return true


end procedure
```

Dequeue Operation

There are two parts to the task of accessing queue data – we access it where the front pointer is pointing and then remove the data after the access. These are the steps for the dequeue operation:

- Look to see if the queue is empty
- If it is, an overflow error is produced and we exit the queue
- If it isn't, we access the data where the front pointer is pointing
- The front pointer is incremented so it points at the next data element available
- It is returned as a success

The dequeue algorithm is:

```
procedure dequeue


  if queue is empty

    return underflow

  end if


  data = queue[front]

  front ← front + 1

  return true


end procedure
```

Chapter 3: Java Web Development

What are Java Web Applications?

Java web applications are, quite simply, web apps built using Java. But, much more than that, they are applications that generate web pages that are fully interactive, each containing different markup language types, such XML, HTML, and so on, along with dynamic content. Typically, a Java web application will be made up of web components that modify data temporarily store the data, interact with web services and with databases and will render content as requested by the application users. Some of the components are JSP – JavaServer Pages, JavaBeans and servlets.

Many of the tasks that are required for the development of web applications can be somewhat repetitive or they may require huge amounts of boilerplate code. We can use web frameworks to take away some of the overhead that goes with the common development activities, for example, many of the frameworks include useful libraries that help you with page templating, session management and they often promote the reuse of code.

What is Java EE?

Java Enterprise Edition (Java EE) is one of the most commonly used platforms and it contains a range of coordinated technologies that take some of the complexity and cost out of the development of server-centric, multi-tier applications, making it much easier to deploy them and manage them. Java EE builds on Java SE and gives us a full set of development APIs that help us run server-side applications that are fully secure, portable scalable, robust, and reliable.

Some of the basic components include:

- EJB (Enterprise JavaBeans) – fully managed server-side architecture for enclosing application business logic. With EJB technology, we can rapidly develop Java-based applications that are distributed, secure, transactional and portable in a simplified way
- JPA (Java Persistence API) – a framework that provides ORM (Object-Relational Mapping) for data management capabilities within applications built using Java technology.

Ajax Development with JavaScript

JavaScript is used mainly in the client-side user interfaces in web applications and is an object-oriented language. Ajax, with stands for Asynchronous JavaScript and XML, is a technique that provides the ability for web pages to change without having to refresh the page each time. JavaScript toolkits can easily be used to implement components enabled by Ajax, along with their functionality, right into a web page.

The Practicalities of Developing Web Applications

Now it's time to get practical because that's the only real way to learn how to build a web application in Java. We're going to look at the basics of using the NetBeans IDE, how to produce a very simple web application, how to deploy it and how to see it in a web browser. This application will use a JSP page for name input and a JavaBeans component to ensure the name persists throughout the HTTP session, retrieving that name so it can be output on the next JSP page.

The first place to start is in setting up your environment so you can follow along.

The software and resources you will need are:

- The NetBeans IDE – v 7.2 onwards, Java EE
- Java Development Kit – v 7 onwards
- Glassfish Server Open Source Edition v 4 onwards OR
- Tomcat Servlet container v 7 onwards OR
- Oracle Web Logic Server – v 10 onwards

If you opt for the Java EE version, you can easily install both the Glassfish and Apache Tomcat servlet containers.

Set Up Your Project

Once you have downloaded everything from above, you can follow this tutorial. Start by opening the NetBeans IDE

Click on File>New Project in the main menu or click CTRL+SHIFT+N if you prefer to use keyboard shortcuts.

Now click on Categories and choose Java Web

Click Projects>Web Application>Next

Go to the text box for Project Name and call it HelloWeb.

Decide the Project Location – it can be any directory on your system. For this tutorial we will be referring to the directory as $PROJECTHOME.

This is an optional step – check the box beside Use the Dedicated Folder for Storing Libraries and decide where the libraries folder will go.

Click on Next and a panel for the Server and Settings will open. Choose which Java EE version you are going to use with the application

Next, choose which server you are going to use for deployment of your application. Note that you will only see those servers that are registered with the NetBeans IDE. Also note the

Context Path (on server) changes to /HelloWeb/ - this is indicative of the name you provided earlier.

Click on Finish

NetBeans IDE will now create a project folder called $PROJECTHOME/HelloWeb. If you go to the Files window in NetBeans or press CTRL+2, you can see the file structure for this project; go to the Projects window, or press CTRL+1 and you can see the logical structure.

This project folder is where all of your metadata and source will go for this project. HelloWeb will open directly in NetBeans IDE while the Welcome page, which is index.jsp, will open in the main window in the Source Editor.

Note – The NetBeans IDE may generate the default welcome page as index.html but this will depend on which server and which version of the Java EE that you chose when the project was created. You have two choices – follow this tutorial using the index.html file or go to the New File wizard and create an index.jsp file – if you choose the latter, make sure you delete index.html to avoid confusion.

Create and Edit Application Source Files

The NetBeans IDE serves many useful functions but one of the most important is the creation and editing of the source files for your web application. That, in all honesty, is what most web app developers spend the bulk of their time doing. With the IDE, you get a huge selection of tools that will suit all types of developer and the individual style that they have, regardless of whether you prefer the IDE to generate much of the code or whether you prefer to code manually.

Creating the Java Package and Source File

Go to the Projects window and find the Source Packages node; expand it. Do note that it contains only a default package node which is empty.

Now right-click on the Source Packages node and, from the menu, click on New>Java Class

In the Class Name box, type in NameHandler and in the Package box type in org.mypackage.hello

Click on Finish. The new file, NameHandler.java, will open in the Source Editor.

Find the class declaration in the Source Editor and, just beneath it type in:

String name;

Now type this constructor into the class:

public NameHandler() { }

And add this line to that constructor:

name = null;

Getter and Setter Methods

In the Source Editor, go to the name field and right-click on it; from the menu, click on Refactor>Encapsulate Fields.

You will see a dialog box open, called Encapsulate Fields and in it is the name filed – note that, by default, Visibility for the Field is set as private and the Accessors Visibility is set as public. This indicates that the access modifier for the declaration of the class variable will be set as private while the getter method is generated with a public modifier and the setter method with a private modifier.

Click on Refactor and the getter and setter methods will be generated for that name field. Note that the class variable modifier is private and both getter and setter are public modifiers. Your class should now look like this:

```
package org.mypackage.hello;


public class NameHandler {


    private String name;


    /** Creates a new instance of NameHandler */
    public NameHandler() {
        name = null;
    }


    public String getName() {
        return name;
    }


    public void setName(String name) {
        this.name = name;
    }
```

}

Edit Default JSP File

In the Source Editor, click the tab at the top for the index.jsp file to refocus it

Go to the Palette window, to the right side of the Source Editor or press on CTRL+SHIFT+8, find HTML Forms and expand it. Drag one Form item to somewhere in the Source Editor after the <h1> tags. You will see the Insert Form dialog box open

The following values need to be specified:

- Action – response.jsp
- Method – GET
- Name – Name Input Form

Click on OK and you will see the HTML form added into your index.jsp file.

Next, from the Palette window, as above drag one Text Input item to the Source Editor just before where the </form> tag is and then specify these values:

- Name – name
- Type – text

Click on OK and the HTML <input> tag will be added in between your <form> tags. Make sure the value attribute is deleted from the tag.

Now drag one Button item to the Source Editor, and drop it just in front of the <form> tag; these values need to be specified:

- Label – OK
- Type – submit

Click on OK and an HTML button will be placed in between your form tags.

Go to where the initial <input> tag is and just before it, type in Enter Your Name. In between the <h1> tags, you will see the default text of Hello World!; delete this and type in Entry Form.

Right-click somewhere in the Source Editor and click on Format (or just press ALT+SHIFT+F) so your code format is tidied up. Your index.jsp file should look something like this:

```
<html>

<head>

        <meta http-equiv="Content-Type" content="text/html; charset=UTF-8">
```

```
        <title>JSP Page</title>
<title>Insert title here</title>
</head>
<body>
        <h1>Entry Form</h1>

        <form name="Name Input Form" action="response.jsp">
        Enter your name:
      <input type="text" name="name" />
      <input type="submit" value="OK" />
   </form>
</body>
</html>
```

Creating a JSP

Go the Projects window, find the project node for HelloWeb and right-click on it; from the menu, click on New>JSP

You will see the New JSP file wizard; call your file Response and then click on Finish. You will see a response.jsp file appear in the Project window, underneath index.jsp and the file will open in your Source Editor.

Go to the Palette window, find JSP and expand it. Drag one Use Bean item to the Source Editor, just underneath the <body> tag.

A dialog box for Insert Use Bean will open and the following values must be specified:

- ID – mybean
- Class – org.mypackage.hello.NameHandler
- Scope – session

Click on OK and you will see, under the body tag, a <jsp:useBean> tag

From the Palette, drag one Set Bean Property to the Source Editor, just ahead of the <h1> tag; click on OK

The <jsp.setProperty> tag will appear; delete the value for the empty attribute and edit it as per the code below. Make sure that the value of the ="" is deleted if it was created by the IDE otherwise it will overwrite the name value passed in index.jsp:

<jsp:setProperty name="mybean" property="name" />

If you scan through the <jsp:setProperty> documentation, you will see that there are several methods of setting value properties. In our case, the user input that comes from our index.jsp file will be a name and value pair that gets passed to our request object. When the <jsp:setProperty> tag is used for setting the property, the value can be specified as per the property name in the request object. So, when you set the property as name, the value input by the user can be retrieved.

Go to the <h1> tags and edit the text to read <h1>Hello, !</h1>

From the Palette, drag one Get Bean Property item to the comma in between the <h1> tags (after Hello, before !). The Insert Get Bean Property box opens, specify these values:

- Bean Name – mybean
- Property Name – name

Click on OK and you will see that there is a <jsp:getProperty> tag appearing inside the <h1> tags.

Be aware that case sensitivity must be observed for property names. The property called name must be in the same case in both response.jsp and the index.jsp input form.

In the Source Editor, right-click anywhere and, from the menu, click on Format (ALT+SHIFT+F) and tidy up your code format. You should now see something like this for the response.jsp <body> tags:

```
<body>

        <jsp:useBean id="mybean" scope="session"
class="org.mypackage.hello.NameHandler" />

   <jsp:setProperty name="mybean" property="name" />

   <h1>Hello, <jsp:getProperty name="mybean" property="name" />!</h1>

</body>
```

Running Your Project

The NetBeans IDE builds web applications and runs them using an Ant build script. This script is generated based on what you have specified in the New Project Wizard and from the options specified in the dialog box for Project Properties. To see this, go to the Project window, right-click on the Project node and click on Properties.

Staying in the Project window, go to the HelloWeb project node and right-click on it. From the menu, click on Run (or press F6). When the web application is run, these steps are carried out by the IDE:

- Builds the application code and runs it. By default, it will be created with a feature called Compile on Save so there is no need for compiling first to run it in the IDE. This step can be done in isolation – go to the Project node, right-click on it and click on either Clean and Build or just Build.
- Launches the server and deploys the applications. Again, this can be done in isolation by right-clicking the Project node and clicking on Deploy.
- Displays your application in a web browser.

An output window gets opened by the IDE, showing the progress of the application run. Have a look at the tab titled HelloWeb – you can see all of the steps carried out by the IDE and, if there are any problems, you will see error information here.

An output window is opened showing the status of the server. Look at the tab that has your server name on it.

Important note – If the Glassfish server does not start, you can manually start it and run your program. Do this by going to the Services window, finding the server node and right-clicking on it; click Start in the menu.

The server output window offers a lot of useful information regarding issues with running web apps and the server logs are also very useful. You can find these in the domain directory for the server. And if you click on View>IDE Log you can see the IDE Log.

Opens the index.jsp page in your browser (if you use more than one, it will be the default browser). Do note that you may see the browser window before the server output is displayed by the IDE.

In the text box, type your name in and click on OK. You will see the response.jsp page showing you a simple greeting.

Troubleshooting

Nothing ever runs as smooth as you would like and there are a couple of problems that you may come across.

You've built your project and you've run it but when you click on OK for the index.jsp page, you get an error page telling you that response.jsp is not there. What do you do?

Go to the Output window in the IDE or press on CTRL+4. The Click on the Project or the Server tab and see if there are any error messages. Check which JDK is being used by your project and see what server is in use> For JDK 7 or above you need either Glassfish 3 or above or Tomcat 7 or above. Go to the Project window, right click on the Project node and click on Properties. Go to the Java Platform field and look in Libraries to see which JDK is being run. For the server, go to the category called Run.

You've built the project and run it and all you see is "Hello, !", no name appears.

Check the <jsp:setProperty> tag – is the ="" attribute value there? This should be deleted as it will override whatever value was passed in index.jsp and will put an empty string in its place instead.

You've built your project and run it but you get a "Hello, null!".

Go to the IDE output window for Application and for Server and also look at the server log. Is your server actually running? Did your application get deployed? If yes to both of these questions, check to see if you get an exception – it will read org.apache.jasper.JasperException:Java.lang.NullPointerException. If you do, it means that one of your values has not been properly initialized. For the sale of this tutorial, it most likely means a type error in a Property name inside the JSP files. Remember – all property names follow case sensitivity rules!

Java EE Technology Support in NetBeans IDE

The NetBeans IDE was developed with very close cooperation between the Glassfish and the Java EE teams to ensure that full integration is achieved and that the Java EE spec is as easy as it could be to use. The very best way to learn Java EE programming to a productive level is to learn the NetBeans IDE. You've already seen it in use so now we will delve a little further into it.

Using Annotations In Place of Deployment Descriptors

With the Java EE platform, you get simplified development because you don't need to use deployment descriptors, with the exception of one – the descriptor that the servlet specification requires. Some of the other descriptors, like those related to web.xml web services, are now obsolete and the J2EE descriptors from v 1.4 were so complex, mistakes were common with completing them. The Java EE platform now uses annotations instead, which are Java modifiers. They are much like private and public modifiers that are specified by you when you write your code. For example, the specification EJB3 is a Java EE subset and is used for defining the annotations for several types, including interface type, bean type, transaction attributes, resource references, security and many more.

The specification, JAX-WS 2.0 also provides annotations for web services; some are for the generation of artifacts, others are for code documentation, for logic specific to runtime, security and other enhanced services. To summarize, with Java EE you get annotations for these:

- Definition and usage of web services
- Development of EJB applications
- Map Java tech classes to databases and to SML
- Map methods to relevant operations

- Specification of external dependencies
- Specification of information for deployment, including the security attributes

All annotations are prefixed with @. When a type that uses annotations is created in the NetBeans IDE, in the code that gets generated, you will see related placeholders. For example, if you created a session bean in the IDE with no state, you would see this code which, as you can see, contains the annotation, @Stateless():

```
package mypackage;


import javax.ejb.*;


@Stateless()

public class HelloWorldSessionBean implements mypackage.HelloWorldSessionLocal {


}
```

Every attribute has its own default values. As such, there is no need for attributes to be specified unless you need a value that is not the default one. Most of the time, you will find that the default value is more than sufficient and that means there is no need to provide a single attribute.

EJB Software Development Simplified

With the EJB 3.0 or higher API, software development is significantly easier because the amount of work needed by the developer is less and is not so complex. In other words, you don't need so many classes and you don't need so much code. The is made possible because the container takes care of performing most of the work. Some of the main features and benefits of using the API are:

- Not so many classes or interfaces needed. There is no longer any need for EJB component object or home interfaces because the container takes over the responsibility for exposing the methods that are necessary. All you need to supply is a business interface and annotations can be used for declaring the EJB components; the container takes care of the transactions.
- No need to use any deployment descriptors. Instead, annotations can be used in the class directly, telling the container about the configuration and the dependencies that were defined originally within the descriptors. If no instructions are provided, the container will handle the common situations using the default rules.

- Simpler lookups. With EJBContext, you can lookup JNDI namespace objects in the class.
- Simpler ORM. With the Java Persistence APU, object-relational mapping is more transparent and much easier because annotations can be used to map the Java objects to the databases.

In the NetBeans IDE, it is possible to code an enterprise bean in the same way as you would code a Java class. This would be done using editor hints and code completion to ensure the right methods are implemented and the classes retain synchronization with their own interfaces. There is no need for any special dialog boxes or commands to generate web service operations, business methods, or the like, although you can still use the commands for help with the Java EE syntax.

Accessing Resources Using Dependency Injection

With dependency injection your objects can make use of annotations for the direct request of an external resource. The result of this is code that is much cleaner, code that is easier to read. There is no longer any need for code that is cluttered with lookup code and resource creation code. Instead, resource injection can be used in the web containers, components, and the clients.

A component will request resource injection by using the @Resource annotation or, if the resource is specialized, the @WebServiceRef and the @EJB annotations. Resources available for injection include:

- Connection factories for the resource adapters
- DataSources object
- EntityManager interface
- Message queues and topics
- Other enterprise beans
- SessionContext object
- Web services

The Source Editor in the NetBeans IDE provides you with code completion for the annotations for resource injection that the Java EE platform provides. As well as that, the IDE can inject the resources directly into your files when commands such as Use Database and Call EJB are run.

The Java Persistence API Model

With the Java EE Platform we get the Java Persistence API which may also be used externally to the EJB components. For example, it can be used in application clients and web applications and in Java SE applications. The API has these main features:

- All entities are Plain Old Java Objects (POJOs). Where the EJB components make use of CMP (container-managed persistence), any entity object that uses the newer APIs are not classed as components and they do not need to be inside EJB modules.
- Standardized ORM. ORM handling has been standardized, giving the developer a break from having to learn strategies that are specific to vendors. Annotations are used by the Java Persistence API for the specification of ORM information but XML descriptors are still supported.
- Named queries. These are now expressed in metadata and are static queries. They may be native queries or they may be Persistence API queries and this allows for queries to be reused very easily.
- Simplified packaging rules. Entity beans are nothing more than a Java technology class and this means that they can be packaged just about anywhere within the EE application. For example, they could be in an application-client JAR, an EJB JAR, a WEB-INF class, a WEB-INF/lib class, an EAR file (Enterprise Application Archive, and more. Using the simplified rules for packaging there is no longer any need to create EAR files for entity beans form application clients or web apps to be used.
- Detached entities. As you now know, an entity bean is a POJO and that means it can easily be serialized. It can then be sent to another address space across the network and used in an environment that is persistence unaware. Because of this, there is no longer any requirement to make use of DTOs (data transfer objects).
- EntityManager API. Programmers can now make use of a standardized EntityManager API for CRUD (Create, Read, Update, Delete) operations where entities are involved.
- With the NetBeans IDE you get a series of tools to help you work with the new API, allowing you to code your entity classes manually or automatically generate the code from databases. There are also a number of graphics editors and templates to help create persistence units and maintain them.

Web Services

The use of annotations has significantly improved within the Java EE platform and has made support for web services much simpler. The specifications that contributed to this are:

- JSR 224 - Java API for JAX-WS 2.0 (XML web-based services)
- JSR 22 - JAXB 2.0 (Java Architecture for XML Binding
- JSR 181 – Web Services Metadata
- JAX-WS 2.0

This is the newest API for Java EE web services, succeeding JAX-RPC 1.1. The natural RPC model for programming has been retained while improvements have happened in protocol and transport independence, data binding, REST web service support and much easier developing.

There is one critical difference between the two – data binding is now taken care of by JAXB 2.0. This means that all JAX-WS web services can now use XML schema in its entirely which makes interoperability much better and much easier to use. Both of the technologies have been integrated so there is no longer any need to use two lots of tools. JAXB 2.0 can now generate embedded XML schema documents – these are in a WSDL (web service description language) document so users no longer have to manually integrate them, saving a lot of errors.

JAX-WS 2.0 provides out of the box support for the following protocols:

- SOAP 1.1
- SOAP 1.2
- XML/HTTP

One of the major goals right from the start was extensibility of the protocols and JAX-WS 2.0 now provides vendors with the ability to perform better or provide specialized web apps by supporting additional encodings and protocols such as FAST Infoset. If a web service uses an attachment to make sending and receipt of larger binary data much easier, they can use the MTOM/XOP (Message Transmission Optimization Mechanism/XML Binary Optimized Packaging) standard contained in W3C without any negative effects on the model.

Before we had the Java EE technology, the process of defining web services meant using long descriptors that were messy and unwieldy. Now all we have to do is add the @WebService annotation in our Java tech class and all the class's public methods will be published automatically as web service operations; JAXB 2.0 maps the arguments to XML Schema data types.

Asynchronous Web Services

Invoking a web service is done over the network and we have no way of predicting how long these calls will take. This can cause a serious downturn in performance with many clients, especially those that are interactive, like desktop apps based on JFC/Wing/ To get away from this downturn, JAX-WS 2.0 offers a new API, an asynchronous client. Using this API means that programmers do not need to manually create threads. Instead, the JAX-WS runtime manages remote, long-running invocations.

We can use asynchronous methods together with any interface generated in WSDL, and the Dispatch API, which is more dynamic. For the sake of convenience, asynchronous methods can be generated for operations that a web service defines when you import any WSDL document.

There are two models for usage:

- If you have a polling model, a call is made. When you want the results, you request them.
- If you have a callback model, a handler is registered. You get notified as soon as the response is received.

Support for asynchronous invocation is wholly client-side implemented so there is no need to make any changes to the target service.

The NetBeans IDE also provides a range of tools that work with JAX-WS. By going into the New File wizard, you can make use of templates that help with the generation of artifacts and you can create asynchronous web services by using a Web Service Customization Editor. And, with the code completion function, there are a number of annotations included that can be used in your web services.

Java EE Applications – Getting Started

We're going to take a brief look at some of the best features brought in with Java EE 6 and, to do that, we'll be following another practical tutorial. This time, we'll look at creating a web application based in Java EE with an entity class made up from an EJB bean façade with a stateless session. There are wizards contained in the IDE that you can use for generating both the bean and the entity class and the code the wizard generates makes use of queries that the Criteria API defines. Next a managed bean is created and named and this will access the presentation layer that makes use of the Facelet view framework and also accesses the session façade.

You will need the following resources and software:

- NetBeans IDE – v 7.2 or above, Java EE
- JDK – v 7 or 8
- Glassfish Server Open Source – v 3 or 4

Creating the Web App Project

We are going to start by creating a very basic web application and you will specify the target EE container as the Glassfish Server. This is fully compatible with Java EE and contains the libraries (JSF 2.x) that you will need in the application.

In the IDE, open the New Project Wizard. Choose your Java EE version – 6 or 7 are best as they are lightweight and they have subsets for the whole EE platform. The web profiles are also designed for uncomplicated, simple web applications that don't require any advanced technology like the JMS API (Java Message Service), the entire specification for EJB 3.1 or remote interface support.

The web profiles also have full support for the persistence management and transaction processing seen commonly in web apps for enterprises. The Java EE web profiles can be used in applications that use session beans with to without a local interface. If you have a remote interface included in the application, you will need the whole EE profile.

From the main menu, click on File>New Project or press CTRL+SHFT+N on the keyboard

Click on Java Web and then on Web Application; click on Next

Call the project SimpleEE6App and specify the location for the project. Ensure the Use Dedicated Folder option is unselected and click on Next

Choose the server (Glassfish) and set your EE version to 6 or y; click on Next

Go to the Frameworks pane and choose JavaServer Faces and then click on Finish

The IDE will choose the JSF 2.x library by default if your web app is Java EE and is being deployed to Glassfish. This library lets you make use of Facelets as the language for the page and provides JSF 1.2 and JSP support.

When you have clicked Finish, the project will be created and opened in Projects. The index.html page will be automatically created and opened in the editor.

The Entity Class and Session Facade

Now we are going to create our entity class and then a session façade for that class. Entity classes are POJOs, nothing more than simple Java classes with the @Entity annotation to denote it as an entity class. Entity classes may be used as persistent objects as a way of representing database tables. The Persistence API in Java lets you make use of persistence in a web app without having to create EJB modules.

In our application the entity class façade session is a session bean with no state. With Enterprise JavaBean 3.1, you get the ability to create any session bean without needing to use business interfaces that would have been required before this version. You can also package your EJB components straight into a WAR archive. The removal of needing EJB modules packaged in JAR archives in EAR archives has made the whole process of developing small web apps much easier. However, where the large enterprise apps are concerned, those that get distributed over multiple different machines, you will still require EAR archives to keep business logic separate from the presentation layer.

Creating Your Entity Class

We're going to make use of the New Entity Class wizard to come up with a very simple little persistent entity class. The wizard can also be used for creating persistence units for defining the entity manager and the data source that the application will use. One field will be added to our class for representing data in the table and you will also generate one getter and one setter for the field.

Entity classes require one primary key. When the class is created with the wizard, by default the NetBeans IDE will generate the id for the field and will use the @Idannotation to annotate the field, declaring it as a primary key. The IDE will also put the @Generated Value annotation in and will specify the strategy to be used for generating the key for the primary id field.

When you use Persistence, your application development is significantly simplified because there is no need for ORM to be provided for the persistent properties or field. Instead, annotations are used for defining the properties in a Java class.

The EntityManager API is used to manage entity persistence, handling the context; each context is one group of instances of an entity. When you develop the application, annotations may be used in the entity class to specify what the persistent context instance is of the entity instance. The container will then take over the handling of the entity instance lifecycle.

To create your class:

Find the project node and right-click on it; click on New>Other

Click on Persistence and then on Entity Class; click on Next

To name the class, type in Message

For the package, type in entities

Click on Create Persistence Unit and then click on Next

Choose your data source, i.e. if you want Java DB then choose jdbc/sample as your source. This one is already included in the JavaBeans IDE but you can use whichever one you want.

The other default options may be retained for the EclipseLink persistence provider and the persistence unit name. Make sure you confirm the Java Transaction API is being used by the persistence unit and that you set Table Generation Strategy to Create. This will ensure that your entity class-based tables are created on the deployment of the application.

Click on Finish and the entity class will be created and opened in the editor. Have a look at it and you will see the id field private long id has been created and the field has been annotated with @Id and with @GeneratedValue(strategy = GenerationType.AUTO).

Go to the editor and, underneath the id field, type the following in bold:

private Long id;

private String message;

In the editor, right-click anywhere and click on Insert Code (ALT+CTRL); click on Getter and Setter

In the dialog box called Generate Getters and Setters, choose the Message field and then click on Generate. The IDE will generate both methods for the message

Save all your changes

Your entity class is representing a database table. When the application is run, a Message database table is created automatically and this will have two columns – id and message.

In the XML editor, have a look at the persistence unit. You will see that your application is going to use the JTA API (transaction-type="JTA". What this does is specifies that the container now has the responsibility to manage the entity lifecycle within the persistence context. The result of this is less code because the application is not doing the managing.

Creating Your Session Facade

Now we are going to create a stateless session façade for our Message entity. According to EJB 3.1, it is now optional to have a business interface for a session bean and in our application, you have two options. Because it is a local client accessing the bean, you can have a no-interface view or a local interface exposing the bean.

To create the bean:

Find and right-click on the Project node and select New>Other

Click on Enterprise JavaBeans and then on Session Beans for Entity Classes. Click on Next

Click on Message Entity and then click Add>Next

For the package, type in boundary and click on Finish

Note that there was no business interface created for the bean; instead, we will use a no-interface view to expose it to a locally managed bean.

When you have finished, the session façade class, MessageFacade.java and the class called AbstractFacade.java and opens them in the editor. The @Stateless annotation is used for declaring the first class as a component of the stateless session bean. This class also extends the second class which is where you will find the business logic. It will also manage the entire transaction:

```
@Stateless

public class MessageFacade extends AbstractFacade<Message> {

   @PersistenceContext(unitName = "SimpleEE6AppPU")

   private EntityManager em;
```

When the entity façade is created with the wizard, the IDE will add an annotation by default – @PersistenceContext(unitName= "SimpleEE6AppPU". This will take care of resource injection into the bean components and will specify what the persistence unit name is. In our example we have explicitly declared the persistence unit name but, if there is only one unit then naming is optional.

The NetBeans IDE will also generate AbstractFacade.java methods for creating entities, editing, removing and finding them. The methods used for interaction with the persistence context are defined by the EntityManager API. The IDE will generate a few default query methods that are used commonly for finding entity objects. The Criteria API will define the count, findRange and findAll methods for the creation of Queries.

Creating the JSF and JSF Managed Bean Pages

Next, we need to create the application's presentation layer and we'll use JavaServer Faces, or JSF for this, along with a managed backing bean that the JSF pages use. Facelets are the view technology preferred for this and support is added into JSF, along with the ability to use the annotation, @ManagedBean, in your code, declaring the class as a managed bean. You do not need to declare managed beans in JSF by putting entries into faces-config.xml and bean names can be used in JSF pages to access the managed bean methods.

Creating the managed bean:

Go the Project node and right-click on it; click on New>Other

Click on JavaServer Faces and click JSF Managed Bean; click on Next

For the class name, type in MessageView

This is also the name you will use for the commandButton and inputText values in index.html for the JSF page when methods are called in the bean.

For the package, type in my.presentation

For the managed bean type in MessageView.

When you use the wizard to create your managed bean, the IDE will give the bean a name by default that is based on the bean class name and starting with a lower-case letter. For the purposes of this tutorial, we explicitly name the bean with an upper-case letter. When the bean is referenced in a JSF page, you use MessageView and not messageView.

Set Scope as Request and click on Finish

The bean class is created and the file opens in the editor. You can see that two annotations were added to the code, along with the bean name. The annotations are @ManagedBean and @RequestScope.

@ManagedBean(name="MessageView")

@RequestScoped

```
public class MessageView {


   /** Creates a new instance of MessageView */
   public MessageView() {
   }


}
```

Now we need to add another annotation, @EJB, and this will get a reference to our session bean called MessageFacade by using dependency injection. We also need to call two exposed methods in the façade – create and findAll. Make use of the code completion ability in the IDE to type in your method names.

In the editor, right-click anywhere and then, from the menu, click on Insert Code (ALT+Insert) and then on Call Enterprise Bean

The dialog box will appear, click on MessageFacade and then click OK. The IDE will put the following code in, in bold, for bean injection:

```
public class MessageView {


   /** Creates a new instance of MessageView */
   public MessageView() {
   }


   // Injects the MessageFacade session bean using the @EJB annotation
   @EJB
   private MessageFacade messageFacade;
}
```

Add the following code to create a new instance.

```
/** Creates a new instance of MessageView */
   public MessageView() {
```

```
    this.message = new Message();
  }
```

Add the following code to the class.

```
  // Creates a new field
  private Message message;



  // Calls getMessage to retrieve the message
  public Message getMessage() {
    return message;
  }


  // Returns the total number of messages
  public int getNumberOfMessages(){
    return messageFacade.findAll().size();
  }


  // Saves the message and then returns the string "theend"
  public String postMessage(){
    this.messageFacade.create(message);
    return "theend";
  }
```

Right-click somewhere in the editor and click on Fix Imports (ALT+SHIFT+I); save the changes.

The postMethod() method returns a string of theend. Explicit navigation rules are enabled in JSF for any application that makes use of the Facelets technology. We haven't configured any navigation rules in faces-config.xml because the navigation handler will instead look for a page that fits in the application. In our application, the handler looks for a page called theend.xhtml whenever postMethod is invoked.

Index Page Modification

Now we are going to change our index.xhtml page by adding a few user interface components. We will start by adding a form that has a button and an input text field. Go to the editor and open index.xhtml.

Add the following form in between the <h:body> tags:

```
<h:body>

  <f:view>

    <h:form>

      <h:outputLabel value="Message:"/><h:inputText
value="#{MessageView.message.message}"/>

      <h:commandButton action="#{MessageView.postMessage}" value="Post
Message"/>

    </h:form>

  </f:view>

</h:body>
```

Use JSF code completion if needed to complete this code.

Do NOT copy and paste this code; type it in yourself. Not only will it give you a better feel for it, but copying and pasting will also throw up a warning, which you will see in the left-hand margin beside the code line with <f:view> in it. If you put your cursor into this line and press ALT+SPACE, you will see a hint about this error, telling you that, to resolve it, you need to input a library declaration – thexmlns:f=http://xmlns,jcp.og/jsf.core.

Add this in and save your changes.

What happens now is that two components, commandButton and inputText will invoke the MessageView methods. The navigation handler looks for theend.xhtml while postMessage() returns 'theend'.

The Results Page

Now we will create our results page, a JSF page called theend.xhtml. This page gets displayed when the Post Message button from the index.html page is pressed by a user. This involves the postMessage method from the managed bean.

Find the project node and right-click it; click on New>Other

Click on JavaServer Faces and then click on JSF Page; click on Next

Call the File Name theend

Make sure that the option for Facelets is enabled and click on Finish

Now we can modify the file; find the <h:body> tags and type this code in between them:

```
<h:body>
   <h:outputLabel value="Thanks! There are "/>
   <h:outputText value="#{MessageView.numberOfMessages}"/>
   <h:outputLabel value=" messages!"/>
</h:body>
```

As you begin to type this in, the IDE will add the library definition tag xmlns:h="//xmlns.jcp.org/jsf/html into the JSF elements file. This is why I recommend typing the code in and not copying and pasting.

Run Your Application

Your application is now fully coded, it's time to test it in the browser.

Go to the Project window and right-click on the project node; click on Run

The IDE will now build your application and deploy it, opening index.xhtml in the browser

Go to the text field and type any message in; click on Post Message

Your message gets saved to the application database and the messages are then retrieved and shown.

If you want, you can look at a few project sources; NetBeans provides samples which you can access in this way:

From the main IDE window, go to the main menu and click on Team>Subversion and then on Checkout

In the dialog box, type in this URL – https://svn.netbeans.org/svn/samples~samples-cource-code and then click on Next

Click on Browse and a dialog box will open; find the root node and expand it

Choose samples/javaee/SimpleEE6App and then click on OK

Specify which folder for the sources – it must be an empty local folder

Click on Finish and the local folder will be initialized as one of the Subversion repositories; the project sources are checked out and a dialog box appears. Click on Open Project and take a good look at the source codes.

Introducing JavaServer Faces

JSF is a UI framework used by web applications written in Java. It was originally designed as a way of easing the time-consuming job of writing applications and maintaining them. These applications will run on Java web servers and their user interfaces are rendered to a target client. With JSF, you get the following features to make things easier for you:

- Allows reusable user interface components to be used to construct a user interface with ease
- Makes migrating application data to the UI and from it simpler
- Provides assistance with managing UI states over requests from the server
- Provides users with an easy model to wire events that are client-generated to application code on the server side.
- Makes it easy to build UI components and reuse them

We're going to look at a way of using NetBeans to give your web application support for JSF. We start by adding the JSF framework to a simple application and we then move on to do this:

- Handle data requests by creating a managed bean in JSF
- Wire that bean to the web pages in the application, and
- Turn those web pages into template files (Facelets).

To do all this, you should already have most of the programs required – NetBeans, JDK and Glassfish Server. You will also need the jsfDemo web app project.

To add JSF support to a simple web application:

Open the Demo file from above in NetBeans IDE. From here, we can go to the Properties window to provide the project with framework support.

From the main menu in the IDE, click on Open Project (CTRL+SHIFT+O) and a dialog box opens

In the box, find the location of your tutorial project (unzipped), select it and then, in the IDE click on Open Project, which will then open in the NetBeans IDE

If the Junit plugin was not installed when you installed NetBeans IDE, you may well be promoted to do it when you open the project. If you get an error reference, resolve it before continuing.

Now run this project in your browser – click on Run Project from the main toolbar or, from the Projects window, right-click on the node and click on Run. Your project will be packaged up and deployed to Glassfish; your browser will open to the index.xhtml page, which is your welcome page

Click on Submit and you will see the response page, response.xhtml, displayed.

Right now, both of these pages are static. Together with duke.png (image file) and stylesheet.css, they are the only files in the application that may be accessed via the browser.

Go to the Projects window (CTRL+1) and find the project node. Right-click it and then click on Properties; this will open your Project Properties window

Click on Frameworks and then on Add

In the dialog box that opens, click on JavaServer Faces and then click OK.

You will now see several options for configurations. Go to Libraries; here we will specify the way the project will gain access to the JSF libraries. What JSF version you see will depend on the IDE and Glassfish versions installed. By default the libraries that came with Glassfish are used but you can choose the JSF libraries too.

Click Configuration. Here, you can specify the way the deployment descriptor for the project registers the Faces servlet. You can also determine which pages are to be used in the project – JSP or Facelets.

If you want to use any of the JSF component suites, click on Components. Whichever suite you choose will require the right libraries to be downloaded and the Ant Library manager needs to be used to create a brand-new library that contains the libraries from the component suite.

Click on OK when you are done to save all your changes and come out of Project Properties.

Once all this has been down, the web.xml deployment descriptor in your project has been changed so it now looks like this:

```
<web-app version="3.0" xmlns="http://java.sun.com/xml/ns/javaee"
xmlns:xsi="http://www.w3.org/2001/XMLSchema-instance"
xsi:schemaLocation="http://java.sun.com/xml/ns/javaee
http://java.sun.com/xml/ns/javaee/web-app_3_0.xsd">

  <context-param>

    <param-name>javax.faces.PROJECT_STAGE</param-name>

    <param-value>Development</param-value>

  </context-param>

  <servlet>
```

```
    <servlet-name>Faces Servlet</servlet-name>
    <servlet-class>javax.faces.webapp.FacesServlet</servlet-class>
    <load-on-startup>1</load-on-startup>
  </servlet>
  <servlet-mapping>
    <servlet-name>Faces Servlet</servlet-name>
    <url-pattern>/faces/*</url-pattern>
  </servlet-mapping>
  <welcome-file-list>
    <welcome-file>faces/index.xhtml</welcome-file>
  </welcome-file-list>
</web-app>
```

Important note. Make sure that there is just a single entry for <welcome-file> in web.xml and that 'faces/' is included in that entry. Doing this will make sure that the welcome page is only displayed on your browser after going through the Faces servlet. This is a necessary step to ensure that the tag library components for Facelets are properly rendered.

The Faces servlet is now registered to your project and, when it is requested, your welcome page will now go through the servlet. Also take note that a PROJECT_STAGE context parameter has been included. If you ensure that the parameter is set as Development, it will be helpful when it comes to running the debugger on your application.

If you go to the Projects window and expand the node for Libraries, you will find the JSF libraries. If it is the Glassfish default libraries you are using, they will be shown as javax.faces.jar under the server node.

The JSF support in NetBeans includes quite a few wizards specific to JSF and the Facelets editor provides quite a lot of special functionality which we will be delving into next.

JSF Managed Beans

JSF managed beans can be used for processing user data and hanging onto it in between requests. Managed beans are POJOs used for storing data and managed by the container that used the framework, for example, Glassfish server. POJOs are Java classes with one public constructor that contains no arguments and that fully conforms, in terms of properties, to the naming conventions in JavaBeans.

When you run your project, if you take a look at the static page that is produced, you should be able to see that a mechanism is required to work out whether a number entered by a user matches the current one selected and that a view is returned appropriate to the outcome. To do this, we can create a managed bean using the Managed Bean Wizard in the NetBeans IDE. Shortly, you will be creating some Facelets pages and these are going to need access to the user-entered number, along with the response that is generated. To do this, we will be adding response properties and add userNumber to our bean.

The Managed Bean Wizard

Go to the Projects window, find the jsfDemo project node and right-click on it. Click on New>JSF Managed Bean. If this isn't in the list, click on Other. Then click JavaServer Faces>JSF Managed Bean. Click on Next.

In the Managed Bean wizard, input the following:

Class Name – UserNumberBean

Package – guessNumber

Name – UserNumberBean

Scope – Session

Click on Finish and the new class will be generated and opened in the editor. Note that these annotations have been included:

```
package guessNumber;


import javax.faces.bean.ManagedBean;

import javax.faces.bean.SessionScoped;


/**

 *

 * @author nbuser

 */

@ManagedBean(name="UserNumberBean")
```

```
@SessionScoped
public class UserNumberBean {


   /** Creates a new instance of UserNumberBean */
   public UserNumberBean() {
   }


}
```

All of your components specific to JSF can be declared through annotations.

Create the Constructor

We need a constructor called UserNumberBean now and this must be able to randomly generate any number between 0 and 10 and store that number inside an instance variable. This is what will form part of the application's business logic.

To define the constructor, input this code for the UserNumberBean class:

```
public class UserNumberBean {


   Integer randomInt;


   /** Creates a new instance of UserNumberBean */
   public UserNumberBean() {
      Random randomGR = new Random();
      randomInt = new Integer(randomGR.nextInt(10));
      System.out.println("Duke's number: " + randomInt);
   }


}
```

This will randomly generate our number, outputting it in the server log.

The next thing to do is fix the imports. In the left margin of the editor you will see the hint icon; click on this and click on import java.util.Random – this will be imported into the UserNumberBeans class.

Now run your project again; either click on Rin Project or press F6 on your keyboard. You should see the log file open in the Output window.

The constructor indicated that you would see Duke's number but you won't see it. By default, JSF makes use of lazy instantiation so there was no UserNumberBean object created. What lazy instantiation means is that beans inside specific scopes will only be created and then initialized when the application needs them.

According to the @ManagedBean annotation Javadoc, if the eager() attribute value is true and value of the managed-bean-scope is 'application' then the class must be instantiated by runtime at the point the application starts. Instantiation must take place and the value stored before servicing any requests takes place. If the eager() attribute is false or is unspecified, or managed-bean-scope is anything else, and not 'application', lazy instantiation will happen by default.

Our UserNumberBean has been session scoped so the Serializable interface must be implemented by it.

```
@ManagedBean(name="UserNumberBean")

@SessionScoped

public class UserNumberBean implements Serializable {
```

Again, click the hint icon in the left margin and import java.io.Serializable.

Adding Our Properties

We are going to be creating our Facelets pages next and these must be able to access whatever number a user inputs, along with the response that gets generated. To do this, we will be adding response and userNumber properties to our class.

The first step is to declare an integer and call it userNumber:

```
@ManagedBean(name="UserNumberBean")

@SessionScoped

public class UserNumberBean implements Serializable {


    Integer randomInt;

    Integer userNumber;
```

Right-click anywhere inside the editor and click on Insert Code (ALT+Insert)' click on Getter and Setter.

Click on userNumber : Integer and then click on Generate

Note that two methods have been added to your class – setUserNumber() and getUserNumber().

Next, we need a response property which is created with the code below, by declaring a string called response:

```
@ManagedBean(name="UserNumberBean")

@SessionScoped

public class UserNumberBean implements Serializable {


   Integer randomInt;

   Integer userNumber;

   String response;
```

Now we need a getter method for the response. Note, we don't need a setter for this application. Input this method in the class:

```
public String getResponse() {

   if ((userNumber != null) && (userNumber.compareTo(randomInt) == 0)) {


      //invalidate user session

      FacesContext context = FacesContext.getCurrentInstance();

      HttpSession session = (HttpSession) context.getExternalContext().getSession(false);

      session.invalidate();


      return "Yes! You got it!";

   } else {


      return "<p>Sorry, " + userNumber + " isn't it.</p>"
```

```
        + "<p>Guess again...</p>";
    }
}
```

This method does two things:

It will test if userNumber (the number input by the user) is equal to the randomly generated number (randomInt) for the current session; a string response is returned

If a user guesses the number correctly (userNumber is equal to randomInt), the method will invalidate the user session. This is so that a new number can be generated if the user wishes to play the game again.

Go to the editor, right-click anywhere and click on Fix Imports (ALT+SHIFT+I). This will automatically create import statements for:

javax.servlet.http.HttpSession

javax.faces.context.FacesContext

If you press on CTRL+SPACE on any item in the editor, suggestions for code completion and documentation support will be invoked. Try this with FacesContext to see what the Javadoc class description is; in the documentation window you will see a browser icon. Click this and the Javadoc opens in an external browser.

Using Managed Beans in Web Pages

One of the main purposes of JSF is to do away with having to write reams of boilerplate code for managing the POJOs and the way they interact with the application views. We saw this earlier when JSF invoked lazy instantiation for the UserNumberBean object when the application was run. We call this IoC – Inversion of Control – and this provides the container with the responsibility to manage parts of the application, freeing the developer up from having to keep writing repetitive code.

Previously, we created a managed bean for the purpose of randomly generating a number from 0 to 10. We also created the response and userNumber properties, representing the response and the user input number respectively.

Now we are going to look at how the UserNumberBean and all its properties in your application web pages. With JSF, you can do this with the expression language included in JSF. This language (EL) is used for binding the values in the properties to the UI components in the application pages. We're also going to look at how we can use the implicit navigation feature in JSF to navigate between your index page and your response page. This is supported by the IDE with support for code completion and for documentation.

We'll do this by changing the index.xhtml page and then the response.xhtml file. In both of these, the HTML form elements will be replaced with their JSF versions as defined in the tag library, JSF HTML. Lastly, we will use the EL for binding the property values to chosen UI components.

Go to the editor and open index.xhtml. You can either double-click on the node or press ALT+SHIFT+O to open the dialog box for Go To File.

Next, the HTML form element needs to be commented out so highlight it and press CTRL+/ on your keyboard. Highlighting can be done by click and drag with the mouse or SHIFT+ the arrow keys on the keyboard.

Toggle the comments by pressing CTRL+/ - you may need to repeat this to make sure the code is uncommented.

The editor will now indicate that the tags <h:form>, <h:commandButton> and >h:inputText> have not yet been declared. To do this, we can use the code completion features for adding the namespace for the tag library to the <html> tag on the page:

Put your mouse cursor over any one of these tags and press on ALT+ENTER.

Click on Enter and the library will be added. If there is more than one choice for the tag library, ensure that you choose the one that matches the tag in the editor before you hit the Enter key.

The tag library namespace for JSF HTML will now be added to that <html> tag and you should see all the error indicators removed.

If there is no option in the IDE to add a tag library, then manual modification of the <html> element will need to be done:

```
<html xmlns="http://www.w3.org/1999/xhtml"

    xmlns:h="http://xmlns.jcp.org/jsf/html">
```

The JSF expression language may be used for binding the userNumber property of UserNumberBeans to the component for inputText. We can then use the value attribute for specifying what the rendered component's current value is. Change your code so it looks like this:

```
<h:form>

   <h:inputText id="userNumber" size="2" maxlength="2"
value="#{UserNumberBean.userNumber}" />
```

The expression language makes use of the #{} syntax. Inside of these delimiters the managed bean name and the property to be applied are specified, separated with a period (.). The value will be saved automatically in the property for userNumber when the form data gets wired to the server. This is done using setUserNumber(), the setter method for the property. And, when a request for the page is made and the userNumber value has been set, the values will be displayed automatically in the rendered component, inputText.

So, we need to specify where the invoked request will go when the form button is pressed. When we used the HTML form, this was done by using the action attribute for the <form> tag. With JSF, we use the action attribute for commandButton and, because JSF offers explicit navigation, we only need the destination file name specified; we don't need to use the file extension too. Change the relevant code so it looks like this:

```
<h:form>

   <h:inputText id="userNumber" size="2" maxlength="2"
value="#{UserNumberBean.userNumber}" />

   <h:commandButton id="submit" value="submit" action="response" />

</h:form>
```

JSF runtime will now look for a file with the name of response. It will automatically assume that the file extension is identical to that of the file the request came from (index.xhtml} and it will look for a file called response.xhtml in the directory that index.xhtml comes from.

These next steps are optional ones. If you prefer, you can skip these and go straight to the response.xhtml section.

We need to see if the EL expression we used earlier calls setUserNumber on the processing of the request. We use the debugger in the IDE to do this.

Press on CTRL+TAB and click on UserNumberBean from the list.

We need to set a breakpoint now for the setUserNumber() signature so click the left margin and you will see a red badge; this tells you that you have set the method breakpoint.

In the main toolbar in the IDE, click on Debug Project and a debugging session will begin. You will see your browser open at the welcome page.

You may well be asked to confirm what the server port is for the application debugging. If you see the dialog box for Debug Project, click on Server Side Java, which is the default, and then click on Debug.

Go to the form that is open in your browser and input a number; click on Submit

Go back to the IDE and have a look at the UserNumberBean class; you should see that the Debugger has paused in the method setUserNumber().

Click on Window>Debugging and choose Variables (CTRL+SHIFT+I) and the variables window for the debugger will open. Where the debugger has paused, you will see the values for the variable at that point.

Go to the Debugger toolbar and click on Step Into. The line that the debugger has stopped on will now be executed and the Variables window will refresh, showing you the changes made when the line was executed. You should now see the property of userNumber set to the number you input on the form.

Go to the main menu and click on Debug>Finish Debugger Session (SHIFT+F5) and the debugger will stop.

Those were the optional steps; the next set is required.

response.xhtml

We now need to comment out the response.xhtml form:

In the editor, open response.xhtml by clicking on the node in Projects or by pressing ALT+SHIFT+O to open the dialog box for Go to File

Next, click and drag your cursor over both the opening and the closing HTML<form> tags, including the code that goes between them and press on CTRL+/

Now you can uncomment the JSF version of the HTML form component. Highlight it in the same way as above and press on CTRL+/.

Right now you should see the following code in between your <body> tags:

```
<body>

  <div id="mainContainer">


    <div id="left" class="subContainer greyBox">


      <h4>[ response here ]</h4>


      <!--<form action="index.xhtml">


        <input type="submit" id="backButton" value="Back"/>
```

```
        </form>-->

        <h:form>

          <h:commandButton id="backButton" value="Back" />

        </h:form>

      </div>

      <div id="right" class="subContainer">

        <img src="duke.png" alt="Duke waving" />
         <!--<h:graphicImage url="/duke.png" alt="Duke waving" />-->

      </div>
    </div>
  </body>
```

After the form component has been uncommented, the editor will tell you that neither the <h:commandButton> tag nor the <h:form> tag has been declared so we need to declare them. We can do this by adding the tag library namespace into the <html> tag for the page. Then you can add the JSF namespaces. When you use code completion to select a Facelets or JSF tag, the namespace will be automatically placed into the root element of the document.

To declare the tag, put your cursor over any undeclared one and press on CTRL+SPACE. You will see the completion suggestions and the documentation display.

Click on Enter. If there is more than one option, again make sure you choose the one that matches the tag in the editor. You will see the namespace for the JSF HTML tag library in the <html> tag and the error indicators will be cleared.

```
<html xmlns="http://www.w3.org/1999/xhtml"
    xmlns:h="http://xmlns.jcp.org/jsf/html">
```

Next, we need to specify where the request will go when invoked by the user clicking on the button on the form. We'll set it so that, when it is clicked, the user goes back to the index page. We make use of the action attribute for the commandButton for this so change the relevant code so it looks like this:

```
<h:form>
   <h:commandButton id="backButton" value="Back" action="index" />
</h:form>
```

When you type in action= "index", you rely on the implicit navigation supported by JSF. When the form button is clicked by the user, JSF runtime looks for a file with the name of index. It will assume that the file extension is that of the file from the originating request, response.xhtml. As such, it will try to find a file called index.xhtml and it will look in the directory that the originating file is in.

Where you see '[response here]", which is static, you can replace it with the response property of UserNumberBeans. We use the expression language to do this so change the relevant code to read:

```
<div id="left" class="subContainer greyBox">


   <h4><h:outputText value="#{UserNumberBean.response}"/></h4>
```

Click on Run Project (F6) to run it. The welcome page will load in the browser; input a number and click on the Submit button. The response page will be displayed if you input the wring number.

There are a couple of things wrong with this page at the moment:

- You can see the html <p> tags in the message
- The incorrect location is being displayed by the Back button

To fix these, do these two steps:

Set the escape attribute for <h:outputText> as false. To do this, put your cursor in between outputText and the value and add a space in. Press on CTRL+SPACE and click on the escape attribute; have a look at the documentation. Then click on Enter and input the value as false.

```
<h4><h:outputText escape="false" value="#{UserNumberBean.response}"/></h4>
```

Set the prependID attribute for the <h:form> as false. To do this, put your cursor after the 'm' in the <h:form> tag and add a space in. Press on CTRL+SPACE and click on the prependID attribute; have a look at the documentation. Click on Enter and input the value as false.

<h:form prependId="false">

JSF will apply internal IDs as a way of tracking the UI components. In our example, if you look at the rendered page's source code, you will what looks like this:

<form id="j_idt5" name="j_idt5" method="post" action="/jsfDemo/faces/response.xhtml" enctype="application/x-www-form-urlencoded">

<input type="hidden" name="j_idt5" value="j_idt5" />

<input id="j_idt5:backButton" type="submit" name="j_idt5:backButton" value="Back" />

<input type="hidden" name="javax.faces.ViewState" id="javax.faces.ViewState" value="7464469350430442643:-8628336969383888926" autocomplete="off" />

</form>

The form element ID is j_idt5 and this has been prepended to the form's Back button ID. The Back button is relying on the style rule that stylesheet.css defines, the #backButton rule and, because of this, when we prepend the JSF ID, the rule gets obstructed. We get around this by setting the prependID value as false.

Now run your project again and input a number into the welcome page; click the Submit button. On the response page, you will now see the response message but the <p> tags won't be showing this time and our Back button is in the right location.

Click on that Back button. You will now see the earlier number you input in the text field. This happens because we bound the UserNumberBeans current value to the component for JSF inputText.

Go to the Output window in the IDE and look at the server log to find out what the correct guess would be.

If the server log is not visible for some reason, go to the Services window and click on the Server node to expand it. Find Glassfish server (this is the server being used for project deployment) and right-click on it; click on View Server Log. If the number is not shown in the server log, go back to the project node, right-click on it and click on Clean and Rebuild. This will rebuild your application.

Input the right number and click on the Submit button. The application will look at your input and the saved number and compare them, displaying the right message

Click on Back again and note that the number you entered earlier is now no longer shown in the Text field. Remember; the current user session is invalidated by the getResponse() method for UserNumberBean when the correct number is guessed.

Applying Facelets Templates

Facelets is now the standard display technology for JSF; it is light-weight, a template framework with support for all of the UI components in JSF and is commonly used for building and rendering the JSF application view component tree. It also has support built in for developers for when expression language errors happening; this is done by allowing you to look at the stack trace, the component tree and all of the scoped variables.

You may or may not have realized but the response.xhtml and the index.xhtml files you have been using are Facelets pages. Every Facelet file has the .xhtml extension and because our project is built using JSF with the Facelet JAR files included in the libraries, the application views could rend the component tree properly.

What I am going to do in this part is to get you familiar with using Facelets templates. If a project has got multiple views it is often better to apply template files that define the appearance and structure specifically for multiple views. When requests are services, the application will add content that is dynamically prepared into the template and pass the client the result. Our project has just two views, the response and welcome pages but we can still see that there is a great deal of content that is duplicated. This can be factored out into a template and then create template files that will handle the content specifically for our two pages.

The NetBeans IDE includes a wizard for the Facelets templates along with a wizard for creating those files that require a template. We'll be using both wizards here. There is also a wizard for JSF pages that you can use for creating single Facelet pages.

Our first step is to create the template so press on CTRL+N and the File wizard will open. Click on JavaServer Faces and then on Facelets Template. Click on Next.

For the file name input Template.

There are 8 layout styles to choose from; pick one and click on Finish. It doesn't matter which one you choose because we'll be using the stylesheet that already exists.

The File wizard will now generate t and the stylesheets that go with based on the selection you chose. These go into a folder in the Webroot directory called resources>css.

Once you have finished with the Wizard, the template file will open up in the editor. Right-click anywhere in the editor and click on View to see it in your browser.

Take a look at the markup for the template file and note these points:

You can see the Facelets tag library has been declared in the <html> tag for the page and it has a prefix of ui

```
<html xmlns="http://www.w3.org/1999/xhtml"
    xmlns:ui="http://xmlns.jcp.org/jsf/facelets"
    xmlns:h="http://xmlns.jcp.org/jsf/html">
```

The <h:head> tag and <h:body> tag are used on the Facelets page rather than the html head and body tags. By doing this, Facelets can build a tree of components encompassing the whole page.

The stylesheets that got created after you finished the wizard are referenced on the page

```
<h:head>
   <meta http-equiv="Content-Type" content="text/html; charset=UTF-8" />
   <link href="./resources/css/default.css" rel="stylesheet" type="text/css" />
   <link href="./resources/css/cssLayout.css" rel="stylesheet" type="text/css" />
   <title>Facelets Template</title>
</h:head>
```

The body of the page uses <ui:insert> tags for each of the compartments that are related to your chosen layout style. Each of these tags has got a name attribute identifying which compartment it goes with. An example:

```
<div id="top">
   <ui:insert name="top">Top</ui:insert>
</div>
```

Have another look at your two pages, welcome and response. You should see that only the title and the text inside the grey square changes between them and that means the template can be used for the rest of the content.

Use the following code to replace the whole content in your template file:

```
<?xml version='1.0' encoding='UTF-8' ?>

<!DOCTYPE html PUBLIC "-//W3C//DTD XHTML 1.0 Transitional//EN"
"http://www.w3.org/TR/xhtml1/DTD/xhtml1-transitional.dtd">

<html xmlns="http://www.w3.org/1999/xhtml"
```

```
    xmlns:ui="http://xmlns.jcp.org/jsf/facelets"
    xmlns:h="http://xmlns.jcp.org/jsf/html">

  <h:head>
    <meta http-equiv="Content-Type" content="text/html; charset=UTF-8" />
    <link href="css/stylesheet.css" rel="stylesheet" type="text/css" />

    <title><ui:insert name="title">Facelets Template</ui:insert></title>
  </h:head>

  <h:body>

    <div id="left">
      <ui:insert name="box">Box Content Here</ui:insert>
    </div>

  </h:body>

</html>
```

This code implements:

The stylesheet.css file in the project will replace the references to the template stylesheet that the wizard created

None of the <ui:insert> tags remain, and that includes the <div> tags that contain them, with the exception of one named box.

There is now a pair of <ui:insert> tags around the named title and the page title

Go to either the index.xhtml file or the response.xhtml file and find the relevant code, copying it to the template and then add the relevant code from below to the <h:body> tags in the template file:

```
<h:body>
   <div id="mainContainer">
      <div id="left" class="subContainer greyBox">
         <ui:insert name="box">Box Content Here</ui:insert>
      </div>
      <div id="right" class="subContainer">
         <img src="duke.png" alt="Duke waving" />
      </div>
   </div>
</h:body>
```

Run your project and, when the Welcome page loads in your browser, the URL should be modified to read:

http://localhost:8080/jsfDemo/faces/template.xhtml

Your project views structure and appearance are now provided by a template file and client files can be created to involve that template.

Create the Template Client File

We now want to create the template client file for the welcome page and for the response page. The welcome page file will be named as greeting.xhtml and the response file will be named as response.xhtml.

greeting.xhtml

Press on CTRL+N and the New File wizard will open. Click on JavaServer Faces and then click on Facelets Template Client. Click on Next

For the file name, type in greeting

Beside the Template field is a Browse button; click on it and a dialog box will load. Find the template.xhtml file created earlier and click on Finish.

You will see the greeting.xhtml file displayed in the editor. Have a look at the markup:

```
<html xmlns="http://www.w3.org/1999/xhtml"
   xmlns:ui="http://xmlns.jcp.org/jsf/facelets">
```

```
  <body>

    <ui:composition template="./template.xhtml">

      <ui:define name="title">
        title
      </ui:define>

      <ui:define name="box">
        box
      </ui:define>

    </ui:composition>

  </body>
</html>
```

In the template client file is a reference to another template that uses the template attribute for the <ui:composition> tag. Because there are <ui:insert> tags for both the box and the title, the client will have a <ui:define> tag for each of those names. The content that you put in the <ui:define> tags is what gets put in the template <ui:insert> tags for the name that corresponds to them.

Call the file title greeting and make sure the relevant code looks like this:

```
<ui:define name="title">
  Greeting
</ui:define>
```

Press on CTRL+TAB and call up the index.xhtml file. Find the content that would be in the grey square you see on the rendered page and copy it. Go back to greeting.xhtml and paste that code into the client file:

```
<ui:define name="box">
```

```
<h4>Hi, my name is Duke!</h4>


<h5>I'm thinking of a number


  <br/>
  between
  <span class="highlight">0</span> and
  <span class="highlight">10</span>.</h5>


<h5>Can you guess it?</h5>


<h:form>
  <h:inputText size="2" maxlength="2" value="#{UserNumberBean.userNumber}" />
  <h:commandButton id="submit" value="submit" action="response" />
</h:form>
</ui:define>
```

Now the tag library for JSF HTML needs to be declared so put your mouse cursor on a tag that has an error flagged beside it, any of those with the prefix, 'h', and press CTRL+SPACE on your keyboard. From the code completion list, choose the right tag and the relevant namespace goes in the <html> tag in the file and error flags are removed:

```
<html xmlns="http://www.w3.org/1999/xhtml"
   xmlns:ui="http://xmlns.jcp.org/jsf/facelets"
   xmlns:h="http://xmlns.jcp.org/jsf/html">
```

In the <h:form> tag, click your cursor just after the m and press on CTRL+SPACE; the namespace will be placed into the file automatically. If there is only one option that is logical it will be applied immediately to the file. When code completion is invoked on any tag, the JSF tag libraries will be declared automatically.

response.xhtml

Your project already has a response.xhtml file in it and you now know what the client file looks like so make your changes to response.xhtml so it becomes the client file. All you need to do here is copy and paste the code provided below or type it in if you prefer.

From the editor, open response.xhtml and put the code below in place of the code already in it.

```
<?xml version='1.0' encoding='UTF-8' ?>

<!DOCTYPE html PUBLIC "-//W3C//DTD XHTML 1.0 Transitional//EN"
"http://www.w3.org/TR/xhtml1/DTD/xhtml1-transitional.dtd">

<html xmlns="http://www.w3.org/1999/xhtml"

    xmlns:ui="http://xmlns.jcp.org/jsf/facelets"

    xmlns:h="http://xmlns.jcp.org/jsf/html">


   <body>


      <ui:composition template="./template.xhtml">


         <ui:define name="title">

            Response

         </ui:define>


         <ui:define name="box">

            <h4><h:outputText escape="false"
value="#{UserNumberBean.response}"/></h4>


            <h:form prependId="false">


               <h:commandButton id="backButton" value="Back" action="greeting" />
```

```
        </h:form>

      </ui:define>


    </ui:composition>


  </body>

</html>
```

Have you spotted that this is an identical file to greeting.xhtml, with one exception? That exception is the content in the title and box <ui:define> tags.

Go to the web.xml deployment descriptor for your project and make a change to the entry for the file; you want greeting.xhtml to be the opening page when you run the application.

Go to the Projects window, find Configuration Files and double-click it. Click on web.xml so it will open in the editor and then click on Pages. Modify the field for Welcome Files so it reads faces/greeting.xhtml.

Run your project so you can see it in the browser; it will be deployed and opened by the Glassfish server.

When you use Facelets template and client files, your applications will act as it did before. All you have done is removed all the duplicated code in the application pages, thus reducing the application in size and so that you don't have to write any more duplicate code if you add extra pages later. This is a more efficient way of developing and maintaining your code becomes easier when you have larger projects.

Introducing Ajax for Java

We are now going to take a look at Ajax and at some of the NetBeans IDE features that allow programming of web applications far more efficient and faster when you use Ajax technologies. As you learn more about Ajax and its low-level functionalities, you will be building an application that used text field auto-completion.

Ajax is an acronym for Asynchronous JavaScript and XML. In brief, Ajax provides a much more efficient way for user interaction with pages to be handled by the application. This way cuts down on the requirement for page reloads or refreshes with each interaction. This provides us with an experience similar to web applications based on plugins or desktop applications when a browser is used. The asynchronous part comes from the Ajax interactions and the way they are handled in the background. While this is going on, users can carry on interacting with the page.

JavaScript code is used to initiate the interactions and modifications are immediate, no page refresh required. We can use Ajax interactions to do all sorts of things, like validation of form entries as a user is inputting data, retrieving data from the server, server-side logic, dynamic data update on pages, submitting partially completed forms and so on.

For this part of the tutorial you will need the Java EE bundle for the NetBeans IDE, the JDK, and the Glassfish or Tomcat server. All I am going to do is give you an overview of what functionality the code provides but I won't be explaining the code in depth.

Application Overview

Think about this. A web page that allows a user to look up information on musical composers. On the page is a field that the user can type in the composer name. In our application, this field will have a functioning auto-complete feature so the user only needs to type in part of the name; the application will try to finish the name by showing a list of all the composers whose name (first or last) starts with what the user types in. This feature eliminates the need to type in long names or to have to remember the full name of a composer; it is intuitive and gives us a more straightforward pathway to the information we want.

We can use Ajax to add the autocomplete feature to a search field. Ajax uses XMLHttpRequest objects for asynchronously passing the requests and their corresponding responses from the client to the server and back again.

The process can be described like this:

- An event is triggered by the user. For example, that event could a key release when a name is typed. The result is a call in JavaScript to the function responsible for initializing the XMLHttpRequest object.
- A request parameter is included in the XMLHttpRequest object and this will have the ID of the event-triggering component along with any user-entered value. An asynchronous request is made by the object to the web server.
- That request is handed on the server by an object like a listener or a handler. Data is pulled from the data store and the response drawn up with the data in an XML document form.
- Lastly, the XML data is received via a callback function by the XMLHttpRequest object. It is processed and the HTML Document Object Model is updated to show the new data on the page.

We're going to be constructing this scenario following that process flow. The client-side files are created first, for both the presentation layer and for the functionality required for the generation of the XMLHttpRequest object. We then go to work on the server-side; we create the business logic and the data store using Java technology and, lastly, we go back to the client side and implement the callback function along with any other functionality needed for the HTML Document Object Model (DOM) to be updated.

The Client-Side

We'll start with making a brand new project; the NetBeans IDE has several templates built-in for all types of projects.

From the main menu, click on File>New Project. Click Categories, click on Java Web then go to Projects and click on Web Application>Next.

Go to the panel for Name and Locations and, where it says Project Name, type in MyAjaxApp. In the field for Project Location, chose where the project will be saved on your computer and leave the rest as their default settings.

Go to the panel for Server and Settings and choose which of the IDE-registered servers you wish to use for deployment. Accept the other settings as their defaults suggest and click on Finish. The project will now be generated and it will open in the NetBeans IDE.

When you create web projects in Java, Ant build scripts are automatically generated. These allow for easy compilation of the project so deployment is immediate and the project can run straightaway on a NetBeans IDE-registered server.

A default entry page gets generated and opened in the Source Editor and, depending on what server the target is, that page will be an index.html or index.jsp page.

Before you start coding, run the application quickly just to make sure that the configuration is set correctly between the IDE, browser and server

Now go to the Project window, find the Project node and right-click on it; click on Run

The application server will start, the application is compiled and then deployed to the server and run. Your browser is opened by the IDE and entry page is shown.

The HTML Editor

Now that you have your environment set up right, you can begin to change your index page to the next stage, the auto-completion interface that your application users will see. There is one huge advantage to using an IDE; the editor tends to provide facilities for code completion and if you can learn to use this when you are writing your code, you can quickly become more efficient and more productive. The Source Editor in the IDE also tends to adapt very quickly to whatever technology you are working with so, for example, if it was an HTML page you were working on, the code completion key combination (CTRL+SPACE) would produce HTML attribute and tag suggestions. As you will see, the same thing applies to when you use JavaScript, CSS and any other technology.

Another useful feature in the IDE is the Palette. From here you have access to simple templates that are very easy to use for elements that are common in the technology you use to code your programs in. All you do is choose the item you want, click on it and drag it to where you want it in your file, which is in the Source Editor. If you right-click somewhere in the Palette window you can choose the option for Show Big Icons, making the icons much larger.

Staying with your open file, we are going to change the <title> and the <h1> tags so they say Auto-Completion using AJAX. We do not need to use server-side script code with the index page so it is perfectly safe to delete whatever was created by default. You should now see your index page code looking something like this:

```
<!DOCTYPE html>


<html>

  <head>

    <meta http-equiv="Content-Type" content="text/html; charset=UTF-8">

    <title>Auto-Completion using AJAX</title>

  </head>

  <body>

    <h1>Auto-Completion using AJAX</h1>

  </body>

</html>
```

Add a bit of text that explains what the text field is for – you can copy and paste what's below or just write your own just underneath the <h1> tags:

<p>This demonstrates real-time auto-completion with AJAX interactions</p>

<p>Add a name into the form below. Possible matches will be displayed underneath the form. For example, try typing Stravinsky, Mozart or Bach and then click a selection to see details of the composer.</p>

Now we will add another form to the page. This is an HTML form and we add it by using the elements provided to us in the Palette. If you haven't got the Palette open yet, go to the main menu and click on Window>Palette.

Click on HTML Forms and select a Form element; drag this to the page just under the <p> tags we just added. You will see a dialog box for Insert Form. Make sure the following are specified:

- Action: autocomplete
- Method: GET

- Name: autofillform

Click the OK button and you will see the <form> tags added to the page; they will have the attributes in them that you specified. By default, GET is applied and, as such, it will not be explicitly declared.

Now we want an HTML table added so in the Palette, click on HTML and then select a Table element. Drag it to the page to a point between your <form> tags. The dialog box for Insert Form opens, specify these:

- Rows: 2
- Columns: 2
- Border Size: 0
- Cell Padding: 5

In the Source Editor, right-click anywhere and click on Format. Your code will now be tidied up and should look like this:

```
<form name="autofillform" action="autocomplete">
 <table border="0" cellpadding="5">
  <thead>
   <tr>
    <th></th>
    <th></th>
   </tr>
  </thead>
  <tbody>
   <tr>
    <td></td>
    <td></td>
   </tr>
   <tr>
    <td></td>
    <td></td>
```

```
    </tr>
   </tbody>
  </table>
</form>
```

Go to the first row in your table and, in the first column, input this:

```
<td><strong>Composer Name:</strong></td>
```

In the second column, rather than getting a TextInput field from the Palette, type in this code:

```
<td>
   <input type="text"
     size="40"
     id="complete-field"
     onkeyup="doCompletion();">
</td>
```

Try using the code completion features to help you type the code in. Type an i for example and then press on CTRL+SPACE; you will see the options suggested by the feature just beneath your cursor and, in another box above, you will see a description of each element you select. You could press on CTRL+SPACE at any time in the Source Editor to help you, no matter what you are coding. And, if there is only one option for input, when you press on CTRL+SPACE, it will be completed automatically.

Now, we typed in an onkeyup attribute; this is pointing to a JavaScript function with a name of doCompletion(). Whenever a key gets pressed in a text field, this function gets called and it will map to the relevant JavaScript call.

The JavaScript Editor

The IDE also has a JavaScript editor that gives us several useful and advanced capabilities for editing, like code completion, instant renaming, semantic highlighting, refactoring, and much more.

When you are coding in .js files, code completion is provided automatically. It is also provided when you code in <script> tags when you are working with another technology, such as JSP, HTML, RHTML, and so on. When you are working with JavaScript code, the IDE can give hints for editing purposes. Options for JavaScript hints can be specified by clicking on Tools and then on Options. This launches the Options window where you can click on Editor>Hints and JavaScript. There is also the ability to add templates of your own; in the Options window, click on Code Templates.

We're going to start by adding a JavaScript file to our application and start implementation of doCompletion().

Go to the Projects window, find the Web Pages node and right-click on it. Click on New>JavaScript (if this option is not available, click on Other. Then click on New File Wizard, Web and then JavaScript.

Give your file the name, javascript, and click on Finish. You will the new file in the Projects window; look in the folder called Web Pages. Input the following code into the file:

```
var req;

var isIE;


function init() {

  completeField = document.getElementById("complete-field");

}


function doCompletion() {

    var url = "autocomplete?action=complete&id=" + escape(completeField.value);

    req = initRequest();

    req.open("GET", url, true);

    req.onreadystatechange = callback;

    req.send(null);

}


function initRequest() {

  if (window.XMLHttpRequest) {

    if (navigator.userAgent.indexOf('MSIE') != -1) {

      isIE = true;
```

```
    }
    return new XMLHttpRequest();
  } else if (window.ActiveXObject) {
    isIE = true;
    return new ActiveXObject("Microsoft.XMLHTTP");
  }
}
```

This will perform a basic check on browser compatibility for Explorer and Firefox.

Go back to the index page and go to the <head> tags. In between them, we want the JavaScript file to be referenced so type this code in:

```
<script type="text/javascript" src="javascript.js"></script>
```

If you press on CTRL+TAB, you can easily switch between open pages in the Source Editor.

Next, go to the opening <body> tag and add an init() call in:

```
<body onload="init()">
```

This will make sure that, whenever the page is loaded, init() is called.

doCompletion() plays a couple of roles in our code:

It will provide a URL that has no data that the server-side can make use of

It is used for initializing the XMLHttpRequest object

It is used for prompting that object to send the server an asynchronous request.

XMLHttpRequest is at the very core of Ajax and has now become the go-to standard to enable asynchronous passing of XML data over HTTP. With asynchronous interaction, we get the implication that the browser can carry on processing page events after a request has been sent. Data passing happens in the background and can be loaded to a page automatically, with no need to refresh the page.

initRequest() is responsible for creating the XMLHttpRequest object called doCompletion(). initRequest() will look to see if the browser understands XMLHttpRequest and if it does it will create the object. If it can't, initRequest() will then check ActiveXObject, and, if identified, will create the ActiveXObject.

When an XMLHttpRequest object is created, 3 parameters are specified:

- URL
- HTTP method, which is either GET or POST
- If the interaction is asynchronous or not

The parameters in our example are:

URL auto-complete along with the text the user inputs in the complete-field:

var url = "autocomplete?action=complete&id=" + escape(completeField.value);

GET, telling us that the GET method is used by the HTTP interactions

True, which tells us that we do have asynchronous interaction:

req.open("GET", url, true);

If asynchronous interaction is set, we must then specify a callback function and we use the following statement to do this:

req.onreadystatechange = callback;

Later, we will need to define a callback() function. HTTP interaction starts at the point we call XMLHttpRequest.send(). This will result in mapping to the HTTP request that gets sent to the server.

Server-Side Programming

Support is bundled into the IDE for server-side programming. This support includes simple editor support for many of the programming languages, it also included web services, like REST, SOAP, MVC-oriented frameworks, and SaaS. You can also go to the plugin portal for NetBeans to get plugins for frameworks driven by Ajax.

The business logic in your application will go to the data store to get the data to process requests. It will then prepare the response and send it. We use a servlet to implement this but before we can write the servlet, we need to set the data store up, along with the functionality the servlet needs to access the data.

The Data Store

This is a simple application so all we need is a class named ComposerData – this uses a HashMap to retain the composer data. HashMaps let you store data in pairs of items that are linked – these are key-value pairs. We also need a class called Composer. This will allow the servlet to get the data from the HashMap entries.

Go to the Projects window and find the Project node; right-click on it and click on New>Java Class

Give the class a name of ComposerData and, in the Package field, type in com.ajax. This will result in a new package being created containing the class, along with the other classes that will be created later.

Click on Finish and the class will be created, opening in the Source Editor.

Go to the Source Editor and add this code:

```
package com.ajax;


import java.util.HashMap;


/**
 *
 * @author nbuser
 */
public class ComposerData {


    private HashMap composers = new HashMap();


    public HashMap getComposers() {
        return composers;
    }


    public ComposerData() {


        composers.put("1", new Composer("1", "Johann Sebastian", "Bach", "Baroque"));
        composers.put("2", new Composer("2", "Arcangelo", "Corelli", "Baroque"));
        composers.put("3", new Composer("3", "George Frideric", "Handel", "Baroque"));
        composers.put("4", new Composer("4", "Henry", "Purcell", "Baroque"));
```

```
composers.put("5", new Composer("5", "Jean-Philippe", "Rameau", "Baroque"));
composers.put("6", new Composer("6", "Domenico", "Scarlatti", "Baroque"));
composers.put("7", new Composer("7", "Antonio", "Vivaldi", "Baroque"));

composers.put("8", new Composer("8", "Ludwig van", "Beethoven", "Classical"));
composers.put("9", new Composer("9", "Johannes", "Brahms", "Classical"));
composers.put("10", new Composer("10", "Francesco", "Cavalli", "Classical"));
composers.put("11", new Composer("11", "Fryderyk Franciszek", "Chopin",
"Classical"));
composers.put("12", new Composer("12", "Antonin", "Dvorak", "Classical"));
composers.put("13", new Composer("13", "Franz Joseph", "Haydn", "Classical"));
composers.put("14", new Composer("14", "Gustav", "Mahler", "Classical"));
composers.put("15", new Composer("15", "Wolfgang Amadeus", "Mozart",
"Classical"));
composers.put("16", new Composer("16", "Johann", "Pachelbel", "Classical"));
composers.put("17", new Composer("17", "Gioachino", "Rossini", "Classical"));
composers.put("18", new Composer("18", "Dmitry", "Shostakovich", "Classical"));
composers.put("19", new Composer("19", "Richard", "Wagner", "Classical"));

composers.put("20", new Composer("20", "Louis-Hector", "Berlioz", "Romantic"));
composers.put("21", new Composer("21", "Georges", "Bizet", "Romantic"));
composers.put("22", new Composer("22", "Cesar", "Cui", "Romantic"));
composers.put("23", new Composer("23", "Claude", "Debussy", "Romantic"));
composers.put("24", new Composer("24", "Edward", "Elgar", "Romantic"));
composers.put("25", new Composer("25", "Gabriel", "Faure", "Romantic"));
composers.put("26", new Composer("26", "Cesar", "Franck", "Romantic"));
composers.put("27", new Composer("27", "Edvard", "Grieg", "Romantic"));
```

```
composers.put("28", new Composer("28", "Nikolay", "Rimsky-Korsakov",
"Romantic"));

composers.put("29", new Composer("29", "Franz Joseph", "Liszt", "Romantic"));


composers.put("30", new Composer("30", "Felix", "Mendelssohn", "Romantic"));

composers.put("31", new Composer("31", "Giacomo", "Puccini", "Romantic"));

composers.put("32", new Composer("32", "Sergei", "Rachmaninoff", "Romantic"));

composers.put("33", new Composer("33", "Camille", "Saint-Saens", "Romantic"));

composers.put("34", new Composer("34", "Franz", "Schubert", "Romantic"));

composers.put("35", new Composer("35", "Robert", "Schumann", "Romantic"));

composers.put("36", new Composer("36", "Jean", "Sibelius", "Romantic"));

composers.put("37", new Composer("37", "Bedrich", "Smetana", "Romantic"));

composers.put("38", new Composer("38", "Richard", "Strauss", "Romantic"));

composers.put("39", new Composer("39", "Pyotr Il'yich", "Tchaikovsky",
"Romantic"));

composers.put("40", new Composer("40", "Guiseppe", "Verdi", "Romantic"));


composers.put("41", new Composer("41", "Bela", "Bartok", "Post-Romantic"));

composers.put("42", new Composer("42", "Leonard", "Bernstein", "Post-Romantic"));

composers.put("43", new Composer("43", "Benjamin", "Britten", "Post-Romantic"));

composers.put("44", new Composer("44", "John", "Cage", "Post-Romantic"));

composers.put("45", new Composer("45", "Aaron", "Copland", "Post-Romantic"));

composers.put("46", new Composer("46", "George", "Gershwin", "Post-Romantic"));

composers.put("47", new Composer("47", "Sergey", "Prokofiev", "Post-Romantic"));

composers.put("48", new Composer("48", "Maurice", "Ravel", "Post-Romantic"));

composers.put("49", new Composer("49", "Igor", "Stravinsky", "Post-Romantic"));

composers.put("50", new Composer("50", "Carl", "Orff", "Post-Romantic"));
```

```
    }
}
```

In the left margin you will spot a warning. This is because the ComposerClass can't be located so do the following to create that class:

Go to the Projects window, find the project node and right-click on it; click on New>Java Class

Call the class Composer, click on Package and click on com.ajax in the drop-down menu

Click on Finish and the class is created by the IDE and opened in the Source Editor. Go to the Source Editor and add this code:

```
package com.ajax;


public class Composer {


    private String id;

    private String firstName;

    private String lastName;

    private String category;


    public Composer (String id, String firstName, String lastName, String category) {

        this.id = id;

        this.firstName = firstName;

        this.lastName = lastName;

        this.category = category;

    }


    public String getCategory() {
```

```
        return category;
    }

    public String getId() {
        return id;
    }

    public String getFirstName() {
        return firstName;
    }

    public String getLastName() {
        return lastName;
    }
}
```

When a class has been created, go to the editor and look at ComposerData; you will see that the warning has gone. If there are still any there, look into them and add import statements that may be missing – the error hints will help you there.

Create the Servlet

Now we need the servlet that will take care of the autocomplete URL that the incoming request receives.

In the Projects window, find the project node and right-click on it. Click on New>Servlet and the New Servlet Wizard will open. If you don't see that option listed, click on Other>Web>Servlet.

Call your servlet AutoCompleteServlet and then click on com.ajax in the drop-down menu for Package. Click on Next

Go to the Configure Servlet Deployment panel and modify the URL pattern so it reads /autocomplete – this will make it match with the URL you set earlier in the XMLHttpRequest object. Using this panel makes it easier for you add details into the deployment descriptor without having to do it manually.

Click on Finish, the servlet will be created and opened in the Source Editor.

There are only two methods that need to be overridden – doGet(), which is defining the way the autocomplete GET request is handled by the servlet, and init() which must initiate a ServletContext, allowing the servlet the ability to access other application classes when needed. To override superclass methods, we use the Insert Code menu in the IDE.

First, we do the following to implement init():

- In the Source Editor, find the class declaration, AutoCompleteServlet, and place your mouse cursor beneath it. Press on ALT+INSERT and the Generate Code menu will appear.
- Click on the Override Method and a dialog box will load. You will see all of the classes that AutoCompleteServlet will inherit from. Go to the GenericServlet node and expand it; click on init(Servlet Config config).
- Click on OK and the init() method gets added to the Source Editor

Now we need a variable added in; this is for the ServletContext object. We also need to modify init() so change the relevant code so it looks like this:

```
private ServletContext context;


@Override

public void init(ServletConfig config) throws ServletException {

   this.context = config.getServletContext();

}
```

ServletContext requires an import statement so go to the left margin in the Source Editor and click the lightbulb icon.

The request URL must be parsed by the doGet() method. This method must also get the relevant data from the store and prepare an XML format response. When the class was created, the method declaration was automatically generated so, to see it, go to the left margin and click the expand icon so the HttpServlet methods are expanded.

Go to the AutoCompleteServlet class declaration and add in these variable declarations below it:

```
private ComposerData compData = new ComposerData();

private HashMap composers = compData.getComposers();
```

A HashMap of the composer data is created; this will be used by doGet() so, go down to doGet() and do the following to implement this method:

```
@Override
public void doGet(HttpServletRequest request, HttpServletResponse response)
      throws IOException, ServletException {

   String action = request.getParameter("action");
   String targetId = request.getParameter("id");
   StringBuffer sb = new StringBuffer();

   if (targetId != null) {
      targetId = targetId.trim().toLowerCase();
   } else {
      request.getRequestDispatcher("/error.jsp").forward(request, response);
   }

   boolean namesAdded = false;
   if (action.equals("complete")) {

      // check if user sent empty string
      if (!targetId.equals("")) {

         Iterator it = composers.keySet().iterator();

         while (it.hasNext()) {
            String id = (String) it.next();
            Composer composer = (Composer) composers.get(id);
```

```
        if ( // targetId matches first name
            composer.getFirstName().toLowerCase().startsWith(targetId) ||
            // targetId matches last name
            composer.getLastName().toLowerCase().startsWith(targetId) ||
            // targetId matches full name
            composer.getFirstName().toLowerCase().concat(" ")
              .concat(composer.getLastName().toLowerCase()).startsWith(targetId)) {

          sb.append("<composer>");
          sb.append("<id>" + composer.getId() + "</id>");
          sb.append("<firstName>" + composer.getFirstName() + "</firstName>");
          sb.append("<lastName>" + composer.getLastName() + "</lastName>");
          sb.append("</composer>");
          namesAdded = true;
        }
      }
    }

    if (namesAdded) {
      response.setContentType("text/xml");
      response.setHeader("Cache-Control", "no-cache");
      response.getWriter().write("<composers>" + sb.toString() + "</composers>");
    } else {
      //nothing to show
      response.setStatus(HttpServletResponse.SC_NO_CONTENT);
    }
```

```
  }
  if (action.equals("lookup")) {

    // put the target composer in the request scope to display
    if ((targetId != null) && composers.containsKey(targetId.trim())) {
      request.setAttribute("composer", composers.get(targetId));
      request.getRequestDispatcher("/composer.jsp").forward(request, response);
    }
  }
}
```

You can see from this that you don't really need to learn anything new for writing server-side code for Ajax. Where you want XML documents exchanged, you do need to set the response content type to text.xml and, with Ajax, you can also make exchanges on plain text or on snippets of JavaScript which might be executed or evaluated by the client callback function. Note as well that your browser might cache the result and, if it does, you may need to modify the Cache-Control HTTP header so it reads no-cache.

In our example, the XML document is generated by the servlet. This document has all of the composer names (first or last) that start with the user-input characters. The XML document will map to the XML data. Have a look at this example – it's an XML document that gets returned back to the XMLHttpRequest object:

```
<composers>
  <composer>
    <id>12</id>
    <firstName>Antonin</firstName>
    <lastName>Dvorak</lastName>
  </composer>
  <composer>
    <id>45</id>
    <firstName>Aaron</firstName>
```

```
    <lastName>Copland</lastName>
  </composer>
  <composer>
    <id>7</id>
    <firstName>Antonio</firstName>
    <lastName>Vivaldi</lastName>
  </composer>
  <composer>
    <id>2</id>
    <firstName>Arcangelo</firstName>
    <lastName>Corelli</lastName>
  </composer>
</composers>
```

Once the application is finished, the HTTP Monitor in the IDE can be used to see the returned XML data.

The Server-Side

Now it's time to get to work on the server-side; first, we need a callback function that will handle the response from the server and provide any necessary functionality to reflect any changes on the page that the user sees. To do this, we must make a change to the HTML DOM and that requires JSP pages for showing a successful request response or failed request error messages. Then we can make a stylesheet for the presentation layer.

Our callback function will be asynchronously called during the HTTP interaction at certain points, when there is a change to the XMLHttpRequest object's readyState property. In our application, the callback function is called callback() and you may remember that, in our doComplete function, we set callback as XMLHttpRequest on the readystatechange property to a specific function; now we need to implement our callback function:

In the Source Editor, launch javascript.js and input the code below:

```
function callback() {
  if (req.readyState == 4) {
    if (req.status == 200) {
```

```
        parseMessages(req.responseXML);
      }
    }
}
```

Where you see readyState ==4, this is signifying that the HTTP interaction is complete. The XMLHttpRequest.readyState API says that there are a total of 5 potential values that may be set and they are:

readyState Value	Object Status Definition
Uninitialized	0
Loading	1
Loaded	2
Interactive	3
Complete	4

Did you also spot that we only call the parseMessages() function when the status of XMLHttpRequest.readyState is 4and the HTTP status code definition for the request is 200; this is telling us it was successful. We will be defining parseMessages() next.

Updating HTML DOM

This function will take care of the XML data that comes in and, to do this it will rely on a number of contributing functions, like getElementY(), appendComposer(), clearTable() etc. We will also need to try introducing additional elements to our index page, like another HTML table for the auto-complete box, and element IDs so that they can better be referenced in the javascript.js file. Lastly, we will need some new variables that correspond to the element IDs on our index page. The init() function will need to initialize these and it will add extra functionality that is required whenever the page gets loaded.

All the elements and functions we are going to create all work interdependently.

In the Source Editor, open the Index page and go to the HTML table we created earlier. Underneath the code for row 2, add the following code:

```
<tr>
   <td id="auto-row" colspan="2">
      <table id="complete-table" />
   </td>
```

```
</tr>
```

Row 2 of this table has another HTML table in it and this is representing our auto-complete box; this box will be used for populating the names of the composers.

In the Source Editor open javascript.js and add these variables at the top:

```
var completeField;

var completeTable;

var autoRow;
```

Now go to the init() function and add these lines:

```
function init() {

   completeField = document.getElementById("complete-field");

   completeTable = document.getElementById("complete-table");

   autoRow = document.getElementById("auto-row");

   completeTable.style.top = getElementY(autoRow) + "px";

}
```

One thing that init() does is make the elements within the index page so that they can be accessed by other functions that can make changes to the DOM on the index page.

Add the following to javascript.js – this is appendComposer() function:

```
function appendComposer(firstName,lastName,composerId) {


   var row;

   var cell;

   var linkElement;


   if (isIE) {

      completeTable.style.display = 'block';

      row = completeTable.insertRow(completeTable.rows.length);

      cell = row.insertCell(0);
```

```
    } else {
        completeTable.style.display = 'table';
        row = document.createElement("tr");
        cell = document.createElement("td");
        row.appendChild(cell);
        completeTable.appendChild(row);
    }

    cell.className = "popupCell";

    linkElement = document.createElement("a");
    linkElement.className = "popupItem";
    linkElement.setAttribute("href", "autocomplete?action=lookup&id=" + composerId);
    linkElement.appendChild(document.createTextNode(firstName + " " + lastName));
    cell.appendChild(linkElement);
}
```

This will make another table row and will add a link into it; this link is to a composer it uses data that passes to the function through the 3 function parameters. The row is inserted into the complete-table element on the index page.

Now add the following getElementY() function code to javascript.js:

```
function getElementY(element){

    var targetTop = 0;

    if (element.offsetParent) {
        while (element.offsetParent) {
            targetTop += element.offsetTop;
```

```
        element = element.offsetParent;
      }
    } else if (element.y) {
      targetTop += element.y;
    }
    return targetTop;
}
```

This function looks at the parent element to find the vertical position of it. This must be done because, when it is displayed, the element positioning depends on the browser being used, including the browser version. Note that, when the complete-table element is displayed with the names of the composers, it is moved to the bottom right of the table it resides in. getElementY() will determine the proper height positioning of it.

Now add this clearTable() function code to javascript.js:

```
function clearTable() {
    if (completeTable.getElementsByTagName("tr").length > 0) {
      completeTable.style.display = 'none';
      for (loop = completeTable.childNodes.length -1; loop >= 0 ; loop--) {
        completeTable.removeChild(completeTable.childNodes[loop]);
      }
    }
}
```

This will set the complete-table element display to none, which effectively makes it invisible, and it gets rid of any composer name entries that already exist.

Next, we are going to make a change to the callback() function so it calls clearTable() whenever new data comes in from the server. If there are any composer entries in the auto-complete box, these will be removed before new entries are added:

```
function callback() {


    clearTable();
```

```
    if (req.readyState == 4) {
        if (req.status == 200) {
            parseMessages(req.responseXML);
        }
    }
}
```

Add this parseMessage() function code to javascript.js:

```
function parseMessages(responseXML) {

    // no matches returned
    if (responseXML == null) {
        return false;
    } else {

        var composers = responseXML.getElementsByTagName("composers")[0];

        if (composers.childNodes.length > 0) {
            completeTable.setAttribute("bordercolor", "black");
            completeTable.setAttribute("border", "1");

            for (loop = 0; loop < composers.childNodes.length; loop++) {
                var composer = composers.childNodes[loop];
                var firstName = composer.getElementsByTagName("firstName")[0];
                var lastName = composer.getElementsByTagName("lastName")[0];
                var composerId = composer.getElementsByTagName("id")[0];
```

```
        appendComposer(firstName.childNodes[0].nodeValue,
          lastName.childNodes[0].nodeValue,
          composerId.childNodes[0].nodeValue);
      }
    }
  }
}
```

This function will receive an object representation as a parameter. This representation is of the XML document that the AutoComplete servlet returns. The function will traverse the document and pull out 3 pieces of information for each entry – firstName, lastName and ID. This data is then passed to appendComposer() and the result is that the contents in the complete-table element will dynamically update. For example, the following could be an entry that gets generated and put into complete-table:

```
<tr>
<td class="popupCell">
<a class="popupItem" href="autocomplete?action=lookup&id=12">Antonin Dvorak</a>
</td>
</tr>
```

The last step in the communication flow when using Ajax for the communication is the dynamic update to the element. The update will map to the CSS and the HTML data that is sent to the presentation layer.

Display the Results

Displaying the results of all this requires a JSP file called composers.jsp. This page will be called during the lookup action from AutoCompleteServlet. We will also require an error.jsp file which we call from AutoCompleteServlet in the event that the composer isn't found.

To show the results and the errors:

Go to the Project window, find the folder called Web Pages and right-click it; click on New>JSP and the New JSP wizard will open.

Type composer into the field for File Name and look in the Created File field – there should be a path that ends in /web/composer.jsp

Click on Finish and the composer.jsp file will open in the Editor. In the Projects window, go to the Web Pages folder and you will see a node for the composer.jsp file.

In the composer.jsp file, find the placeholder code and replace it with this code:

```
<html>
 <head>
  <title>Composer Information</title>

  <link rel="stylesheet" type="text/css" href="stylesheet.css">
 </head>
 <body>

  <table>
   <tr>
    <th colspan="2">Composer Information</th>
   </tr>
   <tr>
    <td>First Name: </td>
    <td>${requestScope.composer.firstName}</td>
   </tr>
   <tr>
    <td>Last Name: </td>
    <td>${requestScope.composer.lastName}</td>
   </tr>
   <tr>
    <td>ID: </td>
    <td>${requestScope.composer.id}</td>
   </tr>
```

```
    <tr>
     <td>Category: </td>
     <td>${requestScope.composer.category}</td>
    </tr>
   </table>

   <p>Go back to <a href="index.html" class="link">application home</a>.</p>
  </body>
</html>
```

If your index page is called index.jsp, the link that returns to the page will need to be changed.

In Projects, click on Web Pages and create a second JSP file, calling it error.jsp. Take the placeholder code out of it and input this instead:

```
<!DOCTYPE html>

<html>
   <head>
      <link rel="stylesheet" type="text/css" href="stylesheet.css">
      <meta http-equiv="Content-Type" content="text/html; charset=UTF-8">
      <title>Search Error</title>
   </head>
   <body>
      <h2>Search Error</h2>

      <p>An error occurred while performing the search. Please try again.</p>

      <p>Go back to <a href="index.html" class="link">application home</a>.</p>
```

```
  </body>
</html>
```

Again, if your index page is index.jsp, the return link must be changed.

Attaching Stylesheets

Right now, you have all the code you need for the application functionality so run the application to see your results. Go to Projects and find the project node; right-click on it and click on Run. Your project will now be recompiled and sent to the server; your browser will open and you will be able to see your index page.

Adding stylesheets is as simple as creating a .css file and linking to it from the application presentation page. For working with .css files, the NetBeans IDE gives you the same code completion features, along with support for generating stylesheet rules and editing them through these windows:

- CSS Style – here you can edit the rules declarations for the HTML elements and the selectors within a CSS file
- Create CSS Rules – this dialog box lets you create some new rules in the style sheets
- Add CSS Property – this dialog box lets you add CSS rule declarations in style sheets through properties and their values.

Adding a stylesheet:

Go to the Projects window, find the Web Pages node and right-click on it. Click on New>Cascading Style Sheet. If this option is not there, click on Other>New File>Web Category> Cascading Style Sheet.

Type in stylesheet in the text field for CSS File Name and click on Finish. The file is created and is opened in the editor.

In the Editor, open the stylesheet.css file and add these rules in, using support for code completion if necessary (CTRL+SPACE):

```
body {
  font-family: Verdana, Arial, sans-serif;
  font-size: smaller;
  padding: 50px;
  color: #555;
  width: 650px;
}
```

```
h1 {
  letter-spacing: 6px;
  font-size: 1.6em;
  color: #be7429;
  font-weight: bold;
}

h2 {
  text-align: left;
  letter-spacing: 6px;
  font-size: 1.4em;
  color: #be7429;
  font-weight: normal;
  width: 450px;
}

table {
  width: 550px;
  padding: 10px;
  background-color: #c5e7e0;
}

td {
  padding: 10px;
}
```

```
a {
  color: #be7429;
  text-decoration: none;
}

a:hover {
  text-decoration: underline;
}

.popupBox {
  position: absolute;
  top: 170px;
  left: 140px;
}

.popupCell {
   background-color: #fffafa;
}

.popupCell:hover {
  background-color: #f5ebe9;
}

.popupItem {
  color: #333;
```

```
  text-decoration: none;
  font-size: 1.2em;
}
```

From the main menu, click on Window>Web>CSS Styles to open the Styles window. In the top pane of the style window you can select rules to edit; clicking on a rule will show you the properties of it in the bottom pane. If you click on Edit CSS Rules in the toolbar at the top, you add new Rules to your stylesheet and, in the bottom pane, you can make changes to the rules; click on Add Property in the toolbar for the bottom pane and you can add properties and edit the sheet.

In the Source Editor go to the index page and locate the <head> tags; add the following stylesheet reference between the tags:

```
<link rel="stylesheet" type="text/css" href="stylesheet.css">
```

Now we want to add a class to our complete-table element. The class is called popupBox and it has been defined in the stylesheet. Change your complete-table element code so it looks like this:

```
<tr>
   <td id="auto-row" colspan="2">
      <table id="complete-table"    />
   </td>
</tr>
```

Again, make use of code completion to help you choose the right style rule for the selector.

This rule is used to position our complete-table element so it will show just on the right of the parent element.

When the index page is saved, the application is deployed automatically to the server again. If you still have your browser open to the index page, just refresh it and you will see that it has been rendered as per the CSS stylesheet rules.

Running Your Project

When your application is run again, it will show in your browser with the newly created stylesheet. Whenever you input a character, a request is sent asynchronously to the server and XML data is returned from AutoCompleteServlet. As more characters are input, the number of composer names will reduce, reflecting the changes in the matches to the name.

HTTP Server Monitor

The IDE contains an HTTP Server monitor that you can use for verification that the HTTP communication taking place as requests and as responses are correctly passed from the client-side to the server-side and back again. The Monitor will show you information like the headers for the client and the server, details of cookies, properties for the session, request parameters and more.

Before you start using the monitor it must be enabled on your chosen server.

Go to the main menu, click on Tools>Servers and the Servers window will open

Loo in the left pane; click on the name of the server that your project is using and then go to the right pane; click the option to Enable HTTP Monitor to enable it. If you are using Tomcat server, this will be under Connection while in Glassfish, it is under Common. Click on close

Restart your server if it is already running otherwise the changes cannot be effected. To do this, click on Window>Services> and then click on Servers node and right-click the name of your server. Click on Restart.

When the application is run this time, you will see the HTTP monitor open at the bottom of the IDE. IN the left pane you will see records; select one and then go to the main window; click on tabs and you will see a load of information on each request.

When a user inputs a character into the autocomplete field, an asynchronous request is made and the response is XML data sent back from the server. You can verify this data by looking at the left of the HTTP Monitor where you will see a tree-view. Right-click on any request record and click on Replay. You will see the response in your browser. In our case, because we have XML data, it will be displayed in your browser's XML viewer.

We've covered a basic introduction to building web applications using Ajax. As you have seen, it is about far more than just an exchange of information over HTTP and dynamic page updates. Next we'll look at using a MySQL database to build a Java web application.

Connecting to a MySQL Database

We are now going to turn our attention to using a MySQL database. We will build a simple application that connects to a server and we'll also look into basic technologies and ideas in Java web development, like JSP, (JavaServer Pages), JSTL (JavaServer Pages Standard Tag Library), JDBC (Java Database Connectivity), API, and the architecture for two-tier client servers. First, we'll start by learning how to connect to a MySQL database from the NetBeans IDE.

This will allow you to start using MySQL in the NetBeans Database Explorer, creating new tables and databases, adding data to tables, and running SQL queries on databases and their content. My SQL is one of the most popular of all the RDBMS (relational database management systems) in place today and tends to be favored for building web applications because it is fast, flexible and highly reliable. To access the data in a database and to process is MySQL makes use of Structured Query Language.

As well as NetBeans and JDK, you will also need to download the latest MySQL Database Server. Once you have that installed, you can continue with the tutorial.

Configuring MySQL

With the NetBeans IDE you get full support for MySQL RDBMS. However, you will need to configure the properties for the SQL server before you can access it through NetBeans.

Go to the Services window, find the Databases node and right-click on it. Click on Register MySQL Server and the server properties dialog box will open.

Check that the name and port for the server are right. Note that, by default, localhost is inserted as the name and the default port is 3306.

You will need administrative access if you want to create databases and remove them so, if the Admin username is not on display, input it, along with a password. Note the default password is set to blank which may also be a password.

Now click on Admin Properties from the tabs at top of this dialog box. Here you can input the information needed to control the MySQL server. Go to the filed for Path/URL to Admin Tool and input the location of your admin application – it will be MySQL Admin Tool. Browse to find the location if you don't know where it was saved but, by default, it will be in the directory for MySQL inside the folder called bin.

Next, we want to add our arguments for this tool so go to the Arguments field and add what you need – you won't need any for this application, this is just for reference

Find the Path to Start Command field and input the location of the start command for MySQL – in the bin folder you will find a file called mysqld.

Again, go to the Arguments field and input any arguments you need – you shouldn't need any for this application

Now go to the Path to Stop Command field and enter the MySQL stop command location; this is the path that leads to the bin file to mysqladmin. In Arguments, to give root permission to stop the server, type in -u root stop.

When you are done, if you are happy with the way your configuration looks, click on OK.

Starting the Server

Before connecting to the server, you need to ensure that it is running on your computer. Go to the Service window and look for the MySQL Server node; if it says disconnected beside the username it is not running and the node won't expand.

To enable connection, make sure the server is running and go to the Service window. Right-click on Databases and then on MySQL Server; click on Connect and, if asked, type in the requested connection password.

When you are fully connected, the server node will expand and you will be able to see all the MySQL databases available.

Create and Connect to a Database Instance

One of the most common database interaction methods is via an SQL editor. In the NetBeans IDE you will find a SQL-editor built-in and, to get to it, go to the Connection node and right-click on it, clicking on Execute.

Now that we have a connection to the MySQL server, we can create a database instance using the editor.

Go to the Service window and find the MySQL Server node; right-click on it and click on Create Database

The dialog box for Create MySQL Database will open, type in the name of the database – for this tutorial, call it MyNewDatabase. Don't select the checkbox at the moment

Although the admin user is the only one with permission to carry out some commands by default, you can grant access to a specific user. The drop-down menu will allow you to assign this but we don't need to do that right now.

Click on OK and go to the Service window; the new database will be visible under the node for the MySQL Server.

Right-click on the newly created database, and click on Connect; this will open the database connection and, in the Service window, you will see a Complete Connection node.

Create a Database Table

With the connection to MyNewDatabase in place we can start to look at how tables are created, how we add data and modify the data already in a maintained window. This will give you the option of looking closely at what functionality the Database Explorer offers as well as the support that the NetBeans IDE has for SQL files.

Right now, MyNewDatabase is empty. We can a table in the NetBeans IDE in two ways – with the Create Table dialog box or by inputting and running an SQL query from the SQL editor. We'll use the editor to create a table called Counselor and we'll use the dialog box to create a table called Subject. Once the tables are created, we'll populate them using an SQL script.

The SQL Editor

Open the Database Explorer and expand the connection node for MyNewDatabase. You will see 3 subfolders named Tables, Views and Procedures.

Right-click on the Tables subfolder and click on Execute Command. IN the main window you will see a blank space in the SQL Editor. Input the query below – this is the definition of the table called Counselor that we are going to create:

```
CREATE TABLE Counselor (
  id SMALLINT UNSIGNED NOT NULL AUTO_INCREMENT,
  firstName VARCHAR (50),
  nickName VARCHAR (50),
  lastName VARCHAR (50),
  telephone VARCHAR (25),
  email VARCHAR (50),
  memberSince DATE DEFAULT '1900-01-01',
  PRIMARY KEY (id)
     );
```

If you form any query in the SQL Editor, it will be parsed in SQL; the language sticks to very strict rules as far as syntax goes. When an SQL query is run, the SQL engine provides feedback which you will see in the Output window; this will tell you whether the query was successfully executed or not.

Either go to the Run SQL button in the top taskbar (CTRL+SHIFT+E) or go to the SQL Editor and right-click in it; click on Run Statement.

The Counselor table will now be generated by the IDE in the database and you will see a message in the Output window that will tell you whether the execution was successful.

In Database Explorer, right click on the node for Tables and click on Refresh. The UI component of Database Explorer will be updated whatever the status of the specific database is at the time. You will now see the new node for the Counselor table in Database Explorer under Tables. Expand that node and you will see the fields that you created in the form of columns; the first will be the primary key.

The Create Table Dialog Box

Go to Database Explorer and right-click on the node for Tables; click on Create Table and you will see the dialog box open

In the text field for Table, type in Subject and click on Add Column

Input id as the column name and, from the drop-down menu for Type, click on SMALLINT – this is the data type. Click on OK.

Go to Add Column and check the box beside Primary Key. This is where we specify the primary key for the table – every table in any relational database has to have a primary key. When you select the primary key, you will note that both Unique and Index boxes are checked automatically and the Null checkbox is unchecked. The reason for this is that a primary key is used for the identification of a unique database row and forms the index of the table by default. All rows must be identified so the primary key may not have Null as a value.

Repeat to add the columns below:

Name – id – Key, Index and Unique checked. SMALLINT data type, size 0

Name – name – Null box checked, VARCHAR data type, size 50

Name – description – Null box checked, VARCHAR data type, size 500

Name – FK_CounselorID – Null box checked, SMALLINT data type, size 0.

We are going to create a table called Subject. This table will have data in it for these records:

- Name – subject name
- Description – subject description
- Counselor ID – the ID that will correspond to one in the Counselor table

The fields that are in the dialog box for Create Table must be the same as those above; check that they are and then click on OK.

You will see the Subject table generated in the database and a node called Subject will show up in the Explorer under Tables.

Table Data

To work with the data in a table, you can use the SQL editor supplied by NetBeans. When you run queries on databases, you can add new data, modify existing data, and delete data from any database structure.

Adding a new row to Counselor:

In Database Explorer, click on Tables>Execute Command. A blank space opens in the Editor

Type the following into the Editor:

INSERT INTO Counselor

VALUES (1, 'Ricky', '"The Dragon"', 'Steamboat','334 612-5678', 'r_steamboat@ifpwafcad.com', '1996-01-01')

Right-click inside the Editor and click on Run Statement. Look in the Output window and you will see a message telling you that execution was successful.

Now we'll check that that record has been successfully added; go to Database Explorer and right-click on the node for the Counselor table; click on View Data.

In the main window you will see a new Editor pane open. Clicking on View Data automatically generates a query that will select all the table data – this appears in the top of the SQL Editor and the statement results appear at the bottom in a table view. You will see the Counselor table appear; a new row has been inserted containing the data that came from your query.

Running a Script

You can also manage the table data by running external scrips in the NetBeans IDE. This works if you created your script elsewhere; just open it in NetBeans and use the SQL Editor to run it.

Download this file - ifpwafcad.sql and save it on your computer. We will be using this for demonstration purposes; it will create a couple of tables much like those you already created and will fill them with data straight away.

As this script is going to overwrite tables that already exist, remove both the Counselor and the Subject tables now – this will make it obvious when the script is run that new tables are going to be created.

To delete a table:

Go to Database Explore and, in turn, right-click on the Counselor and Subject tables and click on Delete.

When you see the Confirm Object Deletion box, click on Yes. The nodes will be removed from Explorer.

To run the script on MyNewDatabase:

Go to the main menu in the IDE and click on File>Open File.

Find the location where you saved the file you downloaded earlier, ifpwafcad.sql. Click on Open and you will see the script opened in the Editor

Go to the toolbar at the top, click on Connection and ensure you are connected to MyNewDatabase.

Click on Run SQL and the script will be executed against MyNewDatabase; feedback will appear in the Output window.

In the Runtime window, find and right-click on the connection node for MyNewDatabase and click on Refresh. The UI component will be updated and you will see two tables in Database Explorer, under MyNewDatabase.

Select one of the table nodes and right-click on it; Click on View Data and you will see what data is in the table. Compare it to the script to make sure they match.

Using a MySQL Database to Build Web Applications

This is a continuation from above; Ensure that you have the MySQL Connector/ J JDBC Driver installed along with Glassfish Server.

Planning Your Structure

You can easily design a simple application using a two-tier architecture; the client and server communicate directly with one another. For our purposes, we will have a Java web app using the Java Database Connectivity API to directly communicate with a MySQL database. The driver that enables this communication is the MySQL Connector/J JDBC Driver.

For the application we are going to build, we will create two JSP pages. Each one will use both CSS and HTML for implementing simple interfaces. We will also use JSTL technology to enable the logic to be performed that queries the database directly, and puts the retrieved data into the new pages. The database tables are in MyNewDatabase which you created earlier and are called Counselor and Subject.

Consider this scenario:

Index.jsp is the welcome page and it will show the user a simple form created in HTML. When the page is requested by a browser, the JSTL code in the page will kickstart the query to MyNewDatabase. It will get the required data from the Subject table and put it on the page before the browser request is completed. When a user chooses a selection on the HTML form, the Submit button will start a request for response.jsp, which is the response page the user sees. Once again, the JSTL code starts the query to MyNewDatabase and gets the data from both tables – Counselor and Subject – and adds it to the page. This lets the users see the data they requested on the browser page.

Implementation of this scenario requires that we create an application for an organization that we call IFPWAFCAD:

In the IDE main menu, click on File>New Project (CTRL+SHFT+N). Click on Java Web>Web application and click on Next. The New Project Wizard opens

Here, you can create a web application that is empty inside a standard project which will use an Ant build script, generated by the IDE, to compile the application, deploy it to the server and run it.

For the Project Name, type in IFPWAFCAD. Specify where you want the project saved on your PC and click on Next. By default, it will be placed into your home directory in NetBeansProjects.

Go to the Server and Settings panel and choose Glassfish as your server for running the application.

Go to the field for Java EE version and choose the version you downloaded. For the purposes of this choose version 5.

Higher versions of Java EE don't use the web.xml deployment descriptor and the web.xml file is not included in the NetBeans project template.. However, I want to show you how data sources are declared in deployment descriptors so use Java EE 5. This method doesn't rely on any features specific to a newer version. If you want to use a later version, do so then you need to go to the New File wizard, click on Web>Standard Deployment Descriptor and create a web.xml descriptor.

Click on Finish and the project template will be created for the whole application, opening a blank index.jsp page in your browser. This is going to be your welcome page.

The Web Interface

We start with the preparation of the index.jsp and response.jsp pages. Index.jsp, your welcome page has an HTML form used for capturing data input by the user. Both pages use HTML tables to show the data in a more structured way. We will also be creating a stylesheet to make both pages look better.

Setting the welcome page up:

Make sure that you have index.jsp opened in the editor; go to the Projects window, click on the IFPWAFCAD project and click on Web pages then index.jsp.

Go to the editor and find the <title> tags; change the text in between them to read IFPWAFCAD Homepage

Go to the <h1> tags and edit the text to read Welcome to IFPWAFCAD.

Open the Palette window in the ID; go to the main menu and click on Window>Palette (CTRL+SHIFT+8)

Go to HTML and place your mouse cursor over the Table icon. You will see the default snippet of code appear.

Configure the Palette how you want. Right-click in the window and click on Show Big Icons. Then click on Hide Item Names and see how it displays

Back to the code, go to the <h1> tags and place your mouse cursor just after them. This is where the new table will go.

In Palette, double-click on Table and you will see an Insert Table dialog box. Make sure the following values are specified and then click on OK:

- Rows: 2
- Columns: 1
- Border Size: 0

The code gets generated and placed in the page.

The next code needs to be added to the Table heading and to the cell in the first row of the table:

```
<table border="0">
  <thead>
    <tr>
      <th>IFPWAFCAD offers expert counseling in a wide range of fields.</th>
    </tr>
  </thead>
  <tbody>
    <tr>
      <td>To view contact details of an IFPWAFCAD certified former
        professional wrestler in your area, select a subject below:</td>
</tr>
```

We now want an HTML table in the bottom row. Go to the second <td> tags, double-click on the icon of the HTML table in Palette and the dialog box appears. For the Action field, type response.jsp and click on OK

Go to the <form> tags and make sure the content reads as follows:

```
<tr>
  <td>
```

```
<form action="response.jsp">
  <strong>Select a subject:</strong>
</form>
</td>
</tr>
```

Press the Enter key so an empty line appears under this content and go to Palette; double-click on the Drop-Down list and the dialog box for Insert Drop Down will appear

In the Name field, type in subject_id and click on OK. You will see the code snippet is added into the form.

Right now, it isn't important how many options are in the drop-down but later, we will add some JSTL tags to generate options dynamically based on what data we get from the Subject table.

Just after the list we added, we need a Submit button. You can do this through Palette or you can use code completion. Click on the Insert Button dialog, give the Label and Name fields the name of submit and then click on OK.

Now we want to format our code so right-click somewhere in the editor and click on Format (ALT+SHIFT+F). Your code will be formatted and it should now look like this:

```
<body>
  <h2>Welcome to <strong>IFPWAFCAD</strong>, the International Former
    Professional Wrestlers' Association for Counseling and Development!
  </h2>


  <table border="0">
    <thead>
      <tr>
        <th>IFPWAFCAD offers expert counseling in a wide range of fields.</th>
      </tr>
    </thead>
    <tbody>
```

```
<tr>
  <td>To view the contact details of an IFPWAFCAD certified former
    professional wrestler in your area, select a subject below:</td>
</tr>
<tr>
  <td>
    <form action="response.jsp">
      <strong>Select a subject:</strong>
      <select name="subject_id">
        <option></option>
      </select>
      <input type="submit" value="submit" name="submit" />
    </form>
  </td>
</tr>
</tbody>
</table>
</body>
```

Right-click inside th Editor, click on Run File (SHIFT+F6) and the JSP pate will be compiled and deployed. Your browser will open and the page will be displayed.

The Response Page

To prepare our response page, we need the file created in the project. Most of what will be seen on this page will use JSP technology to dynamically generate. So, in these steps, we will be adding placeholders; these will later be replaced with the right JSP code.

In Projects, go to the IFPWAFCAD node and right-click on it. Click on New>JSP and the dialog box will open

Go to the field for JSP File Name and type in response. At the moment, Location is currently set as Web Pages – this means that the file gets created in the web directory for the project, the same place as the index.jsp page.

Accept the default settings and click on Finish. In the editor you will see the response.jsp template page open and a JSP node will appear in Projects under Web Pages.

Go to the Editor and where the placeholder code is for the title, replace it with IFPWAFCAD.

Go to the <body> tags and remove the line that says<h1>Hello World!</h1>; input this code into the page body:

```
<table border="0">

  <thead>

    <tr>

      <th colspan="2">{placeholder}</th>

    </tr>

  </thead>

  <tbody>

    <tr>

      <td><strong>Description: </strong></td>

      <td><span style="font-size:smaller; font-style:italic;">{placeholder}</span></td>

    </tr>

    <tr>

      <td><strong>Counselor: </strong></td>

      <td>{placeholder}

        <br>

        <span style="font-size:smaller; font-style:italic;">

        member since: {placeholder}</span>

      </td>

    </tr>

    <tr>
```

```
        <td><strong>Contact Details: </strong></td>
        <td><strong>email: </strong>
          <a href="mailto:{placeholder}">{placeholder}</a>
          <br><strong>phone: </strong>{placeholder}
        </td>
      </tr>
    </tbody>
</table>
```

Right-click somewhere in the editor and click on Run File (SHIFT+F6). The page is compiled, deployed to Glassfish and opened in the browser

The Stylesheet

Now we want a stylesheet to make our interface look better.

Go to the main toolbar in NetBeans IDE and click on New File; the wizard opens, click on Web>Cascading Style Sheet and then click on Next

For the file name, type in style and click on Finish. The empty CSS file is created and put in the same places as both response.jsp and index.jsp. You will also see the style.css node in Projects and the file is opened in the Editor

Go to the editor and add this code to the file:

```
body {
  font-family: Verdana, Arial, sans-serif;
  font-size: smaller;
  padding: 50px;
  color: #555;
}

h1 {
  text-align: left;
  letter-spacing: 6px;
```

```
font-size: 1.4em;
color: #be7429;
font-weight: normal;
width: 450px;
}

table {
width: 580px;
padding: 10px;
background-color: #c5e7e0;
}

th {
text-align: left;
border-bottom: 1px solid;
}

td {
padding: 10px;
}

a:link {
color: #be7429;
font-weight: normal;
text-decoration: none;
}
```

```
a:link:hover {
  color: #be7429;
  font-weight: normal;
  text-decoration: underline;
}
```

Now we want this stylesheet linked to index and response.jsp files. In each of the pages, go the <head> tags and add in this code:

```
<link rel="stylesheet" type="text/css" href="style.css">
```

Application and Database Communication

The best way for the communication between the server and database to be implemented is by setting a database connection pool up. It can take a long time to create new connections for each request, especially where you have an application that gets loads of new requests on a continuous basis. To fix this, we create and maintain all the connections in a pool. When requests are completed, instead of closing down the connection, the connection gets sent back to the pool.

Once the data source and the connection pool have been prepared for the server, we then need to tell the application that it should use the data source. To do this, we create an entry in the deployment descriptor for the application. Lastly, we need to make sure that the database driver can be accessed by the server. For all of this, we will need MyNewDatabase and the Counselor and Subject tables we set up earlier. Your database must be protected by a password otherwise the data source can't be set up and it can't connect to Glassfish. We'll be using the password, nbuser, so to set it up, open your command line prompt and navigate to the bin directory in MySql; type the following code in:

```
shell> mysql -u root

mysql> UPDATE mysql.user SET Password = PASSWORD('nbuser')

WHERE User = 'root';

mysql> FLUSH PRIVILEGES;
```

The JDBC Data Source and the Connection Pool

In Glassfish, there are the libraries for Database Connection Pooling (DBCP); these are used to provide the functionality for pooling the connections in a way that a developer can easily see. We will need a Java Database Connectivity (JDBC) data source configured for the server that your application can make use of for pooling the connections.

There are two ways to do this; either configure it in the Admin Console for Glassfish or, as I describe below, using the glassfish-resources.xml file. When employment happens, the server will read the declarations in and create the resources needed.

We're going to declare the pool along with the data source that depends on the pool and we can do both of these using the JDBC Resource Wizard in NetBeans.

In the main toolbar, click on New File and the wizard will open. Choose Glassfish and click on JDBC Resource; click on Next

Click on Create New JDBC Connection Pool and, for the JNDI text field, type jdbc/IFPWAFCAD.

JDBC data sources require JNDI – Java Naming and Directory Interface – API to provide a consistent way for applications to find data sources and access them.

As an optional step, you can input a description for the source. Click on Next and then on Next again.

For JDBC Connection Pool, type IfpwafcadPool and ensure that the option for Extract from Existing Connection is selected. From the drop-down list, click on jdbc:mysql://localhost:3306/MyNewDatabase and then click on Next.

Click on Resource Type and choose javax.sql.ConnectionPoolDataSouece from the list

The IDE will get information out of the specified database connection and the name-value properties are set for the connection pool.

Click on Finish and the glassfish-resources.xml file is generated; this will have entries in it for the specified data source and the connection pool.

Go to Projects window, click on Server Resources and open the newly created xml file. Note that the data source and the connection pool have been declared between the <resources> tags and these will have the specified values in them.

To make sure the source and pool have been properly registered with the server, go to the Projects window and right-click on the node for IFPWAFCAD project; click on Deploy and the server will start if it isn't running already. The project will be compiled and then deployed to the server.

Go to the Services window (CTRL+5) and expand the following nodes in turn:

- Servers
- Glassfish
- Resources

- JDBC
- JDBC Resources and connection pools

The new source and pool will now be displayed.

Reference the Data Source

The JDBC resource we configured now needs to be referenced from the application and to do this, we need a new entry in the deployment descriptor. The descriptor is an xml file that determined how applications are deployed in certain environments. Normally, they are used for specifying the context parameters for an application, along with the security settings, the patterns of behavior, and the mappings for the listeners, filters and servlets. If you specified a higher version of EE than 5, open the New File Wizard, click on Web and then Standard Deployment Descriptor to create the file.

To reference the source:

Open Projects, click on Configuration Files to expand it and then double-click on web.xml. The file will open in the Editor.

Click References at the top and expand the heading for Resource References; click on Add and the Add Resource Reference dialog box will open.

Type in the name of the resource you provided when you configured the data source – jdbc/IFPWAFCAD

In Resource Type, input javax.sql.ConnectionPoolDataSource and click on OK

You can optionally complete the description field if you want.

You will see the new Resource listed under Resource References.

In the editor, click on Source and you will see that the <resource-ref> tags have now been included:

```
<resource-ref>
    <description>Database for IFPWAFCAD application</description>
    <res-ref-name>jdbc/IFPWAFCAD</res-ref-name>
    <res-type>javax.sql.ConnectionPoolDataSource</res-type>
    <res-auth>Container</res-auth>
    <res-sharing-scope>Shareable</res-sharing-scope>
</resource-ref>
```

Add The Driver's JAR File

The next step is to add the JAR file from the database driver to the server; this is important in allowing communication between the server and the database. The Server management feature in the IDE can detect if the JAR file was added when the application is deployed; if it hasn't been, it will add the file.

To see this, from the main menu, click on Tools>Servers and look for the option for JDBC deployment; if enabled, a check will be initiated to see whether the applications deployed on the server require any drivers. If a SQL driver is needed and it is not there, the IDE will deploy its bundled driver to the right server location.

Open Tools>Server and click on the Glassfish server on the left

Note down the path that you see in the text field for Domains. When a connection is made to the Glassfish server you are connecting to an application server instance. Each of the instances uses unique domains to run applications and the path in Domain name tells you the domain name in use by your server.

Click on Close and the Server Manager will close.

Find where your installation folder is for Glassfish on your computer and click on domains>domai1>lib. As the project has already been deployed to the server, you should see the .jar file.

If the file is not there, go to Projects in the NetBeans IDE and right-click on the Project node; click on Deploy. You will see the progress in the output window telling you the driver has been deployed to a Glassfish location

Go back to the lib subfolder you opened and you will see that the .jar file is now there

Add Dynamic Logic

Let's get back to our index and response placeholders that we made earlier; we can now implement our JSTL code enabling dynamic generation of the content, for example that input by a user. To do this, we need to do 3 things:

Add JSTL Library to Project Classpath

The JavaServer Pages Standard Tag Library, or JSTL, can be applied so that we can access data from the database and display it. JSTL is included in Glassfish by default and to verify it, we can go to the Project window and click on Libraries. Expand the node for the Glassfish server and look for javax.servlet.jsp.jstl.jar. By default, libraries in Glassfish are automatically added to the classpath in your project so you don't need to do anything here.

With JSTL, we get 4 areas of functionality:

- Core functionality – common tasks for structure, like conditionals and iterators, for flow control handling
- fmt functionality – formatting of localization and internationalization messages
- sql functionality – database access
- xml functionality – for handling XML content

We will be focusing our attention on the core functionalities and the SQL functionalities and their tag libraries.

Implementation of JSTL Code

We can now implement the JSTL code that will dynamically retrieve the data and display for both our pages. An SQL query is required on both pages to make use of the data source that we made earlier.

If you go to the Palette (CTRL+SHIFT+8) you can choose from a number of JSTL snippets, provided by NetBeans and specific to databases.

index.jsp

To display the form contents dynamically in index.jsp, we must be able to get the names from the Subject table.

In the Palette window, place your mouse cursor over DB Report. This creates an SQL query by using the <sql:query> tag and then loops through the result set from the query, outputting the data, using the <c:forEach> tag.

Find the declaration on line 7 that reads %@page ... % and then go back to the DB item in Palette; double-click on it and a dialog box will open. Input these details:

- Variable Name: subjects
- Scope: page
- Data Source: jdbc/IFPWAFCAD
- Query Statement: SELECT subject_id, name FROM Subject

Click on OK and you will see the code below generated inside the index.jsp file:

```
<%@taglib prefix="c" uri="http://java.sun.com/jsp/jstl/core"%>

<%@taglib prefix="sql" uri="http://java.sun.com/jsp/jstl/sql"%>

<%--

   Document   : index

   Author     : nbuser
```

```
--%>


<sql:query var="subjects" dataSource="jdbc/IFPWAFCAD">
  SELECT subject_id, name FROM Subject
</sql:query>


<table border="1">
  <!-- column headers -->
  <tr>
  <c:forEach var="columnName" items="${subjects.columnNames}">
    <th><c:out value="${columnName}"/></th>
  </c:forEach>
</tr>
<!-- column data -->
<c:forEach var="row" items="${subjects.rowsByIndex}">
  <tr>
  <c:forEach var="column" items="${row}">
    <td><c:out value="${column}"/></td>
  </c:forEach>
  </tr>
</c:forEach>
</table>


<%@page contentType="text/html" pageEncoding="UTF-8"%>
<!DOCTYPE HTML PUBLIC "-//W3C//DTD HTML 4.01 Transitional//EN"
"http://www.w3.org/TR/html4/loose.dtd">
```

Note that the taglib directives required by the JSTL tags in <sql:query> and in <c:forEach>, the generated content, are automatically added by the IDE. A taglib directive is used for declaring that custom tags should be used by the JSP page, to name the defining library and to specify what the tag prefix is.

Go to the Project window, right click on the node for the project and click on Run. The project is deployed to the server and the welcome page gets opened in the browser.

The DB Report that you clicked on earlier will let you test the database connection quickly and to see the database table data that displays in the browser. This is a very useful feature for when you are building prototypes.

Next we look at the integration of the code into the drop-down list we created a while back. Have a look at the generated code, in specific the data in the column. As you can see, we have 2 <c:forEach> tags, nested one inside the other. This will result in the JSP container, which is the Glassfish server, performing loops on every row in the table. For each of the rows, the tag will loop through every column, thus displaying all the data in the whole table.

Next, we need the >c:forEach> tags to be integrated into our HTML form. Each item's value will become the subject_id while the output text is the name as listed in our database.

```
<form action="response.jsp">

  <strong>Select a subject:</strong>

  <select name="subject_id">

    <c:forEach var="row" items="${subjects.rowsByIndex}">

      <c:forEach var="column" items="${row}">

        <option value="<c:out value="${column}"/>"><c:out
value="${column}"/></option>

      </c:forEach>

    </c:forEach>

  </select>

  <input type="submit" value="submit" name="submit" />

</form>
```

There is, however, an easier way to integrate these tags into the form:

```
<form action="response.jsp">

<strong>Select a subject:</strong>
```

```
<select name="subject_id">
<c:forEach var="row" items="${subjects.rows}">
<option value="${row.subject_id}">${row.name}</option>
</c:forEach>
</select>
<input type="submit" value="submit" name="submit" />
</form>
```

Whichever way you do it, the tags will loop through every subject_id and every name value that comes from the SQL query. The tags will then insert every id and value pairs into the <option> tags, resulting in the data being inserted into the drop-down list in the form.

Find the table that the DB Report item generated and delete it:

```
<%@taglib prefix="c" uri="http://java.sun.com/jsp/jstl/core"%>
<%@taglib prefix="sql" uri="http://java.sun.com/jsp/jstl/sql"%>
<%--
   Document   : index
   Created on : Dec 22, 2009, 7:39:49 PM
   Author     : nbuser
--%>


<sql:query var="subjects" dataSource="jdbc/IFPWAFCAD">
   SELECT subject_id, name FROM Subject
</sql:query>


<table border="1">
   <!-- column headers -->
   <tr>
   <c:forEach var="columnName" items="${subjects.columnNames}">
```

```
    <th><c:out value="${columnName}"/></th>
  </c:forEach>
</tr>
<!-- column data -->
<c:forEach var="row" items="${subjects.rowsByIndex}">
  <tr>
  <c:forEach var="column" items="${row}">
    <td><c:out value="${column}"/></td>
  </c:forEach>
  </tr>
</c:forEach>
</table>
```

```
<%@page contentType="text/html" pageEncoding="UTF-8"%>
<!DOCTYPE HTML PUBLIC "-//W3C//DTD HTML 4.01 Transitional//EN"
"http://www.w3.org/TR/html4/loose.dtd">
```

Save the changes and refresh your welcome page; the drop-down list will now contain all the subject names that came from our database.

There isn't any need for redeploying the project because there is a very handy feature enabled by default on the project – compile-on-save. What this means is, whenever you make changes to a file and save them, it will be compiled automatically and deployed without you needing to do anything else. This feature can be enabled or disabled by going to the Properties window in your project and clicking on Compiling.

response.jsp

On our response page we have the counselor details that correspond to the relevant subject from the welcome page. The query we need must be able to choose the counselor record with a counselor_id matching the counselor_idfk from the subject record selected.

Put your mouse cursor over line 7 where is says %@page ... % and then go to the Palette window can double-click on the DB Query; this will open the dialog box for Insert DB Query. Add these details:

- Variable Name: counselorQuery
- Scope: page
- Data Source: jdbc/IFPWAFCAD
- Query Statement: SELECT * FROM Subject, Counselor WHERE Counselor.counselor_id = Subject.counselor_idfk AND Subject.subject_id = ? <sql:param value="${param.subject_id}"/>

Click on OK and you will see this code in the response.jsp file:

```
<%@taglib prefix="sql" uri="http://java.sun.com/jsp/jstl/sql"%>

<%--

   Document   : response

   Created on : Dec 22, 2009, 8:52:57 PM

   Author     : nbuser

--%>


<sql:query var="counselorQuery" dataSource="jdbc/IFPWAFCAD">

   SELECT * FROM Subject, Counselor

   WHERE Counselor.counselor_id = Subject.counselor_idfk

   AND Subject.subject_id = ? <sql:param value="${param.subject_id}"/>

</sql:query>


<%@page contentType="text/html" pageEncoding="UTF-8"%>

<!DOCTYPE HTML PUBLIC "-//W3C//DTD HTML 4.01 Transitional//EN"

"http://www.w3.org/TR/html4/loose.dtd">
```

Again, the IDE added our taglib directive automatically for the <sql:query> tag. Also, this time we had an >sql:param> tag right inside the query. Because the query relies heavily on the value for the subject_id that the index.jsp page submits., we can also get the value by using an expression language (EL) statement – this is a ${param.subject_id} that then gets passed to <sql.param> tag; this allows it to be used at runtime instead of the SQL question mark.

Add the code below to set a variable using a <c:set> tag. This variable will correspond to the first row of resultset that the query returned:

```
<sql:query var="counselorQuery" dataSource="jdbc/IFPWAFCAD">
  SELECT * FROM Subject, Counselor
  WHERE Counselor.counselor_id = Subject.counselor_idfk
  AND Subject.subject_id = ? <sql:param value="${param.subject_id}"/>
</sql:query>
<c:set var="counselorDetails" value="${counselorQuery.rows[0]}"/>
```

There should be just one record in the resultset but this is an important step because the response page needs to be able to access the record's values through EL statements. Remember; in the index.jsp page, we could access the resultset values just with a <c:forEach> tag; this sets variables for each row in the query, allowing you to get the values just by adding the row variable into the statement.

At the top of the file, add this ode for the JSTL core library taglib directive; this will allow the <c:set> tag to be understood:

```
<%@taglib prefix="c" uri="http://java.sun.com/jsp/jstl/core"%>
<%@taglib prefix="sql" uri="http://java.sun.com/jsp/jstl/sql"%>
```

Go to the HTML markup and put EL statements in place of the placeholder code; these statements will show the data that the counselorDetails variable holds:

```
<html>
  <head>
    <meta http-equiv="Content-Type" content="text/html; charset=UTF-8"/>
    <link rel="stylesheet" type="text/css" href="style.css">
    <title>${counselorDetails.name}</title>
  </head>


  <body>
    <table>
      <tr>
        <th colspan="2">${counselorDetails.name}</th>
      </tr>
```

```
<tr>

  <td><strong>Description: </strong></td>

  <td><span style="font-size:smaller; font-
style:italic;">${counselorDetails.description}</span></td>

</tr>

<tr>

  <td><strong>Counselor: </strong></td>

  <td><strong>${counselorDetails.first_name} ${counselorDetails.nick_name}
${counselorDetails.last_name}</strong>

    <br><span style="font-size:smaller; font-style:italic;">

    <em>member since: ${counselorDetails.member_since}</em></span></td>

</tr>

<tr>

  <td><strong>Contact Details: </strong></td>

  <td><strong>email: </strong>

    <a href="mailto:${counselorDetails.email}">${counselorDetails.email}</a>

    <br><strong>phone: </strong>${counselorDetails.telephone}</td>

</tr>

</table>

</body>

</html>
```

Running Your Application

The application is now built so run it and see what it looks like in your browser. Provided you have the Compile on Save feature enabled, you don't have to think about compiling your application again or redeploying it. That way, whenever your application is run, you can be sure that all your changes are contained in it.

From the main toolbar, click on run Project and you will see the index.jsp page in the default browser.

Click on the dropdown list in the page and choose any subject; click on Submit and you should be redirected to the response.jsp page, where you will see the details that correspond to what subject you chose.

You have learned how to use a MySQL database with Java and NetBeans to create a web application. This may have been a simple one but you can build on this to create more complex applications using the technologies you have learned about. Before we move on to jQuery, we'll go over a few problems that you may come up against.

Troubleshooting

Most of the issues that are likely to arise will be to do with communication between the Glassfish server and MySQL database server. If your application doesn't look as if it is displaying correctly, cast your eye over these possible solutions.

Are There Any Database Resources?

You can use the Service window in NetBeans (CTRL+5) to make sure that the MySQL server is properly running and that it can access MyNewDatabase. You can also check that MyNewDatabase has the right table data.

Right-click on the node for MySQL Server and click on Connect

If you do not see the MyNewDatabase connection node in Services, right-click the node and click on Connect Using; when the dialog box opens, input the correct details. You will notice that the fields in the dialog box are identical to those in the URL string you can see in the option for Show JDBC URL. If you know what the URL is, simply paste it into the filed for Show JDBC URL and all the other fields will populate automatically.

Now you need to ensure that the tables are there and that they have the right data. Expand the connection node for MyNewDatabase and look for the corresponding catalog node. Expand this node and you will see what tables are there. To see the data in a table, right-click on it and click on View data.

Are the Data Source and Connection Pool On the Server?

After the application has been deployed to the Glassfish server, the file called glassfish-resources.xml should tell the server that a JDBC resource and a connection pool need to be created. You can work out whether this has been done using the Services window.

Go to the Services window and expand the Servers node. Click on Glassfish Server and then on Resources.

Now click JDBC resources and you will see the data source called jdbc/IFPWAFCAD that glassfish-resources.xml created. Expand the node for Connection Pools and you should be able to see the correct connection pool.

Can the Glassfish Server Access the MySQL Connector/J Driver?

You need to ensure that the connector/J driver has actually been deployed to Glassfish.

Find the folder on your computer where the Glassfish server was saved and click it.

Click on Glassfish Domains>domain1>lib; in this subfolder you should see the .jar file for the MySQL connector.

Do You Have Password Protection on the Database?

The database must have a password on it otherwise the data source for the Glassfish server will not work correctly. If you are using the MySQL root account, the default one, and it has a blank password, you need to use a command prompt to set the password to nbuser.

Open a command prompt and navigate to the bin directory for your MySQL installation. Type the following at the command prompt:

```
shell> mysql -u root

mysql> UPDATE mysql.user SET Password = PASSWORD('nbuser')

   ->    WHERE User = 'root';

mysql> FLUSH PRIVILEGES;
```

Have the Connection Pool Properties Been Set Correctly?

You need to check that the connection pool works as it should for the server.

Go to the Services window and expand the node for Servers.

Find the Glassfish node and right-click on it; click on View Admin Console

If asked, input the username and the password (you can see what this is in Server manager).

Look at the left of the console and you will see a tree; click Resources>JDBC>JDBC Connection Pools and then on the node for Ifpwafcad. You will see the details of the pool in the main window

Click on Ping and, if the pool has been correctly set up, a message will appear telling you the ping was successful.

If it isn't successful, click Additional Properties and check the values are set correctly.

These are the main issues you are likely to come across. If in any doubt, simply go back over the tutorial and make sure you followed it correctly.

Using jQuery to Improve a Web Page

No doubt you have heard of jQuery and you probably already know that it is a JavaScript library. We use jQuery as an easy way of enhancing the way a web page looks and behaves. The syntax for jQuery is very concise and uses CSS selectors as variables to connect any effect with a DOM element, whether it is an id (a unique element) or a class (a set of elements). Because jQuery is written in JavaScript we can add it to any project where we can use JavaScript.

We're going to look at how to use jQuery in a project built using NetBeans. We'll use the IDE features when we work in a front-end project that involves JavaScript, CSS or HTML files. First, we'll be looking at using code completion on our functions and we'll also be making good use of the API support integrated into the IDE. We will go over some of the main concepts that surround jQuery, like the function call $(document).ready, using jQuery objects that are much like CSS selectors and chaining jQuery effects and their behaviors together. We'll also be setting up a simple document, a Contacts List, using the jQuery UI library and the jQuery Accordion widget.

You will need:

- NetBeans IDE and Java EE
- JDK
- jQuery Core Library
- jQuery Accordion Widget
- Project Resources – these are .jpg files that you will need for this.

Setting Up Your Project

You already know how to do this; we want a new NetBeans project:

In NetBeans, click on File>New Project. Click on the category for Java Web and then on Web Application

Click on Next and call your project jqproject. Make sure you choose the location to save and click on Next

Accept all the default settings that are in the wizard and click on Finish. The new project will be created and it will open in Projects; the welcome page will open in the editor.

Now we want a plain HTML file created to work with through this tutorial. The jQuery code we are going to use will not need to communicate with any back-end server so we can see our results by running the HTML file in a browser.

Right click on the node for jqproject and click on New>HTML file (CTRL+N)

Give the new file the name of index and click on Finish. You will see that the index.html file now appears in your project in the Projects window and is opened in the editor.

Now we want to see what our new welcome page looks like so go to the Projects window and right-click on the node for index.html. Click on View and you will see the page open in the browser window. You can also see it by right-clicking the file in the editor and choosing View.

In the editor, go to the <title> tags and input jQuery Test Project in between them. Now create two <style> tags in the <head>tags:

```
<html>
 <head>
  <title>jQuery Test Project</title>
  <meta http-equiv="Content-Type" content="text/html; charset=UTF-8">
  <style type="text/css">


  </style>
 </head>
 <body>
  TODO write content
 </body>
</html>
```

Next, the project must be configured so that, when we deploy and run the application, the index.html file shows as the Welcome page. To do this, in Projects window, right-click on the node for jqproject and click on Properties.

Click on Run and then go to the Relative URL field and input index.html

Click on OK and the window will close and your changes are saved.

You can now remove the index file that was originally created with the project, the index.jsp file. In the Project window, right-click on index.jsp and click on Delete. Click on Yes in the dialog box.

Adding jQuery Library

Before we can even think about using jQuery, we need the jQuery library added to our project. If you haven't got the jQuery library yet, download it from http://jquery.com/, choosing the Development or Uncompressed version to download. This allows you to see the JS code in your editor and helps when it comes to debugging.

Adding the library is simply a case of copying the folder from where it is on your computer and then pasting it into the Project window in the IDE:

In the NetBeans IDE, click on New File in the toolbar. (CTRL+N). Click on Other Category>Folder and call the folder js. Make sure it is saved in the web root of your project; click on the field for Parent Folder and type in web. Click on Finish

Find the library folder where it was saved on your computer and copy it to your Clipboard (CTRL+C).

Go to the new js folder you just created and paste in the library file. To do this, right-click on the js file and click on Paste (CTRL+V). You will see the file node display in the folder.

Go to the Editor; we want the jQuery library referenced from the index.html file so we need two <script> tags and we need the src attribute pointing to the location of the library:

```
<html>
  <head>
    <title>jQuery Test Project</title>
    <meta http-equiv="Content-Type" content="text/html; charset=UTF-8">
    <script type="text/javascript" src="js/jquery-1.4.2.js"></script>


    <style type="text/css">


    </style>
  </head>
...
```

Save your file and look at the project. You will see the jQuery library added ad that it is now referenced from the index.html file. Now we can start to put some jQuery functionality on our pages.

Getting to Grips with jQuery

The way that jQuery works is that it connects JavaScript behaviors and attributes that have been dynamically applied to certain DOM elements. We'll start by adding an element and seeing if we can affect the properties. What we want is a heading that changes from one color to another when it is clicked on.

The first thing to create is the heading. In structural terms, this is an <h1> element. Delete the TODO write content comment from your earlier code and, between the <body> tags, add this:

```
<h1>Test.</h1>
```

Now we need a CSS class to make our element turn from black to blue when we apply it. Go to the <head> tag and, in between the <style> tags, add this:

```
.blue { color: blue; }
```

Next, we need somewhere for our jQuery commands to go. Again, in the document <head> find the <script> tag that links to our jQuery library and, just after those add another set of the <script> tags:

```
<html>

  <head>

    <title>jQuery Test Project</title>

    <meta http-equiv="Content-Type" content="text/html; charset=UTF-8">

    <script type="text/javascript" src="js/jquery-1.3.2.js"></script>


    <script type="text/javascript">



    </script>



    <style type="text/css">

      .blue { color: blue; }

    </style>

  </head>

...
```

In the editor, right-click and click on Format. This will tidy your code up.

The jQuery instructions that we are going to be adding can only be executed once all the DOM elements are loaded by your browser. This is very important – jQuery behavior is connected to DOM elements and those elements must be accessible via jQuery to get the right results. jQuery will sort this for us by using the (document).read built-in function, represented by a $ and appearing after the jQuery object.

In between your new <script> tags, add the following:

```
$(document).ready(function(){


});
```

You could also use a shorter version of the above code if you wanted to:

```
$(function(){


});
```

Our jQuery instructions are in the format of JavaScript methods. You may have an optional object literal to represent the parameters array and this must go inside a set of {} curly braces within the (document).ready function. This is to ensure that it will execute only when needed, when the DOM is loaded fully.

Right now, your index.html file should look like this:

```
<!DOCTYPE HTML PUBLIC "-//W3C//DTD HTML 4.01 Transitional//EN">

<html>

<head>

<title>jQuery Test Project</title>

<meta http-equiv="Content-Type" content="text/html; charset=UTF-8">

<script type="text/javascript" src="js/jquery-1.3.2.js"></script>


<script type="text/javascript">

$(document).ready(function(){


});

</script>
```

```
<style type="text/css">

.blue { color: blue; }

</style>

</head>

<body>

<h1>Test.</h1>

</body>

</html>
```

To give you an idea of the way that jQuery syntax works, we'll do something very simple. We want jQuery instructions added to the page that will make a word, in this case "Test", change from black to blue when it is clicked on. To do this, we need jQuery to include a CSS class called .blue in the <h1> element in the DOM when it is clicked on.

Go to the (document).ready function and, inside the curly braces {}, add this code:

```
$("h1").click(function(){

        $(this).addClass("blue");

});
```

Save it and go to the editor. Right-click anywhere and click on View; the page will be loaded into the web browser. Test it out; click on "Test" and, if all is correct, you should see it change to blue.

jQuery offers another important quality; we can chain functions together so that we can create behaviors that are sequenced or more complicated. Let's have a go at this by adding a new jQuery instruction. We want to add a slow fadeout to the click(function).

In your code, go to the addClass() function and add a fadeout("slow") function. The line should look like this:

```
$(this).addClass("blue").fadeOut("slow");
```

And the entire function should look like:

```
$(document).ready(function(){

        $("h1").click(function(){

                $(this).addClass("blue").fadeOut("slow");
```

```
    });
});
```

Refresh the page in the browser and click the Test button. The word will turn to blue and will then slowly fade out, gradually disappearing off the page.

Code Completion and API Support in NetBeans

When you type anything in the NetBeans editor, you can press on CTRL+SPACE to invoke the code completion feature. The IDE will provide you with suggestions based on what you type in and you will also get an API documentation defining the items on the list, giving you examples in the form of code snippets and showing you support for the target browser.

The target browser can be specified for the API documentation and code completion very easily; simply open the JavaScript Options window in the IDE; click on Tools>Options and then click Miscellaneous and JavaScript.

Add the jQuery Accordion Widget

We already came up with a simple test that makes use of JavaScript behaviors from the jQuery library. Now we can move on to something a little more complex by looking at a real-world example. We'll set up a contact list for employees making use of HTML markup and then we will add the Accordion Widget to our list.

The widget is included in the jQuery UI library which is built on the core jQuery library. The UI library gives us a modular approach to enabling the interactions, effects and widgets on our page. File sizes can be kept to a minimum and we can select only those components that we require from the jQuery download interface, which can be found at http://jqueryui.com/download.

If you haven't downloaded the widget yet, go ahead and do so. When you select this widget, you will see that both Widget Factory and UI Core Library also get selected automatically. Also, you should see that the UI Lightness theme has also been automatically selected and will be downloaded. This is the theme that will be applied to the contact list we are going to build.

Go to your code and, where it says <h1>Test.</h1>, replace it with this code:

```
<div id="infolist">


  <h3><a href="#">Mary Adams</a></h3>

  <div>

    <img src="pix/maryadams.jpg" alt="Mary Adams">

    <ul>
```

```
        <li><h4>Vice President</h4></li>
        <li><b>phone:</b> x8234</li>
        <li><b>office:</b> 102 Bldg 1</li>
        <li><b>email:</b> m.adams@company.com</li>
    </ul>
    <br clear="all">
</div>

<h3><a href="#">John Matthews</a></h3>
<div>
    <img src="pix/johnmatthews.jpg" alt="John Matthews">
    <ul>
        <li><h4>Middle Manager</h4></li>
        <li><b>phone:</b> x3082</li>
        <li><b>office:</b> 307 Bldg 1</li>
        <li><b>email:</b> j.matthews@company.com</li>
    </ul>
    <br clear="all">
</div>

<h3><a href="#">Sam Jackson</a></h3>
<div>
    <img src="pix/samjackson.jpg" alt="Sam Jackson">
    <ul>
        <li><h4>Deputy Assistant</h4></li>
        <li><b>phone:</b> x3494</li>
```

```
      <li><b>office:</b> 457 Bldg 2</li>
      <li><b>email:</b> s.jackson@company.com</li>
    </ul>
    <br clear="all">
  </div>


  <h3><a href="#">Jennifer Brooks</a></h3>
  <div>
    <img src="pix/jeniferapplethwaite.jpg" alt="Jenifer Applethwaite">
    <ul>
      <li><h4>Senior Technician</h4></li>
      <li><b>phone:</b> x9430</li>
      <li><b>office:</b> 327 Bldg 2</li>
      <li><b>email:</b> j.brooks@company.com</li>
    </ul>
    <br clear="all">
  </div>
</div>
```

Note that the closing <div> element has an id attribute with infolist as its value. Inside the <div> element, we have 4 <h3> tag sets and <div> tags containing images and lists that have not been put in order.

We want the following code added to our markup. Find the .blue style rule in your code, delete it and add these rules instead:

```
<style type="text/css">
  ul {list-style-type: none}
  img {padding-right: 20px; float:left}
```

#infolist {width:500px}

</style>

When you are typing in the <style> tags, use the CSS code completion feature to help you.

Save your file.

Next we want the JPG portrait images that we referenced in this code added to the project.

Go to the resources file you downloaded at the start and copy the whole directory to the Project folder. Make sure it goes on the same level in the folder as index.html. Give it a minute and NetBeans should update the Project window showing the new, manually added directory in the project.

Go back to your browser and refresh it

There are several issues that we need to look at with this document. First, quickly scanning the list to find a specific person is not very easy. You need to scroll through the page and look at an awful lot of info that is likely not of any interest to you. If you had just 4 or 5 contacts in the list, it wouldn't be so bad but if you have 20, 30 or more, then it gets very difficult.

Second, the document looks far too plain and uninteresting and won't blend in aesthetic terms with most of the website designs, especially those that are quite strong on graphics. We can fix both these issues with the accordion widget and the default theme in the jQuery UI.

Go to where the accordion widget was downloaded on your computer and open it. Inside the folder you will see one called development-bundle. In this, click on the ui folder to expand it and find these 3 scripts:

- jquery.ui.core.js
- jquery.ui.widget.js
- jquery.ui.accordion.js

When you use a development version of any toolkit script, you will find that they have not been minimized. This means that the human eye can read them in an editor, making life so much easier for developers.

Use CTRL+C to copy all 3 scripts and go back to the NetBeans IDE. Right-click on the js folder we created at the start and paste the scripts in by clicking on Paste.

It is worth noting that, in development-bundle>ui, you will also see a file with the name of jquery-ui. All 3 scripts are combined in here so you could copy and paste this instead – it's your choice.

We now want these referenced in the index.html page and we do that by adding 3 <script> tags, each linking to a file. You can put these directly after the <script> tag that references the jQuery library; use your existing tags as models for these 3.

Remove the test code from inside (document).ready as we don't need it anymore.

Your <head> tags should now look like:

```
<head>
   <title>jQuery Test Project</title>
   <meta http-equiv="Content-Type" content="text/html; charset=UTF-8">


   <script type="text/javascript" src="js/jquery-1.4.2.js"></script>
   <script type="text/javascript" src="js/jquery.ui.core.js"></script>
   <script type="text/javascript" src="js/jquery.ui.widget.js"></script>
   <script type="text/javascript" src="js/jquery.ui.accordion.js"></script>


   <script type="text/javascript">
      $(document).ready(function(){


      });
   </script>
</head>
```

Making the list we have, the static and style-less list, take the accordion behavior, all we need is 1 line of code. Go to the (document).ready function where you deleted the test code and input this instead:

```
$(document).ready(function(){
   $("#infolist").accordion({
      autoHeight: false
   });
});
```

#infolist is just a CSS selector that has been connected to a DOM element with an id attribute that has a value of infolist. Basically, this is our list of contacts. The connection is made using the normal dot notation in JavaScript and it connects to the jQuery instruction that displays the element using the accordant() method.

Note that auto height has been specified as false. This stops the widget from using the highest part of the content in the markup to set each panel height.

Save your file, return to the web browser and refresh the page. Click on any name apart from the top one, and you will see the accordion effect. The widget takes cared of handling the DOM and any response needed to mouse clicks from a user.

jQuery Default Theme

We now have the project behaving as we want it to but it still looks somewhat plain and it isn't all that well organized in appearance. We can change this by adding the UI Lightness theme that comes with jQuery as default.

Find where the accordion widget was saved on your computer and look in the folder. Expand development_bundle and click on Themes>ui-lightness.

Use CTRL+C to copy the css file in ui-lightness, along with the file that has all the images needed for correct rendering of the theme.

Go to the IDE, find the project node and right-click on it. Click on New>Folder to create a new folder. Call the folder css and add to the same directory that index.html resides in. Make sure it goes into the web root of the project – click the Parent Folder filed and input web.

Paste your 2 files into the folder by right-clicking the folder and clicking Paste.

We now need the css file referenced from the index.html web page so open the page, go the <head> tag and add this link in:

<link rel="stylesheet" href="css/jquery-ui-1.8.1.custom.css" type="text/css">

Save your file, go back to the web browser and refresh it. The list should now be shown with the default Lightness theme, looking much better than it did before.

That concludes our tutorial on using jQuery to brighten up the way your web pages look. We looked at adding the jQuery library to a project, and using basic jQuery syntax to write some instructions. We also looked at the way jQuery will interact with DOM (the document object model) by using variables that are like CSS selectors, changing how the page elements looks and behave. Lastly, we also took a brief look at what the UI library offers and how to use the accordion widget and default style theme. With all these, you can see how jQuery helps to create web pages that are dynamic, improving usability and appearance.

This also concludes our look at web development using Java. It is easier than it seems, especially when you use NetBeans as much of the hard work is taken away and done for you. Next, we are going to look at Java GUI programming.

Chapter 4: Java GUI Programming

Up to now, we have looked at the basics of Java programming, including constructs like data types, arrays, loops, methods and variables and we looked at the Java data structures and algorithms. In the last part we looked at web development in Java, with a practical chapter that gave you a good idea on how to build web apps. Later, we'll be looking at OOP, or object-oriented programming but, for now, it's time to look at GUI programming.

We will start by looking at ways to reuse the Java graphics classes, found in the Java Development Kit, to write your own GUI, or graphical user interface, applications. It really isn't worth even trying to build your own graphics classes; it is nigh on impossible and you may as well just use what has already been built for you. These classes have been developed by experts in Java programming and are incredibly complex, with loads of advanced patterns in them. Reusing them is simple by comparison, so that is what we will do.

Currently, there are three sets of APIs for Java graphics programming:

- AWT – Abstract Windowing Toolkit
- Swing
- JavaFX

The AWT API first came in with JDK 1.0 and most of the components are now obsolete; the newer Swing components should replace these.

The Swing API is far more complex, a full set of graphics libraries that are used for enhancing AWT. It was introduced as a part of the JFC – Java Foundation Classes – that followed JDK 1.1. The JFC is made up of Swing, Accessibility, Java2d, Pluggable Look-and-Feel Support APIs and Internationalization and, since JDK 1.2, it has been fully integrated into Java.

JavaFX, integrated with JDK 8, is designed to replace Swing.

Other than those three APIs from the JDK, there are other graphical APIS, provided by other vendors, that will work with Java, including:

- SWT – Standard Widget Toolkit for Eclipse
- GWT – Google Web Toolkit, used for Android
- Java Bindings for Open GL (JOGL), a 3D graphics API
- Java 3D

GUI Programming with AWT

To give you a full picture of the Java Graphics, we'll start with AWT and then move onto Swing.

AWT Packages

AWT is massive, with 12 packages containing 370 classes. Swing is bigger, 18 classes containing 737 classes. Luckily, we only really need two of these – java.awt and java.awt.event.

Inside java.awt, you will find the core graphics classes for AWT:

- The GUI component classes, like Label, TextField, Button, etc.
- The GUI container classes, like Panel, Frame, etc.
- Layout Managers, like GridLayout, BorderLayout, FlowLayout, etc.
- Custom graphics classes, like Font, Color, Graphics, etc.
- Event handling is supported by java.awt.event and includes:
- Event classes, like MouseEvent, WindowEvent, KeyEvent, ActionEvent, etc.
- Event Listener interfaces, like MouseListener, KeyListener, WindowListener, MouseMotionListener, etc.
- Event Listener Adaptor classes, like KeyAdaptor, MouseAdaptor, WindowAdaptor, etc.

In short, AWT provides an interface that is independent of any device or platform for the development of graphical programs that will run on any platforms, including Unix, Windows and Mac OS X.

AWT Containers and Components

GUIs have two different types of elements:

- Components – these are basic GUI components, like TextField, Label and Button
- Containers – including Panel or Frame, these are used for holding the components in a specified layout, like GridLayout or FlowLayout. Containers may also have sub-containers.

Let's say that we have three containers – two Panels and one Frame. The Frame is a top-level container and it contains a title bar, which has a title, an icon and buttons for Maximize, Minimize, and Close. Frame may also contain a menu bar (optional) and the display area for the content. The Panel is a rectangle shaped area that is used for grouping together related components in a specific layout.

So, we have a top-level Frame that contains two Panels. We have five components:

- Label – provides the description
- TextField – where users can input text
- Buttons – three of, used for triggering specified actions that have been programmed in.

In any GUI program, components must be stored in containers and it is down to the programmer to identify that container. Each container will have an add() method. Let's assume we have a container called c. The container can invoke, for example c.add(aComponent) so it can add aComponent inside itself. For example:

Panel pnl = new Panel();   // Panel is a container

Button btn = new Button("Press"); // Button is a component

pnl.add(btn);   // The Panel container will add a Button component

We also know GUI components by other names:

Controls, for example Microsoft ActiveX Control

Widgets, for example SWT from Eclipse, or GWT

And these allow the user to control or have some kind of interaction with the application.

AWT Container Classes

Every GUI program will have one top-level container and the three that are used the most commonly in AWT are Frame, Applet and Dialog.

The Frame is the main window for the application and it will contain the title bar with an icon, a title and the three buttons you see in the top corner of the page – minimize, maximize, close. It will also have the area for displaying the content and, optionally, a menu bar. When we write GUI programs, we start by using a subclass that extends from java.awt; this is done so that the main window may be inherited, like this:

import java.awt.Frame; // Using Frame class in package java.awt

// GUI programs are written as subclasses of Frame - the top-level container

// The subclass will inherit all the properties from Frame, e.g., title, icon, buttons, content-pane

public class MyGUIProgram extends Frame {

// private variables

......

// Constructor to setup the GUI components

public MyGUIProgram() { ...... }

```
  // methods
  ......
  ......

  // The entry main() method
  public static void main(String[] args) {
    // The constructor is invoked to set the GUI up by allocating an instance
    new MyGUIProgram();
  }
}
```

AWT Dialogs are popup windows that are provided for users to interact with the application. In a Dialog, we have the title bar, which contains a title, an icon and a button to close it down; there is also an area for displaying the content.

AWT Applets, found in the package called java.applet, are the top level applet containers. An applet is a small Java program that runs within a browser.

We also have two secondary containers called Panel and ScrollPane. These go inside the top level containers or inside another secondary container:

Panel is a box, rectangular in shape that is used for laying out specified components in a specified pattern

ScrollPane - this provides the automatic scrolling, horizontal, vertical or both for one child component.

AWT Component Classes

Inside AWT, you will find a large number of GUI components already made and ready to reuse. These are found inside the package called java.awt and the most commonly used are:

- TextField
- Button
- Checkbox
- Label
- CheckboxGroup – these are radio buttons

- List
- Choice

Let's look at these a little closer.

Label

The java.awt.Label is used for a string of text that is a description. Be aware that System.out.println() will NOT print to the graphics screen, only to the console. You can also use Label to provide a label for any other component that needs a text description.

Constructors for Label:

public Label(String strLabel, int alignment); // Construct a Label with the specified text String, of the text alignment

public Label(String strLabel); // Construct a Label with the specified text String

public Label(); // Construct an initially empty Label

There are three constructors in the Label class:

The first one will construct a Label object that has the specified text in the specified alignment. There are three static constants that have been defined in the class for you to use – Label.RIGHT, Label.LEFT and Label.CENTER. These make it easy to specify which alignment you want, rather than having to go through the headache of remembering arbitrary integer values.

The second one will construct a Label object with a specified string of text with a default alignment of left.

The third one will construct a Label object that will, to start with, contain an empty string. When you need to, the label text can be set through the method called setText().

Constants for Labels

public static final LEFT; // Label.LEFT

public static final RIGHT; // Label.RIGHT

public static final CENTER; // Label.CENTER

The above three constants are used to specify what alignment the text in the label will have, as you saw in the constructor above:

Public Methods

// Examples

public String getText();

public void setText(String strLabel);

public int getAlignment();

public void setAlignment(int alignment); // Label.LEFT, Label.RIGHT, Label.CENTER

The methods called getText() and setText() may be used for modifying and reading the text in the label. In the same way, the methods called getAlignment() and setAlignment() are used for the retrieval and modification of the text alignment.

Construction of Components and Addition to a Container

To create a GUI component and then add it into a container requires these three steps:

- Using an identifier, or name, the component must be declared
- Invoke the right constructor, using the new operator, to construct the component
- Identify which container, i.e. Frame or Panel, will hold the component. Once this is down, the container will be able to add the component inside itself using the aContainer.add(aComponent) method. Note; the container explicitly adds the component into itself. The component cannot add itself into the container.

Here's an example:

Label lblInput; // Declare an Label instance called lblInput

lblInput = new Label("Enter ID"); // Construct by invoking a constructor via the new operator

add(lblInput); // this.add(lblInput) - "this" is typically a subclass of Frame

lblInput.setText("Enter password"); // Modify the Label's text string

lblInput.getText(); // Retrieve the Label's text string

Anonymous Instances

Labels may be created without having to specify identifiers first and these are called anonymous instances. In this case, the Java compiler assigns the allocated object with an anonymous identifier. However, the anonymous instances cannot be referenced in your program. This is okay as far as Label instances go, though, as you won't often have the need to reference Labels once they have been constructed.

Here's an example:

// Allocate an anonymous Label instance.

// "this" container adds the instance.

// You can't reference any anonymous instance to carry out any further operations.

add(new Label("Enter Name: ", Label.RIGHT));

// Same as

Label xxx = new Label("Enter Name: ", Label.RIGHT)); // xxx assigned by compiler

add(xxx);

Button

The java.awt.Button GUI component will trigger off a specific action that has been programmed to happen when a button is clicked.

Constructors for Buttons

public Button(String btnLabel);

// Construct a Button with the specified label

public Button();

// Construct a Button with an empty label

There are two constructors in the Button class; the first one is used for creating a Button object that has the specified label over the top of the button and the second one is used for creating a Button object that doesn't have any label.

Public Methods

public String getLabel();

// Get the label of this Button instance

public void setLabel(String btnLabel);

// Set the label of this Button instance

public void setEnable(boolean enable);

// Enable or disable this Button. Disabled Button cannot be clicked.

The methods called getLabel() and setLabel() are used for reading what the label currently says and modifying a button label, respectively.

Note – we'll be talking about Swing later but it is worth noting now that these two methods have been replaced with the JButton methods of getText() and setText().

Events

We'll talk more about event handling later but, for now, understand that, when a button is clicked, an ActionEvent will trigger off an action programmed in.

Here's an example:

Button btnColor = new Button("Red"); // Declare and allocate a Button instance called btnColor

add(btnColor); // "this" Container adds the Button

...

btnColor.setLabel("Green"); // Change the button's label

btnColor.getLabel(); // Read the button's label

...

add(Button("Blue")); // Create an anonymous Button. It CANNOT be referenced later

TextField

The java.awt.TextField is a text box with just one line, allowing users to input some text. There is one for several lines, called TextArea.

Constructors for TextField

public TextField(String initialText, int columns);

// Construct a TextField instance with the given initial text string with the number of columns.

public TextField(String initialText);

// Construct a TextField instance with the given initial text string.

public TextField(int columns);

// Construct a TextField instance with the number of columns.

Public Methods

public String getText();

// Get the current text on this TextField instance

public void setText(String strText);

// Set the display text on this TextField instance

public void setEditable(boolean editable);

// Set this TextField to editable (read/write) or non-editable (read-only)

Event

Pressing the Enter key on any TextField object will trigger an ActionEvent and a specific action that has been programmed.

Here's an example:

TextField tfInput = new TextField(30); // Declare and allocate an TextField instance called tfInput

add(tfInput);   // "this" Container adds the TextField

TextField tfResult = new TextField(); // Declare and allocate an TextField instance called tfResult

tfResult.setEditable(false) ;   // Set to read-only

add(tfResult);   // "this" Container adds the TextField

......

// Read an int from TextField "tfInput", square it, and display on "tfResult".

// getText() returns a String, need to convert to int

int number = Integer.parseInt(tfInput.getText());

*number *= number;*

// setText() requires a String, need to convert the int number to String.

tfResult.setText(number + "");

Note that the getText() and setText() both operate on strings and strings may be converted into primitive data types, such as a double or an int. This is done using the static Integer.parseInt() method or the Double.parseDouble() method. Converting strings to primitive is simply a matter of concatenating the desired primitive with a string that is empty.

AWTCounter Example

Let's do a bit of practical work. We're going to pull a few components together to form a GUI counter program. This program will have Frame as a top-level container and this will have three components – a Label called Counter, a TextField that cannot be edited (this will show the current count) and a button called Count. To start with, the TextField will have a count of 0. Every time the button is clicked, the count will increase by a value of 1:

```
import java.awt.*;       // Using AWT container and component classes

import java.awt.event.*; // Using AWT event classes and listener interfaces


//AWT programs inherit from the top-level container java.awt.Frame
public class AWTCounter extends Frame implements ActionListener {
        private Label lblCount;    // Declare a Label component
        private TextField tfCount; // Declare a TextField component
        private Button btnCount;   // Declare a Button component
        private int count = 0;     // Counter's value

        // Constructor to setup GUI components and event handlers
        public AWTCounter ()
        {
                setLayout(new FlowLayout());

                // "super" Frame, which is a Container, sets its layout to FlowLayout to
arrange
            // the components from left-to-right, and flow to next row from top-to-bottom.
                lblCount = new Label("Counter");  // construct the Label component
                add(lblCount);                    // "super" Frame container adds Label component

                tfCount = new TextField(count + "", 10); // construct the TextField component
with initial text
                tfCount.setEditable(false);       // set to read-only
                add(tfCount);                     // "super" Frame container adds TextField
component
```

```
        btnCount = new Button("Count");  // construct the Button component
        add(btnCount);                   // "super" Frame container adds Button
component

        btnCount.addActionListener(this);

        // "btnCount" is the source object that fires an ActionEvent when clicked.
     // The source add "this" instance as an ActionEvent listener, which provides
     //  an ActionEvent handler called actionPerformed().
     // Clicking "btnCount" invokes actionPerformed().
        setTitle("AWT Counter");  // "super" Frame sets its title
        setSize(250, 100);        // "super" Frame sets its initial window size

        // For inspecting the Container/Components objects
        // System.out.println(this);
        // System.out.println(lblCount);
        // System.out.println(tfCount);
        // System.out.println(btnCount);
        setVisible(true);         // "super" Frame shows

        // System.out.println(this);
        // System.out.println(lblCount);
        // System.out.println(tfCount);
        // System.out.println(btnCount);
    }

    // The entry main() method
    public static void main(String[] args) {
      // Invoke the constructor to set up the GUI, by allocating an instance
      AWTCounter app = new AWTCounter();
```

```
        // or simply "new AWTCounter();" for an anonymous instance
    }

    // ActionEvent handler - Called back upon button-click.
    @Override
    public void actionPerformed(ActionEvent evt) {
        ++count; // Increase the counter value
        // Display the counter value on the TextField tfCount
        tfCount.setText(count + ""); // Convert int to String
    }
}
```

Exiting out of this program requires you to press CTRL+C on your CMD console to close the CMD-shell. This can also be done, if you are using Eclipse, by clicking the Close button (red button) in the Application Console. We have to do this because we haven't yet written the handler for the Close button in Frame; we'll do that later.

Breaking it Down

Lines one and two in the code are the import lines and they are required because the component classes and the AWT container are stored in the package called java.awt. The events and the event listener interfaces, on the other hand, are stored in the package called java.awt.event.

All GUI programs require a top-level container and this is sometimes written as a Frame subclass, as you can see in the fifth line of the code. Basically, the AWTCounter class is a Frame and it will inherit all of Frame's behaviors and attributes, like the content pane and the title bar.

In lines 12 through 46, we are defining a constructor and this is used to set the GUI components up and to initialize them. Line 13 has the setLayout() method, which has been inherited from the Frame superclass, and this is used for setting up how the container layout will look. We have used FlowLayout which will arrange all the components in a left-to-right order and flows down to the next row and through all the others from top to bottom.

We are constructing a Label, a TextField that cannot be edited, and a Button. The add() method is invoked so that these components can be added to the container.

In lines 33 to 34, the setSize() and setTitle() methods are invoked to set the Frame's initial size and title. Then, in line 42, we invoke the setVisible() method so that display can be seen.

In line 27, we have a statement that says btnCount.addActionListener(this); this is used for setting up the mechanism for event handling, something we will talk more about later. Briefly, though, clicking the button calls the actionPerformed() method; in this method, seen in lines 57 through 63, we see the counter value incremented by 1 and the value is shown on the TextField.

In lines 51 through 55 we have the main() method in which we construct the AWTCounter instance. This constructor then gets executed so that the GUI components are initialized and the event handling mechanism is set up. The program will then wait until a user inputs some text.

Using the toString() Method to Inspect Containers and Components

This is an interesting method of inspecting GUI objects. We could add this code before setVisible() and after it:

System.out.println(this);

System.out.println(lblCount);

System.out.println(tfCount);

System.out.println(btnCount);

setVisible(true); // "super" Frame shows

System.out.println(this);

System.out.println(lblCount);

System.out.println(tfCount);

System.out.println(btnCount);

You can see the output, together with comments, below, giving you some idea of the variable that have been defined in the class:

// Before setVisible()

AWTCounter[frame0,0,0,250x100,invalid,hidden,layout=java.awt.FlowLayout,title=AWT Counter,resizable,normal]

// name (assigned by compiler) is "frame0"; top-left (x,y) at (0,0); width/height is 250x100 (via setSize());

java.awt.Label[label0,0,0,0x0,invalid,align=left,text=Counter]

// name is "Labelo"; align is "Label.LEFT" (default); text is "Counter" (assigned in constructor)

java.awt.TextField[textfieldo,o,o,oxo,invalid,text=o,selection=o-o]

// name is "Textfieldo"; text is "o" (assigned in constructor)

java.awt.Button[buttono,o,o,oxo,invalid,label=Count]

// name is "buttono"; label text is "Count" (assigned in constructor)

// Before setVisible(), all components are invalid (top-left (x,y), width/height are invalid)

// After setVisible(), all components are valid

AWTCounter[frameo,o,o,250x100,layout=java.awt.FlowLayout,title=AWT Counter,resizable,normal]

// valid and visible (not hidden)

java.awt.Label[labelo,20,41,58x23,align=left,text=Counter]

// Top-left (x,y) at (20,41) relative to the parent Frame; width/height = 58x23

java.awt.TextField[textfieldo,83,41,94x23,text=o,selection=o-o]

// Top-left (x,y) at (83,41) relative to the parent Frame; width/height = 94x23; no text selected (o-o)

java.awt.Button[buttono,182,41,47x23,label=Count]

// Top-left (x,y) at (182,41) relative to the parent Frame; width/height = 47x23

AWTAccumulator

In this example, we have the Frame as the top level container and this has four components:

- A Label called Enter an Integer
- A TextField that accepts user input
- A Label called The Accumulated Sum is
- And another TextField, that cannot be edited, to display the sum. All the components are in FlowLayout.

The number in the TextField for input will be accumulated and the outputTextField will show the sum.

import java.awt.;   // Using AWT container and component classes*

```
import java.awt.event.*; // Using AWT event classes and listener interfaces

// An AWT GUI program inherits from the top-level container java.awt.Frame
public class AWTAccumulator extends Frame implements ActionListener {
        private Label lblInput;     // Declare input Label
        private Label lblOutput;    // Declare output Label
        private TextField tfInput;  // Declare input TextField
        private TextField tfOutput; // Declare output TextField
        private int sum = 0;        // Accumulated sum, init to 0

        // Constructor to set up the GUI components and event handlers
        public AWTAccumulator() {
                setLayout(new FlowLayout());
                // "super" Frame (container) sets layout to FlowLayout, which arranges
    // the components from left-to-right, and flow to next row from top-to-bottom.

                lblInput = new Label("Enter an Integer: "); // Construct Label
                add(lblInput);          // "super" Frame container adds Label component

                tfInput = new TextField(10); // Construct TextField
                add(tfInput);           // "super" Frame adds TextField

                tfInput.addActionListener(this);
    // "tfInput" is the source object that fires an ActionEvent upon entered.
    // The source add "this" instance as an ActionEvent listener, which provides
    //  an ActionEvent handler called actionPerformed().
    // Hitting "enter" on tfInput invokes actionPerformed().

                lblOutput = new Label("The Accumulated Sum is: "); // allocate Label
                add(lblOutput);         // "super" Frame adds Label
```

```
        tfOutput = new TextField(10); // allocate TextField
        tfOutput.setEditable(false);  // read-only
        add(tfOutput);              // "super" Frame adds TextField

        setTitle("AWT Accumulator");  // "super" Frame sets title
        setSize(350, 120);  // "super" Frame sets initial window size
        setVisible(true);   // "super" Frame shows
    }

    // The entry main() method
    public static void main(String[] args) {
        // Invoke the constructor to set up the GUI, by allocating an anonymous
instance
        new AWTAccumulator();
    }

    // ActionEvent handler - Called back upon hitting "enter" key on TextField
    @Override
    public void actionPerformed(ActionEvent evt) {
        // Get the String entered into the TextField tfInput, convert to int
        int numberIn = Integer.parseInt(tfInput.getText());
        sum += numberIn;      // Accumulate numbers entered into sum
        tfInput.setText("");  // Clear input TextField
        tfOutput.setText(sum + ""); // Display sum on the output TextField
            // convert int to String
    }
}
```

Breaking it Down

AWT GUI programs extend from java.awt.Frame, which you can see in line 5 above, and this is our top-level container. In line 13, we have our constructor where four components are constructed – two java.awt.Label components and two java.awt.TextField components. The components are added by the Frame ad FlowLayout is used.

The source object is tfInput, which is the TextField, and this will trigger an ActionEvent when the Enter key is pressed. The instances are added by tfInput as an ActionEvent handler, as seen in line 24, and the listener class must then implement the interface for ActionListener and the actionPerformed() method. When the Enter key is pressed on the TextField, actionPerformed() gets invoked.

Using toString() to Insect the Container and Components

When we print toString() following the setVisible() method, we get:

AWTAccumulator[frame0,0,0,350x120,layout=java.awt.FlowLayout,title=AWT Accumulator,resizable,normal]

java.awt.Label[label0,72,41,107x23,align=left,text=Enter an Integer:]

java.awt.Label[label1,47,69,157x23,align=left,text=The Accumulated Sum is:]

java.awt.TextField[textfield0,184,41,94x23,text=,editable,selection=0-0]

java.awt.TextField[textfield1,209,69,94x23,text=,selection=0-0]

AWT Event Handling

The programming model adopted by Java for event handling is the event-driven model, sometimes called event delegation. In this programming model, event-handling code gets executed when a specified event is triggered by a specific user input, like pressing Enter or clicking on a mouse button, for example.

Call Back Methods

In the examples shown previously, we used a method called actionPerformed() and this is a callback method. What that means is that the actionPerformed() method is never explicitly invoked on your program. Instead, the graphics subsystem calls it back under specific circumstances as a response to specific user actions.

Source, Listener and Event Objects

The event handling classes for AWT are stored in a package called java.awt.event. To handle an event, three object types are required. A source object – this may be a TextField or a Button, an object that the user can interact with. When the source object is triggered, an event object is created; this will capture whatever action was performed. The event object is then messaged to every listener object that is registered and the correct listener event handler method is called back to give the response. In other words, when a source is triggered, an event is sent to all the associated listeners and the right event handler is invoked.

For a listener to express any interest in the event for a source, it has to be registered with that source. This means that the listener will subscribe to the event and the source will publish the event to every subscriber when it is activated. This is called the observable-observer or subscribe-publish design pattern:

The listener is registered to the source object for a specific event type

When the source is triggered, the event will happen, i.e. a Button click starts an ActionEvent, a mouse button click starts a MouseEvent, clicking a key starts a KeyEvent, and so on

So, how do the listener and the source understand one another? The answer to that is through an interface agreed on between the two. Let's say that a source can kick off an event that we'll call XxxEvent, a MouseEvent for example. That involves a number of operational modes, such as mouse-pressed, mouse-released, mouse-exited, mouse-entered, etc.

The first thing we do is declare the interface called XxxListener, in this example, MouseListener. That interface will contain the names of all the handler methods, for example with the MouseListener, there are five operational modes that go with the declared interface:

// A MouseListener interface, this declares the signature of the handlers

// for the various operational modes.

public interface MouseListener {

public void mousePressed(MouseEvent evt); // Called back upon mouse-button pressed

public void mouseReleased(MouseEvent evt); // Called back upon mouse-button released

public void mouseClicked(MouseEvent evt); // Called back upon mouse-button clicked (pressed and released)

public void mouseEntered(MouseEvent evt); // Called back when mouse pointer entered the component

public void mouseExited(MouseEvent evt); // Called back when mouse pointer exited the component

}

Next, all of the XxxEvent listeners will need to implement that XxxListener interface. That means that each of the listeners needs to provide an implementation or a programmed response to every abstract method declared in that interface. This way, we get the right response from the listener. For example:

// An example of MouseListener, which provides implementation to the event handler methods

```
class MyMouseListener implement MouseListener {
  @Override
  public void mousePressed(MouseEvent e) {
    System.out.println("Mouse-button pressed!");
  }

  @Override
  public void mouseReleased(MouseEvent e) {
    System.out.println("Mouse-button released!");
  }

  @Override
  public void mouseClicked(MouseEvent e) {
    System.out.println("Mouse-button clicked (pressed and released)!");
  }

  @Override
  public void mouseEntered(MouseEvent e) {
    System.out.println("Mouse-pointer entered the source component!");
  }

  @Override
  public void mouseExited(MouseEvent e) {
    System.out.println("Mouse exited-pointer the source component!");
  }
}
```

Next, a list of the XxxEvent listener objects must be maintained in the source and two methods defined – addXxxListener() and removeXxxListener. These will, respectively, add and remove a listener to or from the list. The method signatures are:

public void addXxxListener(XxxListener lis);

public void removeXxxListener(XxxListener lis);

Note; addXxxListener() will take just one parameter and that will be an XxxListener object. That means the only objects it can add are those of the XxxListener type and sub-type. Because XxxListener is an interface, there is no way to create an instance of it but, instead a subclass instance can be created to implement that interface.

To summarize, the source is identified, along with the listener object and the event-listener interface. The listener then implements that interface and the source object will register the listener object using the addXxxListener() method.

The user will trigger the source and an XxxEvent object is created; this will capture all the information needed about the activation. Lastly, the source will invoke the right handler for each of the listeners in the list and programmed response will be triggered.

Examples

AWTCounter – ActionListener Interface and ActionEvent

When a user clicks on a Button or presses the Enter key on a TextField, an ActionEvent signal is sent to all the related ActionEvent Listeners. These listeners will them implement the ActionListener Interface and this, in turn declares a single abstract method which is called actionPerformed(). You can see this below:

public interface ActionListener {

public void actionPerformed(ActionEvent evt);

// Called back on button-click (on Button), enter key pressed (on TextField)

}

The steps for the event-handling are:

btnCount() is identified as the source object

An ActionEvent is sent to all related ActionEvent listeners when a Button is clicked

The listener implements the ActionListener interface and overrides the method called actionPerformed() to get the correct response. For the sake of simplicity, we have used an object called "this" (an AWTCounter) as the ActionEvent listener. As such, the "this" class must implement the interface and provide the response that actionPerformed() is programmed to provide:

```
public class AWTCounter extends Frame implements ActionListener {

   // "this" is the ActionEvent listener, as such, it must

   // implement ActionListener interface

  ......


  // Implementing ActionListener interface requires this class to provide implementation

  // to the abstract method actionPerformed() declared in the interface.

  @Override

  public void actionPerformed(ActionEvent evt) {

    // Programmed response upon activation

    // Increment the count value and display on the TextField

    ++count;

    tfCount.setText(count + "");

  }

}
```

The method called addActionListener() is used by the source object to register the listener; in the above example, btnCount(Button) adds the object called "this" as a listener, like this:

```
btnCount.addActionListener(this);
```

Note; addActionListener() will take one argument and that will be of ActionListener type. The object, "this", which is implementing the addActionListener which is, in turn a subclass of ActionListener, gets passed up to the method called addActionListener().

When a button is clicked, btnCount will create the ActionEvent object and the actionPerformed() method for all the related listeners is called back by the ActionEvent object:

```
ActionEvent evt = new ActionEvent( ...... );

listener.actionPerformed(evt);   // for all its listener(s)
```

AWTAccumulator – ActionEvent and ActionListener Interface

In the example from before:

The source object is identified as tfInput(TextField)

When the Enter button is pressed on the TextField an ActionEvent is sent to all the related listener

"this" is chosen as the ActionEvent listener

The listener is registered by tfInput(TextField) using tfInput.addActionListener(this)

The ActionEvent listener implements the interface and overrides the method called actionPerformed() to provide the correct response when activated.

WindowEvent and WindowListener Interface

When a window, for example a Frame, is opened or closed, activated or deactivated, using the buttons in the top corner of the window, a WindowEvent is sent to all the related listeners. The WindowEvent source is always a top-level container, like a Frame.

WindowEvent listeners implement the WindowListener interface and this will declare no less than seven abstract event-handling methods. Among those, the most common one is the windowClosing() method, called back when the button is clicked to close a window:

public void windowClosing(WindowEvent evt)

// Called back when the user attempts to close the window by clicking the window close button.

// This is the most commonly used handler.

public void windowOpened(WindowEvent evt)

// Called back the first time a window is made visible.

public void windowClosed(WindowEvent evt)

// Called back when a window has been closed as the result of calling dispose on the window.

public void windowActivated(WindowEvent evt)

// Called back when the Window is set to be the active Window.

public void windowDeactivated(WindowEvent evt)

// Called back when a Window is no longer the active Window.

public void windowIconified(WindowEvent evt)

// Called back when a window is changed from a normal to a minimized state.

public void windowDeiconified(WindowEvent evt)

// Called back when a window is changed from a minimized to a normal state.

In the next program you can see that support has been added to the first AWTCounter example for a close window button:

```
import java.awt.*;        // Using AWT containers and components
import java.awt.event.*; // Using AWT events classes and listener interfaces

// An AWT GUI program inherits the top-level container java.awt.Frame
public class WindowEventDemo extends Frame
        implements ActionListener, WindowListener {
        // This class acts as listener for ActionEvent and WindowEvent
        // A Java class can extend only one superclass, but it can implement multiple
interfaces.

        private TextField tfCount; // Declare a TextField component
        private Button btnCount;   // Declare a Button component
        private int count = 0;     // Counter's value

        // Constructor to setup the GUI components and event handlers
        public WindowEventDemo() {
                setLayout(new FlowLayout()); // "super" Frame sets to FlowLayout

                add(new Label("Counter"));  // "super" Frame adds an anonymous Label

                tfCount = new TextField("0", 10); // Construct the TextField
                tfCount.setEditable(false);     // read-only
                add(tfCount);                   // "super" Frame adds TextField
```

```
            btnCount = new Button("Count");  // Construct the Button
            add(btnCount);                 // "super" Frame adds Button

            btnCount.addActionListener(this);
   // btnCount (source object) fires ActionEvent upon clicking
   // btnCount adds "this" object as an ActionEvent listener

            addWindowListener(this);
   // "super" Frame (source object) fires WindowEvent.
   // "super" Frame adds "this" object as a WindowEvent listener.

            setTitle("WindowEvent Demo"); // "super" Frame sets title
            setSize(250, 100);         // "super" Frame sets initial size
            setVisible(true);          // "super" Frame shows
      }

// The entry main() method
public static void main(String[] args) {
        new WindowEventDemo();  // Let the construct do the job
}

/* ActionEvent handler */
@Override
public void actionPerformed(ActionEvent evt) {
        ++count;
        tfCount.setText(count + "");
}

/* WindowEvent handlers */
```

```
  // Called back upon clicking close-window button
  @Override
  public void windowClosing(WindowEvent evt) {
         System.exit(0);  // Terminate the program
  }

  // Not Used, BUT need to provide an empty body to compile.
  @Override public void windowOpened(WindowEvent evt) { }
  @Override public void windowClosed(WindowEvent evt) { }
  // For Debugging
  @Override public void windowIconified(WindowEvent evt) {
System.out.println("Window Iconified"); }
  @Override public void windowDeiconified(WindowEvent evt) {
System.out.println("Window Deiconified"); }
  @Override public void windowActivated(WindowEvent evt) {
System.out.println("Window Activated"); }
  @Override public void windowDeactivated(WindowEvent evt) {
System.out.println("Window Deactivated"); }
}
```

What we are doing is modifying our first AWTCounter example so that it will handle a WindowEvent. Remember; when you press the close window button on AWTCounter it won't do anything as handling was not built in for the windowClosing() method WindowEvent. We added the handling codes for that in this new example.

The steps are:

The super Frame is identified as the source object

The WindowEvent is sent by the Frame to all related WindowEvent listeners

"this" is chosen as the WindowEvent object

"this" is registered as the WindowEvent listener to the Frame using the addWindowListener(this) method

The WindowListener interface must be implemented by the WindowEvent listener and the seven abstract methods are declared. Those methods are:

windowOpened()

windowClosed()

windowClosing()

windowActivated()

windowDeactivated()

windowIconified()

windowDeiconified()

The windowClosing() handler is overridden so the program will exit when System.exit(0) is triggered; the rest of the handlers are ignored but they are needed in empty body format for the code to be compiled.

MouseEvent and MouseListener Interface

When a mouse button is pressed, clicked or released at the source object, or the mouse pointer is positioned at (enter) and away (exit) from that object, a MouseEvent is sent. MouseEvent listeners will implement the interface and this will declare the five abstract methods you see below:

public void mouseClicked(MouseEvent evt)

// Called back when the mouse button has been clicked (pressed followed by released) on the source.

public void mousePressed(MouseEvent evt)

public void mouseReleased(MouseEvent evt)

// Called back when a mouse-button has been pressed/released on the source.

// A mouse-click invokes mousePressed(), mouseReleased() and mouseClicked().

public void mouseEntered(MouseEvent evt)

public void mouseExited(MouseEvent evt)

// Called back when the mouse-pointer has entered/exited the source.

The code is:

import java.awt.;*

import java.awt.event.;*

```
public class MouseEventDemo extends Frame implements MouseListener {
    private TextField tfMouseX; // to display mouse-click-x
    private TextField tfMouseY; // to display mouse-click-y

    // Constructor - Setup the UI components and event handlers
    public MouseEventDemo() {
        setLayout(new FlowLayout()); // "super" frame sets its layout to FlowLayout

        // Label (anonymous)
        add(new Label("X-Click: ")); // "super" frame adds Label component

        // TextField
        tfMouseX = new TextField(10); // 10 columns
        tfMouseX.setEditable(false);  // read-only
        add(tfMouseX);                // "super" frame adds TextField component

        // Label (anonymous)
        add(new Label("Y-Click: ")); // "super" frame adds Label component

        // TextField
        tfMouseY = new TextField(10);
        tfMouseY.setEditable(false);  // read-only
        add(tfMouseY);                // "super" frame adds TextField component

        addMouseListener(this);
        // "super" frame (source) fires the MouseEvent.
        // "super" frame adds "this" object as a MouseEvent listener.

        setTitle("MouseEvent Demo"); // "super" Frame sets title
        setSize(350, 100);           // "super" Frame sets initial size
```

```
        setVisible(true);        // "super" Frame shows
    }

    public static void main(String[] args) {
        new MouseEventDemo();  // Let the constructor do the job
    }

    /* MouseEvent handlers */
    // Called back upon mouse clicked
    @Override
    public void mouseClicked(MouseEvent evt) {
        tfMouseX.setText(evt.getX() + "");
        tfMouseY.setText(evt.getY() + "");
    }

    // Not used - need to provide an empty body to compile.
    @Override public void mousePressed(MouseEvent evt) { }
    @Override public void mouseReleased(MouseEvent evt) { }
    @Override public void mouseEntered(MouseEvent evt) { }
    @Override public void mouseExited(MouseEvent evt) { }
}
```

So, what we did here was set a GUI up with four components – two of these are labels and two are TextFields (non-editable)all within a Frame and arranged in the FlowLayout.

The steps are:

- The Frame is identified as the source object
- A MouseEvent is sent to all related listeners by the Frame when the mouse button is used
- "this" is chosen as the MouseEvent listener
- "this" is registered as the listener to the source object using the addMouseListener(this) method.

The listener implements the interface and this will then declare these five abstract methods:

- mouseClicked()
- mousePressed()
- mouseReleased()
- mouseEntered()
- mouseExit()

the mouseClicked() method is overridden so the x and y coordinates of the mouse click on the TextFields is shown. All the other handlers are ignored; they are there just for compilation

MouseEvent and MouseMotion Listener Interface

When the mouse pointer is moved or dragged at the source object, a MouseEvent is also sent but, the handle the move and drag, we need a MouseMotion Listener. The interface for this will declare these two abstract methods:

public void mouseDragged(MouseEvent e)

// Called back when a mouse button is pressed on the source component and then dragged.

public void mouseMoved(MouseEvent e)

// Called back when the mouse-pointer has been moved onto the source component but no buttons have been pushed.

This is the code:

```
import java.awt.*;

import java.awt.event.*;

// An AWT GUI program inherits from the top-level container java.awt.Frame
public class MouseMotionDemo extends Frame
        implements MouseListener, MouseMotionListener {
        // This class acts as MouseListener and MouseMotionListener

        // To display the (x, y) of the mouse-clicked
        private TextField tfMouseClickX;
```

```
private TextField tfMouseClickY;
// To display the (x, y) of the current mouse-pointer position
private TextField tfMousePositionX;
private TextField tfMousePositionY;

// Constructor to setup the GUI components and event handlers
public MouseMotionDemo() {
        setLayout(new FlowLayout()); // "super" frame sets to FlowLayout

        add(new Label("X-Click: "));
        tfMouseClickX = new TextField(10);
        tfMouseClickX.setEditable(false);
        add(tfMouseClickX);
        add(new Label("Y-Click: "));
        tfMouseClickY = new TextField(10);
        tfMouseClickY.setEditable(false);
        add(tfMouseClickY);

        add(new Label("X-Position: "));
        tfMousePositionX = new TextField(10);
        tfMousePositionX.setEditable(false);
        add(tfMousePositionX);
        add(new Label("Y-Position: "));
        tfMousePositionY = new TextField(10);
        tfMousePositionY.setEditable(false);
        add(tfMousePositionY);

        addMouseListener(this);
        addMouseMotionListener(this);
// "super" frame (source) fires MouseEvent.
```

```
// "super" frame adds "this" object as MouseListener and MouseMotionListener.

        setTitle("MouseMotion Demo"); // "super" Frame sets title
        setSize(400, 120);          // "super" Frame sets initial size
        setVisible(true);          // "super" Frame shows
    }

    // The entry main() method
    public static void main(String[] args) {
        new MouseMotionDemo();  // Let the constructor do the job
    }

    /** MouseListener handlers */
    // Called back when a mouse-button has been clicked
    @Override
    public void mouseClicked(MouseEvent evt) {
        tfMouseClickX.setText(evt.getX() + "");
        tfMouseClickY.setText(evt.getY() + "");
    }

    // Not Used, but need to provide an empty body for compilation
    @Override public void mousePressed(MouseEvent evt) { }
    @Override public void mouseReleased(MouseEvent evt) { }
    @Override public void mouseEntered(MouseEvent evt) { }
    @Override public void mouseExited(MouseEvent evt) { }

    /** MouseMotionEvent handlers */
    // Called back when the mouse-pointer has been moved
    @Override
    public void mouseMoved(MouseEvent evt) {
```

```
        tfMousePositionX.setText(evt.getX() + "");
        tfMousePositionY.setText(evt.getY() + "");
    }

    // Not Used, but need to provide an empty body for compilation
    @Override public void mouseDragged(MouseEvent evt) { }
}
```

We are showing both the MouseListener and the MouseMotion Listener; these are the steps:

The Frame is identified as the source; this will send the MouseEvent to the related MouseListener and the MouseMotion listener.

"this" is chosen as both the MouseListener and the MouseMotion listener

"this" is registered as the Frame listener using the addMouseListener(this) and addMouseMotionListener(this) methods

MouseMotionListener() will implement two abstract methods called mouseMoved() and mouseDragged(), both declared in the interface for the MouseMotionListener.

The mouseMoved() method is overridden so the x and y coordinates of the mouse pointer are shown and the MouseDragged() handler is ignored.

KeyEvent and KeyListener Interface

When a key is pressed, typed and released on a source object, a KeyEvent is sent. The KeyListener interface is implemented by the KeyEvent listener and will then declare these three abstract methods:

```
public void keyTyped(KeyEvent e)
  // Called back when a key has been typed (pressed and released).
public void keyPressed(KeyEvent e)
public void keyReleased(KeyEvent e)
  // Called back when a key has been pressed or released.
```

This is the code:

```
import java.awt.*;
import java.awt.event.*;
```

```
// An AWT GUI program inherits from the top-level container java.awt.Frame
public class KeyEventDemo extends Frame implements KeyListener {
        // This class acts as KeyEvent Listener

        private TextField tfInput;  // Single-line TextField to receive tfInput key
        private TextArea taDisplay; // Multi-line TextArea to taDisplay result

        // Constructor to setup the GUI components and event handlers
        public KeyEventDemo() {
                setLayout(new FlowLayout()); // "super" frame sets to FlowLayout

                add(new Label("Enter Text: "));
                tfInput = new TextField(10);
                add(tfInput);
                taDisplay = new TextArea(5, 40); // 5 rows, 40 columns
                add(taDisplay);

                tfInput.addKeyListener(this);
                // tfInput TextField (source) fires KeyEvent.
                // tfInput adds "this" object as a KeyEvent listener.

                setTitle("KeyEvent Demo"); // "super" Frame sets title
                setSize(400, 200);        // "super" Frame sets initial size
                setVisible(true);         // "super" Frame shows
        }

        // The entry main() method
        public static void main(String[] args) {
                new KeyEventDemo();  // Let the constructor do the job
```

```
        }

        /** KeyEvent handlers */
        // Called back when a key has been typed (pressed and released)
        @Override
        public void keyTyped(KeyEvent evt) {
                taDisplay.append("You have typed " + evt.getKeyChar() + "\n");
        }

        // Not Used, but need to provide an empty body for compilation
        @Override public void keyPressed(KeyEvent evt) { }
        @Override public void keyReleased(KeyEvent evt) { }
}
```

The steps are:

- The source object is identified as tfInput(TextField)
- A KeyEvent is sent by the source object when the key is pressed/released/typed to all the related KeyEvent listeners
- “this” is chosen as the KeyEvent listener
- “this” is registered as the source-listener through the input.addKeyListener(this) method
- The listener will implement the interface and this will declare these three abstract methods – keyTyped(), keyReleased(), and keyPressed().
- keyTyped() is overridden to display the key that was typed on the TextArea and the other methods are ignored.

Nested Classes

Nested classes, sometimes known as inner classes, are classes defined inside other classes. As the example below shows, MyNestedClass1 and MyNestedClass2 are defined within the outer class definition of MyOuterClass:

```
public class MyOuterClass {   // outer class defined here

  ......

  private class MyNestedClass1 { ...... }  // a nested class defined inside the outer class
```

public static class MyNestedClass2 { ...... } // a "static" nested class defined inside the outer class

......

}

Nested classes have the following properties:

- Nested classes are proper classes, i.e. they may contain member variables, constructors and member methods. Instances can be created of nested classes by using the new operator and constructor.
- Nested classes are members of the outer classes, just as any member method or variable defined within a class.
- Very important – nested classes can have access to private member methods or variables in the outer class as if they were of the same level. This is what makes the inner class so useful.
- Nested classes may have one or more of four types of access – public, private, protected or default – just as any of the member methods and variables that are defined in a class. Private inner classes can only be accessed via the outer classes that enclose them; no other class may have access. It is worth noting that, because no-one else may use private outer classes, you cannot make a top-level outer class private.
- Nested classes may also be declared as final, static or abstract, just as ordinary classes can.
- Nested classes are not subclasses of outer classes, i.e. nested classes cannot inherit any methods or variables from the outer class. Nested classes are just ordinary classes that are self-contained. However, you can use the keyword 'extends OuterClassName' within the definition of the nested class as a way of declaring it as a subclass of the relevant outer class.

Nested classes are used to:

- Control the visibilities of the member methods and variables between the inner and outer classes. Nested classes can access the outer class private members because they are defined within an outer class.
- Put a class definition code nearer to where it will be used so that the program is much easier to understand, much clearer to read.
- Manage namespace.

Named Inner Classes as Event Listeners

If you need a smaller class that relies on the outer class for private methods and variables then the nested classes are useful. They are also ideal to use for the implementation of event handlers in event-driven environments. The reason for this is that methods for event handling in listeners often need to gain access to the outer class private variables.

In our next example, , which we have modified from the AWTCounter example from earlier, we are defining a new class as the Button's ActionEvent listener – BtnCountListener. We also create one instance of the class for btnCount's ActionEvent listener. BtnCountListener must implement the interface for the ActionListener and it will override the handler called actionPerformed(). Because we are not using 'this' any longer as the ActionListener, we also delete 'implements ActionListener' from the class definition for 'this'.

We need to define BtnCountListener as an inner class because it needs access to tfCount and count, which are private variables in the outer class:

```
import java.awt.*;

import java.awt.event.*;


// AWT GUI programs inherit from the top-level container java.awt.Frame
public class AWTCounterNamedInnerClass extends Frame {
        // This class is NOT an ActionListener, so it does not implement ActionListener
interface


        // The event-handler actionPerformed() needs to access these "private" variables
        private TextField tfCount;
        private Button btnCount;
        private int count = 0;


        // Constructor to setup the GUI components and event handlers
        public AWTCounterNamedInnerClass () {
                setLayout(new FlowLayout()); // "super" Frame sets to FlowLayout
                add(new Label("Counter"));   // An anonymous instance of Label
                tfCount = new TextField("0", 10);
                tfCount.setEditable(false);  // read-only
                add(tfCount);               // "super" Frame adds tfCount


                btnCount = new Button("Count");
```

```
        add(btnCount);            // "super" Frame adds btnCount

        // Construct an anonymous instance of BtnCountListener (a named inner
class).
        // btnCount adds this instance as a ActionListener.
        btnCount.addActionListener(new BtnCountListener());

        setTitle("AWT Counter");
        setSize(250, 100);
        setVisible(true);
    }

    // The entry main method
    public static void main(String[] args) {
        new AWTCounterNamedInnerClass(); // Let the constructor do the job
    }

    /**
     * BtnCountListener is a "named inner class" used as ActionListener.
     * This inner class can access private variables of the outer class.
     */
    private class BtnCountListener implements ActionListener {
        @Override
        public void actionPerformed(ActionEvent evt) {
            ++count;
            tfCount.setText(count + "");
        }
    }
}
```

Breaking This Down

BtnCountListener is an inner class that is used as ActionListener

We construct an anonymous instance of the inner class, BtnCountListener, and btnCount, which is a source object, will add the instance as one of the listeners, like this:

```
btnCount.addActionListener(new BtnCountListener());
```

Our inner class may have access to tfCount and count, which are private variables from the outer class.

Because 'this' isn't a listener anymore, 'implements ActionListener' is removed from its class definition

Our inner class gets compiled into a class called AWTCount$BtnCountListener.class and this is formatted as OuterClassName$InnerClassName.class

Advanced Example

Take BtnCountListener class outside and then define it into an ordinary class. A reference of AWTCounter will need to be passed to the BtnCountListener constructor and this reference is then used to access count and tfCount variables – this is done by giving them public access or by using public getters:

```
// An ordinary outer class used as ActionListener for the Button

public class BtnCountListener implements ActionListener {

  AWTCounter frame;

  public BtnCountListener(AWTCounter frame) {

    this.frame = frame;

  }


  @Override

  public void actionPerformed(ActionEvent evt) {

    frame.count++;

    frame.tfCount.setText(frame.count + "");

  }

}
```

This is not an example of clean code! Using an inner class would provide a much better solution.

Anonymous Inner Classes as Event Listeners

Rather than a named inner class, this time we'll use an unnamed inner class. These are called anonymous inner classes; in this example, we have the ActionListener:

```
import java.awt.*;

import java.awt.event.*;


// AWT GUI programs inherit from the top-level container java.awt.Frame

public class AWTCounterAnonymousInnerClass extends Frame {

        // This class is NOT an ActionListener, hence, it does not implement ActionListener
interface


        // The event-handler actionPerformed() needs to access these private variables

        private TextField tfCount;

        private Button btnCount;

        private int count = 0;


        // Constructor to setup the GUI components and event handlers

        public AWTCounterAnonymousInnerClass () {

                setLayout(new FlowLayout()); // "super" Frame sets to FlowLayout

                add(new Label("Counter"));   // An anonymous instance of Label

                tfCount = new TextField("0", 10);

                tfCount.setEditable(false);  // read-only

                add(tfCount);                // "super" Frame adds tfCount


                btnCount = new Button("Count");

                add(btnCount);               // "super" Frame adds btnCount


                // Construct an anonymous instance of an anonymous class.

                // btnCount adds this instance as a ActionListener.
```

```
        btnCount.addActionListener(new ActionListener() {
            @Override
            public void actionPerformed(ActionEvent evt) {
                ++count;
                tfCount.setText(count + "");
            }
        });

        setTitle("AWT Counter");
        setSize(250, 100);
        setVisible(true);
    }

    // The entry main method
    public static void main(String[] args) {
        new AWTCounterAnonymousInnerClass(); // Let the constructor do the job
    }
}
```

Breaking This Down

Once again, we haven't used the class called 'this' as our ActionEvent Listener so 'implements ActionListener' is taken out of the 'this' class definition

The compiler generates a name for the anonymous inner class and it gets compiled to OuterClassName$n.class. n is the running number of inner classes for the outer class.

We then construct an anonymous instance of our anonymous inner class and it is passed as an argument of the method called addActionListener(), like this:

```
btnCount.addActionListener(new ActionListener() {
  @Override
  public void actionPerformed(ActionEvent evt) {
    ++count;
    tfCount.setText(count + "");
```

```
  }
});
```

This code will compile as:

```
private class N implements ActionListener { // N is a running number of the inner classes created
  @Override
  public void actionPerformed(ActionEvent evt) {
    ++count;
    tfCount.setText(count + "");
  }
}
btnCount.addActionListener(new N());


// Or
N = new N();
btnCount.addActionListener(n);
```

From JDK 8 onwards, the event handler can be written on one line with a lambda expression, like this:

```
btnCount.addActionListener(evt -> tfCount.setText(++count + ""));
```

Anonymous Inner Class Properties

Anonymous inner classes are defined within methods rather than being members of an outer class. They are local to the methods and you cannot mark them with any access modifier, like static, public, or private, like local method variables.

Anonymous inner classes always have to either implement interfaces or extend superclasses. You do not need to use the keywords implement or extends when you declare it. The anonymous inner class has to implement every abstract method in the interface or superclass.

Anonymous inner classes will always use the no-arg, default constructor out of their superclasses to create instances. If the anonymous inner class is used for implementation of interfaces, they use java.lang.object().

Anonymous inner cases are compiled into classes called OuterClassNamre$n.class – n is the running number of the inner classes inside the outer classes.

We use the following syntax to construct instances of anonymous inner classes:

```
new SuperClassName/InterfaceName() { // extends superclass or implements interface
                    // invoke the default no-arg constructor or Object[]
  // Implement abstract methods in superclass/interface
  // More methods if necessary
  ......
}
```

The instance that has been created may be used as a method argument or assigned to a variable.

Anonymous Inner Classes For Each Source

Ok, let's have a play about with our AWTCounter example. We want three buttons included – count up, count down and reset count. The listener for each of these buttons will be an anonymous inner class.

```
import java.awt.*;
import java.awt.event.*;

// AWT GUI programs inherit the top-level container java.awt.Frame
public class AWTCounter3Buttons extends Frame {
        private TextField tfCount;
        private Button btnCountUp, btnCountDown, btnReset;
        private int count = 0;

        // Constructor to set up the GUI components and event handlers
        public AWTCounter3Buttons () {
                setLayout(new FlowLayout());
```

```
add(new Label("Counter"));  // an anonymous instance of Label
tfCount = new TextField("0", 10);
tfCount.setEditable(false);  // read-only
add(tfCount);              // "super" Frame adds tfCount

btnCountUp = new Button("Count Up");
add(btnCountUp);
// Construct an anonymous instance of an anonymous inner class.
// The source Button adds the anonymous instance as ActionEvent listener
btnCountUp.addActionListener(new ActionListener() {
        @Override
        public void actionPerformed(ActionEvent evt) {
                ++count;
                tfCount.setText(count + "");
        }
});

btnCountDown = new Button("Count Down");
add(btnCountDown);
btnCountDown.addActionListener(new ActionListener() {
        @Override
        public void actionPerformed(ActionEvent evt) {
                count--;
                tfCount.setText(count + "");
        }
});

btnReset = new Button("Reset");
add(btnReset);
btnReset.addActionListener(new ActionListener() {
```

```
            @Override
            public void actionPerformed(ActionEvent evt) {
                count = 0;
                tfCount.setText("0");
            }
        });

        setTitle("AWT Counter");
        setSize(400, 100);
        setVisible(true);
    }

    // The entry main method
    public static void main(String[] args) {
        new AWTCounter3Buttons();  // Let the constructor do the job
    }
}
```

Breaking This Down

This one is simple – each Button's ActionEvent listener is an instance of an inner class, both anonymous.

Three Buttons – One Listener Instance

If we were to use one listener instance attached to all three of the Buttons, we would need to work out which of the buttons sent off the event. All three of the Buttons will be triggering just one event-handler method

The getActionCommand() for ActionEvent

In the next example, we are going to use a named inner class instance that is the same as that of the listener for all three Buttons. Our listener must work out which Button sent the event and we can do this using the getActionCommand() method of ActionEvent; this will return the label of the Button:

```
import java.awt.*;
import java.awt.event.*;
```

```
// AWT GUI programs inherit the top-level container java.awt.Frame
public class AWTCounter3Buttons1Listener extends Frame {
        private TextField tfCount;
        private Button btnCountUp, btnCountDown, btnReset;
        private int count = 0;

        // Constructor to set up the GUI components and event handlers
        public AWTCounter3Buttons1Listener () {
                setLayout(new FlowLayout());
                add(new Label("Counter"));
                tfCount = new TextField("0", 10);
                tfCount.setEditable(false);
                add(tfCount);

                // Construct Buttons
                btnCountUp = new Button("Count Up");
                add(btnCountUp);
                btnCountDown = new Button("Count Down");
                add(btnCountDown);
                btnReset = new Button("Reset");
                add(btnReset);

                // Allocate an instance of the "named" inner class BtnListener.
                BtnListener listener = new BtnListener();
                // Use the same listener instance for all the 3 Buttons.
                btnCountUp.addActionListener(listener);
                btnCountDown.addActionListener(listener);
                btnReset.addActionListener(listener);
```

```
            setTitle("AWT Counter");
            setSize(400, 100);
            setVisible(true);
      }

      // The entry main method
      public static void main(String[] args) {
            new AWTCounter3Buttons1Listener();  // Let the constructor do the job
      }

      /**
       * BtnListener is a named inner class used as ActionEvent listener for all the
Buttons.
       */
      private class BtnListener implements ActionListener {
            @Override
            public void actionPerformed(ActionEvent evt) {
                  // Need to determine which button fired the event.
                  // the getActionCommand() returns the Button's label
                  String btnLabel = evt.getActionCommand();
                  if (btnLabel.equals("Count Up")) {
                        ++count;
                  } else if (btnLabel.equals("Count Down")) {
                        --count;
                  } else {
                        count = 0;
                  }
                  tfCount.setText(count + "");
            }
      }
}
```

The getSource() of the EventObject

getActionCommand() can only be used for ActionEvent so you could use getSource(), which can be used for all event objects. We would use this for getting the reference of the source object that sent the event and a java.lang.Object will be returned. You might have to downcast it to the correct type that matches the source object. For example:

```
import java.awt.*;

import java.awt.event.*;


// AWT GUI programs inherit the top-level container java.awt.Frame
public class AWTCounter3Buttons1Listener extends Frame {
        private TextField tfCount;
        private Button btnCountUp, btnCountDown, btnReset;
        private int count = 0;

        // Constructor to set up the GUI components and event handlers
        public AWTCounter3Buttons1Listener () {
                setLayout(new FlowLayout());
                add(new Label("Counter"));
                tfCount = new TextField("0", 10);
                tfCount.setEditable(false);
                add(tfCount);

                // Construct Buttons
                btnCountUp = new Button("Count Up");
                add(btnCountUp);
                btnCountDown = new Button("Count Down");
                add(btnCountDown);
                btnReset = new Button("Reset");
                add(btnReset);

                // Allocate an instance of the "named" inner class BtnListener.
```

```
        BtnListener listener = new BtnListener();
        // Use the same listener instance for all the 3 Buttons.
        btnCountUp.addActionListener(listener);
        btnCountDown.addActionListener(listener);
        btnReset.addActionListener(listener);

        setTitle("AWT Counter");
        setSize(400, 100);
        setVisible(true);
    }

    // The entry main method
    public static void main(String[] args) {
        new AWTCounter3Buttons1Listener();  // Let the constructor do the job
    }

    /**
     * BtnListener is a named inner class used as ActionEvent listener for all the
Buttons.
     */
    private class BtnListener implements ActionListener {
        @Override
        public void actionPerformed(ActionEvent evt) {
            // Need to determine which button fired the event.
            // the getActionCommand() returns the Button's label
            String btnLabel = evt.getActionCommand();
            if (btnLabel.equals("Count Up")) {
                ++count;
            } else if (btnLabel.equals("Count Down")) {
                --count;
            } else {
```

```
                    count = 0;
                }
                tfCount.setText(count + "");
            }
        }
}
```

Adaptor Class Event Listeners

WindowAdaptor for WindowListener

A WindowEvent listener is required for the implementation of the WindowListener interface and this will declare seven abstract classes. We are really only looking at windowClosing() but the other classes will need empty bodies so that the program can be compiled. This is rather time-consuming; we could rewrite out WindowEventDemo form earlier with an inner class that implements that ActionListener, like this:

```
import java.awt.*;
import java.awt.event.*;

// AWT GUI programs inherit the top-level container java.awt.Frame
public class WindowEventDemoWithInnerClass extends Frame {
    private TextField tfCount;
    private Button btnCount;
    private int count = 0;

    // Constructor to setup the GUI components and event handlers
    public WindowEventDemoWithInnerClass () {
        setLayout(new FlowLayout());
        add(new Label("Counter"));
        tfCount = new TextField("0", 10);
        tfCount.setEditable(false);
        add(tfCount);
```

```
btnCount = new Button("Count");
add(btnCount);
btnCount.addActionListener(new ActionListener() {
        @Override
        public void actionPerformed(ActionEvent evt) {
                ++count;
                tfCount.setText(count + "");
        }
});

// Allocate an anonymous instance of an anonymous inner class
// that implements WindowListener.
// "super" Frame adds this instance as WindowEvent listener.
addWindowListener(new WindowListener() {
        @Override
        public void windowClosing(WindowEvent evt) {
                System.exit(0);  // terminate the program
        }
        // Need to provide an empty body for compilation
        @Override public void windowOpened(WindowEvent evt) { }
        @Override public void windowClosed(WindowEvent evt) { }
        @Override public void windowIconified(WindowEvent evt) { }
        @Override public void windowDeiconified(WindowEvent evt) { }
        @Override public void windowActivated(WindowEvent evt) { }
        @Override public void windowDeactivated(WindowEvent evt) { }
});

setTitle("WindowEvent Demo");
setSize(250, 100);
setVisible(true);
```

```
    }

    // The entry main method
    public static void main(String[] args) {
        new WindowEventDemoWithInnerClass();  // Let the constructor do the job
    }
}
```

The WindowAdaptor Superclass

Because of this, there is an adaptor class that we can use to make things easier. It's called WindowAdaptor and this will implement the WindowListener interface, providing us with default implementations needed for each of the abstract methods. Then, a subclass can be derived from WindowAdaptor to override the methods we want, leaving the remaining ones with the defaults For example:

```
import java.awt.*;

import java.awt.event.*;

// AWT GUI programs inherit the top-level container java.awt.Frame
public class WindowEventDemoAdapter extends Frame {
    private TextField tfCount;
    private Button btnCount;
    private int count = 0;

    // Constructor to setup the GUI components and event handlers
    public WindowEventDemoAdapter () {
        setLayout(new FlowLayout());
        add(new Label("Counter"));
        tfCount = new TextField("0", 10);
        tfCount.setEditable(false);
        add(tfCount);
```

```
        btnCount = new Button("Count");
        add(btnCount);
        btnCount.addActionListener(new ActionListener() {
            @Override
            public void actionPerformed(ActionEvent evt) {
                ++count;
                tfCount.setText(count + "");
            }
        });

        // Allocate an anonymous instance of an anonymous inner class
        // that extends WindowAdapter.
        // "super" Frame adds the instance as WindowEvent listener.
        addWindowListener(new WindowAdapter() {
            @Override
            public void windowClosing(WindowEvent evt) {
                System.exit(0);  // Terminate the program
            }
        });

        setTitle("WindowEvent Demo");
        setSize(250, 100);
        setVisible(true);
    }

    /** The entry main method */
    public static void main(String[] args) {
        new WindowEventDemoAdapter();   // Let the constructor do the job
    }
}
```

As you can see, using this adaptor makes things much easier.

Other Adaptor Classes

There are other adaptor classes, like KeyAdaptor(), MouseMotionAdaptor() MouseAdaptor(), and FocusAdaptor, all available for KeyListener, MouseMotionListener, MouseListener, and FocusListener.

ActionListener does not have an ActionAdaptor because the ActionListener interface declares just one abstract method – actionPerformed() this method must be overridden and there is no requirement for an adaptor.

Layout Managers and Panel

In a container, we have a layout manager, used for arranging the components within the container. Layout managers provide an abstraction level that helps you to map the user interface onto all of the windowing systems; this makes the layout independent of any specific platform.

In AWT, we have these layout managers, all found in the java.awt package. Swing adds more but we'll talk about those later.

setLayout() method for Container:

Containers have a setLayout() method used for setting the layout manager:

// java.awt.Container

public void setLayout(LayoutManager mgr)

To set up a Container's layout, like JPanel, JFrame, Frame or Panel, the sequence of steps is:

An instance of the layout object must be constructed, using constructor and new, for example, new FlowLayout()

Next the Container's setLayout() method must be invoked; create the layout object as the argument

The GUI components go into our Container next, with the add()method; they must be placed in the right zones or added in the right order, for example:

// Allocate a Panel (container)

Panel pnl = new Panel();

// Allocate a new Layout object. The Panel container sets to this layout.

pnl.setLayout(new FlowLayout());

```
// The Panel container adds components in the proper order.

pnl.add(new JLabel("One"));

pnl.add(new JLabel("Two"));

pnl.add(new JLabel("Three"));

......
```

getLayout() Method for Container

The current layout can be obtained through the getLayout() method of the Container:

```
Panel pnl = new Panel();

System.out.println(pnl.getLayout());

    // java.awt.FlowLayout[hgap=5,vgap=5,align=center]
```

Initial Layout of Panel

AWT's Panel, and JPanel in Swing, provide us with a constructor that we can use for setting the initial layout manager. We use this because one of the primary Panel functions is to layout the components in a specific layout pattern:

```
public void Panel(LayoutManager layout)

  // Construct a Panel in the given layout

  // By default, Panel (and JPanel) has FlowLayout


// For example, create a Panel in BorderLayout

Panel pnl = new Panel(new BorderLayout());
```

FlowLayout

In the package, java.awt.FlowLayout, all the components are arranged in the Container in a left-to-right pattern and they are always in the order that they got added through the aContainer.add(aComponent) method. When the first row has been filled, the next row starts. The appearance will depend on what the display windows width is.

Constructors

```
public FlowLayout();

public FlowLayout(int alignment);
```

public FlowLayout(int alignment, int hgap, int vgap);

// alignment: FlowLayout.LEFT (or LEADING), FlowLayout.RIGHT (or TRAILING), or FlowLayout.CENTER

// hgap, vgap: horizontal/vertical gap between the components

// By default: hgap = 5, vgap = 5, alignment = FlowLayout.CENTER

The code example of this:

```
import java.awt.*;

import java.awt.event.*;


// AWT GUI programs inherit the top-level container java.awt.Frame
public class AWTFlowLayoutDemo extends Frame {
        private Button btn1, btn2, btn3, btn4, btn5, btn6;

        // Constructor to setup GUI components and event handlers
        public AWTFlowLayoutDemo () {
                setLayout(new FlowLayout());
                // "super" Frame sets layout to FlowLayout, which arranges the components
                // from left-to-right, and flow from top-to-bottom.

                btn1 = new Button("Button 1");
                add(btn1);
                btn2 = new Button("This is Button 2");
                add(btn2);
                btn3 = new Button("3");
                add(btn3);
                btn4 = new Button("Another Button 4");
                add(btn4);
                btn5 = new Button("Button 5");
                add(btn5);
                btn6 = new Button("One More Button 6");
```

```
            add(btn6);

            setTitle("FlowLayout Demo"); // "super" Frame sets title
            setSize(280, 150);       // "super" Frame sets initial size
            setVisible(true);        // "super" Frame shows
      }

      // The entry main() method
      public static void main(String[] args) {
            new AWTFlowLayoutDemo();  // Let the constructor do the job
      }
}
```

GridLayout

In the java.awt.GridLayout package, the components are all arranged inside the Container in grid or matrix format, consisting of rows and columns. The components are added in a left-to-right, top-to-bottom pattern and this will be in the order that the aContainer.add(aComponent) method added them.

Constructors

```
public GridLayout(int rows, int columns);
public GridLayout(int rows, int columns, int hgap, int vgap);
   // By default: rows = 1, cols = 0, hgap = 0, vgap = 0
```

The code example is:

```
import java.awt.*;
import java.awt.event.*;

// AWT GUI programs inherit the top-level container java.awt.Frame
public class AWTGridLayoutDemo extends Frame {
      private Button btn1, btn2, btn3, btn4, btn5, btn6;
```

```
    // Constructor to setup GUI components and event handlers
    public AWTGridLayoutDemo () {
        setLayout(new GridLayout(3, 2, 3, 3));
        // "super" Frame sets layout to 3x2 GridLayout, horizontal and vertical gaps
of 3 pixels

        // The components are added from left-to-right, top-to-bottom
        btn1 = new Button("Button 1");
        add(btn1);
        btn2 = new Button("This is Button 2");
        add(btn2);
        btn3 = new Button("3");
        add(btn3);
        btn4 = new Button("Another Button 4");
        add(btn4);
        btn5 = new Button("Button 5");
        add(btn5);
        btn6 = new Button("One More Button 6");
        add(btn6);

        setTitle("GridLayout Demo"); // "super" Frame sets title
        setSize(280, 150);         // "super" Frame sets initial size
        setVisible(true);         // "super" Frame shows
    }

    // The entry main() method
    public static void main(String[] args) {
        new AWTGridLayoutDemo();  // Let the constructor do the job
    }
}
```

BorderLayout

In the package, java.awrt.BorderLayout, the Container is in five separate zones:

EAST

WEST

SOUTH

NORTH

CENTER

Each component is added with the aContainer.add(aComponent, zone) method, where zone will be one of the following:

BorderLayout.NORTH or PAGE_START

BorderLayout.SOUTH or PAGE_END

BorderLayout.WEST or LINE_START

Border.Layout.EAST or LINE_END

BorderLayout.CENTER

It is not necessary to have components in every zone. It is also worth remembering that you can vertically stretch the EAST and WEST components, horizontally stretch the NORTH and SOUTH components and choose horizontal or vertical stretching (or both) for CENTER so that any empty space is filled.

Constructors:

public BorderLayout();

public BorderLayout(int hgap, int vgap);

// By default hgap = 0, vgap = 0

The code example is:

```
import java.awt.*;

import java.awt.event.*;


// AWT GUI program inherits the top-level container java.awt.Frame

public class AWTBorderLayoutDemo extends Frame {
```

```
    private Button btnNorth, btnSouth, btnCenter, btnEast, btnWest;

    // Constructor to setup GUI components and event handlers
    public AWTBorderLayoutDemo () {
            setLayout(new BorderLayout(3, 3));
            // "super" Frame sets layout to BorderLayout,
   // horizontal and vertical gaps of 3 pixels

            // The components are added to the specified zone
            btnNorth = new Button("NORTH");
            add(btnNorth, BorderLayout.NORTH);
            btnSouth = new Button("SOUTH");
            add(btnSouth, BorderLayout.SOUTH);
            btnCenter = new Button("CENTER");
            add(btnCenter, BorderLayout.CENTER);
            btnEast = new Button("EAST");
            add(btnEast, BorderLayout.EAST);
            btnWest = new Button("WEST");
            add(btnWest, BorderLayout.WEST);

            setTitle("BorderLayout Demo"); // "super" Frame sets title
            setSize(280, 150);           // "super" Frame sets initial size
            setVisible(true);            // "super" Frame shows
    }

    // The entry main() method
    public static void main(String[] args) {
            new AWTBorderLayoutDemo();  // Let the constructor do the job
    }
}
```

Organizing Components Using Panels as Sub-Containers

AWT Panels are rectangular and that means they can be used as sub-containers. These are used for organizing groups of components that are related to one another in a particular layout, for example, BorderLayout or FlowLayout. A Panel is a secondary container and this is added to a top-level container, like another Panel or Frame.

Have a look at the following example, showing Frame in a BorderLayout with two Panels called panelResult (inside FlowLayout) and panelButtons (inside GridLayout. panelResult will be added into NORTH and panelButtons to CENTER.

```
import java.awt.*;

import java.awt.event.*;


// AWT GUI programs inherit the top-level container java.awt.Frame
public class AWTPanelDemo extends Frame {
    private Button[] btnNumbers;  // Array of 10 numeric Buttons
    private Button btnHash, btnStar;
    private TextField tfDisplay;

    // Constructor to setup GUI components and event handlers
    public AWTPanelDemo () {
        // Set up display panel
        Panel panelDisplay = new Panel(new FlowLayout());
        tfDisplay = new TextField("0", 20);
        panelDisplay.add(tfDisplay);

        // Set up button panel
        Panel panelButtons = new Panel(new GridLayout(4, 3));
        btnNumbers = new Button[10];  // Construct an array of 10 numeric Buttons
        btnNumbers[1] = new Button("1");  // Construct Button "1"
        panelButtons.add(btnNumbers[1]);  // The Panel adds this Button
        btnNumbers[2] = new Button("2");
        panelButtons.add(btnNumbers[2]);
```

```
        btnNumbers[3] = new Button("3");
        panelButtons.add(btnNumbers[3]);
        btnNumbers[4] = new Button("4");
        panelButtons.add(btnNumbers[4]);
        btnNumbers[5] = new Button("5");
        panelButtons.add(btnNumbers[5]);
        btnNumbers[6] = new Button("6");
        panelButtons.add(btnNumbers[6]);
        btnNumbers[7] = new Button("7");
        panelButtons.add(btnNumbers[7]);
        btnNumbers[8] = new Button("8");
        panelButtons.add(btnNumbers[8]);
        btnNumbers[9] = new Button("9");
        panelButtons.add(btnNumbers[9]);
        // You should use a loop for the above statements!!!
        btnStar = new Button("*");
        panelButtons.add(btnStar);
        btnNumbers[0] = new Button("0");
        panelButtons.add(btnNumbers[0]);
        btnHash = new Button("#");
        panelButtons.add(btnHash);

        setLayout(new BorderLayout());  // "super" Frame sets to BorderLayout
        add(panelDisplay, BorderLayout.NORTH);
        add(panelButtons, BorderLayout.CENTER);

        setTitle("BorderLayout Demo"); // "super" Frame sets title
        setSize(200, 200);           // "super" Frame sets initial size
        setVisible(true);            // "super" Frame shows
    }
```

```
    // The entry main() method
    public static void main(String[] args) {
        new AWTPanelDemo();  // Let the constructor do the job
    }
}
```

An Introduction to Swing

Swing is a part of the Java Foundation Classes (JFC), introduced over 20 years ago; JFC is now an integral part of the JDK and it consists of:

- The Swing API, used for more advanced GUI programming
- The Accessibility API, used for providing assistive technology to disabled users
- The Java 2D API, used for producing top quality 2D images and graphics
- Pluggable supports for the look and feel
- Support for Drag-and-drop between native apps and Java

Java GUI programming has one goal – to let a programmer build GUIs that look great on every platform. AWT in JDK 1.0 was pretty awkward to use and it wasn't object-oriented. With JDK 1.1, AWT brought in the event-delegation or event-driven model, which was a good deal clearer and definitely object-oriented. We also got the inner class with JDK 1.1, along with JavaBeans, which is a programming model for the programming of visual environments, much like Visual Basic.

Swing came along after JDK 1.1 and is one of the easiest sets of the JavaBeans GUI components to use and to understand. It can also be dropped into the visual programming environment as 'GU builders' and is a permanent part of Java.

Swing Features

Swing is massive. It has 18 packages and an impressive 737 classes, not to mention great depth to it. It has a huge collection of GUI components that can be reused, and the main features are:

- With the exception of a couple of classes, it is pure Java and that means it is completely portable
- Its components are lightweight in terms of the utilization of system resources, as opposed to AWT being very heavy. With AWT, each if its components have a native opaque display and are always displayed over the top of the lighter weight components. The components in AWT rely very much on the windowing subsystem of the operating system. For example, AWT buttons are tied to real buttons in the native windowing subsystem and are reliant on that subsystem to be processed and

rendered. With Swing, because the components have been written in Java, they are weighed down with the GUI consideration that subsystem imposes.

- With Swing components, you get support for the look and feel, with a choice of Java look and feel or that of the operating system. If you opt for the operating system look and feel, a Swing button will look and feel like a button from the operating system.
- Swing has support for a mouse-less operation and can be operated wholly by the keyboard
- Swing components also have support for 'tool tips'
- All Swing components a JavaBeans; they can be dragged and dropped to a design form with the help of a GUI builder and double-clicked to attach event handlers.
- Swing also uses the AWT event handling classes from the java.awt.event package. There are a few new classes in the javax.swing.event package but these are not used very often.
- The Swing application makes use of the AWT layout manager in the java.awt package, like BorderLayout and FlowLayout. Again, new managers were added to the javax.swing package, like Struts, Springs, and BoxLayout.
- Swing implements automatic repaint batching and double buffering
- In Swing, we were introduced to JInternalFrame and JLayeredPane which are used for the creation of MDI (Multiple Document Interface) applications
- Swing has support for splitter control, undo and floating toolbars, found in JToolBar.

Using the Swing API

If you kept up with the AWT programming section, especially the event-handling and container/components, moving over to Swing is going to be quite easy to do.

Swing Components:

All Swing component classes, found in the javax.swing package, are prefixed with 'J', for example, JButton, JPanel, JLabel, JTextField, JFrame, JApplet, etc.

In terms of hierarchy, there are two classes groups – Containers and Components. Containers are used to hold the Components and they can also have Containers in them because Containers are subclasses of Components.

As a general rule, you should not mix Swing and AWT components together in one program; AWT components are heavier than Swing components and will be painted over the top of the lighter weight components.

Top-Level and Secondary Containers in Swing

Like the AWT applications, Swing applications also need a top-level container and, in Swing, there are three of these:

- JFrame – used for the main window in the application and has a title, an icon, three buttons for minimize, maximize, and close, a menu bar which is optional, and a content display pane
- JDialog – used for the secondary window that pops up and has a title, one button to close it and a content display pane
- JApplet – used for the content display pane for the applet within the browser window

Like AWT, there are also secondary containers, used for grouping and laying out the relevant components.

Top-Level Container Content Pane

Unlike AWT, JComponents do not get added directly to the top-level container because they are lightweight. Instead, JComponents are to be added to the content pane inside the top-level container. Content-pane is a java.awt.Container used for grouping and laying out the components.

You could go to getContentPane() in the top-level container and add some components to it, like this:

```
public class SwingDemo extends JFrame {

  // Constructor

  public SwingDemo() {

    // Get the content-pane of this JFrame, which is a java.awt.Container

    // All operations, such as setLayout() and add() operate on the content-pane

    Container cp = getContentPane();

    cp.setLayout(new FlowLayout());

    cp.add(new JLabel("Hello, world!"));

    cp.add(new JButton("Button"));

    ......

  }

  .......

}
```

You could also set content-pane to the main panel, JPanel, that was created within the application and that holds the GUI components and this is done through setContentPane() in JFrame:

```
public class SwingDemo extends JFrame {
  // Constructor
  public SwingDemo() {
    // The "main" JPanel holds all the GUI components
    JPanel mainPanel = new JPanel(new FlowLayout());
    mainPanel.add(new JLabel("Hello, world!"));
    mainPanel.add(new JButton("Button"));

    // Set the content-pane of this JFrame to the main JPanel
    setContentPane(mainPanel);
    ......
  }
  .......
}
```

Note – if you add a component straight into a JFrame, you must add it to the content-pane, for example:

```
// Assume that "this" is a JFrame
add(new JLabel("add to JFrame directly"));
// is executed as
getContentPane().add(new JLabel("add to JFrame directly"));
```

Swing Event-Handling

Swing makes use of the AWT event-handling classes, found in java.awt.event. There are some event-handling classes in the javax.swing.event but they don't tend to be used too often.

To write an application in Swing, you must use those Swing components in javax.swing that is prefixed with 'J' for example, JFrame, JTextField, JLabel, JButton, etc. You will also need a top-level container, usually JFrame. You cannot add the JComponents to the top-level container directly; instead, we add them to the content-pane in the top-level container. A reference to that content-pane may be retrieved through the method, getContentPane(), invoked from the top-level container.

Swing applications also used the event-handling classes from AWT, like MouseEvent, MouseListener, ActionEvent, ActionListener, etc.

As you can see in the next example, we would NOT run the constructor in the Main thread; instead it is run in Event Dispatcher Thread, for safety:

```
import java.awt.*;          // Using AWT layouts

import java.awt.event.*; // Using AWT event classes and listener interfaces

import javax.swing.*;    // Using Swing components and containers


// A Swing GUI application inherits from top-level container javax.swing.JFrame

public class ...... extends JFrame {


  // Private instance variables

  // ......


  // Constructor to set up the GUI components and event handlers

  public ......() {

    // Retrieve the top-level content-pane from JFrame

    Container cp = getContentPane();


    // Content-pane sets layout

    cp.setLayout(new ....Layout());


    // Allocate the GUI components

    // .....


    // Content-pane adds components
```

```
    cp.add(....);

    // Source object adds listener
    // .....

    setDefaultCloseOperation(JFrame.EXIT_ON_CLOSE);
      // Exit the program when the close-window button clicked
    setTitle("......"); // "super" JFrame sets title
    setSize(300, 150);   // "super" JFrame sets initial size
    setVisible(true);    // "super" JFrame shows
  }

  // The entry main() method
  public static void main(String[] args) {
    // Run GUI codes in Event-Dispatching thread for thread-safety
    SwingUtilities.invokeLater(new Runnable() {
      @Override
      public void run() {
        new ......(); // Let the constructor do the job
      }
    });
  }
}
```

In the next example you will see this template explained.

SwingCounter

Let's take our AWT application from before and convert it to Swing. Compare the source files and see the changes; note how the look and feel are different between the AWT and Swing GUI components:

```
import java.awt.*;      // Using AWT layouts
import java.awt.event.*; // Using AWT event classes and listener interfaces
import javax.swing.*;    // Using Swing components and containers

// A Swing GUI application inherits from top-level container javax.swing.JFrame
public class SwingCounter extends JFrame {   // JFrame instead of Frame
        private JTextField tfCount;  // Use Swing's JTextField instead of AWT's TextField
        private JButton btnCount;    // Using Swing's JButton instead of AWT's Button
        private int count = 0;

        // Constructor to set up the GUI components and event handlers
        public SwingCounter() {
                // Retrieve the content-pane of the top-level container JFrame
                // All operations done on the content-pane
                Container cp = getContentPane();
                cp.setLayout(new FlowLayout());   // The content-pane sets its layout

                cp.add(new JLabel("Counter"));
                tfCount = new JTextField("0");
                tfCount.setEditable(false);
                cp.add(tfCount);

                btnCount = new JButton("Count");
                cp.add(btnCount);

                // Allocate an anonymous instance of an anonymous inner class that
                //  implements ActionListener as ActionEvent listener
                btnCount.addActionListener(new ActionListener() {
```

```
            @Override
            public void actionPerformed(ActionEvent evt) {
                ++count;
                tfCount.setText(count + "");
            }
        });

        setDefaultCloseOperation(JFrame.EXIT_ON_CLOSE); // Exit program if
close-window button clicked
        setTitle("Swing Counter"); // "super" JFrame sets title
        setSize(300, 100);       // "super" JFrame sets initial size
        setVisible(true);        // "super" JFrame shows
    }

    // The entry main() method
    public static void main(String[] args) {
        // Run the GUI construction in the Event-Dispatching thread for thread-
safety
        SwingUtilities.invokeLater(new Runnable() {
            @Override
            public void run() {
                new SwingCounter(); // Let the constructor do the job
            }
        });
    }
}
```

Content-Pane in JFrame

The getContentPane() method in JFrame will return the content-pane from JFrame. Then the layout can be set and the components added in (note that BorderLayout is the default). Here's an example:

Container cp = getContentPane(); // Get the content-pane of this JFrame cp.setLayout(new FlowLayout()); // content-pane sets to FlowLayout

cp.add(new JLabel("Counter")); // content-pane adds a JLabel component

......

cp.add(tfCount); // content-pane adds a JTextField component

......

cp.add(btnCount); // content-pane adds a JButton component

You can also use the JFrame's setContentPane() method to directly set the content-pane to a JPanel (or a JComponent). For example,

JPanel displayPanel = new JPanel();

setContentPane(displayPanel);

// "this" JFrame sets its content-pane to a JPanel directly

.....

// The above is different to:

getContentPane().add(displayPanel);

// Add a JPanel into the content pane. Appearance depends on the JFrame's layout.

setDefaultCloseOperation() in JFrame

Rather than writing a WindowEvent listener containing a windowClosing() handler for the close-window button to be processed, JFrame contains a simple method. setDefaultCloseOperation() is used to set the default operation when a user closes the frame. Normally, the option JFrame.EXIT_ON_CLOSE is set and this will close the application down through System.exit(), for example:

setDefaultCloseOperation(JFrame.EXIT_ON_CLOSE);

Run GUI Construction Codes on Event-Dispatching Threads

In our last examples, the constructor was invoked in the entry main() method for setting up the GUI components. For example:

// The entry main method

public static void main(String[] args) {

// Invoke the constructor (by allocating an instance) to set up the GUI

```
    new SwingCounter();
}
```

The constructor is executed in the thread for Main Program but this can cause problems with multi-threading, like a deadlock or a user interface that becomes unresponsive. The recommendation is that the GUI setup codes be executed in the thread called Event-Dispatching and not Main Program, to ensure that the thread operations are safe. The Event-Dispatching thread is used for processing events and should be used when the GUI is updated by the code.

Running the constructor on this thread requires the SwingUtilities.invokeLater() static method to be invoked. This will queue the constructor asynchronously on the event-dispatching thread and the codes get run when the pending events have all been processed. For example:

```
public static void main(String[] args) {
  // Run the GUI codes in the Event-dispatching thread for thread-safety
  SwingUtilities.invokeLater(new Runnable() {
    @Override
    public void run() {
      new SwingCounter();  // Let the constructor do the job
    }
  });
}
```

Sometimes, usually with games programming, main() or the constructor might have non-GUI codes in it. As such, one common practice is to make a dedicated method, This is called createAndShowGUI() in Swing or in NetBeans it is called initComponents() and this will handle the GUI codes. Another method, initGame() will take care of initializing the objects in the game and it is run within the event-dispatching thread.

Warning Message

If you see a warning message that reads "The serialization does not declare a static final serialVersionUID field of type long", it means that java.awt.Frame has implemented the interface called java.io.Serializable via the superclass called java.awt.Component. In this interface, the object is written serially to an output stream through writeObject() and then read back in through readObject(). A serialVersionUID number is used by the serialization runtime to make sure that the object is fully compatible with the definition of the class and doesn't belong to a different version.

There are three options:

- Ignore the warning message. If a serialVersionUID is not explicitly declared by a serializable class, then a default UID is calculated by the runtime for the class, based on several different aspects of the class.
- The recommended option is to add in a serialVersionUID, for example:

private static final long serialVersionUID = 1L; // version 1

- The last option is to use annotation to suppress the warning. The annotation is found in the java.lang package and is called @SuppressWarnings:

@SuppressWarnings("serial")

public class MyFrame extends JFrame { ...... }

SwingAccumulator

To demonstrate this, look at the example code below:

```
import java.awt.*;      // Using layouts

import java.awt.event.*; // Using AWT event classes and listener interfaces

import javax.swing.*;   // Using Swing components and containers


// A Swing GUI application inherits the top-level container javax.swing.JFrame

public class SwingAccumulator extends JFrame {

        private JTextField tfInput, tfOutput;

        private int sum = 0;   // accumulated sum, init to 0


        // Constructor to set up the GUI components and event handlers

        public SwingAccumulator() {

                // Retrieve the content-pane of the top-level container JFrame

                // All operations done on the content-pane

                Container cp = getContentPane();

                cp.setLayout(new GridLayout(2, 2, 5, 5)); // The content-pane sets its layout
```

```
        cp.add(new JLabel("Enter an Integer: "));
        tfInput = new JTextField(10);
        cp.add(tfInput);
        cp.add(new JLabel("The Accumulated Sum is: "));
        tfOutput = new JTextField(10);
        tfOutput.setEditable(false);  // read-only
        cp.add(tfOutput);

        // Allocate an anonymous instance of an anonymous inner class that
        //  implements ActionListener as ActionEvent listener
        tfInput.addActionListener(new ActionListener() {
            @Override
            public void actionPerformed(ActionEvent evt) {
                // Get the String entered into the input TextField, convert to int
                int numberIn = Integer.parseInt(tfInput.getText());
                sum += numberIn;      // accumulate numbers entered into sum
                tfInput.setText("");  // clear input TextField
                tfOutput.setText(sum + ""); // display sum on the output
TextField
            }
        });

        setDefaultCloseOperation(JFrame.EXIT_ON_CLOSE);  // Exit program if
close-window button clicked
        setTitle("Swing Accumulator"); // "super" Frame sets title
        setSize(350, 120);  // "super" Frame sets initial size
        setVisible(true);   // "super" Frame shows
    }

    // The entry main() method
    public static void main(String[] args) {
```

```
            // Run the GUI construction in the Event-Dispatching thread for thread-
safety
            SwingUtilities.invokeLater(new Runnable() {
                @Override
                public void run() {
                    new SwingAccumulator(); // Let the constructor do the job
                }
            });
    }
}
```

Using the Visual GUI Builder in NetBeans and Eclipse

If your GUI application has a very complicated layout, you should consider using a proper GUI builder, like Eclipse or NetBeans, to ensure you GUI components are laid out in a drag and drop manner, much like other popular visual languages like Visual Basic.

NetBeans for Java

NetBeans is an open source IDE that started life in 1996 as a student project in Prague, at the Charles University. NetBeans was acquired by Sun Microsystems in 1999 and, in 2010, Sun was acquired by Oracle, and that meant NetBeans was also acquired.

Compared to Eclipse, NetBeans's rival, NetBeans provides smooth support for Java ME Mobility pack, Java AWT/Swing, and Java EE, and is also bundled with one of the best profilers for tuning up performance. Before we can look at using NetBeans for GUI programming, we need to install it and learn the basics.

Installing NetBeans on Windows

The first step to installing NetBeans on Windows is to install the JDK (Java Development Kit):

Go to https://www.oracle.com/technetwork/java/javase/downloads/index.html and download the latest version. Make sure that you check the box b=to accept the license agreement

Choose the right JDK that matches your Windows operating system version and let the JDK download

The next step is to install the JDK and the JRE:

Find the installer that downloaded; by default it is usually stored in C:\\Program Files\Java\jdk -xx.x{x}

Click on it and accept the default settings; follow the instructions on the screen to install the JDK and the JRE.

Go into your File Explorer and go to Program Files\Java to look at the folders and note the installed directory for JDK, in particular, the upgrade number – you will need this next.

Now we need to add the bin directory from the JDK into PATH. Shell in windows will look through the current directory and through the directories in the PATH system variable for an EXE file All the JDK programs are in the bin sub-directory of the installed JDK directory and adding bin to the PATH is done like this:

Open your Control Panel>System and Security>System and click on Advanced System Settings

Click on Advanced and then click on Environment Variables

At the bottom of the pane, you will see System Variables; under this, scroll and click on Path>Edit

Note – if you are using one of the latest Windows 10 releases, you will see a table:\ that has all the PATH entries in it. Click on New and then type the bin directory for the JDK, for example c:\\Program Files\Java\jdk-xx.x{x}\bin. {x} must be replaced with the installation number you got from the earlier step. Move this entry all the way up using the Move UP option.

If you are using an older version of the OS, make sure you understand this fully before you follow this step – there is no way of undoing what you do here so you must be 110% certain. To be on the safe side, open Windows Notepad and copy the contents of the variable value over before you make any changes.

Go to the Variable Value field and add c:\Program Files\Java\jdk-xx.x{x\bin, again replacing {x} with the installation number before all the other directories in the field and then follow it with a ; (semi-colon). This will separate the bin directory from all the other directories. Make sure that you don't delete any entries otherwise you will affect other application and may stop them running.

Next, we need to verify the installation:

Open a CMD shell in one of these ways:

Click on Search and type in CMD; select Command Prompt from the menu, or

Right click on the Start button, click on Run and type in cmd, or,

if you are using a version of Windows earlier than 10

Click on Start>All Programs>Accessories (it may be Windows System) and then select Command Prompt, or in Windows 10,

Click on Start>Windows System>Command prompt

When you have the command window open, type in these commands to verify your installation:

// Display the PATH entries

prompt> path

PATH=c:\Program Files\Java\jdk-xx.x.{x}\bin;[other entries...]

Do NOT type in prompt> - this is your command prompt and is already there.

Now type these commands in to check that both JDK and JRE are installed properly; you should see the version number displayed on your screen:

// Display the JRE version

prompt> java -version

java version "xx.x.{x}" 2018-04-17

Java(TM) SE Runtime Environment 18.3 (build 10.0.1+10)

Java HotSpot(TM) 64-Bit Server VM 18.3 (build 10.0.1+10, mixed mode)

// Display the JDK version

prompt> javac -version

javac xx.x.{x}

Installing NetBeans on Mac OS

First, make sure that JDK isn't already installed. Some Mac systems already have JDK installed so open your Terminal window by searching for Terminal or open Finder>Go>Utilities>Terminal and type this command in:

javac -version

If you see a version number appear on your screen, JDK is installed. If that version number is earlier than 1.8, you will need to install the latest one, as will you if you get the message saying that the command is not found.

If you see a message that reads, 'To open javac, you need a Java runtime', click on Install and follow the onscreen instructions to install the JDK.

Downloading the JDK is done like this:

Go to http://www.oracle.com/technetwork/java/javase/downloads/index.html and click on the Download button

Pick your operating system and download the latest installer.

Make sure you click the button to accept the license agreement

Next we need to install the JDK/JRE so

Find and click the DMG file and follow the instruction on the screen to install it

Eject the DMG

Now we need to verify the installation so open a terminal window and type in these commands:

```
// Display the JDK version

javac -version

javac 10.0.{x}


// Display the JRE version

java -version

java version "10.0.{x}"

......


// Display the location of Java Compiler

which javac

/usr/bin/javac


// Display the location of Java Runtime

which java

/usr/bin/java
```

Launching NetBeans

Launch NetBeans on your system; if you see the Start page open, click the cross beside the title, Start Page, and close it. For every Java application, a new project must be created to store all the source files, resources and classes. To do this,

Click on File>New Project

In the dialog window, go to Categories and click on Java

Click Projects>Java Applications>Next

A new dialog window will open, entitled Name and Location. Name the project FirstProject and then choose a location for saving the work. Make sure the box next to Use Dedicated Folder is unchecked and then uncheck the box next to Create Main Class. Click on Finish

Writing Your First Program

To get things off and running, let's write a Hello World program in Java:

Find and right-click on FirstProject and choose New>Java Class. Alternatively, click on File>New File>Categories and choose Java; then click File Types and choose Java Class and click Next

You will see the Name and Location box again; click on Class Name and type in Hello

If Package is not empty, delete the contents and click Finish

You will now see Hello.java in the editor panel and you can input these codes:

```
public class Hello {
   public static void main(String[] args) {
      System.out.println("Hello, world");
   }
}
```

Compiling and Executing

NetBeans source code does not need to be explicitly compiled because NetBeans will compile it as it gets entered; this is called incremental compilation. So, to run your program, either click on Run>Run File or right-click inside the source; look at the output console to see the output.

Notes:

A new Java project must be created for each Java application. However, in NetBeans, you can have two or more programs in one project, great for when you are running tutorial exercises and the like.

Syntax Error

As I mentioned earlier, NetBeans compiles code as it is entered and, if any line is marked with a red cross, you have a syntax error on it. Point the mouse cursor at the red cross to see what the error message is. No program will run while it has a syntax error so correct all the errors and then run it.

On occasion, you will see an orange colored lightbulb beside the red cross. This is hints and right-clicking on that lightbulb will show you a few hints to solve the relevant syntax error. In line 5 of the above code example you should see both the cross and the light bulb; try clicking the lightbulb and fixing the error.

If you see an orange-colored exclamation sign shaped like a triangle, this is a syntax warning. Warnings don't always cause problems but you should try to fix them; you can run the program with these warnings though.

NetBeans Documentation

As an absolute minimum you should take the time out to read the documentation for Getting Started, IDE Basics and Java Applications, all of which you can access by clicking on Help>Help Contents in NetBeans. Trust me when is say that reading this now can save you so much time later on down the line!

You can also look at Help>Online Doc and Support for plenty of useful tutorials and articles on using NetBeans. And, on the NetBeans Start Page are lots of links that will help you get started too.

Debugging

Before we can debug a program, we need to write one so start a new project, call it Factorial and input the following code. The program will compute and then print the factorial of n, which is (=1*2*3...*n). However, our program has one logical error in it and it will give us a wrong answer for n=20 because, if you know your mathematics, you will know that the factorial of 20 is actually a negative number (2102132736).

```
/** Compute the factorial of n */

public class Factorial {

  // Print factorial of n

  public static void main(String[] args) {
```

```
        int n = 20;
        int factorial = 1;

        // n! = 1*2*3...*n
        for (int i = 1; i <= n; i++) {
          factorial *= i;
        }
        System.out.println("The Factorial of " + n + " is " + factorial);
    }
}
```

Now we will debug this using the graphical debugger in NetBeans.

First, we need to set a breakpoint. This will suspend execution of the program so that you can look at the internal state of your program. Before the debugger is started, a minimum of one breakpoint needs to be set for execution to be suspended. So, we'll set our breakpoint at the main() method and we do that by clicking the left-hand margin of the code line with the main() method in it. You will see an inverted triangle or a red circle telling you that the breakpoint has been set.

Next, we debug. Right-click the code anywhere and select Debug File from the menu that appears. The program will start to execute but will stop where the breakpoint is, at the main() method.

The next step is to step over so click the Debug menus and select Step Over and your program will step through one step at a time. At each step you must look at the variable values, which you will see in the Variable panel on the screen, and the outputs that are produced, seen in the Outputs panel, if there are any. You can also hover your mouse cursor over any variable to see what the content is.

This is absolutely the best way to debug a program because this is the way that a computer runs a program, one step at a tie, examining everything.

As you know, the breakpoint will suspend the execution and let you see what the internal program states are. Setting a breakpoint on a specific statement is done by clicking the left-hand margin where the statement is r going to Run>Toggle Breakpoint. Clicking on Continue will start the execution once more, where it will run up to the end of the program or the next breakpoint, whichever comes first.

Single-stepping through a loop that has a large count takes a lot of time so there are a couple of things you can do. You can set the breakpoint at the statement that comes immediately outside that loop, for example, in the above code that would be on line 11 and then click

Continue to start the execution up to that line. Or you could put your mouse cursor on the specific statement and click on Run To Cursor, so the execution continues to that line.

Clicking Finish will stop the debugging and this is something you should always do – either click Finish or click Continue to go to the end of the program.

Other Features of the Debugger

Modifying Variable Values – variable values can be modified by going to the Variable panel and inputting the new value. This feature is good for when you want to change how the program behaves but not change the source code.

Step-Into/Step-Out – when you have a method that you want to debug, you must use Step-Into to go into the method's first statement. If you wanted to go back to the caller, somewhere in the method you could use Step-Out. Alternatively, you could just set a breakpoint within the method.

NetBeans Tips and Tricks

Before we move onto application development, there are a few very useful features in NetBeans that you should learn:

- Maximize Window – double-click the header of any panel to maximize the panel and, to restore it, double-click again. This is good for when you want a full panel for editing code.
- Code Auto-Complete – otherwise called Intellisense. Type in part of a statement and then press the CTRL-Space buttons on your keyboard; this activates auto-complete which will show you all the matches to your partially typed statement. Just choose the one that you want.
- Javadoc – put your mouse cursor over a class or method and then press the CTRL-Space buttons to see the Javadoc. Alternatively, you can press on ALT+F1 and it will open in your browser.
- Code Shorthand – i.e., if you were to enter 'sout' and then press the Tab key, you would get the full path of System.out.println. Input 'pvsm' and Tab and you get public static void main(Strings[]args){}; 'fori' and tab gives you a for loop, and so one. If you want to see the code template and configure it, click on Tools>Options>Editor>Code Templates.
- Format the Source Code – right-click your mouse on the source code or go to Source>Format and NetBeans will lay the source code using the correct format and indents. If you wanted to change the configuration of the formatting, click on Tools>Options>Editor>Formatting.
- Rename or Refactor – if you want to change the name of a variable, right-click on it and choose Refactor>Rename>Enter. Type the new name in and every instance of that variable will be changed in your project.

- Source Toggle Comment – if you want to comment-off a code block temporarily, click Source>Toggle Comment
- Error Message Hyperlink – if you click any error message, it will hyperlink straight to the source statement that corresponds to it.
- Command-Line Arguments – if you want your Java program to have command-line arguments in NetBeans, right-click on Project and choose Set as Main Project>Set Configurations>Customize>Run; choose Main and go to the Arguments field. Type the command line argument in and click on Run>Run Main Project
- Line Numbers – if you want to see the line numbers, right-click in the left-hand margin and select Show Line Numbers.
- Change the Font Size and Face – click on Tools>Options>Font and Colors>Category. Then choose Default. Do the same but, instead of Category, click Font and choose the size and face that you want.
- Reset Window View – if the window view gets messed up, for example you close a window by accident and you can't find it, go to Window>Reset Windows and it will reset.
- Code Templates – i.e. when a new Java class is created, NetBeans will go to the Java Class code template to get the initial contents. Configuring code templates requires you to click on Tools>Templates>Choose and pick the required template; click on Open in Editor. Setting the value for a variable that is in use in all templates requires you to click Tools>Templates>Settings.
- Displaying Chinese Characters – if you need a font that has support for Chinese characters like Monospace, click Tools>Options>Fonts and Colors>Syntax>Default

Java Application Development

Choose your JDK version; right-click your project and choose Properties>Source Node and then in the drop-down menu for Source/Binary Format, you can choose your JDK level.

Choose your default charset by right-clicking your project and clicking Properties>Source Node>Encoding. Pick your charset for text-file Input/Output (I/O) from the menu.

Enable Unicode Support for File Encoding by right-clicking on your project and clicking Properties>Source Node>Encoding and choosing your Unicode encoding, for example, UTF-8, for the text file I/O.

If you want Javadoc/Source included you need to use either Library Manager – click on Tools>Libraries, or Java Platform Manager – click Tools>Java Platforms.

You can also add external JAR files and Native libraries, for example, .dll, .lib, etc. There are quite a few external Java packages that extend the JDK functions and these usually have a lib directory that has JAR files in it. JAR files are Java Archive files and it is a package of a single file of Java classes. They also have native libraries for Mac and Linux.

If you want an external JAR included, you need to expand the Project Node and right click on the option for Libraries>Add JAR. Choose the JAR you want to add or the folder that has the classes. If there are a lot of JAR files in the package, another option would be to make a user library with all those JARs in it and then add that library to any project that requires the files. Click on Tools>Libraries>New Library>Enter and type a name for the library. To add the JAR files in, click Libraries>Add JAR.

Java GUI Application - NetBeans

Start by creating a brand new Java Application project by opening NetBeans and clicking File>New Project>Categories. Click on Java>Projects and select Java Application>Next.

Click on Project Name and type in FirstNetBeansGUI. Pick your location to save your project and make sure the Create Main Class box is not checked. Click on Finish.

Next, we want to write a JFrame Form Java file.

To do this, right-click your project and choose New>JFrame Form. Click on Class Name and type in NetBeansSwingCounter and then click Finish.

Now we are going to visually create our GUI components. Go to the Palette panel and click Swing Controls>Drag and Drop and then drop a TextField, a Label, and a Button into your design panel.

Now click jLabel1>Properties and type in Count under Text. You could also click once on jLabel1 to change it. Right-click jLabel1 and click on Change Variable Name. Click New Name and type in lblCount.

Do the same with jTextField1, changing Text to 0 and the variable name to tfCount. If needs be, resize the text field.

Lastly, for jButton1, do the same and change Text to Count and the variable name to btnCount.

Double-click on the button and type in the following codes to write an event handler:

```
private void btnCountActionPerformed(java.awt.event.ActionEvent evt) {

  count++;

  tfCount.setText(count + "");

}
```

Just under the class declaration, we need a variable count instance so type in this code:

```
public class Counter extends javax.swing.JFrame {

  int count = 0;
```

Now we can compile our code and execute it so right-click the source and click on Run File.

The next step is to look at the source code generated so expand the code and have a good look at the way the GUI builder declares the GUI components, allocates them and initializes them inside initComponents. Especially take note of the way an ActionEvent listener is registered by JButton and the way that the inner class gets used as the listener and provides the actionPerformed() event handler. Also take note of the way a Swing worker is used by main() for running the GUI, not on the Main thread but on Event-Dispatcher.

```
public class NetBeansSwingCounter extends javax.swing.JFrame {
    int count = 0;

    // Constructor to setup the UI via initComponents()
    public NetBeansSwingCounter() {
        initComponents();
    }

    private void initComponents() {
        lblCount = new javax.swing.JLabel();
        tfCount = new javax.swing.JTextField();
        btnCount = new javax.swing.JButton();


    setDefaultCloseOperation(javax.swing.WindowConstants.EXIT_ON_CLOSE);

        lblCount.setText("Counter");
        tfCount.setText("0");

        btnCount.setText("Count");
        // Create an anonymous inner as the listener for the ActionEvent fired by
btnCount
        btnCount.addActionListener(new java.awt.event.ActionListener() {
            public void actionPerformed(java.awt.event.ActionEvent evt) {
                btnCountActionPerformed(evt);
```

```
      }
        });

        // Laying out the components
        // ......

        pack();
    }

    // ActionEvent handler for btnCount
    private void btnCountActionPerformed(java.awt.event.ActionEvent evt) {
        count++;
        tfCount.setText(count + "");
    }

    public static void main(String args[]) {
        // Setup the Look and Feel
        // .....

        // Run the constructor on the Event-Dispatcher Thread for thread-safe
        java.awt.EventQueue.invokeLater(new Runnable() {
            public void run() {
                new NetBeansSwingCounter().setVisible(true);
            }
      });
    }

    // private variables
    private javax.swing.JButton btnCount;
    private javax.swing.JLabel lblCount;
```

```
    private javax.swing.JTextField tfCount;

}
```

Now we will get down to the nuts and bolts of GUI building using the Java GUI builder.

The Java GUI Builder

In any Java application, all the GUI components are stored in containers and these are called forms. The language gives us a range of these components that we can use to build our GUI forms. The GUI builder helps you design your forms and build them by giving you the tools you need to simplify the whole process.

Java GUI Tools

The tools provided by the IDE are:

- GUI Window – the main workspace that the design happens in within the IDE. The GUI builder helps you to lay the forms out, placing the components where they need to be and giving you guidelines as visual feedback.
- Navigator Window – this shows you all your components in the open form in a tree hierarchy. You will see all the visual components and the containers, like labels, buttons, menus, panels and the non-visual ones like the data sources and the timers.
- Palette Window – this is a list that has all the components you can add to your form. The window can be customized so it only shows icons or you can have the component name shown as well.
- Properties Window – shows you all the settings that can be edited for each selected component.
- Connection Wizard – helps you to set events between the components in your form without the need to manually write any code.
- Manager – helps you to add window components, remove them and organize them, including AWT and Swing Components, beans, and Layouts.

On top of all this, the IDE also provides full support for the Beans Binding spec which gives you a way of synchronizing the bean property values. This also makes it much easier to create a desktop database app.

Working with GUI Builder

So, this is a tool to help you visually design your GUIs. As you create a GUI and modify it, the IDE will generate the code automatically for you to implement your interface. When you look in the windows entitled Projects, Favorites, and Files, you will see the GUI forms indicated by form nodes.

When you launch a GUI form, it will be shown in the editor tab in the IDE, and there will be toggles that let you switch between Design and Source view. Design is where you work with the forms visually and Source is where you can edit the source code. Whenever you are in Design view, you will also see the Palette, Properties and Navigator windows.

We use the window to add the form components and the GUI Builder workspace is used to arrange them. As you go along, GUI Builder will show you guidelines that suggest better alignment and anchor points for each component. The Navigator window can be used with the Properties window to look at the layout and component manager properties, manage event handlers and even define the generation of the code.

Be aware – when you create an interface using GroupLayout, the Swing Layout Extensions Library much be available to the layout manager if the interface is to run externally to the IDE. This library is already included in the JDK.

Designing GUI Applications

The basic steps needed to create a GUI application and deploy it are:

- Create the Form – you can do this inside an existing project. To make handling easier, forms already have components, containers and sub-containers. A layout manager helps control how the components are arranged within the container. You can also create an MDI – Multiple Document Interface – application
- Edit the Form – every component on a form had properties for appearance, behavior and accessibility and these can be modified in two ways – through the Property manager or directly.
- Preview the Form – In Preview Design, your form can be tested without you needing to compile or run it.
- Deploy – Java applications tend to be distributed in JAR file format. Before you deploy, you should make sure that the correct libraries are in the JAR

Now we can break these steps down with more detail.

Creating a New Form

Inside your IDE, JFC, Swing and AWT forms can be created, along with sample skeleton applications, or classes based on the component architecture for JavaBeans using the templates already provided for you. You cannot use the GUI Builder for editing any form built external to the builder.

Within an Existing Project:

In the IDE, click on File>New File

In the Project combo box choose your project

Expand the AWT or Swing forms node – it's in the Categories pane – and choose the template you want to use; click on Next

Enter the class name and the location of the GUI form and click on Finish

A blank form is created of the type you chose and opened in Source Editor Design view.

Make sure you use only Swing/JFC components in a Swing/JFC form and AWT components in AWT forms – this avoids repaint issues at design time and runtime.

Working With Containers

A Java GUI is a form made up of top-level containers. In these are sub-containers and the components needed to give you the information and to control the functionality.

The View Focus

Sometimes you will want to focus on one sub-container and not the whole form displayed by the builder. When you have a large form that has many complex, nested container hierarchies, you can change the scope of the focus to concentrate on certain parts. In the Navigator or GUI Builder window, select the container you want to be edited and right-click it:

From the menu that appears, click on Design this Container

The IDE will now change the display so that the selected container takes up the whole work area, hiding all other components. You can still see the whole hierarchy can still be seen in the Navigator window.

To take the display focus back to the whole form:

In the GUI right-click on the container

From the menu, click on Design Top Container and the IDE will readjust the form so everything is visible.

Changing The Order of Container Components

The order of the components within a container is the order that they were added in. If the container's layout manager does not use the BoxLayout, FlowLayout or GridLayout constraints, the component order is also the way they are visually arranged. The component order can be changed in two ways – by dragging the components around in the form or using the Navigator window.

If the layout manager does use those constraints, the component order inside the container will not determine how they actually appear. You can only change the order of these components through the Navigator window.

Add Components to Forms

When your form has been created, components can be added to show information and for you to control the functionality. There are a few ways to add components in the IDE:

- Pick and Plop
- Drag and Drop
- Navigator window

With the navigator window, you get the hierarchical view of all the components on the form. A form is represented by a single root node and in this you find all the components on the form. The remaining GUI components can be found in one of these sub-nodes:

- Form Container – representative of the hierarchies top-level, contains all visible components that can currently be seen in the GUI builder
- Other Components – all the non-visual components in the form

Adding Components from the Palette

Choose the component you want by clicking the relevant icon. Keeping the mouse button pressed down, drag your chosen component to where you want it in your form.

To add a component into the Other Components node, drag that component into the white area that surrounds the form in the Editor workspace

The IDE will now add your chosen component to the chosen container. If you want to add several components from Palette:

Click on one icon

Press SHIFT and click simultaneously to put the first component in place

Click all the locations

Adding to the Other Components Node is exactly the same as for the single component above.

Using Navigator Window to Add a Component

Go to the Navigator window and select the container you want a component added to

Right-click it and then click Add From; choose the component you want

The component will be added to the container.

Add Beans

You can add beans from the Projects, Favorites or Files windows:

In Files window find the class node for the bean – the class has to be a bean and it has to be compiled. (for any class to be a bean you must be able to use an empty constructor (public) to create a class instance.

Right-click on the node and then click Copy in the menu

Click Paste in the GUI builder or Other Components node from the Navigator window

The bean will be added to the form.

When you are working with a nested container it can sometimes be hard to choose the container you want the component added to. First, choose the container and then choose the component. Hold the ALT key down, click the container and the component will be added.

Selecting Components in Forms

The Navigator window and the GUI builder will always show the same components – when you select one in one window, it will show up automatically in the other. To select one component, click on it in GUI builder or click the node in Navigator.

If you want several components selected, do one of these:

Press the SHIFT key and click on the components you want in the Form editor or on the nodes in Navigator

In GUI builder, hold SHIFT and the left mouse key down simultaneously and drag the mouse over the components you want to add. You will see a rectangle appear and, when you let go of the mouse button, all components in that area are selected

In Navigator, if you want consecutive components, press SHIFT and click the first one; keep the SHIFT key held down and click on the final component in the group

Controlling the Selection Depth

With nested components, like those in a Panel, or another container, when you click in the Builder, the deepest component from the point of clicking will always be selected. However, you use modifier keys to choose nested components that are on different levels.

Right-click to show the menu for the container or the subcomponent. If you want to choose the parent container for the component you selected:

Press the ALT key and hold it down

Click on the component in GUI builder.

If there is no parent container for the component the deepest one at the click-point will be selected instead.

If you want a subcomponent of the container:

Press SHIFT and ALT together and hold them down

Click on the subcomponent

If that component does not have any subcomponent, the container component for the whole form will be selected.

Aligning Components

You can change the alignment of any component you added:

Choose the components to be aligned in GUI Builder workspace

From the GUI Builder toolbar click the align button you want to use. Or you can right-click on each component and choose Align Left or Align Right from the menu

The IDE will move the positions so that the edges are aligned as specified and the anchoring relationships for the components are updated.

Aligning Component Baselines

Choose the component to align in the Builder workspace

Drag it right or left of the chosen component

You will see a horizontal guideline showing you the baseline has been aligned with that of the second one, and a vertical one to suggest what spacing should be between them. Position your component by clicking.

The IDE will put the second component into position, aligning it with the first component's baseline and will show you status lines to indicate the spacing and the anchoring relationships.

Indenting Components

In GUI Builder workspace, choose the component to be indented

Now choose the component below the one to be indented.

When the guidelines appear showing the alignment of the left edge of component one with JLabel, move to the right until another set of indentation lines appear

Position the component by clicking

The second component is indented under the first one.

Sizing Components

Sometimes it is beneficial to set multiple related components, like buttons in a modal dialog, so that they are the same size. This makes them easy to recognize as having the same or similar functionalities. It is also possible to change the resizing behavior of the components to ensure the maintenance of relationships at runtime.

To set multiple components to the same size

In the GUI builder workspace, choose all the components for resizing

Right-click any one and click on Set the Same Size. Choose Set Width or Set Height as required from the menu

All the selected components will be set as the same size and the relationship will be indicated by a small graphic.

To change the resizing behavior

Choose all the components that you want to change the resizing behavior of

Right-click any one and select Auto Resizing. Then choose Horizontal or Vertical as you need from the menu

The components will all be set to resize at runtime and the anchoring relationships and guidelines are also updated.

Editing Component Properties

When a component is added to the form, you can go into the Properties window and modify the appearance and behavior of it by changing the values.

To edit the properties

Choose the component in Navigator or GUI Builder so its properties show up in the Properties window

Select the appropriate property by clicking on a button at the top of the window

Choose the property to be modified and input the new value

The new values are added to the chosen components

To go back to the default values, right-click on the name of the property and click on Restore Default Value.

Using the Connection Wizard to Set Events

You can set events between components in a form without the need to write any code:

On the toolbar on GUI builder, click on the button for Connection Mode

Either in Navigator or GUI builder choose the component that will send the event

Choose the component whose state the event will affect

Go to the Select Source Event page in the Connection Wizard and expand the directory node for the event type. Choose the event that will be sent by the trigger component and either type a new name for the handler method or accept the default one. Click on Next

Go to the Specify Target Operation page and specify which operation will be carried out on the target component – do this by clicking the relevant radio button and picking from the operations list. Click on Next

Go to the Enter Parameters page and specify what the values will be for the target methods or properties on each tab by choosing which source the value will come from – you will see the source code for each parameter in the field titled Generated Parameters Preview.

Click on Finish

The code will be generated automatically to connect the components together

Managing Component Events

Java using events as a way of enabling the behavior of GUI forms. Events can be triggered by source objects; at least one object with an event listener will react to this through an event handler.

Defining an Event Handler

Event handlers can be defined in three ways – through a contextual menu or the property sheet for the component or by using the Connection wizard.

To use the property sheet:

In the Navigator window, choose the component

Go to the Properties window and click on Events at the top

In the list, choose the event you want; initially, every event will have None as its value. when you click on the value field, the value is replaced automatically with the default name for the event

Click the ellipsis for the event (...) and the Handler dialog box opens

Click on Add so the new name is added to the handler list and then click OK

You will now see the generated code for the listener and for the empty hander method body. Note that you do still need to add the code you want for the event handler into the Source Editor.

To use the contextual menu:

Go to the Navigator, Project or Files window and right-click on any form component

Click on Events from the menu – if any items in the menu or the submenus are in bold the event handlers have been defined already.

You will now see the generated code for both the listener and the handler method body and the event handler is assigned with the default name. Again, you need to use the Source Editor to add the code for the event handler.

If you have several events that are all the same type, the same handler can be used for all of them. For example, because focusLost and focusGained are both of the java.awt.event.FocusEvent type, you can set both to use the handler called button1FocusChange.

The style of the code generation can also be set for the way in which the code is generated for the event. To do that:

Click on Tools>Options>Miscellaneous>GUI Builder

Set the property for the Listener Generation Style, for Main Class, one inner class or any anonymous inner class.

Adding Several Handlers for a Single Event

Go to the Navigator window and choose the component that will have several handlers

At the top of the Properties window, click Events

Choose which event you want from the property sheet and then click on the ellipsis (...); the Handlers dialog box will appear. Click Add and complete the form and repeat to add other event handlers

Removing Event Handlers

Go to the Navigator window and choose the component to remove the handlers from

Click Events and then click the ellipsis.

In the Handlers dialog box choose the handler you want to remove and then click on Remove

When an event handler is removed, the code block that corresponds to it also gets deleted. If you have more than one handler sharing the same code and name, just deleting one reference will not delete the code. All references need to be deleted.

Modifying GUI Source Code

As your GUI form is created in the Builder, the IDE generates blocks of code guarded in blue automatically. This guarded text includes:

Blocks containing the variable declarations of the components

An initComponents() method which is where the form is initialized. This method gets called from the constructor and, although it cannot be manually edited, you can edit the properties in the property sheet to change how it is generated.

Initialization code generation can be modified and custom code can be written to go inside the initialization code.

Modifying Form, Component, and Component Property Code Generation

It is also possible to modify how the component, form or component property code is generated and this is done in the Properties window where you can edit the code properties. You can also write your own code and state where it is to go within the initialization code.

To modify a guarded block:

Go to the Navigator window, and choose which component you are editing the code for

Click Code, top of Properties, to see the code properties

Choose the property to edit and input the value you want

The guarded code block for that component will now be updated by the IDE.

You can also do this by going to the Code Customizer Dialog box; right-click on any component in Design View (GUI Builder) and click on Customize Code

Setting a Java Component's Variable Modifier

Java language modifiers for any Java element can be set through the Variables Modifier Property Editor box.

Go to the Navigator window and choose the component you want to edit the variable modifier for

At the top of Properties click Code to see the code properties

Choose Variable Modifiers and click on the ellipsis

In the Variable Modifiers box that opens you can edit whichever modifiers you want.

Modifying a Property's Code Generation

The properties for form components can be initialized in several ways. With the IDE you can initialize the properties from:

- A static value defined by you
- A component that has been written to JavaBeans
- The property from a different component on the same form

- Calling the form method or the method of a form component. There is a list of methods to choose from returning the right data type.
- Code defined by you that is to be added into the generated code

Modifying the initialization code that is generated for the property of a component:

Go to the Navigator window and choose the component

Click Properties – top of the Properties window

Choose the Property for which you want to change the code

Click on the Ellipsis and the Property dialog box will appear

Click on Select Mode>Form Connection

Go to the Property Editor and choose which initialization code type you want to add in. Choose from Bean, Value, User Code, Method Call, or Property.

If you pick User Code or Value, a static value has to be added or you must add your own initialization code in the provided field.

If you pick Property, Bean, or Method Call, a list of options is provided for you to choose from.

The new code will be added by the IDE to the guarded block for the selected component.

It is also possible to add custom code before the property initializer or after it. To do that, follow the first four steps from above. Now click Advanced and you will see the dialog box for Advanced Initialization Code. Input your custom pre or post-initialization code or add both if required.

Modify GUI Form Code Externally

You can also modify the GUI code form externally. Each form in the IDE is made up of two separate files:

- A .java file. This has the java source code for the form
- A .form file. This has the information needed for generating the .java file when changes are made in the GUI Builder to the form. It is not necessary to distribute this file with the application but if you delete it, the GUI Builder cannot be used for changing the form.

.java files can be edited with an external editor but not at the same time that you are using the IDE to edit the form. There are three exceptions to the external editing:

- The initComponents() method content should not be modified, The method body gets regenerated whenever you open the form in the IDE

- The special comments in the source, placed there by the GUI builder, cannot be modified or removed. These are signified by //GEN- and are needed so that the form opens as it should. The comments are not seen within the Source Editor
- The event handler headers and footers should not be modified.

Creating MDI (Multiple Document Interface) Applications

The MDI model is much like that of a traditional window system on a computer – it has a desktop and other windows float above it. In a Swing/JFC MDI application, all the internal windows are contained in one enclosing window which can be resized, positions, minimized and closed.

The steps to creating an MDI are:

Click on File>New and the New Wizard will appear

Click Project in the wizard and choose the project you want the form created for,

Find the Java GUI Form Node and expand it; choose one of these templates:

JFrame Form- to build an MDI app from the bottom up – you will need a JDesktop Pane component for this one

MDI Application – found in Sample Forms, this creates an MDI from scratch with JDesktop Pane already included along with a few common menu items already defined.

Click on Next and go to the Name and Location page. Input the name of the firm in the box for Class Name and then the Package and Location must be specified

Click on Finish and the new file will be displayed in the field for Created File.

Creating Accessible Forms

All your GUI forms and any component contained in them must meet specific accessibility requirements and to make sure they do, you can make changes to the accessibility properties. GUIs are accessible when they work with certain assistive technologies, like screen readers.

You can edit these properties to make accessibility better:

- Accessible Name – sets the component name; the default setting is the value of the component's text property
- Accessible Description – sets the component description
- Accessible Parent – sets the name for the component's accessible parent

If you want to edit your form or any of the accessibility properties:

Go to Navigator and choose the component or form you want to modify the accessibility properties for

Go to Properties window and click on the Properties tab; go down the list and click on Accessibility Properties

Click on the ellipsis and the Property Editor will open. Input the new value and the IDE will update the value for the component

A quicker way is to select the current property value and then input the updated value directly.

Previewing a Form

To see how your form gets displayed after compilation and at runtime, in the GUI Builder toolbar click on Test Form. You will see a dialog box showing you all the components in the arrangement they would show up on your form.

Click in this box and you will be able to see how your components work because mouse events will be sent to each of them. For example, type into a text field, move a slider, and when you click a button it will look as though it has been pressed. What doesn't get executed is event handling and cross-component code.

To test how your form works without compilation and without running it, go to the GUI Builder toolbar and press on Preview Design. You will see the form displayed in the Preview window and you can test it out. If you make any updates to your form though, you must close down any Preview windows with open forms in them and click on Preview Design to see those changes.

Working With a Layout Manager

A layout manager is used to help you to control how visual components are laid out in a GUI form and they do this by working out the position and the size of components inside containers. To do this, we must implement the LayoutManager interface.

Any new form created in the GUI Builder will, by default, use the layout manager called GroupLayout. The IDE has something called Free Design which is a special kind of support for this layout. With Free Design you can take advantage of visual guidelines to lay your form out; these will make automatic suggestions of the best spacing and alignment of your components. As you bring your components in, the Builder will automatically turn your decisions into a UI that is fully functional without the need to specify a particular layout manager. Free Design also uses a dynamic layout so, whenever you change locales or resize your form, GUI will adjust it to take your changes into account without any change between component relationships. Also, Free Design containers can be used together with containers that use different layout managers in one form.

Some of the other layout managers that you can use in your IDE include:

- FlowLayout – the components are arranged in the container much the same way as words are arranged on a page. It starts at the top and works left to right, top to bottom, filling each line with components
- BorderLayout – the components are arranged in the middle or around the edges of the container. This is used for putting components in five locations – NORTH, EAST, SOUTH, WEST, CENTER – which corresponds to the four edges and the middle of the container
- GridLayout – the components are placed into a grid or matrix of cells which are all of the same sizes, working left to right, top to bottom
- GridBagLayout – this is one of the more powerful of the layout managers, giving you explicit control of every layout aspect, even when you resize the container. This is done using constraints and is suited to multi-platform applications as you can create a layout that is free form yet looks the same across all platforms. The components are placed in a grid or matrix of columns and rows, where the cells do not need to be the same size. Components may also go across more than one row, column or both.
- CardLayout – this allows you to manage at least two components that are in the same display area. Each of the components is much like a card within a deck; all are the same size and the only card visible at all times is the top one. Because all the components are in the same space, when it comes to designing, you need to use the Navigator window to choose each component
- BoxLayout – this allows you to arrange several components horizontally or vertically – not both. The components are arranged top to bottom or left to right in the order that they go into the container. Components will not wrap around to the next column or row when more are added or the container gets resized.
- AbsoluteLayout – this comes with the IDE and allows components to be put where you want them, to move them about and resize them. It is suited to prototyping as you don't have any real limitations and there is no need to input any property settings.
- Null Layout – this is used for designing a form without using any layout manager. Again, it is suited to prototyping but not for production as the components are fixed in location and size and will not change with environment changes.

Setting the Layout Manager

When a new container is created, it is usually done with the GroupLayout so you can use Free Design. The layout can be changed for many containers through the window, the Navigator Window or through GUI Builder.

From GUI Builder:

Choose the container you want the layout changed for and right-click it

From the menu click Set Layout and select the layout you want

That layout manager will be applied to the container.

From the Navigator Window:

Find the container you want to change and right-click on the node

In the menu click Set Layout and pick your layout manager

This will be applied to the specified container

When the layout is changed, the IDE will note the properties of the original layout. If you want to go back to it, the IDE will put the form back to its original state.

Using the GridBag Customizer

With the GridBag customizer, you can change the placement of the components, along with the constraints, in the GridBagLayout. You will find a property sheet for all the constraints, buttons that allow you to change those constraints and a rough visual idea of how the components look laid out.

To use it:

Choose which components you want to be added to your form and add them. Make sure that GridBagLayout is enabled for the form

Open the customizer by right-clicking on the node in the Navigator window for GridBagLayout and clicking Customize in the menu

Reposition the components as you want them by dragging them to the right pane. As you do this the Grid X and Y properties will change to show the position.

When you have the layout approximately how you would like it, choose one component and change the constraints as you want them – do this in the left pane. Either directly input the new values or use the buttons provided to make the changes. Keep in mind that you have four buttons for use in the right pane toolbar – Test Layout, Redo, Pad, and Undo.

When you have made all your changes, click on Close and the IDE will update everything.

Adjustable Constraints

- Grid X/Grid Y – set these positions to change the vertical and horizontal positioning of each component
- Grid Width/Grid Height – you can set these to show the number of positions in the grid for a component in both directions. You will need to specify one of these:
- Integer Value – how many cells used by the component
- Remainder – use all the remaining vertical or horizontal space to make a component the last in its column or row
- Relative – specifying that a component is the next to last in its column or row
- Fill – controls whether all the allocated space (horizontal or vertical or both) is used by a component. The Grid Size buttons can be used to change this constraint.

- Internal X and Y Padding – these settings let you increase the vertical and horizontal dimensions of each component; numerical values are required for these properties
- Anchor – this controls where the component is placed in any of 11 positions but, if there isn't any space remaining, this setting will not have any effect. The Grid Size buttons can also be used to change this constraint.
- Weight X/Weight Y – this controls the amount of space a component is given relative to the others in the column or row when you resize a container. Usually, the values go from 0 to 1 and those with large values are given more space. If a component has a weight of 0, it will keep the preferential size for the dimensions. If all components in a column or row have a 0 value, the extra space is allocated to the outer edges and the components will retain their size.
- Insets – this controls the minimum external space on all sides of a component. The values may be manually entered.

Using a Custom Layout Manager

If the layout managers cannot provide the result you want, you can use a custom one. If you want a custom layout manager integrated into the GUI builder, it must follow these three rules:

- It must implement the interface java.awt.LayoutManager
- It must be of JavaBeans type
- It must not use any constraints for the individual components

If your custom manager doesn't meet these rules, you will need to make a special support class so it can be added to the Builder.

To use the Files window to install the custom manager:

Go to Files window and find the class for the layout manager; right-click it and then click Tools>Add in the menu

The dialog box for Select Category will appear; choose a category and then click OK

The custom manager will be added to the window.

To install a custom manager from a JAR file:

Go to the Tools menu and click Palette>Swing/AWT Components

The Palette manager will appear, choose Add from JAR

Click on Install Components to Palette and the file chooser will appear; go to the JAR you want and select it

Complete the wizard and click on Finish

The JavaBean will be installed and the IDE will add the new manager.

Setting Layout Properties

If you want to change how your forms look, you can change the properties for the layout manager and those that are component-specific.

Within the IDE, the following can be modified:

- General properties for the layout that affect every container components, like the component alignment and spaces in between each one
- Layout properties that are component-specific provided that component is managed by a specific layout manager. These are the constraints and apply to individual components.

Setting general properties:

In the Navigator window, choose the node for the layout manager

Go to the Properties window, choose the property to be edited and input the value

All the changed positions will be updated.

Be aware that the properties are going to vary based on which layout manager you use and some managers will not even have properties.

Setting component layout properties:

In the Navigator window, choose the component you want to edit

Go to the Properties window and click on the Properties button

Go to Layout properties, choose the property to be edited and input the value

The layout behavior for that component will be updated.

Adding Beans to a Window

If you want the IDE expanded, you can add Beans to a window that can be used in the visual design. Once you have installed the bean, you can go to the Window, select it, compile and add it to your forms. Beans must be compiled before being added to a window.

If you add a bean that has no icon, it will be given a default one by the IDE.

If a JavaBeans component used in a form is altered, the changes are not going to be reflected automatically in the GUI Builder. If you want your changes applied, the component must be recompiled and you need to go to the GUI builder or the Source Editor and press on CTRL+SHIFT+R to load the form again.

Adding a bean:

Open Tools>Palette and choose Swing/AWT Components

If you need a new category created for your bean go to the Palette window and right-click in it; this opens a context menu, click Create New Category and type the name it BEFORE the bean is added

Now choose where the bean is coming from – Project, Library or JAR – and specify which one has the corresponding class file for the bean you are adding

To add directly from the Palette window, find and right-click on the node for the bean in Projects and click on Tools>Add to Palette

Beans Binding and Database Applications

The basic procedure for beans binding is:

Create your GUI form

Add the components you want; this includes the custom beans you are creating the bindings for.

Bind your component properties:

Choose a component in Source Editor Design or in Navigator and right-click it. The Bind menu appears; select your target property and the Bind Dialog box will open

Click Binding and specify the binding source

Click Advanced, specify binding customizations if needed.

Binding Two Bean Properties

When your Java form has been created and all your components added, the code can be generated to bind the properties of those components. Binding retains value synchronization of the properties.

Preparing your components for binding:

In the GUI builder, add the components to your form

Decide which component will be to binding source and which is the binding target

The source is where the property value originates from. In the GUI Editor you initiate the binding on the target and then, in the dialog box for Bind, you declare which is the source.

Any binding may be two way, i.e. Read/Write, so any changes made to the target will be reflected automatically in the source. However, the initial binding must always go from source to target. If you click the Advanced tab in the Bind dialog box, you can change the binding update behavior.

Binding two properties:

Go to the GUI Builder and choose the target component for the binding. Right-click and click on Bind; now pick which property the binding will come from

Go to Binding Source and choose the component with the property to be bound to

Go to Binding Expression and pick the property to be bound to. Click on OK

Binding Data to Swing Components

Once your Java form is created with all its components, the code can be generated for binding them to data. Binding to Swing JList and JTable components is easy in the IDE but before you bind any component to a database, the following must be done:

Connect to an IDE database

In the GUI Builder, add the relevant component onto a form

Entity classes representing the database tables to bind to must be created

Creating an entity class:

Go to Projects and choose your project; right-click it and click on New>Other. Click Persistence>Entity Classes from Database

A wizard will open; click on Database Tables and choose the right database connection

When you see the column for Available Tables populated, choose which ones are to go into your applications. To move the tables to the column of Selected Tables, click on Add. Click on Next

Go to the Entity Classes age and ensure that the dialog box for Generate Named Query Annotations is selected

Mae the changes to the generated class names and to their location

Click on Persistence Unit and the dialog box will load. Make sure that the Persistence Library selected is TopLink and that the Table Generation Strategy is set to None

Click on Finish and the entity class nodes should appear in Projects.

Binding data to JTable components:

In GUI Builder, choose the component and right-click it; select Bind>Elements

Click on Import Data to Form and, in the resulting dialog box, choose which database table the components are to be bound to; click OK.

Go to the Binding Source box and choose one item that is representative of the entity class result list.

Do not change the Binding Expression; leave it as Null

Go to the Display Expression list and choose the property representing the database column with the values to display

Click on OK

Converting Values Between the Source and The Target Properties

When the values for a pair of properties of a pair of objects, you will occasionally need to convert the values between the differing types. The list below is the conversions which do NOT require a converter:

- BigDecimal to String and vice versa
- BigInteger to String and vice versa
- Boolean to String and vice versa
- Byte to String and vice versa
- Char to String and vice versa
- Double to String and vice versa
- Float to string and vice versa
- Int to string and vice versa
- Long to String and vice versa
- Short to String and vice versa
- Int to Boolean and vice versa

Creating a custom converter starts with creating a class to extend org.jdesktop.beansbinding.Converter. The class must override two methods – convertForward() and convertRelease(). The former converts values from source to target and the latter does the opposite, converts from target to source.

Using a custom converter to within a binding:

In Projects, right-click on the Converter class and click on Compile File

Drag the converter over to the Design View and it will be added as a bean into your form

Choose the binding target, right-click it and click on Bind>Target Property

The Bind dialog box appears, click on Advanced

Click Converter and select the added converter from the list

Click on OK

The conversion code may also be directly added. Just click on the ellipsis, click Select Property Converter and click on Custom Code

Validating Target Value Changes

When the values of a pair of properties for a pair of objects are bound, you will, on occasion, need to validate the target property changes before they get written to the source. Validating a target requires a validator to be specified that will extend org.jdesktop.beansbinding.Validator.

Writing a custom validator requires a call that will also extend org.jdesktop.beansbinding.Validator. The class must implement the validate method and this will return null if the value is valid.

Using a custom validator:

In Projects, choose and right-click the validator class and click on Compile File

Drag the validator to the Design view where it will be added as a bean.

Now choose and right-click the binding target and click on Bind>Target Property

The Bind Dialog box appears, click on Advanced

Go to Validator and, form the list, pick the validator that was added

Click on OK

Again, the validation code can be directly added by clicking the ellipsis and clicking on Select Validator Property>Custom Code.

Deployment of GUI Applications

If you want your applications to work externally to the IDE, a few extra JAR files may need to be included when the application is deployed. You may need to use swing.layour-1.0.0.jar, a library that has the extensions related to the layout, like the GroupLayout manager. There is no need to package the library as it is already included for environments that run JRE.

From JDK 6 onwards, the library for Beans Binding is not included in the Java platform. However, the following JAR files can be found on your system in these folders:

- Beans Binding Library – NetBeans_installation_folder/java/modules/ext/
- Swing Layout Extensions Library – NetBeans_installation_folder/platform/modules/ext/

Preparing to Distribute a GUI Application

To make sure that these libraries can be referenced by the GUI application at runtime, the JAR files from the libraries and from the project classpath are copied by the IDE to a folder called dist/libfolder when the project is built. The JAR files are also added to the manifest.mf file for the application JAR; they are added to the Class-Path element.

If the support for these libraries is not used by the application the library will not be added to the folder.

To prepare for external distribution the dist folder must be zipped into a ZIP archive.

Standalone GUI Applications

When the application archive has been distributed, the application may be run externally using the command line:

Go to the dist folder for the project

Type in java -jar.jar_name.jar

GUI Builder Configuration

The Builder design and the way it generates code can also be changed. If you want to do this for one specific form, you must go to Navigator, choose the root node for the form, go to the Properties window and click on Code.

To change the settings for all the projects:

Go to the main window and click on Tools>Options

Click on Java>GU Builder and the settings that can be edited are shown.

Choose which property to edit and make your changes.

Those settings will now be applied.

That concludes our basic look at GUI building in Java; obviously there is a great deal more to this but you can find out everything you need to know by looking on the internet or signing up for a course in Java GUI Building.

Chapter 5: Object-Oriented Programming

OOP, or object-oriented programming is a style of programming with a firm basis in several concepts. Those concepts revolve around objects and classes and include Polymorphism, Encapsulation, Inheritance, Abstraction and more. Java is one of the most popular of all the object-oriented programming languages, as well as one of the easiest to learn and use. For this section of the guide, I will be talking about object orientation in Java, covering all the concepts it encompasses, particularly objects and classes.

Any application built on objects in Java is an object-oriented application and it is based on the declaration of one or more classes, with objects being created from those classes and the interaction between the objects.

Why OOP?

Let's say that you wanted a computer but, rather than buying one off the shelf, you decide that you want to build your own. So, off you go to the nearest computer parts store and you purchase everything you need – a CPU, a motherboard, a hard drive, some RAM, a graphics card, a nice casing to hold it all together and a power supply to make it all work.

You get home and you assemble your new computer. When you plug the power supply in and switch the computer on, with any luck, it will all work just fine. There is no need to worry about how many cores your CPU has, how many layers are in your motherboard; the number of plates in the hard drive, what its physical size is. You don't need to worry about anything because all you do is assemble the parts and expect that your computer will work.

Obviously, what you do need to worry about is having the right interfaces; for example, if the motherboard you choose supports only IDE then your hard drive must be an IDE hard drive. The RAM you choose must be of the right speed rating, and so on. However, that said, it really is not hard to assemble a PC set up using the right hardware components.

In much the same way, a car is manufactured from multiple components – a chassis, the right number of doors, an engine, transmission, brakes, wheels and more. Each of the components may be reusable, for example, one wheel could be used in multiple cars that meet the same specifications.

Hardware like cars and computers are all made up of a series of hardware components, each of which is reusable.

Could you build a software application in the same way? Perhaps choose this routine, that routine and then expect it all to run correctly? No, of course you couldn't. Where it is relatively easy to assemble a hardware object from components, the same does not apply to software and software components. Since the computer was first designed many decades ago, millions of routines and programs have been written but for every new application, the program has to be written from the ground up.

Why do we need to do this? Why do we need to keep rewriting the same old code over and over again? Could you write the codes any better than the experts do?

Traditional Programming Languages – Procedural-Oriented

Traditional languages like Fortran, Pascal, C and Cobol, are procedural-oriented languages and they have a number of drawbacks when it comes to reusing the components they are built from.

Procedural-oriented languages are built from functions and functions are not as easy to reuse as an object or a class is. Copying a function from a program and then using it in another is not very easy because that function is more than likely going to reference other functions and/or global variables. In basic terms, a function is not properly encapsulated as a unit that is self-contained and reusable.

Also, procedural-oriented programming languages are not really suited to solving real-world problems because they don't have a high enough level of abstraction. For example, in C programming we use constructs, like the for loop, if-else statements, methods, arrays and pointers. These are all low-level and very hard to abstract a real-world problem from, like a computer football game or a CRM (Customer Relationship Management) system.

In short, traditional languages, the procedural-oriented languages, separate the variables (the data structures) and the functions (the algorithms).

Object-Oriented Programming

With object-oriented programming, or OOP as it has become known, are designed to get around these kinds of problems. The basic OOP unit is a class and a class will encapsulate both the static properties and the dynamic operations inside a container or 'box'. It will specify what the public interface is for making use of these boxes too.

Because a class is well-encapsulated, it is much easier to reuse. In short, OOP combines the algorithms and the data structures that make up a software entity inside one box.

With OOP languages we have the ability to use a much higher abstraction level, allowing us to solve real-world problems. While a traditional language, the procedural languages like Pascal and C force you to do your thinking in terms of the computer structure, like bytes, memory, decisions, loops and arrays, instead of in terms of the problem that needs to be solved, the OOP languages, like Java, allow you to do your thinking in the problem space. They make use of software objects that represent the problem space entities, and allow you to abstract them to find a solution to the problem.

Let's say, as an example, that you want to write a computer game based on football. Now, this is quite a complex type of game to build and using a procedural-oriented language would prove quite difficult. With an OOP language, it is much easier because the game can be modeled according to real-life things that happen in the game. For example, your classes could be:

- Player - the attribute for a player would be name, location on the playing field, number, etc. while the operations would include running, jumping, kicking the ball and so on
- Ball
- Field
- Reference
- Weather
- Audience

Perhaps more importantly, some classes, like Audience, or Ball, could easily be reused in a different application, perhaps a basketball game, without the need for too much, if any, modification.

The Benefits of Using OOP

Because procedural-oriented languages concentrate on procedures, using a basic unit of a function, you need to spend time first working out what all of the functions are going to be and then thinking about how they should be represented. With OOP languages, we focus our attention on the components perceived by the user using a basic unit of an object. You work out what all the objects are by combining data with the operations that are used to describe the way a user interacts with them.

The benefits of OOP include:

Much easier to use in terms of designing software. Rather than thinking in terms of bytes and bits, you can think in terms of the problem space instead. You are using abstraction and higher level concepts and, because the design is easier, your application development is much more productive.

The software is easier to maintain because it is much easier to understand. In turn, that makes it easier to test and to debug.

The software is reusable. There is no longer any need to keep writing the same functions repeatedly for different scenarios. Being able to reuse the same code is fast and safe because you are using code that has been fully tested already and is proven to work.

OOP Concepts

Object-oriented programming is the combination of multiple concepts and we're going to discuss the most important ones now.

Java Naming Conventions

One rule that you do need to learn and follow is the naming conventions in Java for when you give identifiers, like methods, constants, variables, classes and so on, a name. Using these conventions makes your code much easier to read, not just by you but by any other developer who might want to take a look at your source code. Readability is incredibly important in Java as it means less time is wasted in trying to work out what a piece of code does.

These are the conventions you should follow:

Name	**Convention**
Class	must be a noun and must begin with an uppercase letter, i.e. System, Thread, Button, etc.
Interface	must be an adjective and begin with an uppercase letter, i.e. Remote, ActionListener, etc.
Method	must be a verb and begin with a lowercase letter, i.e. main(), println(), print(), etc.
Variable	must begin with a lowercase letter for the first word and uppercase for the start of other words, i.e. firstName, lastName, orderNumber, etc.
Package	must be in lowercase letters, i.e. lang, java, util, sql, etc.
Constants	must be all uppercase letters, i.e. MAX_PRIORITY, YELLOW, etc.

CamelCase

For interfaces, classes, variables and methods, Java follows the rules of camelCase for the syntax. This means that, where a name is two or more words, the first starts with a lowercase and all subsequent words in the name start with an uppercase letter, i.e. actionEvent, actionPerformed, RufusRubble, etc.

Java Objects and Classes

Objects and classes are the most important concepts in OOP as they are what we use for writing our programs. Java objects may be both physical and logical entities but classes are only logical entities.

Objects

Objects are entities that have both behavior and state. They may be physical (tangible) or logical (intangible) and each object displays three characteristics:

- State - representative of the data or value of the object
- Behavior – representative of the behavior or functionality of the object
- Identity – usually implemented using a unique ID, the value of which cannot be seen by an external user. The Java Virtual Machine uses it internally to identify the objects

An example of these characteristics would be a pen with a name of Ballpoint, a color of black (its state), and it is used for writing (its behavior).

Objects are instances of classes and the class is a kind of template used for creating the objects.

Object Class Methods

There are quite a few methods in the Object class, including:

Method	**Description**
public final Class getClass()	This will return the class object of the object and the class may be used to retrieve the metadata from the class too.
public int hash code()	This will return the object's hash code number.
public boolean equals(Object obj)	This will compare this object with the given object.
protected Object clone()	This will throw an exception, also creates a clone of the object and returns it.
public String toString()	This will return a string representation of the given object.
public final void notify()	This will wake one thread, waiting on the monitor for the object.
public final void notifyAll()	This will wake all threads waiting on the monitor for the object.
public final void wait(long timeout)	This will throw an InterruptedException error and will make the current thread wait for the specified amount of time in milliseconds until a further thread invokes either notify() or notifyAll().
public final void wait(long timeout,int nanos)	This will throw InterruptedException and makes the current thread wait the specified time in milliseconds and nanoseconds until

	a further thread invokes either notify() or notifyAll().
public final void wait()	This will throw an InterruptedException and makes the current thread wait until a further thread invokes either notify() to notifyAll().
protected void finalize()	This will throw Throwable; garbage collector invokes this just before the object goes for garbage collection.

Classes

A Java class is a group of Java objects all of which have the same or similar properties in common. Classes are logical entities and can never be physical. In a class you may find:

- Fields
- Methods
- Constructors
- Blocks
- Nested classes and an interface

The Java syntax used for declaring a class is:

```
class <class_name>{

 field;

 method;

}
```

Java Instance Variables

When a class is created in a class but external to the method, it is called an instance variable. These variables are not allocated any memory when it comes to compile time; instead, the memory is allocated at runtime, when the object or the instance gets created.

Java Methods

Java methods are similar to functions and they are used for exposing an object's behavior. They make reusing code incredibly easy and are also used to optimize your code.

An Example of Objects and Classes

We have a class called Student; it has 2 data member – name and id. We use the new keyword to create an object of the class and print the value of the object. We are also creating a method in the class – the method is called main():

```
//Shows you how classes and fields are defined
//this defines a Student class.
class Student {
        //this defines the fields
        int id; //field data member or instance variable
        String name;

        //how to create the main method inside the Student class
        public static void main(String args[])
        {
                // this creates an object or instance
                Student s1 = new Student(); // this creates an object of Student

                // this prints the value of the object
                System.out.println(s1.id); // using the reference variable to access the
member

                System.out.println(s1.name);
        }
}
```

The output of this is:

0

Null

Second Example

When it comes to real-time development, we create a class and then we can use it from another class; a much better method that what you saw in the last example. In this code, we are going to add a main() method into another class. It is possible for one source file to have multiple classes or for multiple classes to be used over multiple files. If you opt to define several in one file, make sure your file is saved as the class name containing the main() method:

```
//This demonstrates the main method being in
```

```
//another class
//this creates the Student class.
class Student{
	int id;
	String name;
}

//This creates a second class with them main method in it
class TestStudent1{
	public static void main(String args[]){
		Student s1 = new Student();
		System.out.println(s1.id);
		System.out.println(s1.name);
	}
}
```

The output of this will be:

0

Null

Object Initialization

We can initialize Java objects in 3 ways:

- Using a reference variable
- Using a method
- Using a constructor

Let's look at each of these with an example:

Using a Reference Variable

When we initialize an object, we are storing data in it. Have a look at this example of using a reference variable to initialize an object:

```
class Student{
	int id;
```

```
        String name;
}

class TestStudent2{
        public static void main(String args[]){
                Student s1=new Student();
                s1.id=101;
                s1.name="Suzy";
                System.out.println(s1.id+" "+s1.name);//printing members with a white
space
        }
}
```

The output of this will be:

101 Suzy

Another thing we can do is create several objects and use a reference variable for storing the information in them:

```
class Student{
        int id;
        String name;
}

class TestStudent3{
        public static void main(String args[]){
                //Creating objects
                Student s1=new Student();
                Student s2=new Student();
                //Initializing objects
                s1.id=101;
                s1.name="Suzy";
                s2.id=102;
```

```
            s2.name="Arthur";
            //Printing data
            System.out.println(s1.id+" "+s1.name);
            System.out.println(s2.id+" "+s2.name);
      }
}
```

The output of this will be:

101 Suzy

102 Arthur

Using a Method

Next, we will take the Student class and create two objects of it. The value for these objects will be initialized by a method called insertRecord(). When we invoke the displayInformation() method, the subject data or state is displayed:

```
class Student{
      int rollno;
      String name;
      void insertRecord(int r, String n){
            rollno=r;
            name=n;
      }
      void displayInformation(){System.out.println(rollno+" "+name);}
}

class TestStudent4{
      public static void main(String args[]){
            Student s1=new Student();
            Student s2=new Student();
            s1.insertRecord(111,"Kayleigh");
            s2.insertRecord(222,"Annalise");
            s1.displayInformation();
```

```
		s2.displayInformation();
	}
}
```

The output of this will be:

111 Kayleigh

222 Annalise

Using a Constructor

We'll be looking at constructors shortly so refer to that section as it will explain everything.

Here are a few more examples of classes and objects.

Employee:

In this example, we maintain employee records:

```
class Employee{
	int id;
	String name;
	float salary;
	void insert(int i, String n, float s) {
		id=i;
		name=n;
		salary=s;
	}

	void display(){
		System.out.println(id+" "+name+" "+salary);
	}
}

public class TestEmployee {
	public static void main(String[] args){
```

```
                Employee e1=new Employee();
                Employee e2=new Employee();
                Employee e3=new Employee();
                e1.insert(101,"Adrian",50000);
                e2.insert(102,"Irene",30000);
                e3.insert(103,"Nigel",75000);
                e1.display();
                e2.display();
                e3.display();
        }
}
```

The output of this will be:

101 Adrian 50000.0

102 Irene 30000.0

103 Nigel 75000.0

Rectangle:

In this example we are maintaining records in the class called Rectangle:

```
class Rectangle{
        int length;
        int width;
        void insert(int l, int w){
                length=l;
                width=w;
        }

        void calculateArea(){
                System.out.println(length*width);
        }
}
```

```
class TestRectangle1{
        public static void main(String args[]){
                Rectangle r1=new Rectangle();
                Rectangle r2=new Rectangle();
                r1.insert(11,5);
                r2.insert(3,15);
                r1.calculateArea();
                r2.calculateArea();
        }
}
```

The output of this will be:

55

45

Anonymous Objects

An anonymous object is simply one that does not have a name or any reference. They can only be used at the time objects are created and if you only have a single use for an object, it is a good approach. Have a look at this example:

```
new Calculation();//anonymous object
```

Using a reference to call a method:

```
Calculation c=new Calculation();
c.fact(5);
```

Using an anonymous object to call a method:

```
new Calculation().fact(5);
```

This is a full example of the Java anonymous object:

```
class Calculation{
        void fact(int n){
                int fact=1;
```

```
            for(int i=1;i<=n;i++){
                  fact=fact*i;
            }
            System.out.println("Factorial is "+fact);
      }

      public static void main(String args[]){
            new Calculation().fact(5);//calling the method using an anonymous object
      }
}
```

The output of this will be:

Factorial is 120

Using One Type to Create Several Objects:

We can also create several objects using a single type, as is the case of the primitive data type.

Initializing a primitive variable looks like this:

int a=10, b=20;

Initializing a reference variable looks like this:

Rectangle r1=new Rectangle(), r2=new Rectangle();//creating two objects

Let's have a look at the complete example:

```
//This shows us how to use of Rectangle class which
//contains data members of length and width
class Rectangle{
      int length;
      int width;
      void insert(int l,int w){
            length=l;
            width=w;
```

```
	}

	void calculateArea(){
		System.out.println(length*width);
	}
}

class TestRectangle2{
	public static void main(String args[]){
		Rectangle r1=new Rectangle(),r2=new Rectangle();//creating two objects
		r1.insert(11,5);
		r2.insert(3,15);
		r1.calculateArea();
		r2.calculateArea();
	}
}
```

The output of this will be:

55

45

And here is a real world example, showing the way the banking system works.

```
//This shows us how the banking system works
//with deposits and withdrawals of specified amounts from our bank account
//we create an Account class with two methods -  deposit() and withdraw()
class Account{
	int acc_no;
	String name;
	float amount;
	//this method initializes an object
```

```
    void insert(int a,String n,float amt){
        acc_no=a;
        name=n;
        amount=amt;
    }
    //deposit method
    void deposit(float amt){
        amount=amount+amt;
        System.out.println(amt+" deposited");
    }
    //withdraw method
    void withdraw(float amt){
        if(amount<amt){
            System.out.println("Insufficient Balance");
        }else{
            amount=amount-amt;
            System.out.println(amt+" withdrawn");
        }
    }
    //this method checks the account balance
    void checkBalance(){
        System.out.println("Balance is: "+amount);
    }
    //this method displays the object values
    void display(){
        System.out.println(acc_no+" "+name+" "+amount);
    }
}

//this is a test class to deposit and withdraw the amount amount
```

```
class TestAccount{
    public static void main(String[] args){
        Account a1=new Account();
        a1.insert(832345,"Angel",1000);
        a1.display();
        a1.checkBalance();
        a1.deposit(40000);
        a1.checkBalance();
        a1.withdraw(15000);
        a1.checkBalance();
    }
}
```

The output of this will be:

832345 Angel 1000.0

Balance is: 1000.0

40000.0 deposited

Balance is: 41000.0

15000.0 withdrawn

Balance is: 26000.0

Time to move on to constructors.

Java Constructors

One of the concepts in OOP is the constructor, a code block that makes use of a new object. Constructors look much like Java instance methods but they are not methods because a constructor does not contain any return type. Constructors and methods are different but you often hear people refer to constructors as special methods.

A constructor will share the same name as the class it is for and, in Java code, looks like this:

```
public class MyClass{
    //This is a constructor
    MyClass(){
```

```
        }
        ..
}
```

Note, the constructor name is the same as the class name and there is no return type.

How Constructors Work

In order to understand how a constructor works, we'll need to look at an example. Using the class called MyClass from our previous code example, we need to create an object for it and that would look like this:

```
MyClass obj = new MyClass();
```

We have used a keyword, new, to create the MyClass object. This keyword is also used for invoking the constructor so that it initializes our new object. So that you understand initialization let's take the example of a simple constructor program.

Have a look at this code, to start with:

```
public class Hello {
        String name;
        //Constructor
        Hello(){
                this.name = "MyFirstBook.com";
        }

        public static void main(String[] args) {
                Hello obj = new Hello();
                System.out.println(obj.name);
        }
}
```

The output for this code will be:

MyFirstBook.com

What we have done here is taken the class called Hello and created an object which we called obj. Next, the object's instance variable name is displayed. You can see that the code output is MyFirstBook.com – this is the data that we passed to name while the constructor was initializing the object. You can see that, when the object called obj was created, the constructor was automatically invoked. The keyword we used here was this, referencing the current object called obj.

Different Constructor Types

In the Java language, there are three types of constructor:

- Default
- no-arg
- Parametrized

Let's look at each in a little more details.

The Default Constructor

If you omit implementation of a constructor within your class, a constructor is added by the Java compiler. Each class must have a constructor and the one used is called the default constructor. You won't see it listed anywhere in your Java code as the compiler adds at compilation time into the .class file. Should you implement a constructor in your code, the compiler will not add the default one.

The no-arg Constructor

A no-arg constructor is a constructor that contains no arguments. The no-arg constructor signature is identical to that of the default constructor but the body of this constructor may contain code – the default constructor body is always left empty. There are those who will swear blind that the default and the no-arg constructor are identical but, really, they are not. If, for example, you were to add public Demo() to a class called Demo(), it is not a default constructor because it contains code. Here's an example:

```
class Demo

{

	public Demo()

	{

		System.out.println("This is an example of a no-arg constructor");

	}


	public static void main(String args[]) {

		new Demo();

	}

}
```

The output for this would be:
This is an example of a no-arg constructor

The Parameterized constructor

A constructor that contains arguments, otherwise known as parameters, is called a parameterized constructor. Let's see how it works with an example:

```
public class Employee {

        int empId;

        String empName;


        //this parameterized constructor has 2 parameters

        Employee(int id, String name){

                this.empId = id;

                this.empName = name;

        }


        void info(){

                System.out.println("Id: "+empId+" Name: "+empName);

        }


        public static void main(String args[]){

                Employee obj1 = new Employee(50287,"Smith");

                Employee obj2 = new Employee(84218,"Jones");

                obj1.info();

                obj2.info();

        }

}
```

The output of this would be:

Id: 50287 Name: Smith

Id: 84218 Name: Jones

Here, we have an example of a parameterized constructor that contains 2 constructors – name and id. When we created our objects, called obj1 and obj2, we passed 2 arguments, ensuring that the constructor is invoked once obj1 and obj2 have been created.

Here's another example:

With the second example, we now have both a parametrized constructor and a default constructor. When we create the object, using the new keyword, and we don't pass a parameter, the compiler invokes the default constructor; when you do pass a parameter, the parametrized constructor is invoked, matching the list of passed parameters:

```
class Example2

{

        private int var;

        //default constructor

        public Example2()

        {

                this.var = 20;

        }


        //parameterized constructor

        public Example2(int num)

        {

                this.var = num;

        }


        public int getValue()

        {

                return var;

        }


        public static void main(String args[])

        {

                Example2 obj = new Example2();
```

```
        Example2 obj2 = new Example2(200);
        System.out.println("var is: "+obj.getValue());
        System.out.println("var is: "+obj2.getValue());
    }
}
```

The output would be:

var is: 20

var is: 200

And a third example, showing inly a parametrized constructor implemented in the class:

```
class Example3
{
    private int var;
    public Example3(int num)
    {
        var=num;
    }

    public int getValue()
    {
        return var;
    }

    public static void main(String args[])
    {
        Example3 myobj = new Example3();
        System.out.println("value of var is: "+myobj.getValue());
    }
}
```

The output of this would be a compilation error. Why? Because a default constructor is invoked by the Example3 myobj = new Example3() and we don't have that default constructor in the code.

If we were to take the parametrized constructor out the program would compile and run just fine because the default constructor would be implemented by the compiler.

Chaining Constructors

When one constructor calls for another constructor of an identical class, we call this constructor chaining. The purpose of this is to allow you to pass your parameters through several different constructors while doing the initialization in one place. If we have two constructors that need a certain parameter and you don't chain the constructors, that parameter needs to initialized twice; when there are changes to that initialization you will then need to repeat those changes in all the relevant constructors, not just one.

In general, the constructor that has the fewest arguments should call the constructors that have more. Let's see an example to try to understand this.

We have a number of constructors in this example; one calls another using the this keyword. The very first statement in the constructor must be this(); if it isn't, you will get an error message telling you there is an "Exception in thread "main" java.lang.Error: Unresolved compilation problem: Constructor call must be the first statement in the construct".

```
class Employee

{

   public String empName;

   public int empSalary;

   public String address;


   //The default constructor for the class

   public Employee()

   {

         //this calls the constructor that has the String parameter

      this("Smith");

   }


   public Employee(String name)

   {
```

```
        //this will call the constructor that has the (String, int) parameter
        this(name, 312587);
    }
    public Employee(String name, int sal)
    {
        //this will call the constructor that has the (String, int, String) parameter
        this(name, sal, "Gilly");
    }
    public Employee(String name, int sal, String addr)
    {
        this.empName=name;
        this.empSalary=sal;
        this.address=addr;
    }

    void disp() {
        System.out.println("Employee Name: "+empName);
        System.out.println("Employee Salary: "+empSalary);
        System.out.println("Employee Address: "+address);
    }

    public static void main(String[] args)
    {
      Employee obj = new Employee();
      obj.disp();
    }
}
```

The output of this will be:

Employee Name: Smith

Employee Salary: 312587

Employee Address: Gilly

The Super() Keyword

The super() keyword is used to reference objects for the immediate parent class. This ties in with inheritance, which we will be talking about in some depth later; for now, read through this and then come back to it after the section on inheritance.

Using the Super() Keyword

The super() keyword is used:

- For accessing the parent class data members when the parent and the child contain a member with identical names
- For explicitly calling the parametrized and no-arg constructors for the parent class
- For accessing the parent class method when it has been overridden by the child class.

Now let's see some examples to explain these:

Accessing Parent Class Variables

When you have a child class that contains a variable that is also in the parent class, when you want access to the parent class variable the super() keyword is needed. In the next code example, we have declared a data member called num in our parent class. We cannot access the variable for num in our parent class without the super() keyword:

```
//Parent class, Superclass or base class

class Superclass

{

        int num = 150;

}


//Child class, subclass or derived class

class Subclass extends Superclass

{

        /* The variable called num which is in the superclass

         * is also present in the subclass

         */

         int num = 160;

         void printNumber(){
```

```
            System.out.println(num);
    }
    public static void main(String args[]){
            Subclass obj= new Subclass();
            obj.printNumber();
    }
}
```

The output of this will be:

160

To access the num variable in the parent class, we can call it in the following way, provided the parent and the child class contains the same variable:

super.variable_name

Another example; this we have a print statement where, rather than num, we pass super.num instead:

```
class Superclass
{
    int num = 150;
}

class Subclass extends Superclass{
  int num = 160;

  void printNumber(){
        /* Rather than using num, we are using
         * super.num in our print statement
         * referencing the num variable of Superclass
         */
        System.out.println(super.num);
  }
```

```
    public static void main(String args[]){
                Subclass obj= new Subclass();
                obj.printNumber();
    }
}
```

Output:

150

By using super.num instead of num, we can gain access to the parent class num variable.

Invoking the Parent Class Constructor

The object for the subclass is created, we use the new keyword for invoking the child class constructor. In turn, this implicitly invokes the parent class constructor. The execution order when the child class object is created is a constructor for the parent class gets executed first, followed by the constructor for the child class. The reason for this order is that the compile inserts super() to invoke the parent class no-arg constructor as the initial statement in the child class constructor.

Let's see this by way of an example:

```
class Parentclass
{
        Parentclass(){
                System.out.println("Constructor of parent class");
        }
}

class  Subclass extends Parentclass
{
        Subclass(){
                /* Compile will implicitly add super() at this point as the
                 * initial statement for this constructor.
                 */
                System.out.println("Constructor of child class");
```

```
    }

    Subclass(int num){
        /* Although it is a parameterized constructor.
         * The compiler will still insert the no-arg super() at this point
         */
        System.out.println("arg constructor of child class");
    }

    void display(){
        System.out.println("Hello!");
    }

    public static void main(String args[]){
        /* The default constructor is used for creating the object and this
         * invokes the  child class constructor, which, in turn
         * invokes the constructor for the  parent class
         */
        Subclass obj= new Subclass();
        //We are now calling the subclass method
        obj.display();
        /* We use the arg constructor to create another object
         * which invokes the child class constructor which, in turn
         * will invoke the parent class no-arg constructor automatically
         */
        Subclass obj2= new Subclass(10);
        obj2.display();
    }
}
```

The output for this will be:

Constructor of parent class

Constructor of child class

Hello!

Constructor of parent class

arg constructor of child class

Hello!

Using a Parametrized Super() Call

For the child class constructor we can explicitly call super() but it makes no sense to do so because it would only be redundant. However, for a parent class constructor that takes parameters, we would use a parametrized super() call instead, as a way of invoking the parent class's parametrized constructor from the child class's constructor.

An example will make this clearer:

```
class Parentclass

{

        //no-arg constructor

        Parentclass(){

                System.out.println("no-arg constructor of parent class");

        }


        //arg or parameterized constructor

        Parentclass(String str){

                System.out.println("parameterized constructor of parent class");

        }

}



class Subclass extends Parentclass

{

        Subclass(){
```

```
        /* super() must be added to the initial statement of the constructor
         * otherwise you get a compilation error. Another important
         * point is that when super is explicitly used in the constructor,
         * the compiler will not invoke the parent constructor automatically.
         */
        super("Hahaha");
        System.out.println("Constructor of child class");
    }

    void display(){
        System.out.println("Hello");
    }

    public static void main(String args[]){
        Subclass obj= new Subclass();
        obj.display();
    }
}
```

The output of this will be:

parameterized constructor of parent class

Constructor of child class

Hello

This particular example throws up two important points:

You must have either super() or a parametrized super() as the initial constructor statement otherwise the compilation error we talked of earlier will be thrown.

When super() was placed explicitly in the constructor, note that the no-arg constructor for the parent class was not called by the compiler.

The Super() Keyword and Method Overriding

When a method that is already in the parent class is declared by the child class, it is called overriding. We will talk more about this later; for now, keep in mind that when child classes override parent class methods, when a method is called form the child class object it will be the child version of the method. However, when you use super() in this way – super.method_name, the parent class method, the one that has been overridden, may be called. Have a look at an example:

```
class Parentclass

{

        //The method that has been overridden

        void display(){

                System.out.println("Parent class method");

        }

}



class Subclass extends Parentclass

{

        //The method doing the overriding

        void display(){

                System.out.println("Child class method");

        }


        void printMsg(){

                //This calls the Overriding method

                display();

                //This calls the Overridden method

                super.display();

        }


        public static void main(String args[]){

                Subclass obj= new Subclass();

                obj.printMsg();
```

```
    }
}
```

The output of this would be:

Child class method

Parent class method

To summarize constructors:

- Each class must have a constructor, be it a normal or an abstract class
- A constructor is not the same as a method and does not have a return type
- The name of the constructor must match with the name of the class
- Any access specific may be used with a constructor and they can also be declared as private constructors. However, although these are perfectly possible in the Java language, it must be borne in mind that a private constructor only has scope within the class.
- In the same way as a constructor, a method may also share the same name as the class but a method has a return type. We use this type to identify them as a method and not a constructor.
- If no constructor is implemented within a class, the compiler will implement the default constructor.
- The initial statement in any constructor code must be this() or super(). If you omit these, an error exception is thrown by the compiler.
- It is possible to overload a constructor but not to override one.
- Constructors may not be inherited
- If there is no default or no-arg constructor in a class, the compiler will not add the default constructor to the child class as it would normally
- An interface does not have a constructor
- An abstract class may have a constructor and it may be invoked when the class is instantiated, so long as it is the class that implements an interface
- With the this() keyword, one constructor can invoke other constructors of the same class.

The Static Keyword

We use the static keyword mostly for memory management and the keyword goes with the class itself, not with a class instance. It may be:

- A variable, or class variable
- A method, or class method
- A block
- A nested class
- Static Variable

Static variables are used for referencing common properties of every object – these are properties that are not unique to any one object. An example would be the name of the organization for a group of employees or the name of a college for a group of students.

Static variables are only allocated memory when they are in the class at the time the class is loaded. Because of this, they increase the efficiency of your program memory.

Here's an example that does not have a static variable:

```
class Student{
  int rollno;
  String name;
  String college="ITS";
}
```

Now let's assume that our college has 500 students in it. Every one of the instance data members will be allocated memory every time the object gets created. Every student has their own unique name and roll number so the use of the instance data member is good enough. In the code above, the word 'college' is referencing the property commonly shared between each object. If we were to change that to a static variable, the memory will be allocated just once because the static property gets shared among every object.

Here's the example:

```
//This will demonstrate the use of a static variable
class Student{
        int rollno;//instance variable
        String name;
        static String college ="ITS";//static variable
        //constructor
        Student(int r, String n){
                rollno = r;
                name = n;
        }

        //this method will display the values
        void display (){
```

```
            System.out.println(rollno+" "+name+" "+college);
    }
}

//this test class will show the object values
public class TestStaticVariable1{
    public static void main(String args[]){
            Student s1 = new Student(111,"Kayleigh");
            Student s2 = new Student(222,"Annalise");
            //we can use one line of code to change the college property for all the objects
            //Student.college="BBDIT";
            s1.display();
            s2.display();
    }
}
```

The output of this will be:

111 Kayleigh ITS

222 Annalise ITS

Counter Program – No Static Variable

Here, we are creating an instance variable with a name of count. This variable has been incremented within the constructor. Because the variable is going to be allocated memory when the object is created, each of the objects will contain a copy of that instance variable. Incrementation will not affect the other objects, leaving the count variable in each one with a value of 1:

```
//this will show you how to use an instance variable
//which are allocated memory whenever a class object is created
class Counter{
```

```
	int count=0;//this will be given memory at the time the instance is created

	Counter(){
		count++;//incrementing value
		System.out.println(count);
	}

	public static void main(String args[]){
		//Creating objects
		Counter c1=new Counter();
		Counter c2=new Counter();
		Counter c3=new Counter();
	}
}
```

The output of this will be:

1

1

1

Counter Program – With Static Variable

As we saw above, the static variable is allocated memory just once; if any of the objects modifies the static variable value, the object will retain its own value:

```
//This will demonstrate how a static variable is used
//and which is shared between all the objects
class Counter2{
	static int count=0;//is only allocated memory once and retains its value
```

```
        Counter2(){
                count++;//increments the static variable value
                System.out.println(count);
        }

        public static void main(String args[]){
                //creating objects
                Counter2 c1=new Counter2();
                Counter2 c2=new Counter2();
                Counter2 c3=new Counter2();
        }
}
```

The output of this will be:

```
1
2
3
```

Static Method

If the static keyword is applied to a method, it becomes known as a static method and, like the variable, it will belong to the class and not the class instance. There is no need to create a class instance to invoke a static method and the method may access a static data member and modify its value.

Here's an example:

```
//This shows you how a static method is used
class Student{
        int rollno;
        String name;
        static String college = "ITS";

        //This static method will modify the static variable value
```

```
	static void change(){
		college = "BBDIT";
	}

	//This constructor initializes the variable
	Student(int r, String n){
		rollno = r;
		name = n;
	}

	//This method displays the values
	void display(){
		System.out.println(rollno+" "+name+" "+college);
	}
}

//This is a test class that creates and displays object values
public class TestStaticMethod{
	public static void main(String args[]){
		Student.change();//calling change method
		//creating objects
		Student s1 = new Student(111,"Kayleigh");
		Student s2 = new Student(222,"Annalise");
		Student s3 = new Student(333,"Suzy");
		//calling display method
		s1.display();
		s2.display();
		s3.display();
	}
}
```

The output of this will be:

111 Kayleigh BBDIT

222 Annalise BBDIT

333 Suzy BBDIT

Here's an example of a static method carrying out a normal calculation:

```
//This will use the static method  to retrieve the cube of a specified number
class Calculate{
        static int cube(int x){
                return x*x*x;
        }

        public static void main(String args[]){
                int result=Calculate.cube(5);
                System.out.println(result);
        }
}
```

The output of this will be:125

Static Method Restrictions

The static method has 2 main restrictions:

- A static method may not directly call a non-static method or use a non-static data member
- The keywords, this and super, cannot be used in any static context

Here's an example:

```
class A{
        int a=40;//non static

        public static void main(String args[]){
                System.out.println(a);
```

```
    }
}
```

The output of this will be:

Compile Time Error

Static Block

Static blocks in Java are used for initializing the static data members and are executed at class loading time before execution of the main method.

Here's an example:

```
class A2{
    static{
        System.out.println("static block is invoked");
    }

    public static void main(String args[]){
        System.out.println("Hello main");
    }
}
```

The output of this will be:

static block is invoked

Hello main

The Java OOP Concepts

The Java OOP concepts are what let us create particular interactions between two or more Java objects, making it possible to safely reuse code and make our programs far more readable. There are several main concepts which we will discuss briefly below before going into more depth later on.

Abstraction

Abstraction is designed to show users only the information they need to see, reducing complexity significantly. Let's say, for example, that you want to go for a drive in a car.

There is no need to have any knowledge about the way the car works, only that it goes and stops as it should. The same could be said about the classes in Java. The details of the internal implementation are hidden through the use of abstract classes and/or interfaces. All that needs to be defined on the abstract level is the method signature – the method name and list of parameters. Each class will then implement the signature as they need to and in the way they see fit.

Summary:

Java abstraction:

- Hides the complexity from the user
- Avoids the use of repetitive code
- Only shows the internal functionality signature
- Provides developers with the flexibility to modify how the abstract behavior is implemented
- With abstract classes, partial abstraction may be achieved
- With interfaces, total abstraction may be achieved

Encapsulation

With encapsulation, we can protect any data stored in any class from access across the system. As the name gives away, the internals of the class are safeguarded as if they were inside a real capsule. Implementation of encapsulation is done by ensuring that class variables (the fields) are private but with public getter methods and setter methods pointing to them. One example of a class that is fully encapsulated is a Java Bean.

Summary

Java encapsulation:

- Reduces the direct access to class data members or fields
- The fields are set as private
- A getter method and setter method are provided for each field
- Getter methods are used for returning fields
- Setter methods are used to let us modify a field's value

Polymorphism

Polymorphism is the process by which we can perform a given action in multiple ways. Java polymorphism tends to take two forms – overloading and overriding of methods. With method overloading, we have multiple methods in a class, each with the same name. When each is called, they are separated by their parameters – how many, what type and what order they are in. overriding is when a child class overrides a parent class method.

Summary:

Polymorphism in Java:

- The same name is used for multiple methods in one class
- These methods can all be called from the objects
- Every object in Java is polymorphic
- Static polymorphism is known as method overloading
- Dynamic polymorphism is known as method overriding

Inheritance

With Java inheritance, we can create child classes that inherit methods and fields from the parent class. Child classes are able to override methods and values in a parent class but this is not really necessary. A parent class may also be called a base class or a superclass and the child classes are also called derived classes or subclasses. the inheritance principle is implemented in Java using the extends keyword.

Summary:

Inheritance in Java:

- Child classes may extend parent classes through feature inheritance
- Fully implements the programming principle of DRY – Don't Repeat Yourself. (More about this in Best Practices later)
- Makes it easier to reuse code
- Multilevel inheritance is possible, i.e. a child class can have a child class
- Multiple inheritance is not possible because a class cannot extend any more than a single class

There are three other concepts in Java OOP besides the main ones – association, aggregation and composition. Aggregation is a kind of association and composition is a special kind of aggregation.

Association

Association is all about taking two classes that are not related and making a relationship between them. Let's say you declare a couple of fields, each having a different type inside one class; association would be having the fields interact with one another.

Summary:

Association in Java:

- Two unrelated classes are given an association through objects
- Both classes can exist without the other class

- The relationship or association can be on a one-to-one basis, one-to-many basis or a many-to-many basis

Aggregation

Aggregation is a narrow version of association and it happens where there is a HAS-A (one way) relationship between the associated classes. An example would be that all passengers have a car but not every car will necessarily have a passenger. When the Passenger class is declared, a field may be created for the Car type; this will show the car that the passenger is related to (belongs to). Then, whenever a new Passenger object is instantiated, the data stored in the Car that is part of the relationship may also be accessed

Summary:

Java Aggregation:

- Association in one direction only
- Is representative of a HAS-A relationship between the classes
- One class depends on another but both classes do not depend on each other

Composition

Composition is a form of aggregation but a much stricter one and it happens when the classes that you have associated with one another depend mutually on each other and one cannot exist without the other. Let's take two classes called Car and Engine. Cars need Engines to run while an Engine needs to be built into a Car to function properly. This type of relationship is also known as a PART-OF relationship.

Summary

Java composition:

- A form of aggregation but more restricted
- Representative of a PART-OF relationship between classes
- Both of the classes are mutually dependent upon one another
- If one class no longer exists, the other class cannot survive
- Now we can delve deeper into these concepts, using code examples to help explain them.

Abstraction

Abstraction is one of the major concepts, the biggest building blocks of Java code. We learned earlier that abstraction is all about hiding what goes on inside, the inner workings as it were, and showing only what is absolutely necessary. So you could simplify abstraction by saying it hides complexity and show functionality.

It is important to note that you can only achieve 100% abstraction by using interface and I will go into details on that at the end of this.

Explaining Abstraction

The easiest way to explain abstraction is with the example of a text message. When you send a text message to someone, all you are doing is inputting the number/name to send it to along with your message, and then pressing send. You don't know what is going on in the background to send this message. Abstraction has been used to hide the complexity from you and show only the functionality that you need to see.in Java, we use abstraction and/or interface to achieve this.

Before we move on to the syntax, we'll go over the key points you need to learn about abstraction:

Abstract Class

The abstract keyword is used to declare an abstract class. This may have a body without methods, methods without a body or both. If you declare any class with a method but with no body then it must be declared as an abstract class for the simple reason the method has no functionality and no implementation.

In this example you can see that one of the methods, calling, does not have a body so the class is declared as an abstract class:

```
abstract class Mobile{

        abstract void calling();

        void messaging()

        {

                System.out.println("Messaging");

        }

}
```

Abstract Method

A method that has no body and no methods, and has only a signature is called an abstract method. These methods do not have any implementation and are declared with the abstract keyword in front of the method name. This is an example of an abstract method:

```
abstract void calling();
```

and the correct syntax to use is:

abstract void method_name();

Before you can use an abstract method, that method must be overridden in the child class – more details about overriding at the end of the section on OOP.

Extending Abstract Classes

So, an abstract class may have an abstract method with no implementation and that means not being able to instantiate the abstract class. If we were to attempt to instantiate it, we would find that the object is next to useless because abstract methods have no implementation. To stop this happening, Java does not allow abstract class instantiation.

The first thing to do is to extend the abstract class; here we can implement the abstract method and then the new class can be instantiated. Here's how to do it.

We define the abstract class with an abstract method:

```
abstract class Mobile{

        abstract calling(); //Method without a body

}
```

Next, we extend the abstract class and then implement the abstract methods:

```
class Apple extends Mobile{

        void calling();

        {

                System.out.println("Start Calling");

        }

}
```

Abstraction Syntax

Abstraction syntax begins with the abstract keyword, followed by the name of the class and then a combination of both abstract methods and non-abstract methods.

abstract class <ClassName>{

//Combination of abstract methods without a body or any implementation and non-abstract methods that do have a body and implementation.

//If a class contains one or more abstract methods, it must be declared as an abstract class

```
}
```

Abstraction Examples

We're going to look at some real-life examples of abstraction. In this first example, we'll use the sounds created by different animals and then the sounds will be displayed using abstraction in Java. I have used Eclipse for this example; we have not covered that in this guide but if you want to play along, Eclipse is easy enough to understand and use.

Example 1

Create a new project using Eclipse and then create an abstract class. Call it Sound and add this code:

```
public abstract class Sound {


        //Non-abstract method with implementation
  public void soundmessage(){
    System.out.print("Animal Sound");
  }

  //Abstract method without body or implementation
  abstract void sound();
}
```

Next, create a class called Dog; this will extend Sound. Then implement an abstract method called sound() for Dog and add this code into it:

```
public class Dog extends Sound{


        void sound(){
                soundmessage();
                System.out.println(" of Dog: Bark");
        }
}
```

Now create another class called Horse; this will also extend the Sound class. Then implement that sound method again but, this time, for Horse and add this code:

```
public class Horse extends Sound{

    void sound(){

        soundmessage();

        System.out.println(" of Horse: Neigh");

    }

}
```

Next comes the main class called AnimalSound. We create two objects, one for the Dog class and one for the Horse class. Then the sound() method is called on the objects. Here is the code for AnimalSound():

```
public class AnimalSound {

    public static void main(String[] args)

    {

        Dog dog = new Dog();

        dog.sound();


        Horse horse = new Horse();

        horse.sound();

    }

}
```

Run this program and you would see

Animal Sound of Dog: Bark

Animal Sound of Horse: Neigh

With this example you can see how useful abstraction is. All we did was defined a combination of abstract methods and non-abstract methods in the abstract class and the implemented the abstract class in a child class as per requirement. The same method will provide different results depending on which objects are used from which child class.

Example 2:

In the second example, we will display a text that reads RufusRubble and we'll do this with an abstract method of an abstract class called Base. The child class will implement our Base class and it will override our display method. The text will then be printed.

Here's the Base class code:

```
public abstract class Base {

        abstract void display(); //abstract method

}
```

And here is the code for the child class and the main function of the class:

```
public class Child extends Base{


        void   display() // this method will override the base class display method

        {

                System.out.println("RufusRubble");  //This will print "RufusRubble" as the
output

        }


        public static void main(String args[]) //this is main function of our class

        {

                Child c=new Child(); //this will create an object of the child class

                c.display(); //this calls the child class display method using the object for help

        }

}
```

Running this would give you this output:

RufusRubble

Here, the Base class is an abstract class that has an abstract method called display(). The child class provides the implementation.

Why Abstraction is Important

Abstraction is important because:

- It hides complexity and shows functionality, making the system easier to maintain

- It provides a great deal more power to OOP languages when used together with other OOP concepts like polymorphism and encapsulation
- It helps provide real solutions to real problems

Abstract Class vs Interface

- The abstract class and interface are very similar in that they both have an abstract method and neither can be instantiated. There are also differences between the two:
- Abstract classes may extend only one class at any one time whereas the interface may extend multiple interfaces at any one time
- An abstract class may have abstract and non-abstract classes whereas the interface may only have abstract methods
- The abstract keyword is used to declare an abstract method but the keyword is optional in interface because all methods in interface are abstract
- The abstract class may contain public, private, and public abstract methods whereas interface may only contain public abstract methods
- The abstract class may contain final, static or static final variable using any access specifier whereas interface may only have static final variables.

Before we move onto the next major OOP concept, we'll take some time out to explore interface and how it works with abstraction.

Interface

Java interface is used for achieving 100% abstraction because interface only contains methods without any implementation or body. Any field that is declared inside interface is public, static, and final and by default, any method is a public abstract method.

Interfaces are like class templates; we never build them to represent any object, only to run interference between OOP concepts and Java programs.

Interface Explanation

In much the same way that abstraction does, interface hides the complex details of implementation and shows only the necessary functionality but there is a big difference between them. The methods declared in interface are all abstract while, in abstraction, you can have a combination of abstract and non-abstract.

To show you how interface works using a real-world example. We'll build an interface called Run. This interface could have methods in called runForward() or jumpOver(). There wouldn't be any logic in these methods but any class that implements Run would also need to implement both of the methods. Let's say that we have classes for running birds, like Ostrich and Kiwi, both of which will implement the Run interface.

Declaring Interface

To declare interface, you need to use the keyword, interface:

```
public interface Run {
        void runForward();
        void jumpOver();
}
```

Implementing Interface

Interface is implemented by the class providing a body, i.e. implementation, to every method that has been declared. The implements keyword is used for this and, because the methods in interface do not have bodies, they have to be implemented in another class before we can access them.

Now we'll look at an example showing how a class will implement interface. Bear in mind that, while a class implements an interface, we can also use one interface to extend another and we'll look at how to do that as well.

First we create an interface named Run; this has two methods in it – runForward() and jumpOver():

```
{
    void runForward();
    void jumpOver();
}
```

Next we create another class called Ostrich and this will implement the class called Run

```
public class Ostrich implements Run{

        public void runForward()
        {
                System.out.println("Ostrich running forward");
```

```
        }

        public void jumpOver()
        {
                System.out.println("Ostrich jumping over");
        }
}
```

Next, a class called Kiwi which will also implement Run:

```
public class Kiwi implements Run{
        public void runForward() {
                System.out.println("Kiwi is running forward");
  }

  public void jumpOver() {
    System.out.println("Kiwi is jumping over");
  }
}
```

Our main class, which we create now, is called Bird and in this class both the Ostrich and the Kiwi classes will be instantiated:

```
public class Bird {
  public static void main(String[] args)
  {
    Ostrich Ostrich = new Ostrich();
    Ostrich.runForward();
    Ostrich.jumpOver();

    Kiwi Kiwi = new Kiwi();
```

```
    Kiwi.runForward();
    Kiwi.jumpOver();
  }
}
```

The output from all this will be:

Ostrich running forward

Ostrich jumping over

Kiwi is running forward

Kiwi is jumping over

Extending an Interface

As I mentioned earlier, one interface can extend another but remember that an interface can't implement any other interface; that can only be done by a class.

The next example shows this extension in operation. We are using two interfaces – StaffNoDetails and EmployeeDetails which will extend the StaffNoDetails class.

First, we create the StaffNoDetails interface and give it one method called staffNo

```
public interface StaffNoDetails {
    void staffNo();
}
```

Next we create a further interface called EmployeeDetails. This will extend the StaffNoDetails and will have a name() method declared in it. Because the extends keyword has been used, the StaffNoDetails methods may now be inherited by EmployeeDetails; the latter interface will now have two methods – name() and staffNo().

```
public interface EmployeeDetails extends StaffNoDetails{
    void name();
}
```

A class called Details is created next and this will implement EmployeeDetails. We must give both methods, name() and staffNo() a body because the StaffNoDetails interface methods were inherited by the EmployeeDetails method.

Details is also going to be the main class:

```
public class Details implements EmployeeDetails{
```

```
    public void name(){
        System.out.println("RufusRubble");
    }

    public void staffNo(){
        System.out.println("98639012");
    }

    public static void main(String[] args) {

        Details details = new Details();
        System.out.print("Name: ");
        details.name();
        System.out.print("Roll No: ");
        details.staffNo();
    }
}
```

The output of this will be:

Name: RufusRubble

Roll No: 98639012

Interface vs Class

There are a few differences between interfaces and classes:

- An interface cannot be instantiated whereas a class can
- Every object that is created in an interface after implementation will have identical states; in a class, every object will have a state of its own
- In an interface objects must implement the defined contract to define their own behavior; in a class, unless an object is overridden, all objects have the same behaviors.
- Interface variables are public static finals and, when defined, must have a value assigned. With a class, the variables are instance unless specified otherwise.

- Interfaces cannot inherit classes but they can extend multiple interfaces. Classes can inherit only a single class and can implement multiple interfaces.
- Interface methods are public abstract and have no definition; in a class, every method must be defined unless the abstract keyword has been used as a decorator.

Encapsulation

Encapsulation is a concept whereby data is hidden from users. This is done to protect it from being accessed outside of the class it is in. All the concept involves is wrapping the data member and all the data functions into one class. With encapsulation, an object's internal details are hidden and the public getter and setter methods are set with private fields, enabling data to be set and gotten from them.

Encapsulation Explanation

To make it easier to understand, we'll look at encapsulation with Java examples.

In this example, we have two fields, one set as name and one as email. Both are private fields and both are set in a class called UserInfo. Both fields may only be accessed from inside the class; no external access is allowed. So, we also create a public getter method called getName() and a public setter method called setName(). These allow data to be read and written to the fields from outside the class. In this way, we have hidden the fields and their implementation.

First we create a class called UserInfo. Then we create the two fields, name and Email and set both as private. This is followed by the getter and setter methods, both set as public.

```
public class UserInfo {

    private String name;

    private String email;


    public String getName()

    {

        return name;

    }


    public void setName(String name)

    {

        this.name = name;

    }
```

```
	public String getEmail()
	{
		return email;
	}

	public void setEmail(String email)
	{
		this.email = email;
	}
}
```

Next, we create another class called User. In the main method, an object is created for UserInfo and, on this object, two methods are called to write data – setName() and setEmail, followed by two methods for reading the data – getName() and getEmail().

```
public class User {
	public static void main(String[] args) {
		UserInfo userInfo = new UserInfo();

		userInfo.setName("RufusRubble");
		userInfo.setEmail("info@RufusRubble.com");

		System.out.println("Name: "+ userInfo.getName());
		System.out.println("Email: "+ userInfo.getEmail());

	}
}
```

The output of this will be:

Name: RufusRubble

Email: info@RufusRubble.com

It is important to note that the public methods of setName(), getName(), setEmail() an getEmail() are all access points for the UserInfo class instance variables. In Java these are called getter and setter methods and any external class that wants to access the variables must go through these methods.

Real-World Encapsulation

Another way of looking at encapsulation is to use a real-world example so we'll use a class called VegetableDetails and this will contain the related fields, such as name, color, price.

First, we create a class called VegetableDetails. This is followed by three fields, all set to private, and called name, color, price, respectively. We also need a constructor to initialize the class object and this is followed by the getter and setter methods:

```
public class VegetableDetails

{

    //Data members of class VegetableDetails

    private String name;

    private String price;

    private String color;


    //declaration of constructor

    public VegetableDetails(String name, String price, String color)

    {

        this.name = name;

        this.price = price;

        this.color = color;

    }


    //Declaring Setter for all fields

    public void setName(String name) {

        this.name = name;

    }


    public void setPrice(String price) {
```

```
        this.price = price;
    }

    public void setColor(String color) {
        this.color = color;
    }

    //Declaring Getter for all fields
    public String getName()
    {
        return name;
    }

    public String getPrice()
    {
        return price;
    }

    public String getColor()
    {
        return color;
    }
}
```

Next, create a class called Vegetable and create one object for the class, VegetableDetails. Complete the details for Vegetable – in our case, carrot – in the constructor and then use the getter method to retrieve and print the value. Lastly, we use the setter method to modify the initialized value and the getter method to print the new value:

```
public class Vegetable {

    public static void main(String[] args) {
```

```
            VegetableDetails carrot = new VegetableDetails("Carrot","$1","Orange");
//Use the constructor to initialize


        //Use getter to retrieve the value
            System.out.println("Name: "+ carrot.getName()+" Price:
"+carrot.getPrice()+" Color: "+carrot.getColor());


            //Use Setter to update the price and the color
            carrot.setColor("Purple");
            carrot.setPrice("$4");


            System.out.println("Values of Carrot after updating");


            //Using getter to get the value
            System.out.println("Name: "+ carrot.getName()+" Price:
"+carrot.getPrice()+" Color: "+carrot.getColor());
        }
}
```

The output of this will be:

Name: Carrot Price: $1 Color: Orange

Values of Carrot after updating

Name: Carrot Price: $4 Color: Purple

Summary

In encapsulation:

- Class fields may be read or write only
- A class has complete control over what data is stored in the fields
- No class user will know how the data is stored. Classes can modify field data types and class users will not need to modify any code
- The biggest benefit with encapsulation is that it provides us with that ability to modify code we implemented without breaking the code used by other users. It ensures that our code is extensible, maintainable and flexible and ensures that unit testing is very easy. We can also modify parts of our code without having any effect on the rest.

Important Points

- We achieve encapsulation by using a class to keep the data and related methods together in one unit.
- It is a technique for providing protection for information in one object from other objects
- It gives us access control to control what can be accessed and by what; those controls may be public, private and/or protected.

Abstraction vs Encapsulation

There are several differences between the two:

- Java problems are solved at design level with abstraction and at implementation level with encapsulation
- We use abstraction for hiding unnecessary data and showing only the functionality; with encapsulation, the code and the data are hidden in one unit to provide protection from external access
- With abstraction, we can focus on what an object does and not how it is done; with encapsulation, we are hiding the internal mechanics of how the object does what it does

Real-World Example

We can demonstrate the difference between abstraction and encapsulation by using a real-world example. Let's assume that you have got a mobile phone and you can use the buttons on the keypad to dial a specific number. You do not need to know how all this works, just that it does. In Java, this is abstraction. Now, let's say that you want to know how the mobile phone works internally? How do the keypad buttons connect to internal circuits to make them work? In Java, this would all be rolled into one unit and is called encapsulation.

Inheritance

The next OOP concept is inheritance. This one allows one class to use the behaviors and the states from another class. In simple terms, one class will derive the methods and fields from another. In inheritance, a derived class is a child class or a subclass and the class that is derived from is a superclass or a parent class. A superclass may have multiple subclasses in inheritance but a subclass may one extend a single superclass.

Inheritance Explanation

By default, in inheritance all the parent class data members and functions are made available to a child class, so long as they have not been made private. Inheritance is defined as an IS-A relationship between parent and child classes and is signified by the use of the extends keyword.

Let's see this in terms of an example:

We have a class called Base

```
class Base
{
        //Code of the Base class
}
```

Then we have another class called Child that extend the Base class properties using inheritance:

```
Class Child extends Base
{
        //extends the base class properties
}
```

In this example, our child class inherits both the fields and the methods from the Base class.

Inheritance Types

In Java, we have three types of inheritance:

- Single – where we derive one class from a single parent class
- Multilevel – we have a grandparent class where, for example, class A is inherited by class B which is, in turn inherited by class C
- Hierarchical – we can derive multiple subclasses from one parent class, for example, classes B and C are both derived from class A

Java and Multiple Inheritance

Java does not have any support for multiple inheritance because it causes too much ambiguity. Consider this:

Class D will extend both class B and class C while inheriting the methods from class A. The problems arise when D is used to extend B and C; if D wanted to use a method that appears in both of these classes, which one gets called? You can see where the problems can arise.

Inheritance Examples:

Let's see another example of how inheritance works:

We have our Base class and we want two fields and one method that the child class can inherit:

```
public class Base {
        int x=100;
        int y = 120;

        //The Addition method will return the integer value of x + y
        public int addition(){
                return x+y; //return 220
        }
}
```

Our child class will inherit both the addition method and the x field from our Base class.

```
public class Child extends Base{
        int z;

        public void substraction(){
                //addition method and x filed is inherited from Base Class
                z = addition() - x;
                System.out.println(z);
        }
}
```

In our Main class, the Child object is created and it will call the Subtraction method

```
public class InheritanceRufusRubble {

        public static void main(String[] args) {
                Child child = new Child(); //Child object
                child.substraction();//Subtraction method is called on the child object
        }
}
```

The output of this will be:

110

Have a look at another example:

```
class Base
{
        int x=100;
}
```

Child.java:

```
public class Child extends Base{
        int x=40;
        void show()
        {
                System.out.println(x);
        }
}
```

InheritanceRufusRubble.java

```
public class InheritanceRufusRubble {
        public static void main(String[] args)
        {
                Child c = new Child();
                c.show();
        }
}
```

The output of this will be:

40

You might wonder why the output was x=40 – this is because priority is always given to a local variable. In the child class, in our show() method, parent class members can be accessed, for example, we can access the Base class by using the super keyword. So, if we wanted to print x-100, we could use the super keyword to do so.

Here's an example of the super keyword used in inheritance:

```
public class Base {
```

```
    int x=100;
}
```

Child.java:

```
public class Child extends Base{
    int x=40;

    void show()
    {
        System.out.println(x);
        System.out.println(super.x);
    }
}
public class InheritanceRufusRubble {
    public static void main(String[] args)
    {
        Child c=new Child();
        c.show();
    }
}
```

The output of this is:

40

100

The Importance of Inheritance

There are two main reasons why inheritance is important:

- Code reusability. This is a fundamental feature of inheritance and it allows us to reuse code that already exists rather than having to keep writing and creating identical code over and over. Not only does this save a great deal of time and money because the properties are being reused, but it also makes our code a great deal more reliable.
- Method Overriding. When we use inheritance, we can override the methods in our base class, making the base class easier to use in a derived class.

Important Points:

There are also some important points to remember about inheritance:

- When both a parent and a child class have identical data members, inheritance becomes known as data hiding
- When both a parent and a child class have the same functions, inheritance becomes known as method overriding
- When both a parent and a child class have the same static functions, inheritance becomes known as function hiding
- You cannot print the super keyword; if you tried you would get a syntax error. The super keyword is used by the child class to inherit the data members of a parent class
- If a non-static function is made as final in any class, the child class may not the override it.

Polymorphism

Polymorphism is all about one thing taking on many forms. It is a property used to send one message to multiple objects in different classes and having each object behave in a different way. Polymorphism is an incredibly powerful OOP concept that allows us to create some very flexible applications.

Polymorphism Types

There are two types:

- Compile time
- Runtime

Compile Time Polymorphism

When an object has been bound at compile time with its functionality, it is called compile time polymorphism. When it comes to compile time, Java looks at the method signature to see which is the correct method to call. Compile time polymorphism may also be known as early or static binding.

Implementing Compile Time Polymorphism

To achieve compile time polymorphism we need to do a little method overloading. The rules of overloading state that we may have multiple functions sharing one name in one class. Function or method overloading is the way to achieve compile time polymorphism so let's have a look at an example.

The first step is to create a class named Addition. In this class three separate add() methods are declared, each having different parameters

public class Addition {

```
    public int add(int m, int n)
    {
        return m+n;
    }

    public int add(int m,int n,int o)
    {
        return m+n+o;
    }

    public int add(int m, double n)
    {
        return m+(int)n;
    }
}
```

Next, we need another class named PrintAdd and an object which will be used to call the above methods in the new class:

```
public class PrintAdd {
    public static void main(String args[])
    {
        Addition a=new Addition();

      System.out.println(a.add(2,3));

      System.out.println(a.add(2,3,4));

      System.out.println(a.add(2,3.4));
    }
}
```

The output of this is:

5

9

5

What we have here is three different versions of an add method. The first one has two arguments or parameters, the second one has three parameters, and in the third, we change the parameter type. The Java compiler will look at the signature of the methods and decide which one to call for a specific compile time method call.

Runtime Polymorphism

When an object gets bound at runtime with its functionality, it is called runtime polymorphism. It is possible to have a method inside a subclass that will override a method in the parent class – the methods will have the same names and the same parameters. The Java virtual machine (JVM) will work out which method needs to be called at runtime not at compile time. Runtime polymorphism may also be known as late or dynamic binding.

Implementing Runtime Polymorphism

We implement runtime polymorphism by using method overriding. The rules of method overriding state that a child class and a parent class both have the same method declared in them. If a child class provides the implementation of a method already provided by a parent class, this is called overriding.

Let's see an example of runtime polymorphism.

First, we need a class which we will call Vehicle. In this class, we will declare a method called move()

```
public class Vehicle {

    public void move()

    {

        System.out.println("vehicles may move");

    }

}
```

Next, we need another class called Bicycle; this will extend the Vehicle class:

```
public class Bicycle extends Vehicle{

    public void move()
```

```
        {
                System.out.println("Bicycle may move and may accelerate too");
        }
}
```

Next, a third class called TestVehicle. We create an object in this class which will call the class method form above

```
public class TestVehicle {
        public static void main(String args[])
        {
                Vehicle v= new Bicycle();

          v.move();

          Vehicle v1= new Vehicle();

          v1.move();

        }
}
```

The output of this will be:

Bicycle may move and may accelerate too

Vehicles can move

Note from this code that, with first move() call, we have Vehicle as the reference type. The object that is being referenced is Bicycle. When the call is made to move(), Java will wait until it's runtime before it will look to see which object the reference is pointing to. In the case of our code, Bicycle is the class object so the Bicycle class's move() method is the method that is called. In the next move() call, the object being called is in the Vehicle class. As such, the Vehicle class's move() method is the one that is called at runtime.

Runtime vs Compile Time Polymorphism

There are several fundamental differences between the two types of polymorphism:

- With compile time polymorphism, the compiler will resolve the call; in runtime polymorphism, the compiler does not get involved
- Compile time polymorphism is also called early or static binding; runtime polymorphism is also called late or dynamic binding.
- Compile time polymorphism is achieved by function and operator overloading,; in runtime it is achieved by virtual functions.
- Compile time polymorphism is fast to execute because it already knows which method it wants at compile time; in runtime polymorphism, it is slower because it waits for the runtime to decide on the method call.
- Compile time polymorphism is not so flexible because everything is executed at compile time; in runtime polymorphism things are more flexible because everything is executed at runtime.

The Importance of Polymorphism

Three important reasons for polymorphism are:

- It makes an object far less complex
- We can replace total implementation by reusing identical signatures
- As far as object handling goes, polymorphism reduces the workload

Important Points:

The important points to remember about polymorphism are:

- Java has no direct support for operator overloading
- Java has no support for compile time polymorphism – I only told you about it because it is part of the concept
- There is no role in function overloading for access modifiers or specifiers
- If you wish to make each function have the same number of arguments but still overload them, you will need to change the argument data type.
- If the value is being returned by a function, you do not need to catch the value when you call it
- A function's return type does not have any role to play in function overloading
- You can only achieve function overloading by modifying the arguments.

Association, Aggregation, and Composition

The final OOP concepts that you need to know about are association, aggregation and composition, and we'll start with association.

What is Association?

Association is nothing more than a connection that exists between two classes. We use the objects of these classes to set up the connection. Association can be done in three ways – one-to-one, one-to-many and many-to-many. Let's have a look at an example showing how association is implemented in Java.

```
public class InsuranceCompany {

        private String name;

        // insuranceCompany name

        InsuranceCompany(String name)

        {

                this.name = name;

        }


        public String getInsuranceCompanyName()

        {

                return this.name;

        }

}

class Employee

{

        private String name;


        Employee(String name)

        {

                this.name = name;

        }


        public String getEmployeeName()

        {

                return this.name;
```

```
        }
}
class Association
{
        public static void main (String[] args)
        {
                InsuranceCompany insuranceCompany = new InsuranceCompany("DRPK");
                Employee emp = new Employee("Harry");
                System.out.println(emp.getEmployeeName() +
                " is an employee of " + insuranceCompany.getInsuranceCompanyName());
        }
}
```

The output of this will be:
Harry is an employee of DRPK

In this example, our insurance company has a lot of employees and is connected to multiple objects. That makes this a one-to-many relationship.

Java Association Types

There are two types of association in Java:

Aggregation

- Aggregation is a special association type and it offers these characteristics:
- Aggregation represents a HAS-A relationship
- Aggregation is a unidirectional or one-way relationship
- When you end one entity, it does not affect any others; they can all be independently present.

Here's an example:

```
import java.util.List;
class Employee
{
        String name;
        int id ;
```

```
        String dept;

        Employee(String name, int id, String dept)
        {
                this.name = name;
                this.id = id;
                this.dept = dept;
        }
}
class Department
{
        String name;
        private List<Employee> Employees;
        Department(String name, List<Employee> Employees)
        {
                this.name = name;
                this.Employees = Employees;
        }

        public List<Employee> getEmployees()
        {
                return Employees;
        }
}
class Branch
{
        String branchName;
        private List<Department> departments;

        Branch(String branchName, List<Department> departments)
```

```
        {
                this.branchName = branchName;
                this.departments = departments;
        }

        public int getTotalEmployeesInInstitute()
        {
                int noOfEmployees = 0;
                List<Employee> Employees;
                for(Department dept : departments)
                {
                        Employees = dept.getEmployees();
                        for(Employee s : Employees)
                        {
                                noOfEmployees++;
                        }
                }
        return noOfEmployees;
        }
}
class GFG
{
        public static void main (String[] args)
        {
                Employee s1 = new Employee("Michelle", 1, "CSE");
                Employee s2 = new Employee("Paula", 2, "CSE");
                Employee s3 = new Employee("Joan", 1, "EE");
                Employee s4 = new Employee("Ronald", 2, "EE");
                List <Employee> cse_Employees = new ArrayList<Employee>();
                cse_Employees.add(s1);
```

```
            cse_Employees.add(s2);
            List <Employee> ee_Employees = new ArrayList<Employee>();
            ee_Employees.add(s3);
            ee_Employees.add(s4);
            Department CSE = new Department("CSE", cse_Employees);
            Department EE = new Department("EE", ee_Employees);
            List <Department> departments = new ArrayList<Department>();
            departments.add(CSE);
            departments.add(EE);
            Branch branch = new Branch("BITS", departments);
            int totalNumber = 0;
            for(Department dep : departments)
                totalNumber += dep.getEmployees().size();
            System.out.print("Total number of Employees in the branch: ");
            System.out.print(totalNumber);
    }
}
```

The output of this will be:

the total number of Employees in the branch: 4

What we have here is a Branch which has several offices, such as EE, and CSE. Each of the offices has several employees and we can use this to associate a Branch to the class that references the object or objects in the Department class. The implication is that the Branch class relates to the Department class via the objects. The Department class also references the one or more objects in the Employee class, the implication being there is a relationship with the Employee class because of the objects.

Composition

Composition is a restricted format of aggregation in which the quantities depend very highly on one another. It is representative of a PART-OF relationship in which the entities need one another in order to exist.

Here's an example:

```
import java.util.*;
```

```
public class Book {
    public String title;
    public String author;

    Book(String title, String author)
    {
        this.title = title;
        this.author = author;
    }
}
public class Library {
    private final List<Book> books;
    Library (List<Book> books)
    {
        this.books = books;
    }

    public List<Book> getTotalBooksInLibrary(){
        return books;
    }
}
public class GFG {
    public static void main (String[] args)
    {
        Book b1 = new Book("Jane Eyre", "Charlotte Bronte");
        Book b2 = new Book("Wuthering heights", "Emily Bronte");
        Book b3 = new Book("Emma", "Jane");
        List<Book> books = new ArrayList<Book>();
        books.add(b1);
```

```
        books.add(b2);
        books.add(b3);
        Library library = new Library(books);
        List<Book> bks = library.getTotalBooksInLibrary();
        for(Book bk : bks){
            System.out.println("Title : " + bk.title + " and "
            +" Author : " + bk.author);
        }
    }
}
```

The output of this will be:

The Title: Jane Eyre and Author: Charlotte Bronte

Title: Wuthering heights and Author: Emily Bronte

Title: Emma and Author: Jane

Aggregation vs Composition

There are a couple of differences between the two:

- With aggregation, a child class can be independently present; this cannot happen in composition because each entity requires the others to exist.
- Aggregation is a HAS-A relationship while composition is a PART-OF relationship.
- Aggregation is a weak form of association while composition is a strong form of association.

Here's an example:

```
public class Engine {
    public void work()
    {
        System.out.println("The car engine has been started ");
    }
}
public final class Car {
    private final Engine engine; // Composition
```

```
        Car(Engine engine)
        {
                this.engine = engine;
        }

        // when the engine is started the car starts moving
        public void move()
        {
                engine.work();
                System.out.println("Car is moving ");
        }
}
public class GFG {
        public static void main (String[] args)
        {
                Engine engine = new Engine();
                Car car = new Car(engine);
                car.move();
        }
}
```

The output of this is:

The car engine has been started

The car is moving.

That was a basic view of association, along with aggregation and composition. I haven't gone too much in depth here as the other concepts are far more important.

To finish this section, well take a look at the design principles as far as object-oriented programming goes.

Best Practice Guide for OOP

The idea behind the Java OOP concepts is to save a developer time without reducing ease of use and security and all the design principles are aimed at that idea.

Object-oriented design principles form the very core of OOP programming. Sadly, far too many developers spend far too much time trying to chase design patterns like the Decorator Pattern, the Singleton Pattern, or the Observer Pattern, and not spending nearly enough time or putting anywhere near as much focus as needed on learning OOP design and analysis.

It is very important that you learn the basic concepts of OOP, such as encapsulation abstraction, inheritance and encapsulation. But it is also very important that you learn the design principles of OOP too, so that you can learn how to create programs with a modular, clean design. Too often, developer of all levels of experience either have no idea of the design principles or they just don't know what will have the most benefit for a specific principle or even how the design principles should be applied in their code.

The bottom line is this. You should always be working towards a solution, design or code that is fully cohesive and loosely coupled. Have a look at some of the open source code from Sun or Apache; this will give you some great examples for learning the OOP design principles in Java.

They give us an idea of how the design principles should be properly used in your Java programs and code. If you look into the Java Development Kit, you will see that it follows several design principles, such as the Singleton Pattern in the Runtime class, the Factory Pattern in the BorderFactory class and the Decorator Pattern in many of the java.io classes.

5 of these design principles come under the acronym of SOLID, which stands for:

- Single Responsibility
- Open Closed
- Liskov Substitution
- Interface Segregation
- Dependency Inversion

And all of these are included in this list of design principles for Java OOP.

Design Principle Guide

The very best way of learning any of these design principles is through practice and working on real-world examples. It is important to understand that any violation of a design principle has consequences and practical work is the only way to see what those consequences are. However, here, I will give you an overview of the principles in the hopes that you will be able to apply them to your work.

DRY Principle

Or, don't repeat yourself. I've tried to make it clear throughout this guide that repetitive code is unnecessary and there are always ways to make life easier for yourself. Duplicate code is wrong on so many levels – not only is it boring and time-consuming to write, it doesn't make your code look nice, it makes your code hard to read and it duplicates the chances of errors.

Use Abstraction instead, abstracting common items to one place. If you have a code block that goes in two or more places, you could also consider turning it into a method that you can call wherever needed. And if have a hard-coded value that you use more than once make it into a public final constant.

The major benefit of the DRY principle is that it makes your code far easier to maintain.

Encapsulate the Changes

If there is one thing that remains constant in the field of programming software, it is 'change'. Use encapsulation for code that you know or think is going to change sometime in the future. When you use Java for your coding, get into the habit of making methods and variables private and then adding access one step at a time, i.e. from a private method or variable to a protected one and then public if needs be.

Many of the OOP and SOLID design principles use encapsulation and one common example is the Factory design pattern. This encapsulates the code for creating an object and then gives us the flexibility to add new products at a later time without affecting the code that already exists.

The main benefit of this principle is that it makes code easier to test and encapsulated code is easier to maintain.

Open Closed Principle

As a rule of thumb, all methods, classes, and functions must OPEN so that new functionality can be added and CLOSED to any modification. This is another of the SOLID principles, one that stops anyone else from modifying your code.

This principle helps you to focus on how your code and your system could adapt to changes that might happen in the future. The principle states that any system should be able to have new functionality added with little to no effect on any existing codes. As such, the open-closed principle states that code should be open to extension and closed to modification. Have a look at a code example:

```
public class BusinessLoan

{

   public void Terminate()

   {
```

```
      //Rules related to termination must be processed here; the business loan is terminated
   }
}
public class AutoLoan
{
   public void Terminate()
   {
      // Rules related to termination must be processed here; the business loan is
terminated
   }
}
public class LoanProcessor
{
   public void ProcessEarlyTermination(object loan)
   {
      if ( loan is BusinessLoan )
      {
         //Business Loan processing
      }
      else if (loan is AutoLoan)
      {
         //Auto Loan Processing
      }
   }
}
```

The biggest issues with LoanProcessor is that, as soon as a new type of loan is added, for example a HomeLoan, it would need to change. The structure should really have looked like this:

```
public abstract class Loan

{

   public abstract void Terminate();

}

public class BusinessLoan extends Loan

{

   public override void Terminate()

   {

      // Rules related to termination must be processed here; the business loan is
terminated

   }

}

public class AutoLoan extends Loan

{

   public override void Terminate()

   {

      // Rules related to termination must be processed here; the business loan is
terminated

   }

}

public class LoanProcessor

{

   public void ProcessEarlyTermination(Loan loan)

   {

      loan.Terminate();
```

```
    }
}
```

In this way, when a new Loan type is added, LoanProcessor does not get affected.

SRP – Single Responsibility Principle

Another of the SOLID principles, SRP dictates that there must not be any more than a single reason for a class to be changed nor should a class handle any more than single responsibility.

In Java, if a class has two or more functionalities, the concept of coupling is introduced between the functionalities. If you were to modify one of those functionalities, there is a high chance of breaking the coupled functionality; a further round of tests would be needed to make sure there were no surprises in store!

Dependency Injection

Otherwise known as the Inversion principle, this is one of the better design principles. It states that you should never request dependency because the framework will provide it for you and it is implemented really well in the Spring framework. The real simplicity of this principle is that if you have a class that the D I framework has injected, it will be far easier to use a mock object to test it and much easier to maintain. This is because the code for the object creation has been centralized inside the framework, eliminating the need to scatter it across the client code.

There are several ways that dependency injection may be achieved, such as the use of bytecode instrumentation or proxies.

Composition is Better than Inheritance

Where possible, you should use composition rather than inheritance. There will be developers who argue against this but there is no denying that composition offers far more flexibility than inheritance does.

Composition lets you change a class behavior at runtime by allowing you to set a property at that time. Also, when we use interfaces to compose classes we are making use of polymorphism which is also more flexible.

Loose Coupling

This goes with encapsulation really; if your class behavior is encapsulated properly, your classes can be loosely coupled; this is best achieved with abstraction rather than implementation.

LSP – Liskov Substitution Principle

The Liskov Substitution Principle states that we must be able to substitute a subtype for a supertype. In other words, any function or method that makes use of the superclass type must also be able to work seamlessly with subclass objects.

LSP is related very closely to the SRP principle and the interface segregation principle. If a class has got more functionality than a subclass has, it may not provide support for some functionality and that is a violation of the LSP rules.

To ensure that you follow this design principle, you must ensure that your derived classes or derived subclasses enhance functionality but do not reduce it.

ISP – Interface Segregation Principle

According to the interface segregation principle, client code must not implement any interface that it doesn't use. This tends to happen when an interface has two or more functionalities and the client requires just one of them.

Interface design is not easy; once the interface has been released, it cannot be modified without all the implementation into being broken and that results in an awful lot of work for a developer.

The main benefit to ISP is that the interface implements all the methods before a class can make use of them so having just one functionality means fewer methods to implement.

Program for the Interface and Not Implementation

It is better to program this way because your code will be far more flexible and will be able to work on any additional implementation made in the interface. Where possible, use the interface type for your variables, your method return types and method argument types.

Delegation

Don't try to do everything by yourself. Instead, delegate where you can to the right class. one of the most common examples of the delegation principle is hash code() and equals(). To compare a couple of objects for the purpose of equality, we tell the relevant class to do the comparison and not the client class.

The main benefit of this is that there is no duplication of code and behavior is much easier to modify. Another example is event delegation – events are delegated to event handlers for the purpose of handling.

Cohesive Classes Are Best

You should never have data and behavior spread across multiple classes. When you create your classes, make sure they cannot break or leak the contained implementation details to any other class. What this involves is not including code in any class where that code will go beyond what it exists for.

The Law of Demeter

Otherwise known as the "principle of least knowledge", this principle states that no object should ever know any of the internal details of any object that it has a collaboration with. It comes under the real-life principle that you should always talk to a person directly and not a friend of that person!

Classes should be able to invoke only the public data members from a class that it has a collaboration with; it should never be able to gain access to any data or behavior for a class that is created by the data members. If you don't follow this principle carefully, you end up with tight coupling and that leads to a system that is very difficult to modify.

The Hollywood Principle

Or don't call us, we'll call you! This principle allows the glow of conditional logic to be broken so the code may be executed as per specific events. We do this by using event callbacks or by injection of the interface implementations. Good examples include inversion or dependency injection and it provides strong promotion for loose coupling, enabling easier maintenance of your implementation.

All of these design principles are designed to help you write much better, cleaner and more flexible code that is highly cohesive and offers loose coupling. The theory is only the first stepping stone in Java programming; the most important thing is that you learn how to know when these design principles should be implemented and how you should do it.

Java OOP – Miscellaneous

Java Object Cloning

Object cloning is just a way of creating an identical copy of an object and we use the clone() method to do this. To be successful, the class that we want to create the clone for must have the java.lang.Cloneable interface implemented; if it isn't, the clone() method will throw a CloneNotSupported Exception.

A clone() method is always defined inside the relevant object class using this syntax:

protected Object clone() throws CloneNotSupportedException

The clone() method is useful for eliminating the requirement for additional processing when we want an identical copy of one object. If we were to try doing this using the new keyword it would take forever to achieve; therefore the clone() method is better used.

It may have one or two issues in terms of design but the clone() method is one of the most popular and easiest ways of copying any object. These are the advantages of the clone() method:

There is no need to write time-consuming and repetitive code; simply use one abstract class with a clone() method that is 4 to 5 lines long

It is the easiest way, not to mention the most efficient, of copying an object, even more so if the project has already been developed and/or is an old one. All you do is define the parent class and then implement Cloneable. You then define the clone() method and that's it, job done.

Using the clone() method is the fastest way of copying arrays.

As with everything, though, there are disadvantages to using the clone() method:

- Using the clone() method requires an awful lot of syntax change in your code – you must implement the Cloneable interface, define the clone() method, handle the error, CloneNotSupported, call object.clone(), and so on.
- The Cloneable interface must be implemented without any methods because we are only using it to let the JVM (Java Virtual Machine) know that clone() can be performed on the object.
- Because Object.clone() is protected, we must provide a clone() of our own and then call Object.clone() indirectly from it.
- No constructor is invoked by Object.clone() so we have absolutely no control over the way objects are constructed.
- If you need a clone() method inside a child class, all of the relevant superclasses must define that method or they must inherit it from a parent class otherwise there will be a failure of the super.clone() chain.
- Only shallow copying is supported by Object.clone() but if deep cloning is required we will need to override it.

Have a look at this example of using the clone() method to clone an object:

public class Student18 implements Cloneable{

int rollno;

String name;

Student18(int rollno,String name){

```
        this.rollno=rollno;
        this.name=name;
    }

    public Object clone()throws CloneNotSupportedException{
        return super.clone();
    }

    public static void main(String args[]){
        try{
        Student18 s1=new Student18(101,"Arthur");

        Student18 s2=(Student18)s1.clone();

        System.out.println(s1.rollno+" "+s1.name);
        System.out.println(s2.rollno+" "+s2.name);

        }catch(CloneNotSupportedException c){}

    }

}
```

The output of this will be:

101 Arthur

As you can see, the reference variables both have the same value so the clone() method copies the value of an object over to another. This means there is no need for writing code that explicitly copies the values from one object to another.

If we used the new keyword and create a new object and then assigned it with the values from another project, it would take a lot of work and processing; the clone() method takes the hard work out of it.

Math Class

Java Math classes are also a concept in OOP and there are several provided methods for working on mathematical calculations:

- min()
- max()
- avg()
- sin()
- cos()
- tan()
- round()
- floor()
- ceil()
- abs()
- and so on.

Contrary to some StrictMath class methods, every implementation of the Math class-equivalent function, cannot be defined to return the "bit-for-bit" results. Because this is so relaxed, we get better implementation with more improved performance without the need for strict reproducibility.

If the size is a long or int type and the results go over the value range, certain methods will throw up an ArithmeticException:

- addExact()
- subtractExact()
- multiplyExact()
- toIntExact()

Other operations of an arithmetic nature, such as decrement, increment, absolute value divide and negation, among others, will overflow only with a specified value, either maximum or minimum.

Look at this example:

```
public class JavaMathExample1

{

    public static void main(String[] args)

    {

        double x = 28;

        double y = 4;
```

```
        // return the maximum of two numbers
        System.out.println("Maximum number of x and y is: " +Math.max(x, y));

        // return the square root of y
        System.out.println("Square root of y is: " + Math.sqrt(y));

        //returns 28 power of 4 i.e. 28*28*28*28
        System.out.println("Power of x and y is: " + Math.pow(x, y));

        // return the logarithm of given value
        System.out.println("Logarithm of x is: " + Math.log(x));
        System.out.println("Logarithm of y is: " + Math.log(y));

        // return the logarithm of given value when base is 10
        System.out.println("log10 of x is: " + Math.log10(x));
        System.out.println("log10 of y is: " + Math.log10(y));

        // return the log of x + 1
        System.out.println("log1p of x is: " +Math.log1p(x));

        // return a power of 2
        System.out.println("exp of a is: " +Math.exp(x));

        // return (a power of 2)-1
        System.out.println("expm1 of a is: " +Math.expm1(x));
    }
}
```

The output of this will be:

Maximum number of x and y is: 28.0

Square root of y is: 2.0

Power of x and y is: 614656.0

Logarithm of x is: 3.332204510175204

Logarithm of y is: 1.3862943611198906

log10 of x is: 1.4471580313422192

log10 of y is: 0.6020599913279624

log1p of x is: 3.367295829986474

exp of a is: 1.446257064291475E12

expm1 of a is: 1.446257064290475E12

And another example:

```
public class JavaMathExample2
{
    public static void main(String[] args)
    {
        double a = 30;

        // converting values to radian
        double b = Math.toRadians(a);

        // return the trigonometric sine of a
        System.out.println("Sine value of a is: " +Math.sin(a));

        // return the trigonometric cosine value of a
        System.out.println("Cosine value of a is: " +Math.cos(a));

        // return the trigonometric tangent value of a
        System.out.println("Tangent value of a is: " +Math.tan(a));

        // return the trigonometric arc sine of a
```

```
            System.out.println("Sine value of a is: " +Math.asin(a));

            // return the trigonometric arc cosine value of a
            System.out.println("Cosine value of a is: " +Math.acos(a));

            // return the trigonometric arc tangent value of a
            System.out.println("Tangent value of a is: " +Math.atan(a));

            // return the hyperbolic sine of a
            System.out.println("Sine value of a is: " +Math.sinh(a));

            // return the hyperbolic cosine value of a
            System.out.println("Cosine value of a is: " +Math.cosh(a));

            // return the hyperbolic tangent value of a
            System.out.println("Tangent value of a is: " +Math.tanh(a));
        }
}
```

The output of this will be:

Sine value of a is: -0.9880316240928618

Cosine value of a is: 0.15425144988758405

Tangent value of a is: -6.405331196646276

Sine value of a is: NaN

Cosine value of a is: NaN

Tangent value of a is: 1.5374753309166493

Sine value of a is: 5.343237290762231E12

Cosine value of a is: 5.343237290762231E12

Tangent value of a is: 1.0

Math Methods

In the java.lang.Math class there are a few methods that help us to do basic numerical operations, like cube root, logarithm, trigonometric functions, and so on. These are the Java math methods:

Method	Description
Math.abs()	Returns the absolute value of a specified value
Math.max()	Returns the biggest out of two values
Math.min()	Returns the smallest out of two values
Math.round()	Rounds decimal numbers up or down to the nearest value
Math.sqrt()	Returns a number's square root
Math.cbrt()	Returns a number's cube root
Math.pow()	Returns the value of one argument that is raised to the power of another argument
Math.signum()	It takes a specified value and finds the sign of it
Math.ceil()	It finds the smallest integer value that is greater/equal to the mathematical integer or argument
Math.copySign()	It will find the absolute value of one argument together with the sign that is provided in another argument
Math.nextAfter()	It will return the floating-point number next to the initial argument; it works in the direction of the next argument
Math.nextUp()	It will return the floating-point number that is next to d in positive infinity direction
Math.nextDown()	It will return the floating-point number that is next to d in negative infinity direction
Math.floor()	This is used for finding the biggest integer value less or equal to the specified argument and equal to the integer (mathematical) of a specified double value
Math.floorDiv()	This is used for finding the biggest integer value less or equal to the specified algebraic quotient
Math.random()	This will return a double value that has a positive sign, greater or equal to 0.0 but lower than 1.0

Math.rint()	This will return a double value equal to a mathematical integer and nearest to the specified argument
Math.hypot()	This will return the square root (x2 + y2) without any intermediate over or underflow
Math.ulp()	This will return the size of one ulp of an argument
Math.getExponent()	This will return an exponent (unbiased) to be used in a value representation
Math.IEEEremainder()	This will calculate a remainder operation on a pair of arguments as per the IEEE754 standard, returning the value
Math.addExact()	This will return the sum of the specified arguments; should the result overflow a long or an int, an exception will be thrown
Math.subtractExact()	This will return the difference between the specified arguments; should the result overflow an int, an exception will be thrown
Math.multiplyExact()	This will return the specified argument's products' should the result overflow a long or int, an exception will be thrown
Math.incrementExact()	This will return the argument with an increment of one; should this result in an int overflow, an exception will be thrown
Math.decrementExact()	This will return the argument with a decrement of one; should the result be a long or int overflow, an exception will be thrown
Math.negateExact()	This will return an argument's negation; should a long or int overflow happen as a result, an exception will be thrown
Math.toIntExact()	This will return the value of the specified long argument' if an int is overflown as a result, an exception will be thrown

Logarithmic Math Methods

The following are the Java logarithmic math methods:

Method	Description
Math.log()	This will return the natural logarithm for a specified double value
Math.log10()	This will return a double value's base 10 logarithm
Math.log1p()	This will return the natural logarithm of the argument's sum plus 1

Mat.exp()	This will return E raised up to a double value's power. E is equal to 2.71828 (Euler's number)
Math.expm1()	This will work out the power of E and then take 1 away from it

Trigonometric Math Methods

These are the Java trigonometric math methods:

Method	**Description**
Math.sin()	This will return the value of the trigonometric sine of a specified double value
Math.cos()	This will return the value of the trigonometric cosine of a specified double value
Math.tan()	This will return the value of the trigonometric tangent of a specified double value
Math.asin()	This will return the value of the trigonometric arc sine of a specified double value
Math.acos()	This will return the value of the trigonometric arc cosine value of a specified double value
Math.atan()	This will return the value of the trigonometric arc tangent of a specified double value

Hyperbolic Math Methods

These are the Java hyperbolic math methods:

Method	**Description**
Math.sinh()	This will return the value of the trigonometric hyperbolic sine of a specified double value
Math.cosh()	This will return the value of the trigonometric hyperbolic cosine value of a specified double value
Math.tanh()	This will return the value of the trigonometric hyperbolic tangent of a specified double value

Angular Math Methods

And, finally, the Java angular math methods

Method	Description
Math.toDegrees	This converts the given radians angle to the equivalent in degrees
Math.toRadians	This converts the given degrees angle to the equivalent in radians

The Wrapper Class

The wrapper class in Java is used to convert primitives into objects and vice versa automatically, using the autoboxing and unboxing features built-in. There are 8 wrapper classes in the package called java.lang and they are:

Primitive Type	Wrapper Class
boolean	Boolean
char	Character
byte	Byte
short	Short
int	Integer
long	Long
float	Float
double	Double

Let's look at an example of converting a primitive to a wrapper:

```
public class WrapperExample1{
        public static void main(String args[]){
                //Converting an int into an Integer
                int a=20;
                Integer i=Integer.valueOf(a);//conversion of an int into an Integer
                Integer j=a;//autoboxing, now the compiler will write the Integer.valueOf(a)
internally
```

```
        System.out.println(a+" "+i+" "+j);
    }
}
```

The output of this will be:

20 20 20

And vice-versa:

```
public class WrapperExample2{
    public static void main(String args[]){
        //Converting an Integer to an int
        Integer a=new Integer(3);
        int i=a.intValue();//converting an Integer to an int
        int j=a;//unboxing, now the compiler will write a.intValue() internally

        System.out.println(a+" "+i+" "+j);
    }
}
```

The output of this will be:

3 3 3

Java Calls by Value and Reference

In Java, there is no such thing as a call by reference, only a call by value. If a method that passes a value is called, we are calling by value and any change in the method being called do not get affected in the method used to call.

Where a call by value is used, there is no change to the original value. Have a look at this example:

```
class Operation{
    int data=50;

    void change(int data){
        data=data+100;//changes will only be made in the local variable
```

```
    }

    public static void main(String args[]){
        Operation op=new Operation();

        System.out.println("before change "+op.data);
        op.change(500);
        System.out.println("after change "+op.data);
    }
}
```

The output of this will be:

before change 50

after change 50

And here's another example:

With a call by reference, the original value is only changed id there were modifications to the method that was called. If we were to pass an object rather than a primitive value, then the original value gets changed. Here, the value we are passing is an object:

```
class Operation2{
    int data=50;

    void change(Operation2 op){
        op.data=op.data+100;//changes will be made in the instance variable
    }


    public static void main(String args[]){
        Operation2 op=new Operation2();

        System.out.println("before change "+op.data);
        op.change(op);//passing object
```

```
        System.out.println("after change "+op.data);

    }
}
```

The output of this will be:

before change 50

after change 150

Strictfp Keyword

When you use the strictfp keyword, you can ensure that, regardless of which platform you are using, when you perform any operation within the floating point variable, the result will always be the same.

The correct way to write the strictfp code is on interfaces, methods and classes:

```
strictfp class A{}//strictfp on a class

strictfp interface M{}//strictfp on an interface

class A{

    strictfp void m(){}//strictfp on a method

}
```

The strictfp keyword may not be used on a constructor, variable or method

The Javadoc Tool

We can use the Javadoc tool to create document APIs and to do that, in any Java code file, to post any information to a method, class, constructor, field, etc., we need the documentation comment - /**...*/.

Here's an example:

```
package com.abc;

/** This is a user-defined class containing a method cube.*/

public class M{


    /** The cube method will print the cube of the specified number */
```

```
    public static void cube(int n){System.out.println(n*n*n);}
}
```

Using the Javadoc tool to create the API is done by following the tool with the name of the Java file. You do not need to compile this file. To generate the API, type the following at your command prompt:

javadoc M.java

Now you will see a series of HTML files; look for the one called index.html and open it to see information about all the classes.

Java Command Line Arguments

A command line argument is an argument that gets passed at program runtime. Arguments are passed from your console to the Java program and used as inputs in the file. In this way it provides us with a convenient method of checking a program to see how different values behave. There is no limit on how many arguments can be passed from the command prompt.

Have a look at this example, showing that one argument is received and printed. Running this program requires a minimum of one argument to be passed from the command prompt:

```
class CommandLineExample{
    public static void main(String args[]){
        System.out.println("Your first argument is: "+args[0]);
    }
}
```

compile by > javac CommandLineExample.java

run by > java CommandLineExample Suzy

The output of this will be:

Your first argument is: Suzy

Here's another example showing all the command line arguments being printed. To do this we have used a for loop to traverse the array:

```
class A{
    public static void main(String args[]){
        for(int i=0;i<args.length;i++)
```

```
                    System.out.println(args[i]);
        }
}
```

compile by > javac A.java

run by > java A Suzy Judd 1 3 abc

The output of this will be: Suzy

Judd

1

3

abc

Java Method Overriding

We talked briefly about this earlier but it's time to go into it in more detail. Strictly speaking, this is a follow-on from the OOP concept of polymorphism. Method overriding is used when we want a class, a subclass, or a child class to use a method that the parent class is already using. The subclass or child class method will have the same parameters, return type, signature or name as the method in the parent class.

It is also the method that Java uses to provide support for polymorphism at runtime. The execution method is picked based on the Java object type, not that of the reference variable.

Here's an example of method overriding:

```
//Base Class
class Parent
{
        void show()
        {
                System.out.println("Parent's show()");
        }
}
//Inherited class
class Child extends Parent
```

```
{
        //This method will override the show() in the Parent class
        @Override
        void show()
        {
                System.out.println("Child's show()");
        }
}


//Driver class
class Main
{
        public static void main(String[] args)
        {
                //If a reference to a Parent type refers
                //to a Parent object, then the Parent's
                //show() is called
                Parent obj1 = new Parent();
                obj1.show();
                //If a reference to a Parent type refers
                //to a Child object, then the Child's show()
                //is called. This is known as RUNTIME
                //POLYMORPHISM.
                Parent obj2 = new Child();
                obj2.show();
        }
}
```

Method Overriding and Access Modifiers

Using an access modifier as well provides far more access than the method that has been overridden.

Here's an example:

```
class Parent
{
    // private methods are not overridden
    private void m1()
    {
        System.out.println("From parent m1()");
    }

    protected void m2()
    {
        System.out.println("From parent m2()");
    }
}

class Child extends Parent
{
    // new m1() method
    // unique to Child class
    private void m1()
    {
        System.out.println("From child m1()");
    }

    // overriding method
    // with more accessibility
```

```
    @Override
    public void m2()
    {
        System.out.println("From child m2()");
    }
}

//Driver class
class Main
{
    public static void main(String[] args)
    {
        Parent obj1 = new Parent();
        obj1.m2();
        Parent obj2 = new Child();
        obj2.m2();
    }
}
```

If we don't require a method to be overridden, that method must be declared as final, for example:

```
class Parent
{
    // Cannot be overridden
    final void show() { }
}

class Child extends Parent
{
    // This would produce an error
```

```
    void show() { }
}
```

You also cannot override a static method.

In method hiding a static method will have an identical signature to that of the base class. Here's an example:

```
class Parent
{
    static void m1()
    {
        System.out.println("From parent static m1()");
    }

    void m2()
    {
        System.out.println("From parent non-static(instance) m2()");
    }
}

class Child extends Parent
{
    // This method will hide m1() in Parent
    static void m1()
    {
        System.out.println("From child static m1()");
    }

    // This method will override m2() in Parent
    @Override
    public void m2()
```

```
    {
        System.out.println("From child non-static(instance) m2()");
    }
}

//Driver class
class Main
{
    public static void main(String[] args)
    {
        Parent obj1 = new Child();
        obj1.m1();
        obj1.m2();
    }
}
```

If you want a parent class method called when overriding methods, you need to use the super keyword. Here's an example:

```
//Base Class
class Parent
{
    void show()
    {
        System.out.println("Parent's show()");
    }
}

//Inherited class
class Child extends Parent
{
```

```
        //This method will override show() of Parent
        @Override
        void show()
        {
                super.show();
                System.out.println("Child's show()");
        }
}

//Driver class
class Main
{
        public static void main(String[] args)
        {
                Parent obj = new Child();
                obj.show();
        }
}
```

Overriding and Exception Handling

When you handle Java exceptions, there are a couple of rules to bear in mind:

If a checked expression is thrown, you will get a compile error. If no exception is thrown by the superclass, it will come from the subclass. Here's an example:

```
class Parent
{
        void m1()
        {
                System.out.println("From parent m1()");
        }
```

```
    void m2()
    {
        System.out.println("From parent m2()");
    }
}

class Child extends Parent
{
    @Override
    // no problems arise while throwing unchecked exception
    void m1() throws ArithmeticException
    {
        System.out.println("From child m1()");
    }

    @Override
    // compile time error
    // issue arises while throwing checked exception
    void m2() throws Exception
    {
        System.out.println("From child m2");
    }
}
```

And second, if the exception happens in a parent class, you will get the compile error. Here's an example:

```
class Parent
{
    void m1() throws RuntimeException
    {
        System.out.println("From parent m1()");
```

```
    }
}

class Child1 extends Parent
{
    @Override
    // no issue arises while throwing same exception
    void m1() throws RuntimeException
    {
        System.out.println("From child1 m1()");
    }
}

class Child2 extends Parent
{
    @Override
    // no issue arises while throwing subclass exception
    void m1() throws ArithmeticException
    {
        System.out.println("From child2 m1()");
    }
}

class Child3 extends Parent
{
    @Override
    // no issue arises while not throwing any exception
    void m1()
    {
```

```
        System.out.println("From child3 m1()");
    }
}

class Child4 extends Parent
{
    @Override
    // compile time error
    // issue arises while throwing parent exception
    void m1() throws Exception
    {
        System.out.println("From child4 m1()");
    }
}
```

Multilevel Method Overriding Example:

```
//Base Class
class Parent
{
    void show()
    {
        System.out.println("Parent's show()");
    }
}
```

```
//Inherited class
class Child extends Parent
{
	//This method will override show() of Parent
	void show()
	{
		System.out.println("Child's show()");
	}
}

//Inherited class
class GrandChild extends Child
{
	//This method will override show() of Parent
	void show()
	{
		System.out.println("GrandChild's show()");
	}
}

//Driver class
class Main
{
	public static void main(String[] args)
	{
		Parent obj1 = new GrandChild();
		obj1.show();
	}
}
```

Java Method Overloading

Method overloading is a process that allows methods to have names that are similar but different signatures based on the input parameters which, in turn, are based on the number or the type in Java. Method overloading also supports static polymorphism, that is to say, polymorphism at compile time.

Here's an example:

```
public class Sum

{

    // Overloaded sum(). This sum will take two int parameters

    public int sum(int x, int y)

    {

        return (x + y);

    }


    // Overloaded sum(). This sum will take three int parameters

    public int sum(int x, int y, int z)

    {

        return (x + y + z);

    }


    // Overloaded sum(). This sum will take two double parameters

    public double sum(double x, double y)

    {

        return (x + y);

    }


    // Driver code

    public static void main(String args[])

        {

        Sum s = new Sum();
```

```
            System.out.println(s.sum(10, 20));
            System.out.println(s.sum(10, 20, 30));
            System.out.println(s.sum(10.5, 20.5));
        }
}
```

Method overloading has one major advantage – dealing with methods becomes much easier because there is no need to remember all the different names for one operations; all we do is modify the method parameters.

One thing we can't do is overload methods for a return type. Here's an example:

```
public class Main
{
        public int foo()
        {
        return 10;
        }
        // compiler error: foo() has already been defined
        public char foo()
        {
                return 'a';
        }
        public static void main(String args[]) {}
}
```

Java provides support for both static method overloading and main() method overloading. Here's an example of the latter:

```
public class Test
{
        // Normal main()
        public static void main(String[] args)
        {
                System.out.println("Hi Nerd (from main)");
```

```
        Test.main("Nerd");
    }

    // Overloaded main methods
    public static void main(String arg1)
    {
        System.out.println("Hi, " + arg1);
        Test.main("Dear Nerd","My Nerd");
    }

    public static void main(String arg1, String arg2)
    {
        System.out.println("Hi, " + arg1 + ", " + arg2);
    }
}
```

There are a few ways that Java methods can be overloaded:

By using several parameters inside 2 methods. Here's an example:

```
class Addition
{
    // add two integer values.
    public int add(int a, int b)
    {
        int sum = a+b;
        return sum;
    }

    // add three integer values.
    public int add(int a, int b, int c)
    {
        int sum = a+b+c;
```

```
            return sum;
        }
}

class GFG
{
        public static void main (String[] args)
        {
            Addition ob = new Addition();
            int sum1 = ob.add(1,2);
            System.out.println("sum of the two integer value :" + sum1);
            int sum2 = ob.add(1,2,3);
            System.out.println("sum of the three integer value :" + sum2);
        }
}
```

By using the data types of the method parameters. Here's an example:

```
class Addition
{
        // add three integer values
        public int add(int a, int b, int c)
        {
            int sum = a+b+c;
            return sum;
        }

        // add three double values
        public double add(double a, double b, double c)
        {
            double sum = a+b+c;
```

```
            return sum;
        }
}

class GFG
{
        public static void main (String[] args)
        {
            Addition ob = new Addition();
            int sum2 = ob.add(1,2,3);
            System.out.println("sum of the three integer value :" + sum2);
            double sum3 = ob.add(1.0,2.0,3.0);
            System.out.println("sum of the three double value :" + sum3);
        }
}
```

By using the method parameter order. Here's an example:

```
class Flair
{
        public void flairIdentity(String name, int id)
        {
            System.out.println("flairName :"+ name +" "+"Id :"+ id);
        }

        public void flairIdentity(int id, String name)
        {
            System.out.println("flairName :"+ name +" "+"Id :"+ id);
        }
}
```

```
class GFG
{
    public static void main (String[] args)
    {
        Flair flair = new Flair();
        flair.flairIdentity("Mary", 1);
        flair.flairIdentity("Shipham", 2);
    }
}
```

Difference Between Overloading and Overriding

There are quite a few differences between Java method overloading and overriding:

Overloading

- Method overloading makes a program far more readable
- Method overloading happens inside a class
- With overloading, the parameters must not be the same
- Overloading supports polymorphism at compile time (static polymorphism)
- You cannot perform overloading just by changing the method's return type. The return type can be different or the same but the parameter must be different

Overriding

- Method overriding provides specific method implementation of a method provided by the superclass
- Method overriding happens in a pair of classes that are related by inheritance
- The parameters must be the same for overriding
- Overriding supports runtime polymorphism
- The return type must be the same

An example of method overloading:

```
class OverloadingExample{
    static int add(int a,int b){return a+b;}
    static int add(int a,int b,int c){return a+b+c;}
}
```

An example of method overriding:

```
class Animal{

        void eat(){System.out.println("eating...");}

}

class Dog extends Animal{

        void eat(){System.out.println("eating bread...");}

}
```

That completes our look at object-oriented programming. In the next section, we will take a look at some of the questions you are likely to be asked at a Java interview.

Chapter 6: Java Interview Questions

For this section I am going to provide you with a list of questions that you are likely to be asked in a Java interview, along with the answers. Do study them carefully and do learn the answers as this will give you a huge advantage in the interview process. Millions of developers use Java across the world on billions of devices so the competition at interview is going to be tough. Add to that the fact that Java is used for creating applications for next-generation technology, like AI and big data, right down to the smallest of mobile devices and you can see just how widespread and popular the programming language is.

As a professional in the Java language, it is important that you know the buzzwords, you understand and learn what the right technologies are for any given scenario and how to use them and that you are fully prepared for any Java interview that comes your way.

Let's dive into the first section straight away.

Basic Java Interview Questions

Explain the difference between JDK, JRE, and JVM.

The JDK is the Java Development Kit and it is a necessary tool required for compiling, documenting, and packaging Java programs. Together with JRE, an interpreter or loader is built-into the JDK, a compiler called javac, an archiver (JAR), the Javadoc document generator and many other tools required for successful Java development.

The JRE is the Java Runtime Environment. It is the environment in which the Java bytecode may be executed and it is used for implementing the Java Virtual Machine. The JRE also provides us with all the class libraries and many other support files required at runtime by the JVM. It is, in basic terms, a software package that provides us with everything we need for running Java programs, a physical implementation of the Java Virtual machine.

JVM stands for Java Virtual Machine. The JVM is an abstract machine, a specification that provides us with the JRE in which our bytecode is executed. The JVM must follow these notations – Specification, which is a document describing how the JVM is implemented, Implementation, which is a program meeting the JVM specification requirements, and Runtime Instance, which is the JVM instance that gets created whenever the command prompt is used to write a Java command and run a class.

All three are inextricably linked and each relies on the others to work.

What does public static void main(String args[]) mean?

Breaking it down:

- public – an access modifier that we use for specifying who may access the specified method. Use of the word public dictates that any class can access the method.
- static – this is a Java keyword that tells us the method is class-based. That means we do not need to create a class instance to access the method.
- void – this is the specific return type for the method. Void is used to define a method that does not and will not return any value.
- main – this the name for the method that the JVM searches at the start of an application with a specific signature. The main execution of the program happens in this method.
- String args[] – this is the parameter that we pass to our main method.

Put together we have an access modifier that tells us any class can access our method, which is class-based, does not require a class instance, will not return a value, is inside the Main method and has a parameter containing string arguments.

What Do We Mean By Platform Independence?

Java is a Platform-Independent language which means that you can write the code once and run it anywhere – there is no need to create separate codes for separate platforms. Java contains bytecodes that can be run on pretty much any system regardless of the operating system or platform that underlies it.

Why Is Java NOT Completely Object-Oriented?

Java uses no less than eight separate primitive data types:

boolean

byte

char

int

long

short

double

float

Because none of these are objects, Java cannot be 100% object-oriented.

What is a Wrapper Class?

A wrapper class is a class that we use for converting Java primitive data types into reference data types, or objects. Each of the primitive data types listed has a dedicated class and these are called wrapper classes because they are used for wrapping the primitive into a class object. These are the primitives, their wrapper class and the constructor used:

PRIMITIVE	WRAPPER CLASS	CONSTRUCTOR ARGUMENT
boolean	Boolean	String or boolean
byte	Byte	String or byte
char	Character	char
int	Integer	String or int
float	Float	String, double or float
double	Double	String or double
long	Long	String or long
short	Short	String or short

What is a Java Constructor?

A Java constructor is a code block that we use for initializing an object. The name of a constructor must be the same as the name of the class. Constructors do not have any return type and they are called automatically whenever we create an object. There are two type – a default constructor and a parameterized constructor.

What is the Singleton Class and How is a Class Made Singleton?

A singleton class is one that has just one instance that may be created at a specified time in one Java Virtual Machine. We can make a class into a singleton class by setting the constructor as private.

What is the Difference Between a Vector and an Array?

VECTOR	ARRAY LIST
A vector is synchronized	An array list is NOT synchronized
A vector is slower because it is thread-safe	An array list is faster because it lacks synchronization
A vector will default to doubling its array size	An array list may double in size by 50% if an element is added to it

A vector will define the size of the increment	An array list will not define the size of the increment
With the exception of the Hashtable, a vector the only class that may use both an iterator and enumeration.	an array list may only use an iterator for is the traversal of an array list

Explain the Difference Between == and equals().

The method, equals(), is defined inside a Java object class and is used to see whether there is equality between a pair of objects where business logic was used to define them. == is a binary operator called equality and it is used when we want to compare objects and primitives. The object class provides us with the public boolean equals (Object o) method and the default implementation will use the quality operator (==) to compare the objects. For example, some methods can be overridden, like the String class. Here's an example:

```
public class Equaltest {

    public static void main(String[] args) {

        String str1= new String("EFGH");

        String str2= new String("EFGH");

        if(str1 == str2)

        {

            System.out.println("String 1 == String 2 is true");

        }

        else

        {

            System.out.println("String 1 == String 2 is false");

            String str3 = str2;

            if( str2 == str3)

            {

                System.out.println("String 2 == String 3 is true");

            }

            else

            {

                System.out.println("String 2 == String 3 is false");
```

```
            }

            if(str1.equals(str2))
            {
                System.out.println("String 1 equals string 2 is true");
            }
            else
            {
                System.out.println("String 1 equals string 2 is false");
            }
        }
    }
}
```

Explain the Difference Between Stack Memory and Heap.

There are several differences between them:

- Stack memory is only used by a single execution thread whereas heap memory is used by every part of an application
- Other threads cannot access the stack memory whereas any object that is stored in a heap are accessible globally
- A stack follows the rules of LIFO – Last In First Out – to free up memory whereas, with the heap, memory management depends on the generation that each object has associated with it
- Stack memory will remain in existence until the thread has been executed whereas heap memory remains in existence from the start of the application until the very end.
- Stack memory may only have reference variables and local primitives to objects inside the heap space whereas, whenever an object gets created, it will always be stored in the heap space.

OOPS Java Interview Questions

What is Polymorphism?

Polymorphism is an OOP concept by which we can assign one entity, such as a function, an object, or a variable, with many different meanings in different contexts. There are two types of polymorphism – compile time and runtime. Compile time polymorphism is otherwise known as method overloading while runtime polymorphism makes use of interfaces and inheritance. It is sometimes called method overriding.

Explain Runtime Polymorphism

Runtime polymorphism is otherwise known as dynamic method dispatch and it is a process by which a call to a method that has been overridden gets resolved at runtime and not at compile time. A reference variable from a related superclass is used to call the overridden method. This example explains it better:

```
class Vehicle {
        void run()
        {
                System.out.println("The vehicle is running");
        }
}

class BMW extends Vehicle {
        void run()
        {
                System.out.println("The BMW runs safely at 100 km/h");
        }

        public static void main(String args[])
        {
                Vehicle b= new BMW();    //upcasting
                b.run();
        }
}
```

Explain the Difference Between Interfaces and Abstract Classes

There are several main differences between an abstract class and an interface:

- Abstract classes are able to provide default code that is complete and/or only the details that need to be overridden whereas an interface can only provide a signature, no code.

- Once class can only extend one abstract class whereas one class can implement multiple interfaces.
- Abstract classes may contain non-abstract methods but all of the methods in an interface must be abstract
- Abstract classes may contain instance variables but an interface cannot
- Abstract classes may have public, protected and/or private visibility but, in an interface, visibility can only be public or none
- When we add methods to abstract classes, we may, if we want, provide the default implementation, meaning the existing code should all work K. With the interface, when new methods are added we must find every implementation of that specific interface and define a new implementation for the new method.
- Abstract classes may have constructors while interfaces cannot.
- Abstract classes are very fast but an interface is slower because it needs indirection to locate the method that corresponds to in the class.

Refer to the chapter on OOP concepts for more information.

Explain Method Overloading and Overriding

In method overloading, methods that share a class may have the same name but each must have their own parameters of a different order and/or return type and different numbers of parameters. Method overloading is about adding to the behavior of a method and is known as compile time polymorphism. Every method has a different signature and you may or may not need to use inheritance.

The example below can explain this better:

```
class Adder {

    static int add(int a, int b)

    {

        return a+b;

    }


    static double add( double a, double b)

    {

        return a+b;

    }


    public static void main(String args[])
```

```
    {
        System.out.println(Adder.add(11,11));
        System.out.println(Adder.add(12.3,12.6));
    }
}
```

With method overloading, a sub or child class will have the same name, type and number of parameters and the same return type as its super or parent class. With method overriding we are changing how a method behaves and it is often known as runtime polymorphism. The methods require the same signature and inheritance is also a requirement for method overriding.

Have a look at this example:

```
class Vehicle {
    void run(){
        System.out.println("The vehicle is running");
    }
}

class BMW extends Vehicle{
    void run()
    {
        System.out.println("The BMW runs safely at 100 km/h");
    }

    public static void main(String args[])
    {
        Vehicle b=new BMW();
        b.run();
    }
}
```

Can a Private or a Static Method be Overridden in Java?

The short answer is no, private and static methods may not be overridden in Java. If you were to create a method that is similar, with identical method arguments and return type within the child class, the parent class (superclass) method will be hidden in a process called method hiding. In the same way, a private method in a child class cannot be overridden because there is no way to access it in there. The way around it is to create another method set as private in the child class and give it the same name.

This example will make things clearer:

```
class Base {

    private static void display() {

        System.out.println("The static or the class method from Base");

    }


    public void print() {

        System.out.println("The non-static or the instance method from Base");

    }

}


class Derived extends Base {

    private static void display() {

        System.out.println("The static or the class method from Derived");

    }

    public void print() {

        System.out.println("The non-static or the instance method from Derived");

    }

}


public class Test {

    public static void main(String args[])

    {

        Base obj= new Derived();

        obj.display();
```

```
        obj.print();
    }
}
```

Explain Multiple Inheritance/ Does Java Provide Support?

Multiple inheritance is when a child class inherits a property from several classes. There is no support in Java for multiple inheritance, mainly because it is far too ambiguous. If several parent classes were to share the same method name, when it comes to runtime, the compiler will struggle to determine which method in the child class needs to be executed.

Explain Association

Association is an OOP concept, a relationship where every object will have its own unique lifecycle with no owner. An example would be Teacher and Pupil. Several Pupils can be associated with one Teacher but no ownership exists between objects and both will have their own unique lifecycle. The associate may be one-to-one, one-to-many or many-to-many.

Explain Aggregation

Aggregation is a special type of association in which all of the objects have their own unique lifecycle. However, as opposed to association, in aggregation there is ownership and a child object may not belong to any other parent object. Using an example of Teacher and Department; one Teacher may not belong to several Departments, however if the Department object were deleted, the Teacher object would still exist.

Explain Composition

Composition is a special type of aggregation, sometimes called a "death" relationship. It is a stronger form of aggregation where a child object may not have its own Lifecyle and, if a parent object is deleted, the child object will be deleted as well. Using an example of a House and its Rooms – a House may have several Rooms; no room may belong to more than one House and each Room does not have independence; if the House were deleted, the Rooms would be deleted too.

Servlets Interview Questions

Explain What a Servlet is

A Java servlet is a type of server-side technology that is used for extending web browser capability. It does this by providing full support for data persistence and dynamic response. Java has two built-in servlet packages – javax.servlet and javax.servlet.http. Both of these provide us with classes and interfaces so we may write our own servlets.

Every servlet has a requirement to implement the interface called javax.servlet.Servlet. This is used for defining the lifecycle methods of the servlet. When we implement a generic service, the GenericServlet class that the Java Servlet API provides may be extended. With the HttpServlet class we are given methods like doGet() and doPost() which we can use to handle HTTP-specific services. We extend the HttpServlet class because we use the HTTP protocol to access most web applications.

Explain the Difference between the Get and Post Methods

The two methods offer several differences:

- With the Get method, we can only send a limited amount of data because the header is used for sending the data. In the Post method, the body is used to send the data so we can send much more.
- The Get method is not secure because all the data gets exposed in the URL bar whereas this does not happen in the Post method, making it much more secure.
- The Get method can be bookmarked whereas the Post method cannot.
- The Get method is idempotent* whereas the Post method is non-idempotent.
- The Get method is far more efficient and tends to be used more than the Post method which is not as efficient.
- – this denotes one element in a set whose value does not change when the element is multiplied or when it operates on itself

Explain What a Request Dispatcher is

The RequestDispatcher is an interface used for forwarding a request to a different resource – JSP, HTML, or any other servlet within the same application. It can also be used when we want to add content to the response from another resource. We can define two methods in the RequestDispatcher interface – void forward() and void include().

Explain the Differences between the forward() and sendRedirect() Methods

There are three major differences between these two methods:

- The forward() method is used to send the same request to a different resource whereas the sendRedirect() method must always send a new request because it makes use of the browser URL bar.
- The forward() method is a server-side method while sendRedirect() is a client-side method.
- The forward() method will only work in the server whereas the sendRedirect() method will work both inside and out of the server.

These are the only differences that we need to be aware of.

What is a Servlet's Lifecycle?

A servlet has five stages in its lifecycle:

- The servlet gets loaded
- The servlet gets instantiated
- The servlet gets initialized
- The servlet services the request
- The servlet is destroyed

Every servlet has this basic lifecycle.

Explain How Cookies Work within a Servlet

Cookies are small pieces of text data that go from the server to the client, getting saved on the local machine on the client-side. The Servlet API provides support for cookies with a class called javax.servlet.http.Cookie – this class implements the Cloneable and the Serializable interfaces.

A method called HttpServletRequest getCookies() is provided to retrieve the Cookie array from the request and the HttpServletResponse addCookie() method helps attach the cookie inside a response header. Cookies do not have any getter methods.

Explain the Difference Between ServletContext and ServletConfig.

There are a few differences between ServletContext and ServletConfig:

- The ServletConfig object only represents one servlet whereas the ServletContext object is representative of the entire application that runs on a specific JVM; it is common for all servlets in the application.
- ServletConfig is similar to a local parameter associated with one specific servlet whereas the ServletContext object is similar to a global parameter that is associated with the entire application.
- The ServletConfig object is a name-value pair that is defined in a web.xml file (in the section for servlets); as such its scope is servlet-wide. The ServletContext object is defined external to the servlet tag in the web.xml file and has a scope that is application-wide.
- The getServletConfig() method gets the config object while the getServletContext() method gets the context object.
- In basic terms, a ServletConfig object tends to be tied to a single servlet whereas the ServletContext object has global scope and is open to an entire application.

Explain the Methods used for Servlet Session Management

A Session is described as a "conversational" state between a client and a server; it may consist of several requests and responses between the client and the server. Because both Web Server and HTTP are stateless, a session may only be maintained when information unique to the session id is passed from the server to the client and back in every single request and response.

Some common ways that servlet session management is carried out are:

- HTML Hidden Field
- User Authentication
- Cookies
- Session Management API
- URL Rewriting

JDBC Interview Questions

What is the JDBC Driver?

The JDBC (Java Database Connectivity) Driver is a component of software that allows a Java application to interact with a given database. We have four JDBC driver types:

- Type 1 - JDBC-ODBC Bridge driver
- Type 2 -Native-API driver – this is a partial java driver
- Type 3 - Network Protocol driver – this is a full Java driver
- Type 4 -Thin driver – this is another full driver

Type 1 drivers make use of ODBC drivers for database connections. JDBC method calls are converted to ODBC function calls. The type 1 driver can connect to any database.

Type 2 drivers use the database client-side libraries. JDBC method calls are converted to database API native calls. To connect with different databases, the driver requires a local API.

Type 3 drivers use the application server or middleware to indirectly or directly convert JDBC calls into the database protocol specific to a given vendor.

Type 4 drivers directly interact with a database and do not need any native libraries.

What Steps Are Needed For a Connection to a Java Database.

First the driver class must be registered and then the connection can be created. A statement is created, the queries are executed and the connection is closed.

Explain what the JDBC API Components are

The JDBC API classes and interface can be found in the package called java.sql and they are:

Interfaces:

- Connection interface
- Statement interface
- PreparedStatement interface
- ResultSet interface
- ResultSetMetaData interface

- DatabaseMetaData interface
- CallableStatement interface

Classes

- DriverManager class
- Blob class
- Clob class

This is by no means an exhaustive list but gives you enough to show that you know what you are talking about. Also included are types like SQLException.

What Role Does the JDBC DriverManager Class Have?

The DriverManager class is for management of all registered drivers. We can use the class to register a driver and to unregister a driver when it is no longer needed. The class also provides the factory method that we use to return the Connection instance.

What is the JDBC Connection Interface?

The JDBC connection interface is used for maintaining a database session. We can use it for managing transactions and it also provides the factory methods that will return instances of Statement, CallableStatement, PreparedStatement and DatabaseMetaData.

What Purpose Does the JDBC ResultSet Interface Have?

The ResultSet object is used to represent one row in a table and it can be used for changing the mouse cursor pointer and for retrieving database information.

Explain What the JDBC ResultSetMetaData Interface is

The ResultSetMetaData interface is an interface used for returning table information, like the column name, the total number of table columns, the column type, and so on.

Explain What the JDBC DatabaseMetaData Interface is

The DatabaseMetaData interface is used for returning database information, like driver name and driver version, username, the total number of database tables, how many views, and so on.

What is Meant by Batch Processing in JDBC?

Batch processing is a process that helps us to group SQL statements that are related into one batch for execution rather than executing one query. With batch processing in JDBC, multiple queries may be executed at once, significantly speeding up performance.

Explain the Difference Between execute, executeUpdate and executeQuery

The execute statement is used for the execution of SQL queries. If, for example, you are running a Select query and it results in ResultSet, the statement will return TRUE. FALSE is output when the result is not a ResultSet, such as when you run Update or Insert queries. To get the update count, we can use the getUpdateCount() method and to retrieve the ResultSet, we can use getResultSet().

The statement, executeUpdate, is used for executing Insert, Update and Delete DML or DDL statements that do not return anything. For DML statements, the output will be int and it will be equal to the row count; for DDL, the output will be 0.

The statement, executeQuery, is used for the execution of Select queries and the return will be ResultSet. When ResultSet is returned, regardless of whether there are any records that match the query, it will never be null. When select queries are being executed, the executeQuery method should always be used so if anyone were to attempt to execute an insert/update statement, an exception would be thrown – java.sql.SQLException – saying that the method can't be used for updating.

The execute() method should be used only when you are not certain of the statement type; otherwise executeUpdate or executeQuery should be used.

Spring Interview Questions

What is Spring?

Spring is defined as an application framework that is also a control inversion container for Java. Any Java application may use the core features of the Spring framework but extensions will be required to build web apps on the Java EE platform.

What are the Spring Framework Modules?

Some of the Spring Framework modules are:

- Spring Context, used for dependency injection
- Spring AOP, used for aspect-oriented programming
- Spring DAO, used for database operations that use the DAO pattern
- Spring JDBC, used for DataSource and JDBC support
- Spring ORM, used for support for Hibernate and other ORM tools
- Spring Web Module - used to create web apps
- Spring MVC, the Model-View-Controller (MVC) implementation for the creation of web services, web apps and so on

These are the most important modules in the Spring Framework but is by no means an exhaustive list.

What Are Some of the Annotations in the Annotation-Based Configuration of Spring?

Some of the annotations are:

- @Autowired
- @Required
- @Resource
- @Qualifier
- @PreDestroy
- @PostConstruct

These are the important annotations, there are many more.

Discuss What Bean is in Spring and what Some of the Spring Bean Scopes Are

A bean is an object that is part of the core of a Spring application. The IoC container is responsible for managing Spring beans, which means the container will instantiate, assemble and manage it.

Spring bean scopes:

- Singleton – one bean instance is created per container. A singleton is the default scope; when used, you should ensure that the bean doesn't share any instance variables otherwise issues may arise with data inconsistency because the bean will not be thread-safe.
- Prototype – whenever a bean is requested a new instance gets created.
- Request – the same as for prototype but is used for web applications. For every HTTP request a new bean instance is created.
- Session – for every HTTP session from the container, a new bean gets created
- Global-Session – used Portlet applications, for the creation of global session beans.

These are the five scopes that have been defined in a Spring bean.

What Roles do DispatcherServlet and ContextLoaderListener Play?

DispatcherServlet is a Spring MVC application front controller. It is responsible for loading the configuration file for the Spring bean and for initializing all configured beans. Provided annotations have also been enabled, DispatcherServlet will scan through the packages to ensure that all beans annotated with either @Component, @Repository, @Controller or @Service, are configured.

ContextLoadListener is the listener that starts and finishes WebApplicationContext on the root of Spring. It has several important functions, including tying the Application Context lifecycle to the ServletContext lifecycle and for automating ApplicationContext creation.

Explain the Difference Between Constructor and Setter Injection

Setter injection provides partial injection while constructor injection does now. Setter injection will override the property for the constructor provided both of them have been defined whereas the constructor injection will override the property for setter. Constructer injection will create a new instance should there be any modification while setter injection while setter injection will not create any new instances if the property value is modified. Lastly, the setter injection works best when you don't have many properties while constructor injection works better when you have too many.

Explain Autowiring and Autowiring Modes in Spring

Autowiring allows a programmer/developer to automatically inject the bean without having to write any explicit injection logic. The code using dependency injection to inject the bean is:

<bean id="emp" class="nameofclass" autowire="byName" />

The modes for autowiring are:

no – the default mode, autowiring has not been enabled

byName – this will inject the bean based on the name of the property and uses the setter method

byType – this will inject the bean based on the type of the property and uses the setter method

constructor – this will use the constructor to inject the bean

Autowiring is designed to take some of the load off the developer

Explain How Exceptions are Handled in the Spring MVC Framework

The framework provides three ways to handle exceptions:

Controller

Exception-handler methods may be defined in the controller classes; we just add the @ExceptionHandler annotation to the methods

Global Exception Handler

The Spring MVC framework provides us with an annotation, @ControllerAdvice, that can be used with any class to define global exception handlers

Implementation of HandlerExceptionResolver

Where we have generic exceptions, static pages are mostly served. The framework provides us with the HandlerExceptionResolver interface that can be implemented for creating global exception handlers. This was provided because Spring also gives us a series of default implementation classes that can be defined in the configuration files for Spring beans, allowing us access to the benefits of the Spring exception handling capabilities.

List Some Important Spring Annotations That You Use

The answer to this question will obviously depend on which annotations you have personally used. Some that you are more likely to use include:

- @RequestMapping – this is used for configuration of URL mapping inside the methods for handling controllers.
- @Controller – used for Spring MVC controller classes
- @PathVariable – used for mapping the dynamic values for the method arguments from URL to handler
- @ResponseBody – used to send an Object, usually JSON or XML data, as a response
- @Qualifier – used with the @Autowired annotation to stop any confusion when you several bean type instances
- @Autowired – used to autowire soring bean dependencies
- @Scope – used to configure the spring bean scope
- @Service – used for the service classes

There are many others that you may use so make a note of them and what they are for

Explain How the Spring and Hibernate Frameworks Are Integrated

The Spring ORM module may be used for integrating both frameworks. However, if you are using a version of Hibernate whereby the current session is provided by SessionFactory then you should not use either the HibernateDaoSupport or HibernateTemplate classes – stick to using a DAO pattern that has dependency injection built-in.

Spring ORM also has support for declarative transaction management in Spring so that should be used rather than boiler-plate code.

Hibernate Interview Questions

What is the Hibernate Framework?

Hibernate is an ORM tool based in Java; the framework is for mapping relational database tables to application domain objects and vice versa. In Hibernate is a reference to the Java Persistence API implementation, an API that makes this one of the best choices of ORM (Object-relational mapping) tool that comes with loose coupling as a benefit. The API can be used for CRUD operations and the framework gives us the option of mapping POJOs (plain old Java objects) to database tables using both XML-based configuration and JPA annotations. Configurations in hibernate are very flexible and may be used programmatically or from the XML config file.

Name Some of the Benefits of the Hibernate Framework

Some of the more important benefits include:

- Elimination of JDBC boiler-plate code and resource management, leaving the programmer to concentrate on the business logic
- Support for XML and JPA annotations making implementation of code independent
- Provision of HQL, similar to SQL and very powerful. HQL, however, is a full OOP and can understand concepts such as association, polymorphism and inheritance.
- Open-source and global making it the best choice because there is a smaller learning curve and loads of documentation online, not to mention one of the largest communities with plenty of forums.
- Integrates easily with other EE frameworks and has support built-in to help integrate Hibernate with all Spring applications
- Has support for using proxy objects for lazy initialization and will only do database queries when asked
- Better performance through hibernate cache
- Native SQL queries can be executed

Overall, it is one of the best choices of ORM tool on the market today, containing every feature you should ever need.

Explain the differences Between the get() and load() Methods

There are four main differences between these methods:

If an object is not found, the get() method will return null while the load() method will throw an ObjectNotFoundException. Where the get() method will always hit the database, the load() method won't. Where the load() method will return a proxy object, the get() method will return a real object and, lastly, the get() method is recommended if you can't be certain whether the instance exists and the load() method is recommended when you are certain.

Explain The Advantages of Using Hibernate Over JDBC

There are a number of advantages:

- Hibernate eliminates much of the boiler-plate code that the JDBC API includes, making code look cleaner and easier to read
- Hibernate offers support for collections, associations and inheritance; the JDBC API does not.
- Transaction management is provided implicitly with Hibernate meaning most queries may not be executed externally to a transaction. With the JDBC API there is a need to use rollback and commit to write transaction management code.
- Because the JDBC API will throw a checked SQLException, there is a need to write quite a lot of try-catch blocks into the code. In most JDBC calls, this is redundant and is only used for transaction management. In Hibernate, the JDBC exceptions are

wrapped and only unchecked exceptions, HibernateException and JDBCException, will be thrown, eliminating the need to write handling code. And with the transaction management built into Hibernate, we don't need to use try-catch blocks.

- HQL, or Hibernate Query Language, is fully object-oriented; JDBC isn't and native sql queries must be written.
- Hibernate caching provides a performance boost whereas JDBC does not cache queries, lowering performance.
- In Hibernate we have the option of creating database tables; in JDBC, the tables must already be in the database.
- With the Hibernate configuration we can use both JNDI data source and JDBC-like connections for a connection pool, important for enterprise app development and a feature that is conspicuous by its absence from JDBC.
- We get support for JPA annotations in Hibernate so our code is implementation-independent and may be replaced with another ORM tool whereas JDBC is very tightly coupled to the application.

Java JSP Interview Questions

Explain the JSP Lifecycle Methods

There are three main methods.

- The public void jspInit() method is invoked just once, similar to the servlet init() method.
- The public void _jspService(ServletRequest request,ServletResponse) method will throw a ServletException.IOException. The method is invoked for every request, exactly the same as the servlet service() method.
- The public void jspDestroy() method is invoked just once, similar to the servlet destroy() method.

Name The Implicit Objects Provided by JSP.

There are nine implicit objects:

Object	**Type**
application	ServletContext
config	ServletConfig
exception	Throwable
out	JspWriter
page	Object
pageContext	PageContext
request	HttpServletRequest
response	HttpServletResponse
session	HttpSession

Discuss the Differences Between the Include Action and Include Directive

There are three differences:

- The include action will include content at the time of request whereas the include directive will include the content at the time the page is translated.
- The include action will invoke the include() method from the class provided by the vendor rather than including the original content whereas the include directive does have that original page content, causing an increase in the size of the page at runtime.
- The include action works better on dynamic pages while the include directive works better on static pages.

Explain How Caching on the Browser Back Button is Disabled.

It is disabled using this code:

```
<%
	response.setHeader("Cache-Control","no-store");
	response.setHeader("Pragma","no-cache");
	response.setHeader ("Expires", "0");		//This stops caching at the proxy
server
%>
```

What are the JSTL Tags?

JSTL provides five tags, namely core, sql, internalization, xml and function.

Explain How a Session is Disabled in JSP

A JSP session is disabled using this code:

<%@ page session="false" %>

Explain How JSP Cookies are Deleted

This code provides an explanation of how to delete cookies in JSP:

```
Cookie mycook = new Cookie("name1","value1");


response.addCookie(mycook1);

Cookie destroymycook = new Cookie("mycook1","value1");

destroymycook . set MaxAge ( 0 );

destroymycook . set Path ("/");

destroymycook . addCookie ( destroymycook 1 );
```

What is the jspDestroy() Method?

The jspDestroy() method gets invoked when a JSP page is set to be destroyed. It is invoked from the javax.servlet.jsp.JspPage interfaces. Methods are destroyed by servlets and can be overridden quite easily when cleanup is needed, like when a database connection is closed.

Discuss why JSP Technology is Better Than Servlet?

JSP technology is server-side and is designed to make it easy to generate content. It is document-centric while a servlet is a program. Java Server pages may have Java program fragments which will instantiate and execute a Java class. They happen inside HTML template files and provide the framework necessary for web applications to be developed.

Why Shouldn't JSP Standard Tags Be Configured in web.xml?

It is not necessary to configure these tags in web.xml because they are automatically configured when the web app is loaded by the container and the TLD files are found. They are configured for use in the JSP pages in the application; we must remember to include them in the page that uses the taglib directive.

Exception and Thread Java Interview Questions

Explain the Difference Between Error and Exception

Errors are conditions that happen at runtime and are irrecoverable, like an OutOfMemory error. They are irrecoverable because they are not repairable at runtime. The error may be caught in a catch block, but the application execution will stop and cannot be recovered.

Exceptions are conditions that happen because of wrong input or mistyped words, etc. For example, if a file cannot be found a FileNotFoundException is thrown or if you are attempting to use a null reference a NullPointerException will be thrown. Most of the time, recovery from exceptions is possible by correcting what was wrong in the first place.

How are Java Exceptions Handled?

Java exceptions are handled using five keywords – try, catch, throw, finally, throws.

Explain the Difference Between a Checked and Unchecked Exception

Checked exceptions are classes that extend the Throwable classes with the exception of Error and RuntimeException. They are checked when it comes to compiling and examples include SQLException and IOException.

An unchecked exception is one that extends the RuntimeException; they are not checked when it comes to compiling and examples include NullPointerException and ArithmeticException.

Explain the Purpose of the Final, Finally And Finalize Keywords.

The Final keyword is used when we want restrictions applied to a method, class and variable. We can't override the Final method, inherit the Final class or change the Final variable. This example should explain it better:

```
class FinalVarExample {

    public static void main( String args[])

    {

        final int a=10;  // Final variable

        a=50;            //Error because we can't change the value

    }

}
```

The Finally keyword is used when we need important code placed and it is executed regardless of whether the exception gets handled. This example will explain it better:

```
class FinallyExample {

    public static void main(String args[]){

        try {
```

```
            int x=100;
        }
        catch(Exception e) {
            System.out.println(e);
        }
        finally {
            System.out.println("The finally block is being executed");
        }
    }
}
```

The Finalize keyword is used when we need to perform some clean up immediately before garbage collection on an object. This code will explain it better:

```
class FinalizeExample {
    public void finalize() {
        System.out.println("Finalize is called");
    }

    public static void main(String args[])
    {
        FinalizeExample f1=new FinalizeExample();
        FinalizeExample f2=new FinalizeExample();
        f1= null;
        f2=null;
        System.gc();
    }
}
```

Explain the Difference Between Throw and Throws

The main differences between them are:

- The throw keyword is used when we want an expression thrown explicitly while the throws keyword is used for declaring exceptions.

- The throw keyword cannot be used on its own for the propagation of checked exceptions whereas the throws keyword can.
- The throw keyword is always followed with an instance while the throws keyword is always followed with a class.
- The throws keyword is used inside a method whereas the throws keyword is used in the signature for the method.
- We can't throw multiple exceptions but we can use the throws keyword for declaring multiple exceptions.

Explain the Java Exception Hierarchy

The Java exception hierarchy is:

All Exception classes have a parent class of throwable. There are two exception types, checked and unchecked or runtime. Both can be used for extending the Exception class but errors get classified further into Assertion and Virtual Machine errors.

Explain How a Custom Exception is Created

Creation of a custom exception requires the Exception class or a subclass of the Exception class to be extended. For example:

class New1Exception will extend Exception { } *// this creates a Checked Exception*

class NewException will extend IOException { } *// this creates a Checked exception*

class NewException will extend NullPointerException { } // this creates an Unchecked exception

Explain the Important Methods in a Java Exception Class

There are no specific methods in the Exception or any of the Exception subclasses; all methods get defined in Throwable, which is the base class.

- String getMessage() – Will return a message that reads String of Throwable. The method may be provided while the exception is being created through the constructor.
- String getLocalizedMessage() – this method is only given so that it can be overridden by subclasses. This is so that the calling program can be provided with a locale-specific message. Returning the exception message with the implementation of the throwable class requires the use of the getMessage() method.
- Synchronized Throwable getCause() – this will return the exception cause or, if the cause is not known it will return null id.
- String toString() – this will return some information in string format about throwable. In the string returned, the throwable class name and the localized message will be shown.

- void printStackTrace() – the stack trace information will be printed to the error stream (standard). PrintWriter or PrintStream may be passed as arguments so the stack trace info can be written.

Explain the Difference Between a Process and a Thread.

- A process is the instance of an execution for a program while the thread is a subset of this process.
- Inter-process communication must be used for the communication process with any sibling process whereas a thread can communicate with any threat inside its process.
- A process may only control child processes while threads have a great deal of control over any thread that is the same process.
- If a change is made in a parent process, the child process is not affected whereas changes in main threads could have an effect on the behavior of other process threads.
- Process memory runs in separate spaces in memory whereas thread process shares memory space.
- The operating system controls process and a programmer inside a program controls threads.
- A process is independent, a thread is not.

Explain What a Finally Block is and If There Are Any Cases Where it Won't Execute?

A finally block is a code block that will always execute statement sets. A finally block always has an associate with a try block, whether any exceptions happen or not. If a program calls System.exit() or a fatal error causes process abortion, the finally block will not be executed. In all other cases, it will be.

Explain Synchronization

Synchronization is all about multi-threading. A block of code that has been synchronized may only be executed by a single thread at a time. Java has support for multiple thread execution and that means that two threads or more may have access to the same objects or fields. The process of synchronization ensures that concurrent threads in the execution process are kept synchronized to avoid consistency errors with memory – this happens when there are inconsistent views of the shared memory space. If a method has been declared as synchronized, the thread will hold the method object monitor; should there be another thread executing the same method, the thread will be blocked until the monitor is released.

Can There Be More Than One Catch Block in One Try Block?

Yes. It is possible in Java to have several catch blocks in one try block but we should use a specific to general approach. Here's an example:

```
public class Example {
	public static void main(String args[]) {
		try {
			int a[]= new int[10];
			a[10]= 10/0;
		}
		catch(ArithmeticException e)
		{
			System.out.println("Arithmetic exception in the first catch block");
		}
		catch(ArrayIndexOutOfBoundsException e)
		{
			System.out.println("Array index out of bounds in the second catch
block");
		}
		catch(Exception e)
		{
			System.out.println("Any exception in the third catch block");
		}
	}
}
```

Chapter 7: Java Language and Terminology

A

Absolute filename

An absolute filename is a filename with a full path that is provided from the top or the root of the file system tree, or example c:\Java\bin\javac.exe

Abstract class

An abstract class is one whose header contains the reserved keyword, abstract. An abstract class is distinguishable from other classes by the fact that it is not possible to use the new operator to construct objects from them directly. Each abstract class may have at least zero abstract methods.

Abstraction

Abstraction is a simple representation of a complex situation. In basic terms, abstraction hides how a section of code or program works and shows only the functionality of it. This is designed to make it easier to maintain, read and work on the code. OOP design often revolves around finding an abstraction level to work with when real-life objects are being modeled. Too high a level and insufficient detail is capture; too low and you run the risk of a program being more complicated to create and difficult to understand that it should be.

Abstract method

An abstract method is a method whose header contains the reserved keyword, abstract. Abstract methods do not have a method body. Any method that has been designed inside an interface is considered abstract, with no exceptions. An abstract method's body is defined inside an abstract class subclass or, if a class implements the interface, within that class.

Abstract Windowing Toolkit

The AWT, or Abstract Windowing Toolkit contains a collection of classes that are designed to make creating applications with GUIs (graphical user interface) much simpler. You will find these in the java.awt group of packages and classes included are for buttons, windows, menus, frames, text areas and more.

Accessor method

An accessor method is a method that has been designed specifically to provide access to a class private attribute. By Java convention, accessor methods are prefixed with get and then the attribute name. For example, to gain access to an attribute called speed, the accessor method would be getSpeed(). When attributes are set as private, it stops objects from external classes from modifying the value unless a mutator method is used. We can use accessor methods to provide specific access to the private attribute values and to stop other objects in other classes from accessing the private attribute – the correct visibility needs to be used for the accessor to achieve this.

Actor

See client.

Actual argument

This is the value of the argument passed from outside a method into a method. When the method is called, the values (actual argument) will be copied to the formal arguments that correspond to it. The actual argument type and the formal argument types must be compatible with one another.

Actual parameter

See actual argument.

Address space

This is the virtual memory area that a process runs in.

Agent

See server.

Aggregation

This is an OOP concept, a type of relationship where one object has at least one other subordinate object making up its state. These subordinate objects don't tend to have an independent existence outside the object that contains them. When this object no longer has a reason to exist, neither do its subordinates. For example, you may have a GasStation object that has a few pump objects. Once the GasStation object is destroyed or has no further use, the pump objects follow suit. Aggregation is also known as a HAS-A relationship, distinguishing form inheritance which is an IS-A relationship.

Aliases

Aliases are several references to one object. The object may receive messages from any of the aliases and any change in state the results from a message will be easily detected by all.

Anonymous array

This is an array that has been created with no identifier. Anonymous arrays tend to be created as actual arguments like this:

```
// An anonymous array of integers is created

YearlyRainfall y2k = new YearlyRainfall(

    new int[]{ 10, 8, 9, 9, 5, 3, 2, 0, 3, 3, 8, 11}

);
```

Anonymous arrays can also be returned as the result of a method.

Anonymous class

An anonymous class is one that does not have a class name. this type of class is generally a subclass or an interface implementation and normally gets created as an actual argument or is returned as a result of a method. For example:

```
quitButton.addActionListener(new ActionListener(){

    public void actionPerformed(ActionEvent e){

        System.exit(0);

    }

});
```

Anonymous object

An anonymous object is an object that gets created with no identifier. Usually, they are array elements, results of methods or actual arguments. For example:

```
private Point[] vertices = {

    new Point(0,0),

    new Point(0,1),

    new Point(1,1),

    new Point(1,0),

};
```

Also see anonymous class as, very often, anonymous objects come from anonymous classes

API

See application programming interface.

Append mode

Append mode is a mode of file writing in which the contents of a file are kept when the file gets opened and new content gets appended.

Applet

An applet is a small Java program that is based on the Applet or the JApplet class. Mostly they are used for providing active content on a web page and they have a number of features that set them apart from a standard Java graphical app, including security restrictions that limit them in what they can do and having no main method defined by a user.

Application

Application is sometimes used synonymously for the word program but, as far as Java is concerned, application is the term used to describe GUI programs that aren't applets.

Application programming interface (API)

The API is a set of definitions used for writing a program. In Java, an API is a set of classes, packages and interfaces used for creating complex applications without having to start from the bottom up.

Argument

An argument is the information or data passed to a method. Sometimes arguments are called parameters. If a method expects to be passed arguments the method header must have a declaration for a formal argument for every argument. When the method is called the values for the actual arguments are copied to the formal arguments that correspond with each one.

Arithmetic expression

An arithmetic expression is one that contains numerical values that are of float or int type. For example, the arithmetic operators, like *, +, -, and /, will all take an arithmetic expression as an operand and their results are arithmetic values.

Arithmetic operator

These are a type of operator that will return a numerical result and are part of an arithmetic expression. Operators include +, -, *, /.

Arpanet

Arpanet is the network that came before the global internet.

Array

An array is an object of fixed size that can hold at least zero items of the declared type for the array. For example, an int array will hold int items.

Array initializer

An array initializer is used to initialize an array. It steps in to take the role of the separation creation step and the initialization. For example:

int[] pair = { 4, 2, };

is equivalent to the following four statements.

int[] pair;

pair = new int[2];

pair[0] = 4;

pair[1] = 2;

Assembler

An assembler is a program that is used for translating programs that are written in the assembly language into a binary form of a specified instruction set.

Assembly language

The assembly language is a symbolic one that corresponds very closely to a central processing unit (CPU) instruction set. The assembler (above) is the translation program that transforms the program into binary.

Assignment operator

The assignment operator is an equal sign (=) used for storing an expression's value into a variable; for example, variable = expression. The right side of the operator must be evaluated before the assignment can be made. An assignment may, on its own be used on an expression. This example assignment statement will store a value of zero into both of the variables – x = y = 0.

Assignment statement

An assignment statement is a statement that contains the assignment operator.

Attribute

An attribute is a specific use of an instance variable. The attribute values in one class instance are defining the current state of that specific instance. Class definitions can impose constraints on the valid instance states through a requirement that a given attribute or attributes do not take particular values. For example, if an attribute holds exam results for a class, it should not have negative values. An attribute may be manipulated using mutator and accessor methods.

B

Base case

A base case is a non-recursive route taken through a recursive method

Base type

The base type indicates the item type in an array, i.e. the arrays' defined type. For example:

int[] numbers;

Numbers have a base type of int. If the base case is the type of class, it will be indicating lowest supertype of the objects that the array can store. For example:

Ship[] berths;

All that can be stored in berths are instances of the class called Ship. If an array's base type is Object, it may be used for storing instances for any class.

Behavior

Class methods are what implement the behavior of a class. The behavior of a specific object is a mixture of the class method definitions and the current state of the specific object.

Big-endian

A type of machine. One of the most common differences between machines is how they store each byte of numerical data with many bytes. A big-endian machine will store high-order bytes first, followed by low-order bytes.

Also see little-endian

binary

A binary is base 2 number representation. With base 2 only 1 and 1 are used as digits and the positions of the digits are representing successive powers of 2.

Also see bit

Binary operator

A binary operator is an operator that will take two operands. Java has several binary operators, including some of the arithmetic and Boolean operators.

Binary search

A binary search is a search that looks through sorted data where the central position is looked at first. The search will then go to the left or the right, eliminating the other side of the data space. This is repeated for each step until all the data has been searched or the specific item has been located.

Bit

A bit is a binary digit. It can take only two values, 0 and 1. A bit is a basic block for building both data and programs. A computer will move data around on a regular basis in multiples of units made up of 8 bits, generally called bytes

Bit manipulation operator

A bit manipulation operator, like |, &, and ^, are used for manipulating bits inside data item bytes. The <<, >> and >>> shift operators are bit manipulation operators too.

Blank final variable

A blank final variable is a final variable that wasn't initialized when it was declared. These variables need to be initialized in one of two ways before it can be used – in every class constructor or in an instance initialization block.

Block

A block is a section of code made up of declarations and statements enclosed in a pair of opening and closing curly brackets {}. Both a class body and a method body are blocks. Blocks are also used for enclosing nested scope levels.

Bookmark

A bookmark is used by a web browser as a way of remembering URL details.

Boolean

a Boolean is a primitive data type in Java. It has just two possible values – TRUE or FALSE.

Boolean expression

a boolean expression is one that results in a boolean, i.e. TRUE or FALSE. The && and the | operators, among others, will take a boolean operand, producing a boolean result. Relational operators will take operands of different types and will also produce a boolean result.

Boot

A computer "boots" up when you turn it on and the term is derived from the phrase "pulling yourself up by your bootstraps". When a computer is first switched on it must load everything it needs from its disks before it can be used but, to do this, there is a program it needs and this is called a bootstrap.

Bootstrap classes

A bootstrap class is part of the Java Platform Core API, like those from the java.io and java.lang packages.

Boundary error

A boundary error is one that happens as a result of a mistake happening at the edge of a problem, such as no items of data, indexing off an array edge, a loop termination and more. Boundary errors are very common logical errors.

Bounded repetition

Bounded repetition is where statements in the body of a loop get performed a certain number of times – the number of times is worked out when the loop begins. Java does not have any control structure that will guarantee bounded repetition.

Also see unbounded repetition

Bounds

A bound is the limit of a collection or array. In Java, a lower limit will always be zero and, where arrays are concerned, an upper bound will always be one less than the array length and it is fixed. When you index outside a collection or array bound, you will get an IndexOutOfBoundsException thrown.

Branch instruction

A branch instruction will store an instruction address in the counter for a program. The result is that the next instruction fetched may not be the one that immediately follows the branch instruction and this causes disruption in the normal sequence of instruction execution. The result of this is conditional instruction execution and repetition.

Break statement

A break statement is a statement for breaking out of a loop, a labeled block or a switch statement. In every case, control flow moves to the statement that immediately follows the block containing the statement.

Bridging method

A bridging method is one that provides a bridge between methods in a public interface for a class and the private implementation of that interface. Usually, bridging methods are non-public in terms of visibility.

Byte

A byte is, in computing terms, eight data bits. In Java, it is also a primitive data type with a size of eight bits.

Bytecode

The Java compiler translates Java source files into bytecode which is the instruction set of the JVM. All bytecode is stored in a .class file.

C

Call-by-value

A call-by-value is an explanation of an argument being passed to a method in which a copy is taken of the actual argument and it is put in a different memory space, represented by the formal argument that corresponds to it. The result of this is that any assignment to a method's formal argument will not affect the value that is stored in the actual argument. This is an often misunderstood Java principle. It doesn't mean that objects referred to by actual arguments are not able to be modified through the formal argument. Have a look at this example where the array that the variable numbers refer to is sorted:

Arrays.sort(numbers);

The sort() method is going to change the order in which the values are stored in the object the numbers refer to but it isn't possible for the method to change the array the numbers are referring to.

Carriage return

This is indicated by \r and is also a synonym for the Enter key or the Return key used for terminating a text line. The name is derived from the mechanical typewriter carriage return.

Cascading if-else statement

This is a kind of if-else statement; all of the else parts of the statement with the exception of the final one will have another if-else statement nested inside. These tend to be used for overcoming textual drift issues that arise with nested if statements.

Case label

A case label is a value that is used for selecting a specific switch statement case.

Case sensitive

A test for case sensitivity as to whether a character is upper or lower case.

Cast

Cast is used to force the Java compiler into accepting a source value of a type to use on the target where Java doesn't allow that source type to be used. Great care should be taken when you cast a primitive type value because information can easily be lost. When a cast is made on an object reference, they are checked for legality at runtime. If any are illegal, a ClassCastException is thrown.

Catch clause

The catch clause is the section of a try statement that will handle caught exceptions.

Catching exceptions

The catch clause in a try statement is responsible for catching exceptions which gives a program the chance to bounce back from a problem or to repair the cause of the problem.

Central Processing Unit

This is the CPU which is the part of a computer that enables a computer to follow instructions. Each CPU type will have its own unique instruction set.

Character set encoding

This refers to the set of values that have been assigned to the characters inside a character set. You will often see related characters in groups with consecutive values, like digits or alphabetic characters.

Checked exception

A checked exception is one that must be locally caught in a try statement or it must be generated through a throws clause that has been defined in a method header.

Also see unchecked exception.

Class

A class is a programming concept that lets us group methods and data together and it is one of the building blocks of the OOP language. Class methods define the operations on the class data; the close link between operations and data means that a class instance, or an object, will respond to messages received from the class methods.

Class body

A class body is the body of the definition of a class. In the body are the class member definitions – the methods, fields and nested classes

Class constant

A class constant is a variable that has been defined as both static and final

Class header

Belonging to a class definition, the header names the class and is responsible for defining access. It will also state whether the class is implementing any interfaces or is extending a superclass.

Class inheritance

Class inheritance is when a subclass extends a superclass, creating a relationship between them. The subclass will then inherit all the attributes and methods of the superclass. In Java, inheritance is always single; there is no support for multiple inheritance.

Also see interface inheritance for another inheritance form.

Class method

Class method is another way of saying static method

Classpath

The classpath is the path that the compiler and the interpreter look through for class definitions. It can be set using a command line argument or using an environment variable.

Class scope

If a private variable is defined externally to the class methods, it is said to have class scope. The variable may be accessed from all the class methods, no matter what order they were defined in. A private method will also have class scope, while a method or variable can have a much wider scope if the private access modifier is not used.

Class variable

Class variable is another way of saying static variable.

Client

A client is a service user, for example, web clients place requests for resources from a web server. Clients that are objects send messages to object servers.

Cohesion

Cohesion defines the extent to which one component will one fully defined task. For example, a method that has strong cohesion will carry out one task, i.e. adding one item into a data structure, or data sorting, where a method that has weak cohesion will do a number of contrasting tasks.

Weak cohesive components should really be separated into cohesive components. An example of a weak package is java.util because it has a lot of interfaces and classes that are not related whereas java.io is strongly cohesive.

Command-line argument

These are arguments that get passed to a program at runtime. These are received in the formal argument that goes with a program's main method. For example:

public static void main(String[] args)

In this, the arguments have been stored individually as strings.

Comment

A comment is a bit of text that tells a human who is reading code what the code does. Provided a comment has been input correctly, the compiler will ignore it.

Common Gateway Interface

The CGI or Common Gateway Interface is one of the standards that allow interaction between web clients and programs on web servers. CGI scripts on servers can process arguments or input that comes from the client and provide an appropriate response.

Compilation

Compilation is the translation of a computer programming language. Very often, the translation is from a high-level to a low-level language or the translation of a binary form from a specified instruction set. The Java compiler does the translation, transforming a program into bytecode.

Compiler

The compiler is the program which does the compilation on a high-level computer programming language.

Complement operator

The complement operator is denoted by ~ and it is used for the inversion of bit values in binary patterns. Each bit is inverted individually. Fr example, the complement of 1010010 would be 0101101.

Concurrency

Concurrency is one of the parallel programming features. When program executions are overlapped in time, they are executing concurrently. Java provides support for concurrency in the thread feature.

Condition

A condition is a Boolean expression that controls a conditional statement or a loop.

Conditional operator

A conditional operator is a type of operator that will take three operands and is often called a ternary operator. The condition operator is denoted by a ? and is used like this:

bexpr ? expr1 : expr2

In this, bexpr is a Boolean expression which if it has a value of TRUE will result in a value of expr1 or, if it is FALSE, the result will be a value of expr2.

Connection handshake

A connection handshake is a message exchange between processes to try to get a connection between them.

Constant

A constant is a variable with a value that cannot be changed. In Java we use final variables to implement these.

Constructor

Constructors are called automatically when a class instance is called. Constructors are always named the same as their class and do not have any return type. For example:

```
public class Boat {

  public Boat(String name){

     ...

  }

  ...

}
```

A class that does not have an explicit constructor will be given a no-arg constructor by default; this constructor has an empty body and will not take arguments.

Continue statement

A continue statement is one that can only be used in a loop body. With a while loop or a do loop, control will immediately pass straight to the terminating test of that loop. With a for loop, the control will go to the update expression immediately after the body.

Continuous simulation

In continuous simulation, time passes at a rate applicable to the specific scenario. At every tick of time, every object within the simulation will be told of the passage of time and will be updated.

Also see discrete simulation for another simulation form.

Control structure

A control structure is a statement that has an effect on a method's flow control. If statements and loops are typical examples of control structures.

Copy constructor

A copy constructor is a type of constructor that takes one argument of the class. For example:

```
public class Point {
    // the attribute of 'p' is used to initialize this object.
  public Point(Point p){
    ...
  }
  ...
}
```

This argument is used for defining the new object attribute's initial values.

Coupling

Coupling happens when classes know of one another because of interaction between their instances. The link may be between strong or weak classes. Strong coupling happens when a class is aware of very detailed information about the internal implementation of another class and has been written to use that information to advantage. If anything can reduce how much knowledge is inside the coupling will be weaker which is why we make use of encapsulation and information hiding. The four visibility levels in Java, which are private, package, protected and public will real progressive detail to the other classes, increasing the chance of strong coupling. Interfaces are used to weaken coupling because interaction takes place through an abstract definition and not a concrete implementation.

Critical section

A critical section is a piece of code that contains a high potential for a race hazard. Critical sections used synchronized statements or methods.

Curly brackets

See block.

Cursor

A cursor tells you visually where your mouse pointer is on the virtual desktop. We can set shapes for the cursor as a way of representing the program's current state, i.e. an hourglass to tell a user to wait, or as a way of suggesting what actions are available on a given part of the user interface.

D

Decrement operator

A decrement operator is denoted by – and is used to add one to the associated operand. The operator has two forms - --x, which pre-decrement, and x--, which is post-decrement. For pre-decrement, the expression result will be the argument value following the decrement while, in post decrement the result is argument value before the decrement. For example:

int a = 6, b = 6;

int y,z;

y = --a;

z = b--

After this, y will have a value of 5 and z will have a value of 6; and b will both have the value of 5.

Daemon thread

A Daemon thread is a non-user thread and is normally used for low-priority tasks that shouldn't have priority over the program's main task. When all the other threads have been blocked a Daemon thread may be useful and an example of a daemon thread is the garbage collector.

Datagram

A datagram is an information packet, passed over the network between two processes that communicate with one another. TCP (transmission control protocol) and UDP (user datagram protocol) are both involved indirectly in sending these datagrams to provide reliable communication (TCP) and unreliable communication (UDP) respectively.

Data type

Java has eight primitive data types, five representing numerical types that vary in precision and range. These are float, double, long, short and int. The other three are used for the representation of Boolean values (single-bit), bytes values (single byte) and char values (two-byte characters that are present in the Unicode character set).

Deadlock

A deadlock arises when a pair of thread each gets the lock to one of the resources sets that they both require.

Decimal

A decimal is a base 10 number representation in which all the digits between 0 and 9 may be used. The positions of the digits are representative of powers of 10 in succession.

Declaration and initialization

This is a statement which both declares and immediately initializes a variable. The following are examples of this:

int numPupils = 25;

Boat argo = new Boat();

Pupil[] Pupils = new Pupil[numPupils];

If an instance variable is not explicitly initialized at the time of declaration, they are given a default initialization value that is pertinent to the type. If a local variable is undefined its initial value will be undefined.

Deep copy

A deep copy is when an object is copied and subsequent copies are made of all the object subcomponents. The object that results may be a clone.

Also see shallow copy

Default initial value

This is the default value of a variable that has not been explicitly initialized at the time of declaration. By default, numeric primitive type fields will have a value of zero, Booleans have the default value of false, a char variable will have the default value of \u0000 and an object reference will have the default value of null. Unless they are explicitly initialized, a local variable will have undefined initial values.

Default label

A default label is where the values from a switch statement expression that don't have case labels (explicit) go to. Default labels are optional.

Delegation

Delegation is a process whereby a message is passed by an object to a subordinate object. If inheritance is not in use, delegation is the best alternative to avoid duplication of code, thus promoting the reusability of code.

De Morgan's theorem

De Morgan's theorem is a pair of rules that help make Boolean expressions that contain several logical-not operators combined with other operators of the Boolean type much simpler.

Deprecated

Something that is deprecated is obsolete because a later version of the API has taken over. You should not use a deprecated method because they may not be in existence in future versions of Java.

Direct recursion

Direct recursion happens when a method calls itself.

Discrete simulation

Discrete simulation is a form of simulation in which time passes irregularly; this is determined by the main interest events in the simulation scenario.

Also see continuous simulation

Disk drive

A disk drive is a piece of hardware used for data storage. It may be a compact disk, a hard disk, a floppy drive or an SSD and may be internal or external to the computer.

Divide and conquer

Divide and conquer is a problem-solving approach that tries to reduce one large problem down into several simpler and smaller problems.

Do loop

A do loop is one of the control structures in Java for looping – the others are the for loop and the while loop. Do loops have a loop body and one Boolean expression. Once the loop body has completed the first iteration, the condition will be tested. It is retested after each iteration and will terminate when a false value results from the condition. Loop body statements are always executed a minimum of one time.

Dotted decimal notation

A dotted decimal notation is used for representing an IP address's four-byte value. Each of the bytes is represented as a value somewhere between 0 and 255, for example, 159.35.0.1. The first byte written is the most significant one.

Double buffering

Double buffering is a graphical technique used to make animations smoother. A second image version is drawn in the background and, when the drawing is finished, it is displayed. There is the assumption that it is quicker to display the image fully drawn than it is to compute it and draw it.

Downcast

A downcast is a form of cast that goes to the dynamic type of an object, i.e. it goes down the hierarchy of inheritance. For example:

// Downcast from the Object to the String

String s = (String) o;

Also see upcast.

Dynamic type

The name of a class used for constructing an object is the dynamic type of that object.

Also see static type

E

Edit-compile-run cycle

This is one of the most common parts of the process of program development. Source files are created and then compiled. Any syntax errors need to be corrected using the editor and then the file is compiled once more. After successful compilation the program can be run. At this point, logical errors may be revealed or there may be a need to enhance parts of the program. The result is another iteration of editing, compiling and running.

Encapsulation

Encapsulation is an OOP concept in which an object state is safeguarded. To do this, the attributes of the object are defined as private and access is given only via mutator and accessor methods.

Enumerated type

An enumerated type is a data type that is not available directly in Java. Symbolic names represent a sequence of values, all constant numerics. These types help us to avoid using magic numbers. We can simulate them in Java using interface fields, for example:

public interface States {

public static final int Stop = 0, Go = 1;

}

Exception

An exception is an object that represents one occurrence of a circumstance that is exceptional, usually when something has gone wrong and the program no longer runs smoothly. An exception object is created from a class that extends Throwable.

Also see checked exception and unchecked exception

Exception handler

An exception handler is where an exception object gets caught and then dealt with. The try statement is an exception handler.

Exclusive-or operator

This operator is denoted by ∧ and it is a Boolean and a bit-manipulation operator. With the Boolean version we get a value of TRUE if just one operand is true, False if otherwise. The bit-manipulation version will produce 1 bit at any point where bits in the corresponding operands are not the same.

Expression

An expression is a combination of operators and operands that produce resulting values. An expression has a resulting type that will have an effect on what context they may be used in.

Also see Boolean expression and arithmetic expression

F

Factory pattern

A factory pattern is a class definition pattern. The class is used for generating instances for other classes. It is sometimes used for the creation of local-specific or platform implementations of an interface or an abstract class. This will reduce coupling between the classes as the factory client is freed from its need-to-know about specific implementations.

Fetch-execute cycle

The fetch-execute cycle is a series of steps that are repeated over and over for each instruction of the program; the CPU is responsible for this. Examples of instructions include 'fetch the next instruction the program counter references', 'execute the instruction that has just been fetched', etc.

Field

A field is a class member and is a variable or variables defined in an interface or a class, external to the methods.

File system

A file system is a structure of files made possible by an operating system to use disk drive space. Every file system will have conventions for naming of files, structuring of directories and folders and for splitting large files down into smaller ones, for example. We cannot normally transfer and data from the file system in one operating system directly to that in another operating system because there is likely to be an incompatibility between the conventions.

File transfer protocol

FTP or File Transfer Protocol is a standard rule set that allows files to be transferred from one file system to a different one.

Filter stream

A filter stream is an I/O class that manipulates or filters input or output data stream. DataInputStream and DataOutputStream are two examples.

Final class

A final class has the reserved keyword, final, in the class header. Final classes cannot be extended by other classes.

Finalization

Right before garbage collection is used on an object, the object final method will be called. This allows the object to release any resources it may have.

Finally clause

A finally clause is included in a try statement and is the part that always gets executed. This happens in one of two ways – after a caught exception is handled or after the protected statements terminate normally.

Final method

A final method has the reserved keyword, final, in its header. Final methods cannot be overridden by any method that is defined in a subclass.

Final variable

A final variable has the reserved keyword, final, in the declaration. Final variables cannot be assigned any value after they have been initialized and this normally happens when the variable is declared. However, where a blank final variable or uninitialized final field requires initialization, this may be passed to an initializer or to the class constructor to do.

First in, first out

FIFO, or First In First Out, is the definition of a queue data structure. Items are taken out of the queue in the order that they appeared in the queue i.e. the first item added will be the first item removed.

Also see last in, last out

Floating point number

Also see real number.

For loop

A for loop is a Java looping control structure. The while loop and the do loop are the other two. For loops have a loop header and body. In the header are three expressions, with two semicolons separating them. At least one expression can be left out if not needed. The first of the expressions will be evaluated just once, when the loop is entered. The second expression is always a Boolean expression that represents the termination test of the loop. The TRUE value is represented by an empty expression and the third expression will only be evaluated when the lop body has been iterated once. The loop can only terminate when the FALSE value is given by the termination test. Loop body statements may be executed at least zero times.

Formal argument

A formal argument is a method argument definition which is included in the method header. All formal arguments will have one type associated with them. When a method gets called, the values of the actual argument are copied to the formal argument that corresponds to it. The actual argument types and the formal argument types must be compatible with one another.

Formal parameter

See formal argument.

Fully qualified class name

A fully qualified class name is a call name that also contains a package name and the name of the enclosing class. Have a look at this example:

package oddities;

```
class Outer {
   public class Inner {
      ...
   }
   ...
}
```

Inner has a fully qualified name of oddities.Outer.Inner.

Fully evaluating operator

A fully evaluating operator is one that evaluates every argument in it to get a result. Fully evaluating operators are the arithmetic operators. Conversely, some of the Boolean operators are called short-circuit operators.

Functional programming

This is a programming style that is associated with programming languages like Haskell. These languages are tied closely to the function concept (mathematical) than an imperative language is. This means it is much easier for program-proving techniques to be applied along with logical reasoning to any functional program. The concept of variables does not enter into functional programming in the way you are used to them, i.e. as a location in memory with contents that may be modified as a program is executed.

G

Garbage collector

A garbage collector is a daemon thread that will recycle any object that has no extant reference to it in a program.

Global variable

Global variables tend to be more of a problem in a structures language than in OOP. Within a structured program, like C, global variables are defined externally to any functions and procedures of the program. Usage of these variables is difficult to track because it can be written or read by the entire module or program it is has been defined in. This is why logical errors are common in variables. Instance variables pose problems like this in a class definition because the scope rules in Java ensure that they can be accessed by all class methods. This is why accessor and mutator methods are generally used in Java to allow access, even in a class.

Graphical user interface

A GUI or graphical user interface is the bit of a program where a user may interact using components like buttons, menus, etc. Interaction is usually with a mouse but can also be via the keyboard.

H

Hardware

This refers to the physical hardware that makes up a computer system, like disk drives, printers, keyboards, sound cards, graphics cards, etc.

Has-a relationship

See aggregation.

Hash code

A hash code is a value that a hash function returns. Access to a random-access data structure is often done via a hash code which acts as the index for the structure. This provides a mapping between objects and their locations. Hash codes tend to be used by HashMap and other similar classes.

Hash function

A hash function will provide the hash code from an object's arbitrary contents. The hashValue method, which is inherited from its object class, may be overridden by a class that will then define a hash function of its own.

Heterogeneous collection

This is a collection containing objects that all have dynamic types.

Also see homogenous collection

Hexadecimal

A hexadecimal is a base 16 number representation. With base 16, we can use the letters A to F and the digits 0 to 9. A is representative of 10, which is base 10, B is representative of 11, also base 10, and so on. The digit positions are representing powers of 16 in succession.

High-level programming language

High-level programming languages, like Java, give their programmers many features, including methods, data structures, classes, and packages, etc. The features are, for the most part, independent of a specific instruction set and that means any program written in it have higher portability than those written in low-level languages.

Homogeneous collection

A homogenous collection is a group of objects that all have an identical dynamic type. The most common of these are arrays.

Also see heterogenous collections

Hostname

This is the name given to a host system.

Host system

This is the computer system that runs a process.

Hot spot

A hot spot is part of an image map that has a specific significance. Programs tend to monitor mouse movements and will provide the appropriate response to actions that are associated to the hot spots it passes over. This could include information being displayed, for example. Sometimes, when the mouse is clicked over a hot spot, the program is 'told' to activate an association with it. Hot spot is also used for describing a part of a program that is intensive in computation terms, like inner loops. Places like this are often potential places where the program may be optimized.

HSB color model

An HSB color model is one based on the representation of a color in three components – hue, saturation, and brightness. This is also called the HSV model – hue, saturation, and value.

Also see RGB Color Model

HyperText Markup Language

Better known as HTML, this is a presentation language that is used for web page content markup. HTML tags are often paired where text sections need to be marked for representation in different font colors.

HyperText Transfer Protocol

Better known as HTTP, this is a rule set that is defined to allow interaction between a browser or client and a server.

I

Icon

An icon is a small image that communicates a culturally or language independent meaning.

Identifier

An identifier is a name defined by a programmer for an interface, class, method or variable.

IEEE 754

This is the standard the Institute of Electrical and Electronic Engineers issue and is used for arithmetic pertaining to binary floating points. The arithmetic in Java conforms to this standard.

If-else statement

An if-else statement is one of the control structures in Java. Control structures are used for choosing between two actions to perform. For example:

if(boolean-expression){

// If the expression is TRUE, the statement is performed.

...

}

else{

// If the expression is FALSE, the statement is performed.

...

}

Boolean expressions control these structures.

Also see if statement

If statement

The if statement is another control structure that will decide whether or not to perform any further action.

if(boolean-expression){

```
    // If the expression is TRUE, the statement is performed.
    ...
}
```

Boolean expressions control the statement.

Also see if-else statement

Image map

An image map is an image that has been split into logical areas. Each area will have a hot spot.

Immutable object

An immutable object is one that cannot be changed. For example, String class objects are immutable because, once created, the length and the content of the String class cannot be changed.

Implements clause

An implements clause is part of a class header. It is the part that indicates the interfaces the class will implements. Classes may implement one or more interfaces.

Also see multiple inheritance

Implicit type conversion

The implicit type conversions don't need a cast and do not usually result in any information being lost. For example, if you combine an integer operand and floating point operand inside an arithmetic expression, the result will be an implicit type conversion – the integer to a floating point value that is equivalent.

Import statement

Import statements are used to enable one or more class names or interface names to be available in an alternative package to the one they are defined in. An import statement will come after a package declaration and before interface or class definitions.

Inconsistent state

An inconsistent state is one that an object should never be in. classes must be designed carefully to make sure that no instances can fall into an inconsistent state.

Increment operator

The increment operator is denoted by ++ and will add one to the operand. The increment operator has two forms - ++x, the pre-increment, and x++, the post-increment. In pre-increment, an expression's result is the argument value following the increment while, in post-increment, the expression's result is the argument value before the increment. Look at this example:

int a = 4, b = 4;

int y,z;

y = ++a;

z = b+;

The result of this is that y will have a value of 5 and z will have a value of 4. The values of a and b will be 5.

Indirect recursion

Indirect recursion happens when method Y calls method x while there is already an X to y call happening.

Infinite loop

An infinite loop is one with a termination test that will not ever evaluate as FALSE. This may, on occasion, be set deliberately by a programmer, by using a construct like:

while(true) ...

or

for(; ;) ...

However, it may also be a logical error in the loop condition or in the loop body statements.

Infinite recursion

Infinite recursion is recursion that never terminates. This can happen after direct, indirect or mutual recursion and is normally a result of a logical error. It may also end in a stack overflow.

Information hiding

Information hiding is a process of only allowing enough class implementation information to be seen as is absolutely necessary. By hiding any information that isn't necessary, fewer classes will use that information to aid their own implementation. This produces weaker coupling and also reduces the chance that any modifications in the underlying implementation will result in another class being broken. One way to promote this is to make sure that all class fields have been defined as private.

Inheritance

Inheritance is an OOP concept by which subtypes inherit variables and methods from their supertype.

Inheritance hierarchy

This is the relationship that occurs between super and subclasses. Single inheritance refers to one class having one parent class with the Object class right at the very top. If two classes share an immediate superclass they are called sibling subclasses. Multiple inheritance is a more complex hierarchy structure.

Initializer

An initializer is a block that has been defined at the outer level of a class, much like a method that has no header. All initializer blocks get executed in the order they are in whenever instances are created. This happens before a class constructor but following superclass constructors. An initializer is one place where a blank final variable can be initialized.

Inner class

An inner class is one that is defined within an enclosing method or class and usually refers to nested classes that are non-static.

Instance

Another word for object. Class objects are instantiated following the invoking of a class constructor using the new operator.

Instance variable

An instance variable is a non-static class field. Each class object will have a copy of the field as opposed to class variables which are shared by all class instances. We can use instance variables to model class attributes.

Instantiation

Instantiation is the creation of a class object or instance.

Instruction set

An instruction set is a set of instructions characterizing a specific CPU. Any program that is written in one CPU instruction set can't usually be run on any other CPU type.

Integer

An integer is a whole number, positive or negative. The primitive types of byte, int, short and long all hold values of the integer type, either in narrow or wide ranges.

Interface inheritance

When classes implement interfaces we get an interface inheritance relationship. The class will not inherit any of the interface implementations but it will inherit the static variables and the method signatures. One interface may also extend at least one other interface. This is the only multiple inheritance form in Java.

Also see class inheritance

Internet

The internet is a global network that consists of multiple networks all interconnected.

Internet service provider

An ISP or internet service provider provides the connection to the internet for any user who has no network of their own. Each user is given an IP address and this will allow them to interact with other connected computers.

Interpretational inner class

This is an inner class with the job of providing interpretations or views of the data in its enclosing class bet independently of the actual data representation.

Interpreter

An interpreter is a program responsible for executing a source program that has been translated by a compiler; this is done through the implementation of a virtual machine. An interpreter will simulate a CPU; the Java interpreter implements the JVM, or Java Virtual Machine and executes the code (bytecodes) that the Java compiler produces. There is one advantage of using a compiler in Java; the language is far more portable than fully compiled languages.

Interprocess communication

This is when two or more processes that are completely separate are able to communicate with each other.

Interrupt

This is an asynchronous message that gets sent to a thread or process to interrupt it. Usually, the result of this will be the thread or process receiving an InterruptedException object.

IP address

This is an Internet Protocol address that is given to a networked computer by an ISP. IP addresses have four-byte values in them, displayed in dotted decimal notation, for example 135.15.0.1. At some point in the future, these IP addresses will change to 16-byte values to accommodate the huge rise in the numbers of computers connected to the network.

Is-a relationship

See inheritance.

Iteration

Iteration is when a set of statements is repeated, generally using a control structure – a for loop, a while loop, or a do loop.

Iterator pattern

An iterator pattern is a common pattern where a collection's contents are iterated over in the order they are in. This pattern allows a data client to be released from needing to know the details of the data storage. Support is provided in the form of the ListIterator and Iterator interfaces.

J

Java

Java is a high-level portable programming language that Sun Microsystems released.

Java Archive file

Java archive files, or JAR, allow for several bytecode files to be stored in one file.

Java 2 SDK

The Java 2 SDK is a specific implementation of abstract functionality as described in the Java 2 Platform specifications.

Java virtual machine (JVM)

A JVM is an idealized machine with an instruction set made up of bytecodes. Java programs are compiled into a bytecode form equivalent to the written code and an interpreter will execute them by implementing the JVM.

K

Key value

A key value is an object that generates a lookup hash code inside a data structure (associative).

L

Last in, first out

LIFO is an explanation of a stack data structure in which items get removed in the opposite order they entered the stack. For example, the last item added to the stack will be the first item removed.

Also see first in first out (FIFO)

Layout manager

A layout manager is an object that shares space between all the components in a graphical container.

Left shift operator

Denoted by <<, the left shift operator is also a bit-manipulation operator. It will move bits in the left operand at least zero places left as per the right operand value. the right of the result will get zero bits added.

Lexicographic ordering

This defines the order of words as they would be if they were in a directory. Please note that different locales will use an order whereby words that look similar are grouped as per conventions, although this usually applies to accented characters.

Lightweight process

See thread.

Line feed

See new line.

Little-endian

Little-endian defines a machine that stores low-order bytes first followed by high-order bytes.

Also see big-endian

Livelock

A livelock is when a thread is waiting for notification of a condition but, when it wakes, it will find that a different thread has inverted the condition once again. The original thread will now have to wait and when this continues to happen indefinitely, the thread is livelocked.

Local inner class

A local inner class is a class that has been defined inside a method.

Local variable

A local variable is one that has been designed inside the body of a method.

Logical error

A logical error is an error that appears in the class or method logic. The logical error may not immediately lead to runtime errors but they will have an impact on the program overall.

Logical operators

The logical operators include &, &&, |, ||, and ^ and they all take a pair of Boolean operands, producing Boolean results. They are generally used in Boolean expressions, usually inside a control structure condition.

Look-and-feel

This is what a user interface looks like and how the interaction with it feels. The window manager generally takes responsibility for this, together with the operating system, on the given computer. It refers to the way windows are moved, how they are resized, the title bars on the windows, how a mouse performs operations and so on. Preferably, a consistent look and feel should be maintained in one environment but some window managers do allow some programs to look and feel a little different to the host environment. The components in Java Swing fully support this by letting applications select a different look and feel to the ones provides in the interface manager.

Loop variable

Loop variables are those that control loop operations, like for loops. Usually, loop variables are provided with an initial value and will then be incremented at the end of each iteration until it gets to or goes past a terminating value.

Low-level programming languages

A low-level language is referred to as an assembly language and provides not much more than a basic instruction set for a CPU. As such, programs written in these languages are not as portable as high-level language programs.

M

Magic number

A magic number is a constant value that is significant in a certain context. For example, a value of 12 could have several different meanings, i.e. how many hours worked in a day, how many dollars you own your friend, etc. As far as it is possible, these values should have some association to an identifier that expresses their meaning clearly. For example:

```
final int maxSpeed = 60;
```

Provided a final variable is used for storage, execution overhead is not likely to be incurred.

Main method

The main method is the starting point for the execution of a program, for example:

```
public static void main(String[] args)
```

Manifest file

A manifest is a file stored in a JAR file, holding details about the archive content.

Marking interface

A marking interface is an interface that does not have any methods.

Member

A field, a method or a nested class, all members of classes.

Memory leak

A memory leak is when memory no longer in use does not return to the pool holding the free memory. Garbage collectors are used to return any unreferenced object to this pool so that memory leaks do not occur.

Message passing

Object interactions are characterized as message passing. A client object invokes a server class method to send a message to the server object. A message may be passed with arguments and the server will return the result.

Method

A method is the bit of the class definition responsible for implementing some of the class object behavior. The method body has declarations of statements and local variables that will implement the behavior. Methods receive input through their arguments if there are any and, if not declared void, a result will be returned.

Method body

This the body of a method containing everything that is in a method's outermost block.

Method header

The method header contains the name of the method, the result type, any formal arguments and, if any, thrown exceptions. May also be called a method signature.

Method overloading

When two methods or more are defined in a class and share the same name, they are overloaded. The same applies to a constructor and to any other method. Overloading is applied through class hierarchy so subclasses can overload methods that are defined in their superclasses. One important thing to learn is the difference between overloaded and overridden methods. Methods that are overloaded must be differentiated from one another, whether they have different argument types or different numbers of arguments. With method overriding the formal arguments are identical.

Method overriding

Methods defined inside a superclass can be overridden by a method in a subclass that has the same name. Both methods must have the same name, the same number of formal arguments and their argument types must be the same too. If a checked exception is thrown by the subclass method must be of the same type as the checked exception thrown by the superclass method or it must be a subclass of that type of exception. However, when the superclass method throws an exception, the subclass doesn't have to throw the same. There is a fundamental difference between overloading and overriding – overloaded methods share a name but have different formal arguments.

Also see overriding for chaining, overriding for breadth, overriding for restriction

Method Result

A method result is a value that a method returns through a return statement. The return statement's expression type must be the same as the type the method header declares.

Method signature

Another name for the method header.

Method variable

See local variable.

Micro-chip

A microchip is a tiny electronic device used in electronic equipment and computers. They are usually sued for supplying processing and memory components for a computer.

Also see Central Processing Unit

MIME

MIME stands for Multipurpose Internet Mail Extensions and these are rules that allow email to send content that isn't just text.

Modal

If the parent application of a dialog is blocked from doing anything until the dialog has finished, then the dialog is considered to be modal.

Also see non-modal

Model-view pattern

A modal-view pattern is one which data representation, or the model, is separated from the visualization or view of the model. This type of decoupling enables us to easily change the data representation that underlies it or to provide several views. Very often, another element is used to create the MVC pattern in which any element that can modify or control the model is separately defined.

Modem

A modem, or modulator-demodulator, is a piece of hardware that connects digital networks to analog phone networks. The analog signal is changed into a digital signal or the digital signal is changed to an analog signal.

Module

A module is a group of components (program) which have restricted visibility for programming the components in different modules. Packages are used in Java to implement this.

Monitor

A monitor is an object that has at least one synchronized method.

Multiple-boot options

Some computers have a hardware configuration that allows them to run a different combination of operating system and window manager. Some will let a user pick the combination they want for a specific session when the computer boots up.

Multiple inheritance

Multiple inheritance is when an interface or a class can extend multiple interfaces or classes. Multiple inheritance is only supported in Java in these circumstances:

Interfaces may extend multiple interfaces

Classes may implement multiple interfaces

For one class to extend another class, we can only use single inheritance.

Multiprogramming system

A multiprogramming system is an operating system that can concurrently run several programs.

Mutator method

A mutator method is one that is designed specifically to allow a class's private attribute to be modified in a controlled way. Convention dictates that mutator names are prefixed with set and followed by the attribute name, for example, setSpeed is the name of a mutator for an attribute with a name of Speed. When we set an attribute as private. No other object from any other class can change the value of the attribute in any way that doesn't go through the mutator. Mutators can check the modifying value and reject it if needs be. And, when one attribute is modified it could mean that others need to be modified to ensure the object maintains a consistent state – this can be done by a mutator method. Mutators are used for allowing safe access to a private attribute value and to keep those attributes protected from modification by external sources. The latter is done by selecting the correct mutator visibility.

Mutual Recursion

Mutual recursion happens when two methods recursively call one another.

N

Namespace

A namespace is the part of a program where specific identifiers are made visible. In java packages provide the namespaces and the four visibility rules – private, package, protected, and public – will also have identifiers in their namespaces.

Native method

Native methods are those written in a different language to Java but can be accessed by a Java program.

Nested class

A nested class is one that is defined in an enclosing class.

Also see Inner Class

Newline

This the newline character - \n.

New operator

The new operator is used for creating class instances.

No-arg constructor

A no-arg constructor is a constructor that will not take any arguments. By default, every class that does not have an explicit constructor is given the no-arg constructor, set to public. It has only one role – invoking the no-arg constructor in the superclass that is immediate to it.

Non-modal

If a parent application's dialog has not been blocked from doing anything while the dialog is on display, the dialog is said to be non-modal.

Non-static nested class

See inner class.

Null character

The null character is \u0000. Do not get this mixed up with the null reference.

Null reference

A null reference is a value that means 'no object'. We use it when we have an object reference variable that doesn't refer to any object.

Number base

The number base is the base used for interpretation of numerical characters. For example, the binary notation is base 2 and decimal is base 10.

O

Object

An object is a class instance. Generally, multiple objects may be constructed from the definition of a class. The characteristics of every instance of a specific class are defined by the object class. In these characteristics, an object's behavior will be in accord with the current state of the environment and the attributes.

Object construction

The new operator is used to create an object and then a constructor that is appropriate to the object will be invoked.

Object-oriented language

Java is an object-oriented language, otherwise called OOP. OOP languages allow problem solutions to be expressed as class objects.

Object reference

A reference that points to an object. Do make sure that you are clear on the distinction between objects and their references. For example:

Boat argo;

A variable like argo above is not an object but it can hold an object reference. It may only refer to one object at any one time but, on occasion it can hold different references.

Object serialization

Object serialization refers to the contents of an object being written in a way that restoring its state is possible, be it inside another process or at a future time. We can use this to store object between program runs or for transferring objects over the network.

Octal

Octal is a base 8 number representation. The only digits used in base 8 are 0 to 7 and the digit positions are representative of powers of 8 successively.

Octal character constant

An octal character constant is constant with the form of \ddd; each d is representing an octal digit. This can be used with Unicode character values from 0 to 255.

Operand

Operands are operator arguments. An expression contains a combination of operators and their operands. An expression value is worked out by the operation that has been defined by the operator being applied to the operand value.

Operating system

An operating system allows programs to access hardware devices in a computer system. For example, it provides a file system for the organization of data, the coordinates of a mouse are provided to programs as the mouse gets moved around. An operating system also makes it so that several programs can be concurrently run or for several users to use one machine.

Also see concurrency

Operator

Operators are symbols like ==, -, +, ? and so on, each taking at least one and up to three operands and producing a result. Both arithmetic and Boolean expressions use operators.

Operator precedence

See precedence rules

Out-of-bounds value

Out-of-bounds values are redundant values. They are used for indicating that another action, not the normal one, will be needed at some point. For example, the InputStream read method will return -1, indicating that the streams end has been reached. The normal output is a value of a positive byte-range.

Out of scope

Variables stay in scope so long as the flow control of the program is inside the defining block of the variable; if it isn't, the variable is out of scope.

Overriding for breadth

A type of method overriding; the subclass method will implement its own behavior in the attribute context and subclass behavior before calling the superclass method so that a similar task may be performed in the superclass context.

Overriding for chaining

Another type of overriding; the subclass method will look to see it is able to respond to a message without any help and will only call the superclass method.

Overriding for restriction

The third type of method overriding; the subclass method will call the superclass method first and then manipulate the result.

P

Package

A package is a group of interfaces and classes with a name; they provide a namespace. If a class, class member and interface does not have an explicit access modifier, i.e. public, private or protected, then they have package visibility. An import statement is used to import a public interface or class to another package.

Package access

See package.

Package declaration

A package declaration is what we use for naming a package. The declaration must be the first thing in a source file, before any of the import statements. For example:

package java.lang;

Parallel programming

Parallel programming is a programming style where statements are not always executed in a sequence; instead they may be executed in parallel. These languages make it much easier for programs to be created for hardware with multiple processors. The thread features in Java support a certain amount of parallel programming.

Parameter

See argument.

Parsing

Parsing is normally applied to a compiler's action when they analyze the source file of a program looking for syntax errors. Parsing also means the analysis of the input structure.

Pattern

A pattern is a usage or class design theme that recurs. Iterator and other interfaces encapsulate an access pattern to a collection's items, at the same time, releasing the client for needing to know how a collection is being implemented.

Peer

A peer is a term that the AWT uses to reference underlying classes that implement component classes in a platform-specific way.

Peripheral devices

A peripheral is a device that connects externally to a computer, such as a mouse, a keyboard, etc.

Pipe

A pipe is a link between two components of a program. One is a data source that will write to the pipe while the other is a data receiver and will read from the pipe.

Also see PipedOutputStream and PipedInputStream

Pixel

A pixel is an element of a picture, usually just a dot on the screen.

Polling

Polling is the process of testing a condition over and over until it evaluates TRUE. It may be an inefficient method if the time in between the tests is shorter than the time taken for the condition to test TRUE. Polling threads should sleep in between tests so that other threads can run. An alternative to polling is to use an interrupt for when the condition evaluates TRUE or you can use the mechanism called wait and notify that goes with threads.

Polymorphism

Polymorphism is an OOP concept in which an object reference may be used as if it were referring to an object that has a different form. Java polymorphism is a result of interface inheritance and class inheritance. The different forms result from a variable's static form, where the reference gets sorted.

Popup menu

A popup menu is a menu that contains actions and is not usually visible until a button is clicked on. They are used to keep a user interface clear of clutter.

Port

A port is a number that a process uses to communicate across a network with another process, using UDP or TCP, for example.

Also see TCP Endpoint

Portable

Portability is when a program is built in a way that it can run on multiple systems. Low-level languages don't tend to be as portable as the high-level languages. Low-level languages are tied more closely to a specific characteristic or instruction set of a specific CPU. The high-level languages have more portability but still retain the ability to make assumptions that are non-portable about the file system of a computer.

Post-decrement operator

See decrement operator.

Post-increment operator

See increment operator.

Precedence rules

Precedence rules are those that determine what order an expression is evaluated in when it has two or more operators. The operators that are higher in precedence are evaluated first, followed by those that have lower precedence. For example, take the expression, x+y*z. Because multiplication is higher in precedence it is evaluated first, followed by the addition.

Pre-decrement operator

See decrement operator.

Preempt

A thread that is currently being executed can be preempted. This means that they may be forced to concede control by a thread of higher priority that becomes eligible to run in its timeslice.

Pre-increment operator

See increment operator.

Primitive type

A primitive type is one of the Java data types and there are eight – they are byte, boolean, long, short, int, float, double and char.

Priority level

Every thread is given a level of priority that tells the scheduler where the thread goes in the list to be run. An unblocked eligible thread, for example, always gets run before low-priority eligible threads.

Process

A process is a thread of control which is allocated an execution timeslice by the underlying operating system.

Program counter

Program counters are an important part of the CPU. It will reference the memory address of the instruction due to be fetched during the next fetch-execute cycle. Once the instruction fetch has been given, the counter moves to refer to the next one before the last one is executed. The usual sequence of instruction execution can be changed if a branch instruction is executed – this will store a new address for the instruction in the program counter.

Propagation

When a method throws an exception but does not have the right exception handler, the exception can be propagated to the method caller. With checked exceptions, there must be a throws clause in the method header. This is not needed for propagation of unchecked exceptions.

Protected access

If a class member has been prefixed with a protected access modifier, protected access is possible. Any class that is defined in the enclosing package and any of the subclasses that extend the enclosing class may access that member.

Protected statement

A protected statement is in the try statement as part of the try clause.

Protocol

Protocol refers to a set of rules defining the interaction between a pair of processes. Specification of the protocol is usually found in the URL, indicating how a given resource is to be sent to the client from a web server.

Public interface

Class members that have been given a public access modifier as a prefix; these members can be seen by all classes in a given program.

Punctuation

The compiler uses punctuation, such as semicolons and commas, as a way of understanding a program structure.

Q

Quantum

See timeslice.

Queue

See first in, first out (FIFO) queue.

Quotient

A quotient, along with a remainder, is the result of an integer division operation. The quotient is representing the integer number that is divided into the dividend by the divisor. For example, with 5/3 the dividend is 5 and the divisor is 3. The result is 1 being the quotient and 2 being the remainder.

R

Radio buttons

Radio buttons are a series or group of components, all selectable but only one can be selected. When one component is selected, the previous component that was selected becomes deselected.

Race condition

See race hazard.

Race hazard

A race hazard happens when several threads share one resource. One thread will make an assumption about a resource's state and the actions of a different thread will invalidate that assumption.

Random access memory

Better known as RAM, this is the section of memory in a computer that the processing components of that computer can access easily. Specifically, the time taken to read and/or write to a part of memory is not dependent on the location address that is to be read or written. By contrast a videotape is accessed on a serial basis and read/write operation time is dependent on the distance of the location to be read or written to.

Reader class

A reader class is a subclass of the abstract Reader which you will find in the java.io package. A reader class can translate the input from a Unicode character set that is dependent on the host.

Also see Writer class

Real number

A real number contains one integer and a fraction. The float and double primitive types are used for representing a real number.

Recursion

Recursion is the result of a method that is invoked while an existing call to that method hasn't been returned. For example:

```
public static void countDown(int n){
  if(n >= 0){
    System.out.println(n);
    countDown(n-1);
  }
  // else - base case. End of recursion.
}
```

Also see indirect recursion, direct recursion and mutual recursion

Redundant value

This is a data type value where the data type doesn't have any real meaning or use in a specific context. Negative values, for example, are redundant values in a class that models assignment marks using integer attributes. Redundant patterns can be useful in some applications because they may be explicitly used as escape values or out-of-bounds values.

Reflection

Reflection is a way of determining constructors, fields, methods, etc. have been defined for an object or class. The class called Class supports reflection, along with other classes defined in java.lang.reflect, a Java package. With reflection we can create programs that are dynamic.

Relational operators

Relational operators are used in Boolean expressions, producing Boolean results. The operators include < >, >=, <=, !, and ==.

Relative filename

A relative filename is the name of a file with a full path relative to a specified point inside a file system tree. Usually this will be current working directory. For example:

../bin/javac.exe

Depending on what context a relative filename is used in, it can refer to a different file at a different time.

Also see Absolute filename

Repetition

See iteration.

Reserved word

Reserved words are keywords that are reserved for use by Java. They are for a specific purpose and cannot be used for any other purpose, especially not for naming identifiers. Some reserved words include int, class, public, etc. A full list of the reserved keywords can be found at the start of this guide.

Resource

See Uniform Resource Locator (URL).

Return statement

Return statements are used for terminating method execution. If a method has a type of void return it can only contain return statements in this format:

return;

If a method has any other type of return, it must contain one or more return statements in this format:

return expression;

In this format, the expression type must match the method return type.

Return type

A return type is the declared method type. It must be placed before the name of the method, as in void in the example below:

public static void main(String[] args)

or, in this example, Point[]:

public Point[] getPoints()

Return value

A return value is the value of an expression that is used within a return statement.

RGB color model

RGB is a color model that represents a color in three components – Red, Green, Blue.

Also see HSB color model

Right shift operator

Denoted as >>, the right shift operator is another of the bit-manipulation operators. It is used for moving bits that are in the left operand to the right by zero or more places, as per the right operand value. The most important bit before the right shift happens will be replicated in the position to the far left in a process known as sign extension. An alternative to the right shift operator is >>> which will replace any bits lost with a zero on the left side.

Round robin allocation

A round robin is a timeslice allocation that cycles over and over around a series of eligible threads in an order that is fixed.

Runtime error

A runtime error occurs at runtime and makes a program terminate.

Runtime stack

A runtime stack is a structure that the JVM maintains, recording a list of methods being executed in the current time. The method entered the most recently is at the top while the application main method is near to the bottom of the stack.

S

Scheduler

A scheduler is part of the JVM and is responsible for thread management.

Scheme

See protocol.

Scope

The scope of a language is used to determine the visibility level of classes, methods and variables inside a program or a class. The scope of a local variable, for example, is only the code block it was defined in. Private variables and private methods are limited to the class that defined them. Java has four levels of visibility – public, private, protected and package.

Search path

A search path is a list of the directories or folders that are to be searched, for example, for a class or a program.

Security policy

A security policy limits applet access to a host system's resources.

Semantic error

A semantic error indicates an error in a program's meaning. While there may be no syntax errors in a statement, it can still break the Java rules. For example, if we had ifvar as an int variable, this statement is right in syntax terms:

ifvar = true;

But, in terms of meaning it is wrong because assigning an integer variable with a Boolean value is illegal in Java.

Server

A server provides a service. For example, web servers are used to provide clients with resources. When an object is used as the server, it will receive messages from object clients.

Shallow copy

A shallow copy is an object copy. As opposed to a deep copy, in a shallow copy no copies re made of the subcomponents of an object. Shallow copying an array would provide us with two array objects. Each one would have a reference to the same object set that the original stored.

Also see Deep copy

Shift operator

See right shift operator and left shift operator.

Short-circuit operator

A short-circuit operator is one that evaluates only the number of operands required to determine the operation result. The commonest examples of short-circuit operators are && (logical and) and || (logical or). It is also worth noting that ? (the conditional operator) will only evaluate two of its operands even though it has three.

Shortcut key

A shortcut key is a keyboard key press associated with a GUI component as an alternative to using the mouse to select the operation.

Sibling subclasses

Sibling subclasses are two or more subclasses that share an immediate superclass.

Also see Inheritance hierarchy

Sign bit

A sign bit is the most important bit inside an int value used for determining the value's sign in twos-complement notation. 1 bit is indicative of a negative while 0 bit is indicative of a positive number.

Sign extension

When an int value, from a type that has a specific range, gets stored in a variable that has a larger range, sign extension is used for determining the value that results from this. The extra bits in a new value are filled using the most important (significant) bit from the original value. For example, let's say we have a byte variable that has the 10000000 bit pattern in it. If we were to store this in a short variable the bit pattern that results would be 1111111110000000. Given an original value of 01000000, the bit pattern that results would be 0000000001000000.

Single inheritance

Java does not allow a class to extend any more than a single class. as far as class inheritance goes, Java provides a model for single inheritance only.

Also see Multiple inheritance

Single line comment

A single-line comment is a text comment in a code that goes over one line and indicated by //:

// The compiler will ignore this line.

Singleton pattern

A singleton pattern is a pattern that lets us make sure only one instance of a specified class may exist at any given time. We can also use the singleton pattern when two or more instances are without a unique state and, as such, behave exactly the same.

Software

These are programs that are written specifically to run on computer systems.

Software engineering

This the application of engineering disciplines to the design of a software system, as well as the implementation and the maintenance of the systems.

Software reuse

This is when software components can be reused in alternative contexts. In Java, we can use encapsulation to help promote component reuse.

Soundcard

A soundcard is a hardware device that converts digital data to sound.

Stack

See last in, first out (LIFO) stack.

Stack overflow

When we try to push too many items onto one stack that only has finite capacity, a stack overflow occurs.

Stack trace

Stack trace is when the runtime stack is displayed.

State

Every object has a state. Current object state is represented by the attribute values combined. One of the most important parts of the class design is the protection of an object state from unauthorized modification or inspection – the mutator and accessor methods are used to protect the attribute state and integrity. In class design, we often try to model object state in real-world terms. However, unless a solid match exists between the data types provided by Java and the states we want to model, class design can be incredibly complex. One of the more important principles is to make sure that objects can never enter an inconsistent state as a result of a response to a message.

Statement

A statement is a fundamental building block of a method. There are several types of Java statement, including if statement, assignment statement, while loop, and return statement.

Statement terminator

The statement terminator is a semicolon, (;), which indicates a statement has reached the end.

Static initializer

A static initializer is a standard initializer with the prefix of the Java reserved keyword, static. Static initializers are defined externally to the enclosing class methods and can only have access to the enclosing class static methods.

Static method

Static methods are sometimes called class methods. The method header will contain the reserved keyword, static. A static method is different from any other method because it has no association to any specific instance in the class that it comes from. Static methods are directly accessed using the defining class name.

Static nested class

Static nested classes are nested classes with the header containing the reserved keyword, static. As opposed to an inner class, static nested class objects do not have enclosing objects.

Static type

When a variable refers to an object, the type declared for that variable is the static object type.

Static variable

Static variables are defined in the body of a class. These variables are shared by every object in the class but belong wholly to the class. We can use class variables to define default instance variable values. They are used for holding the dynamic information that every class instance uses, for example, the next account number that would be allocated in a credit account class. Be careful to use synchronization for access to information like this, that is being shared. Class variables also provide application-wide objects or values a name because they can be directly accessed through the name of the containing class and not a class instance.

Stepwise refinement

Stepwise refinement is a divide and conquer approach to computer programming. Complex problems are divided recursively into ever smaller subproblems that are much easier to manage. This tends to be used more often with structured languages.

Stream class

Input stream classes send data from the class source, usually a file system translated to a byte sequence. In the same way the output stream class writes byte-level data. Reader and writer classes should be used to contrast a stream class.

String

A string is String class instance. A string is made up of zero or more characters in Unicode. Once created they are immutable meaning they cannot be changed. Literal strings are written inside a pair of delimiters, usually “”, as in this example:

"hello, everyone"

Structured programming

Structured programming is a programming style that we normally associate with languages such as Pascal, Fortran, C, etc. With structured programming, problems tend to be solved with the divide and conquer approach. A big problem is split into smaller subproblems, each of which gets broke down further into even smaller ones. This stops when the difficulty level is more manageable. At its lowest level, implementation of solutions is done using data structures and procedures. Normally, this is used with programming languages considered imperative as opposed to object-oriented, in which neither procedures nor data structures get implemented as a class.

Subclass

A subclass extends a superclass. Subclasses inherit the superclass members. Every Java class is considered a subclass of the class called Object, found at the inheritance hierarchy root (the top class).

Also see Subtype

Subordinate inner class

A subordinate inner class is one that will perform subordinate tasks that are well defined for the enclosing class.

Subtype

Subtypes are types that have parent supertypes.. The relationship between the subtype and the supertype is general compared to the relationship between the subclass and superclass. Classes that implement interfaces are considered interface subtypes while interfaces that extend interfaces are also called subtypes.

Superclass

Superclasses are classes that at least one subclass extends. Every class in Java has a superclass of Object.

Also see Supertype

Supertype

A supertype is a type that has a child subtype. Interfaces that a class implements are class supertypes and interfaces extended by other interfaces are also called supertypes.

Swapping

Operating systems can sometimes run programs that need more memory than the host system has available in physical terms. To do this, the total amount of memory needed is split down into small pieces and these are swapped in when they are needed and then swapped out when their space is needed by another.

Swing

Swing classes are part of the Java Foundation Classes, otherwise known as JFC. They are defined inside javax.swing packages and provide components that are used for extending the AWT capabilities. They also provide much greater control over the look-and-feel of an application.

Switch statement

Switch statements are selection statements where an arithmetic expression value gets compared against a series of case labels, looking for a match. If there is no match, the default label (optional) is selected. For example:

```
switch(choice){
    case 'q':
        quit();
        break;
    case 'h':
        help();
        break;
```

```
    ...
    default:
        System.out.println("Unknown command: "+choice);
        break;
}
```

Swizzling

Swizzling is when object contents are recursively written using object serialization.

Synchronized statement

A synchronized statement is a statement where an object-lock is required for the target object before the statement body can be accessed. They are used to prevent race hazards by enclosing critical sections.

Syntax error

A syntax error is one that the compiler will detect when it parses a program. They are usually a result of missing punctuation, missing or incorrect bracketing, or symbols being placed in the wring order inside a statement or expression.

T

TCP endpoint

The TCP endpoint is the IP address combined with the TCP (transmission control protocol) port number.

Ternary operator

See conditional operator

This

This is one of the reserved keywords in Java and it has a number of uses. In a constructor, for example, it is the first statement, calling another constructor that exists in the same class. For example:

```
// Initialize with the default values.
public Heater()
{
        // Use the other constructor.
```

```
        this(15, 20);
}

// Initialize with the given values.
public Heater(int min,int max)
{
        ...
}
```

In a method or a constructor it can also be used for distinguishing between fields and parameters or method variables that have the same name. For example:

```
public Heater(int min,int max)
{
        this.min = min;
        this.max = max;
        ...
}
```

And it may be used to reference a current object. Usually this is to pass references to other objects. For example:

```
talker.talkToMe(this);
```

Thread

A thread is a lightweight process that the JVM manages. Thread support is provided in the java.lang package in the Thread class.

Thread starvation

Thread starvation applies to threads that are stopped from running. This is done by threads that are blocked or do not yield.

Throw an exception

Usually a result of logical errors, an exceptional circumstance arises in a program and an exception object gets created and then throw. If an exception handler does not catch the exception, the program terminates, displaying a runtime error.

Throws clause

A throws clause is a method header clause that indicates the propagation of at least one exception from the method. For example:

public int find(String s) throws NotFoundException

Throw statement

A throw statement throws an exception. For example:

throw new IndexOutOfBoundsException(i+" is too big.");

Timesharing system

A timesharing system is an operating system that takes the processor time and allocates multiple processes with a timeslice. When the timeslice has expired, the next process will be able to run.

Timeslice

A timeslice is the amount of time allocated to a thread or process for running before the scheduler decides on another thread or process to be run. If a thread or process becomes preempted or blocked during the timeslice, it will not use its entire timeslice.

Toggle

Toggling allows us to alternate between a pair of values, i.e. 1 and 0, true and false, etc.

Top level class

A top level class is one defined on the outer level of a static nested class or a package.

Transmission control protocol

TCP is a rule set that facilitates communication across a network between processes. The communication is reliable, as opposed to UDP, which is unreliable.

Also see UDP – User Datagram Protocol.

Trusted applet

A trusted applet has more privileges than a standard or an untrusted one.

Try clause

See try statement.

Try statement

The try statement is used as an exception handler, to catch and deal with exception objects. Generally, it will have a try clause, at least one catch clause and a finally clause. For example:

```
try{
   statement;
   ...
}
catch(Exception e){
   statement;
   ...
}
finally{
   statement;
   ...
}
```

You can leave out the catch or the finally clause – you cannot leave out both.

Twos-complement notation

The sign bit is the most important (significant) bit of an int value. 1 bit is indicative of a negative number while 0 bit is positive. To convert a positive to its negative value, the bit pattern must be complemented and 1 added; the same is true of converting negative to positive equivalents.

U

Unary operator

A unary operator is one that only takes one operand. The unary operators in Java are +, -, !, --, and ++.

Unbounded repetition

This is a type of repetition where the loop body statements are carried out an arbitrary number of times. This is in accordance with the effects of the loop body statements. All of Java's loop control structures have support for unbounded repetition.

Also see bounded repetition

Unchecked exception

An unchecked exception is an exception which does not require a local try statement and it isn't necessary to define a throws clause in the method header for propagation. Unhandled exceptions will cause a program to terminate if thrown.

Also see checked exception

Unicode

Unicode is a character set of 16-bits. They are designed to simplify the process of exchanging and displaying information that uses a range of symbols and languages.

Uniform resource locator

A URL is used to extend the file access concept from a local context only to uniform naming of resources, regardless of their physical location. URLs encode locations, names and schemes.

Uninitialized variable

An uninitialized variable is one that has been declared but doesn't have a value. The compiler will throw up a warning of those variable used before they are initialized.

Unnamed package

Every class defined in a file that do not have a package declaration will be put in the unnamed package.

Upcast

An upcast is when a cast goes toward the ultimate supertype of an object, i.e. up the hierarchy for inheritance towards the class of the object. For example:

```
// Upcast from VariableController to HeaterController

VariableController v;

...

HeaterController c = v;
```

The polymorphism rules in Java dictate that explicit upcasting is not normally needed.

Also see downcast.

User datagram protocol

UDP is a rule set that facilitates communication between processes over a network. UDP is an unreliable protocol, meaning there is no guarantee of correct transfer of information between the processes.

Also see TCP – Transmission Control Protocol

UTF

This is the UCS (Universal Character Set) Transformation Format, used to represent characters that are multibyte. It is fully compatible with file systems and programs designed for handling single-byte characters.

V

Variable declaration

A variable declaration is when a variable is associated with a specific type. You must be clear on the difference between declaring primitive type variables and class type variables. Primitive type values act as containers for one declared type value. With the class type, declaring the variable doesn't lead to automatic construction of an object of that specific type. By default, the value of null is assigned to the variable. Class type variables also act as reference holders for objects compatible with the class type of the variable. Under the rules of polymorphism in Java, a class type variable may be a reference holder of objects of the declared type or of any subtype. A variable with an Object type can, therefore, hold references to objects from any class.

Virtual desktop

The name used to describe a user's graphical working area within a window manager. The name arose in the early days of graphical user interfaces when it was thought that these would lead to `paperless offices'. It was anticipated that the computer screen would become a user's desktop, in which virtual documents, as opposed to paper documents, would be created, read and manipulated in various ways.

Virtual machine

See Java Virtual Machine (JVM).

Virtual memory

Computers only have a certain amount of real memory that they can use and a program will sometime need more than that. In multi-programming systems, there is the addition of multiple processes trying to use the same memory at the same time. Operating systems can get around this with virtual memory. A certain amount of virtual memory is given to each process, the size of which may be bigger than the total real memory. This can be done because the parts of the address space that a process does not use are stored on the disk until they are needed. At this point, the memory is swapped in to a bit of the real memory and the previous contents of the real memory are swapped out and stored on disk.

W

Well-known port

A well-known port is a port number where a server will offer a service that is familiar. For example, the well-known port number for a server that uses HTTP, or HyperText Transfer Protocol is port 80.

While loop

The while loop is one the three loop control structures in Java – the others are the for loop and the do loop. While loops contain a loop body and a Boolean expression. The loop condition will be tested before the body is accessed the first time and it will be tested again on completion of the end of the loop body. The loop will terminate when the condition evaluates as FALSE with the loop body statements executing zero or more times.

Whitespace

Whitespace is a characters that is used for adding visual space to a program. It includes the characters for line feed, carriage return, tab and space.

Window manager

A window manager allows the user of a computer to use a virtual desktop which has at least one window and at least one working area where programs can be run. The manager will allow the desktop contents to be arranged through arranging and resizing the windows. It also provides support for drag and drop operations together with the operating system. The window manager monitors movements made by mice to other components, such as popup menus.

Wrapper classes

The primitive types in Java are not object types. The java.lang package defines wrapper classes; one class for each of the primitive types – Byte, Boolean, Character, Float, Integer, Double, Short, and Long. Wrapper classes provide the methods needed for parsing strings that have primitive values and to convert a primitive value into a string. The Float and the Double class provide the methods that detect the bit patterns for the floating point numbers, with representation for values like +infinity, -infinity, NaN, and others.

Writer class

A writer class is a subclass of Write abstract which the java.io package defines. The writer class can translate Unicode output to character set encoding that is host-dependent.

Also see Reader class

Z

Zip file

A zip file is used for the storage of compressed files. However, the JAR (Java Archive) files, together with bytecode files, have pretty much superseded these.

Conclusion

Once again, I would like to thank you for choosing my guide on Java programming. As you can see, it is a simple yet complex language, with so many different aspects to learn. By now you should have a good understanding of the core concepts of Java programming and how to use it.

Your next step is, quite simply, practice. And keep on practicing. You cannot possibly read this guide once and think that you know it all. I urge you to take your time going through this; follow the tutorials carefully and don't move on from any section until you fully understand it and what it all means.

To help you out, there are several useful Java forums to be found online, full of people ready and willing to help you out and point you in the right direction. There are also loads of online courses, some free and some that you need to pay for, but all of them are useful and can help you take your learning to the next level.

Did you enjoy this guide? I hope that it was all you wanted and more and it has put you on the right path to getting your dream job!

Thank you and good luck!

References

https://www.edureka.co

https://www.javaworld.com

https://www.javatpoint.com

http://tutorials.jenkov.com

https://medium.freecodecamp.org

https://hackernoon.com

http://www.vogella.com

https://www.journaldev.com

https://searchmicroservices.techtarget.com

http://www.ntu.edu.sg

https://java2blog.com

https://www.codeproject.com

https://www.tutorialspoint.com

https://netbeans.org

https://medium.com/

https://stackify.com

http://www.doc.ic.ac.uk

https://data-flair.training

https://javarevisited.blogspot.com

https://raygun.com

Made in the USA
Middletown, DE
08 March 2019